DELIBERATION AND DECISION

Law, Ethics and Economics

Series Editors:
Christoph Luetge, University of Munich, Germany
Itaru Shimazu, Chiba University, Japan

Law, Ethics and Economics brings together interdisciplinary books which deal with at least two of the three constituents. Among other subjects, this series covers issues in ethics and economics, law and economics, as well as constitutional issues in law, economics, philosophy and social theory. The focus is on theoretical analysis that goes beyond purely normative considerations, thus aiming at a synthesis of the desirable and the feasible.

Deliberation and Decision

Economics, Constitutional Theory and Deliberative Democracy

Edited by

ANNE VAN AAKEN
Max Planck Institute for Comparative Public Law and International Law, Heidelberg

CHRISTIAN LIST
Department of Government, London School of Economics

CHRISTOPH LUETGE
Department of Philosophy, University of Munich

Routledge
Taylor & Francis Group
LONDON AND NEW YORK

First published 2004 by Ashgate Publishing

2 Park Square, Milton Park, Abingdon, Oxfordshire OX14 4RN
711 Third Avenue, New York, NY 10017

Routledge is an imprint of the Taylor & Francis Group, an informa business

First issued in paperback 2018

British Library Cataloguing in Publication Data
Deliberation and decision : economics, constitutional
theory and deliberative democracy. - (Law, ethics and
economics)
1. Democracy - Philosophy - Congresses 2. Political
philosophy - Congresses 3. Economics - Political aspects -
Congresses
I. Aaken, Anne Van II. List, Christian III. Luetge, Christoph
321.8'01

Library of Congress Cataloging-in-Publication Data
Deliberation and decision : economics, constitutional theory and deliberative democracy /
edited by Anne van Aaken, Christian List and Christoph Luetge.
p. cm. -- (Law, ethics and economics)
Includes bibliographical references.
ISBN 978-0-7546-2358-8
1. Decision making--Citizen participation--Congresses. 2. Democracy--Congresses. 3. Social choice--Congresses. I. Aaken, Anne van. II. List, Christian. III. Luetge, Christoph, 1969-

HD30.23.D443 2003
330'.01--dc22

2003056292

ISBN 13: 978-0-7546-2358-8 (hbk)
ISBN 13: 978-1-138-38346-3 (pbk)

Contents

PART II: DELIBERATION AND SOCIAL CHOICE

PART III: DELIBERATION AND SOCIAL ORDER

List of Contributors

1) Main Papers:

Anne van Aaken, Postdoctoral Research Fellow
Max Planck Institute for Comparative Public Law and International Law, Heidelberg, Germany

Luc Bovens, Professor of Philosophy
University of Colorado at Boulder, Department of Philosophy, Boulder, USA

Geoffrey Brennan, Professor of Social and Political Theory
Australian National University, Research School of Social Sciences, Canberra, Australia

John S. Dryzek, Professor of Social and Political Theory
Australian National University, Research School of Social Sciences, Canberra, Australia

Robert E. Goodin, Professor of Social and Political Theory and Philosophy
Australian National University, Research School of Social Sciences, Canberra, Australia

Christian Kirchner, Professor of German, European and International Civil and Business Law, and New Institutional Economics
Humboldt-University Berlin, Faculty of Law, Berlin, Germany

Christian List, Lecturer in Political Science
London School of Economics, Department of Government, London, UK

Philip Pettit, William Nelson Cromwell Professor of Politics
Princeton University, Departments of Politics and Philosophy, Princeton, USA

Wlodek Rabinowicz, Professor of Philosophy
Lund University, Department of Philosophy, Lund, Sweden

Andreas Suchanek, Professor of Economic and Business Ethics
Catholic University Eichstätt, Faculty of Economics, Ingolstadt, Germany

Axel Tschentscher, Assistant Professor of Law
University of Bern, Faculty of Law, Bern, Switzerland

Stefan Voigt, Professor of Economics
University of Kassel, Faculty of Economics, Kassel, Germany

2) Commentators:

Detlef Aufderheide, Assistant Professor of Economics
University of Münster, Faculty of Economics, Münster, Germany

Natalie Gold, DPhil-candidate in Economics
University of Oxford, Balliol College, Oxford, UK

Michaela Haase, Assistant Professor of Economics
Free University Berlin, Department of Economics, Berlin, Germany

Horst Hegmann, Associate Professor of Political Theory
University of Konstanz, Department of Political Science, Konstanz, Germany

Christoph Luetge, Assistant Professor of Philosophy
University of Munich, Department of Philosophy, Chair for Philosophy and Economics, Munich, Germany

Matthias Meyer, Assistant Professor of Economics
University of Munich, Department of Philosophy, Chair for Philosophy and Economics, Munich, Germany

Martin Rechenauer, Assistant Professor of Philosophy
University of Munich, Department of Philosophy, Munich, Germany

Thomas Schmidt, Assistant Professor of Philosophy
University of Göttingen, Department of Philosophy, Göttingen, Germany

Alois Stutzer, Assistant Professor of Economics
University of Zürich, Institute for Empirical Research in Economics, Zürich, Switzerland

Viktor J. Vanberg, Professor of Economics
University of Freiburg, Faculty of Economics, Freiburg, Germany

Rüdiger Waldkirch, Business Consultant
University of Munich, Department of Philosophy, Chair for Philosophy and Economics, Munich, Germany

Jurgen De Wispelaere, PhD-candidate in Political Science
London School of Economics, Department of Government, London, UK

Michael Wohlgemuth, Managing Research Associate
Walter Eucken Institut, Freiburg, Germany

Preface

The aim of this book is to explore ways of bridging the gap between two influential approaches towards theorizing about democratic institutions: constitutional economics on the one hand, and deliberative democracy, on the other. The two approaches offer partly rival accounts of (i) the functioning and (ii) the legitimacy of democratic institutions. Although both approaches highlight the importance of consent or agreement for the foundations and functioning of institutions, their accounts of the features of such consent or agreement are fundamentally different. Constitutional economists model individuals as self-interested rational utility maximizers, and use criteria such as incentive compatibility for evaluating institutions. By contrast, deliberative democrats model individuals as discursive communicating subjects. On an influential version of this account, the source of legitimacy is reasoned argumentation under certain ideally free and equal speech conditions. Deliberative democrats therefore use what may be called discourse compatibility (a term coined by Philip Pettit) as a criterion for evaluating institutions.

The two approaches are disjoint not only in terms of their assumptions and methodology, but also in terms of the level of communication (or lack thereof) between the corresponding two communities of researchers. The book brings together scholars from both communities, and presents their accounts of the theme of "Deliberation and Decision", all centered around the question of how the apparent gap between constitutional economics and deliberative democracy can be bridged. The book aims not only to provide a comprehensive overview of the recent debate between the two approaches, but also to make new original contributions to that debate.

The book is the result of a conference that was held in Wittenberg, Germany, from 24 to 26 September 2001. Wittenberg is the town where Martin Luther and Philipp Melanchthon lived and where they famously published the theses of reformation. We would like to thank the Volkswagen Stiftung, the Sparkasse Wittenberg, the Landeszentrale für politische Bildung Sachsen-Anhalt, and the Chair for Philosophy and Economics of the University of Munich for generous financial support. We are also very grateful for the assistance given by the Wittenberg Center for Global Ethics, where the conference took place. Finally, we would like to thank Professor Christian Kirchner from the Humboldt University Berlin and all the participants, who made the conference so fruitful and enjoyable.

Anne van Aaken, Christian List, Christoph Luetge

INTRODUCTION

Deliberation and Constitutional Theory – Introduction to Part I

Anne van Aaken

General Remarks

Deliberative democracy and constitutional economics are paradigms that are much discussed in political science, economics, social philosophy and law. The discussion revolves around questions of democratic theory and has normative and positive aspects. There are two competing points of view on the relation between discourse theory and deliberation on the one hand and constitutional economics on the other. One view holds that those theories are incompatible, or that they are mutually exclusive alternatives. The other view suggests that the two theories should be combined in order to give a more fruitful account of how people make choices concerning the social order. The crucial task, on this second account, is to identify the key elements of the theories of democracy and institutions, and to explain – if we wish to link the two paradigms – how the linkage might be achieved.

Contributions

In her contribution 'Deliberative Institutional Economics', Anne van Aaken argues that institutional economics (constitutional economics being a part of that research program) and discourse theory stand unconnected next to each other, although they are both concerned with the legitimacy of institutions (normative aspect) and their functioning and effectiveness (positive aspect). Both use as theoretical constructs rational individuals in a broad sense and the concept of consensus as a source of legitimacy. Van Aaken's paper outlines a theoretical synthesis between the two theories – to be called deliberative institutional economics – by identifying common ground and possibilities of fruitful combination on the problems of legitimacy, institutional design and the effectiveness of legal norms. Discourse theory, on the one hand, emphasizes the conditions and criteria of a legitimate and fair consensus and may thus enable institutional economics to escape the infinite regress of judging a consensus legitimate. It may do so by specifying the conditions of decision-making more precisely. Institutional economics, on the other hand, can provide a tested social science paradigm (rational choice) of explaining and predicting the functioning of institutions. On the question of how a consensus might be reached, van Aaken takes up the distinction drawn by Vanberg and Buchanan between the theory component and the interest component of preferences. A discourse on the theory component of preferences may occur at the constitutional level and may either involve special information provided by experts, or a discourse on the actual consequences of the rules at issue. What is neglected by constitutional economics is a possible change of the interest component of preferences through deliberation. From the viewpoint of discourse theory, the conditions described by constitutional economics are necessary but not sufficient for a legitimate consensus. The former applies substantially stricter conditions than the latter. In doing so, discourse theory may provide a substantive criterion X to break the infinite regress in constitutional economics that stems from a purely procedural understanding of a freely formed consensus. Van Aaken proposes a positive model of man as a homo rationalis communicans, which is a combination of homo communicans and homo oeconomicus. While economists mainly trust incentive-compatible rules (self-interest) for compliance, deliberative theorists focus on the acceptance of the decision through reason-giving. These concepts seem complementary. The discursive element of rule generation is vital in claiming legitimacy, which in turn affects rule-following and therefore the effectiveness of the law. For the purposes of institutional design it thus seems plausible to test not only for incentive-compatibility but also for discourse-compatibility. Institutions may then be criticized not only on the grounds that they are incentive-incompatible, but also on the grounds that they are discourse-incompatible. In van Aaken's view, neglecting the discursive element involves the danger of not being able to sketch adequate institutional design.

Michael Wohlgemuth's comment is sympathetic to van Aaken's general approach. Wohlgemuth suggests that additional theories might strengthen and clarify her approach. He embeds the theory of deliberative institutional economics in the overlapping frameworks of public choice theory, new institutional economics, constitutional political economy and Austrian economics on the one hand and discourse theory on the other, taking into account the concepts of consensus and the models of man in those theories. In discussing the (positive) problem of a combining discourse theory with the assumption of exogenously given preferences in economics, he proposes to bridge the conceptual gap by providing further building blocks for deliberative institutional economics, namely concepts developed by Austrian Economics and theories of public opinion formation. The former adds elements of knowledge-creation, decentralization and communication, commending deliberative democracy as a Hayekian 'discovery procedure'. The latter suggests that in political processes people might act on preliminary opinions, that they might not express their true opinions or that they might be 'rationally irrational' – facts that should be taken into account when we discuss political processes.

Matthias Meyer puts the two paradigms into a broader philosophy of science perspective. Meyer emphasizes the problem-dependency of theories, suggesting that when we discuss theories we have to consider a threefold distinction: problem-theory-reality. He criticizes the concept of homo rationalis communicans, arguing that the required distinction was not sharply drawn by van Aaken, as she includes empirical findings such as experimental economics in her account of rational choice. In Meyer's view, an 'empirically correct' model of man is not the adequate point of departure. Instead Meyer wants to rely on the concept of constant preferences. He points out that the model of homo oeconomicus is a theoretical construct that allows us to predict adjustment reactions to changes of rules with the intention of solving the problem of social order. He argues that the model is necessary to avoid tautologies.

In his paper 'Constitutionalism and its Alternatives', John Dryzek argues that discursive democracy may serve as an alternative to constitutionalism and constitutions. But he acknowledges that constitutions matter and that they may even prove fatal if they do not fit a country's problems. The crucial question, according to Dryzek, is whether alternative sources of order other than constitutions matter more than constitutions themselves. He suggests that we find no empirical difference between countries with a written constitution and countries without one. He also finds that the same formal constitution may generate completely different outcomes when adopted in different countries. It follows, then, that there must be some alternative sources of order such as coercion, markets, discourse and deliberation. In Dryzek's view, liberal constitutionalism carries the threat of coercion as it requires a strong state to prevent a constitution from being misused by single groups such as the mafia. Another alternative is the introduction of a meta-constitution, which relies on a market of constitutions and which would grant an 'exit option' to the individuals concerned. Contrary to the 'exit-option' of constitutionalists, Dryzek stresses the 'voice-option' of discourse for creating a new state of affairs that may or may not take a constitutional form. That discourse may take place within the political and/or public sphere. Such a mechanism also mitigates the emerging unpredictability and unstableness of modern social and political life by using discourse as a means of reflexive modernization. While prevailing constitutional arrangements work only due to a supportive discourse, reflexive modernization means that the ratio of rule-questioning to rule-obedience increases. Failing constitutions or weak constitutional sources of order are therefore in need of an increased discourse by the people. This concern was also advanced by James Buchanan (1989), but Dryzek extends it to non-constitutional devices of social ordering, suggesting a 'network society'.

In his comment on Dryzek, Viktor Vanberg acknowledges the common interest in the legitimacy of collective choice. Although Vanberg is sympathetic to certain elements of deliberative democracy that might be integrated into constitutional economics, he objects to Dryzek's claim that deliberation is the essence of democracy, as opposed to voting, interest aggregation or constitutional rights. He rebuts the claim that deliberation is a superior alternative to liberal constitutionalism. Noting that constitutional economists submit their recommendations to the individuals' consent as the ultimate source of legitimation, Vanberg challenges theorists of deliberation to explain how their recommendation of authentic deliberation can improve the prospect for achieving mutual gains from cooperation. In Vanberg's view, Dryzek fails to explain the preconditions for discourse and deliberation, which on his account should be constitutional provisions.

Axel Tschentscher's comment on Dryzek discusses the distinctions between the notions of participation, legitimacy and legitimation, as well as deliberation, ideal and real discourse. On his account, legitimacy is an empirical concept, while legitimation is a normative one. Participation may enhance legitimacy and also be a source of democratic legitimation. Deliberation is defined as public reasoning among equal citizens prior to a decision. It excludes arguments of those not affected by the decision at stake. While deliberation always precedes a decision, discourse, in Tschentscher's view, does not even require the intent of taking a decision, and is even averse to decision-making. Thus the two concepts are mutually exclusive. Tschentscher therefore considers deliberation a democratically preformed 'sister' of discourse. According to Tschentscher, discourse theory is compatible with non-discursive procedures for deliberation and decision-making and does not claim that institutionalized democracy needs to take the form of deliberative democracy. Rather, real discourse has meaning only where it is explicitly acknowledged as a formal procedure within the institutional setting. Discourse theory with the concept of continuous discursive control provides the new rationale of reevaluating democratic legitimacy.

Axel Tschentscher's paper 'Constitutional Economics in Constitutional Jurisprudence' was originally a comment on a talk to be given by Jules L. Coleman, who was unfortunately unable to attend the conference, following 11 September 2001. Coleman could unfortunately not submit a paper for this volume, and Tschentscher's paper has been included in its place. Tschentscher connects the notions of efficiency and consensus in constitutional economics and discourse theory with constitutional jurisprudence. Tschentscher stresses the differences between discourse theory and rational choice theory with regard to the notions of equality and voluntary action. One focuses on strategic bargaining and the other on moral arguing by the agents. Drawing on Jules Coleman's (1984) distinction between various concepts of efficiency in the economic analysis of law (realist versus counterfactualist and subjectivist versus objectivist), Tschentscher claims that using the efficiency criterion of Kaldor-Hicks as a legal norm would leave the lawmaker with hardly any choice at all. Also, if the Pareto criterion were a constitutionally required principle of law-making, this would mean that laws could always be challenged on the grounds of sub-optimality. This stands in contrast to legal theory where norms claim validity no matter how costly their implementation may be. Tschentscher also analyses the compatibility of constitutional economics with jurisprudence. If one follows Coleman's distinction, one can categorize this approach as realist (transaction costs are taken into account) and subjectivist (efficiency cannot be defined independently of actual agreement). Following Coleman's criticism of constitutional economics, Tschentscher argues that the most pressing question of jurisprudence cannot be answered by constitutional economics, as it leads to a conflict between the subjectivist view of efficiency and the need for an objective criterion to determine the comparative advantage among different institutional settings. Additionally, the ruling principle for determining comparative advantage does not necessarily have to be that of efficiency or optimality.

References

Buchanan, J. M. (1989) "The Ethics of Constitutional Order", in *Essays on the Political Economy*, Honolulu (University of Hawaii Press), 25-31.

Coleman, J. L. (1984) "The Foundations of Constitutional Economics", in McKenzie, R. B. (ed.) *Constitutional Economics: Containing the Economic Powers of Government*, Lexington (Lexington Books), 141-55.

Deliberation and Social Choice – Introduction to Part II

Christian List

General Remarks

The second part of this volume is concerned with the problem of how collective decisions can be made on the basis of individual preferences or views. The challenge of collective decision-making arises when the preferences or views held by different individuals are in conflict with each other. How can such conflict be resolved? Economists and deliberative democrats have suggested what appear to be rival answers to this question. Following the work of Arrow (1951), economists have usually taken the conflict as given and asked how the conflicting individual preferences or views can be summarized – or *aggregated* – into overall collective decisions, for instance by voting. Deliberative democrats, on the other hand, have focused on ways of reducing the level of conflict itself through *group deliberation*, which may transform individual preferences or views and, ultimately, bring about agreement. These two rival answers to the question of how conflict between different individual preferences or views can be resolved reflect different positions on what lies at the core of democracy. According to the first answer, *aggregation* of individual preferences or views lies at the core of democracy, where those preferences or views are *exogenously* given. According to the second answer, *transformation* of individual preferences or views lies at the core of democracy; here individual preferences or views are *endogenous* to the democratic process; they are not only framed, but also revised *within* the democratic process.

The papers in this part take the perspectives of economics and deliberative democracy not as incompatible, but as complementary. They all make some contribution to the following question: How can problems of *aggregation* of conflicting individual preferences or views be solved within a *deliberative* conception of democracy?

The three papers address two different kinds of aggregation problems. We shall briefly introduce the two aggregation problems in turn.

The classical problem concerns the aggregation of the preference rankings of several individuals over a number of alternatives into a single preference ranking for the group as a whole. The difficulties raised by the aggregation of preference rankings are well illustrated by Condorcet's famous paradox. Suppose there are three individuals and three alternatives (candidates). Call the individuals 1, 2 and 3, and the alternatives x, y and z. Suppose the preference rankings of the three individuals are as follows. The symbol '>' is to be read as 'is strictly preferred to':

Individual 1: $x > y > z$
Individual 2: $y > z > x$
Individual 3: $z > x > y$

Then there are majorities (of 2 out of 3 individuals) for x over y, for y over z, and for z over x. The corresponding majority preference ranking is $x > y > z > x$, a 'cyclical' and hence inconsistent preference ranking. In short, the plausible decision procedure of pairwise majority voting can generate inconsistent majority preferences, even when the preferences of all individuals are perfectly consistent, as in the present example. The problem is generalized by Arrow's impossibility theorem. Arrow's theorem shows that pairwise majority voting is not the only decision procedure that has some undesirable properties, such as to sometimes generate inconsistent majority preferences; rather, *any* decision procedure will violate at least one of five seemingly compelling requirements.

Several scholars in social choice theory, led by William Riker (1982), have interpreted these cycling and impossibility results as a decisive challenge to any normatively demanding notion of democracy. On this challenge, democracy is vulnerable to inconsistency, and further, if there is no principled way of resolving that inconsistency, to arbitrariness and manipulation. This raises the question of whether deliberation can provide an answer to this challenge.

The second, less familiar problem concerns the aggregation of the views of several individuals over multiple interconnected propositions into a single set of views for the group as a whole. Just as the problem of preference aggregation is illustrated in a particularly distilled form by Condorcet's paradox, so the problem of aggregation over multiple interconnected propositions is illustrated by a paradox of its own: the 'doctrinal paradox' or 'discursive dilemma' (e.g. Kornhauser, 1992; Chapman, 1998). Suppose a three-member court has to decide on whether a defendant is liable under a charge of breach of contract. Legal doctrine requires that the court should find that the defendant is liable (proposition R) if and only if it finds, first, that the defendant did some action X (proposition P), and, second, that the defendant had a contractual obligation not to do action X (proposition Q). Thus legal doctrine requires $(R \leftrightarrow (P \wedge Q))$. Suppose the views of the three judges are as in Table 1:

	P	Q	$(R \leftrightarrow (P \wedge Q))$	R
Judge 1	Yes	Yes	Yes	Yes
Judge 2	Yes	No	Yes	No
Judge 3	No	Yes	Yes	No
Majority	Yes	Yes	Yes	No

Table 1. The 'Doctrinal Paradox' or 'Discursive Dilemma' (Conjunctive Version)

All three judges accept the rule ($R \leftrightarrow (P \wedge Q)$). Further, judge 1 accepts both P and Q and, by implication, R. Judges 2 and 3 each accept only one of P or Q and, by implication, they both reject R. If the court applies majority voting on each proposition – including on ($R \leftrightarrow (P \wedge Q)$) – it faces a paradoxical outcome. A majority accepts P, a majority accepts Q, a majority (unanimity) accepts ($R \leftrightarrow (P \wedge Q)$), and yet a majority rejects R. Propositionwise majority voting thus produces an inconsistent collective set of views, namely the set $\{P, Q, (R \leftrightarrow (P \wedge Q)), \textit{not-R}\}$ (corresponding to the last row of Table 1). This set is inconsistent in the standard sense of propositional logic: there exists no assignment of truth-values to the propositions P, Q and R that will make all the propositions in the set simultaneously true. And this outcome occurs even though the views of all judges (corresponding to the first three rows of Table 1) are individually consistent. Moreover, in analogy to Arrow's more famous impossibility theorem, the 'doctrinal paradox' can be shown to be illustrative of a more general impossibility result (List and Pettit, 2002).

Although the 'doctrinal paradox' and the problem of aggregation over multiple propositions have not received as much attention by the social-choice-theoretic critics of democracy as their counterpart results on preference aggregation, it is easy to see that they also pose a potential threat to democracy. To the extent that complex decisions over multiple propositions are common in many democratic settings, it is important to find ways of avoiding the paradoxical outcomes illustrated by the 'doctrinal paradox'. Why is it important?

First, one might argue that it is undesirable in itself for a democratically organized group to endorse a logically inconsistent set of collective views. Second, such inconsistencies might make the group prone to erratic choices. Specifically, inconsistencies make collective outcomes highly sensitive to the chosen decision procedure. In the example of the three-member court, it is far from clear whether the defendant should be held liable or not. The two reasons for liability are each accepted by a majority of judges, and yet the conclusion that the defendant is liable is not. On a reason-driven decision procedure the court would therefore find that the defendant is liable, whereas on the basis of a majority vote on the conclusion, the court would reject that charge. The challenge for deliberative democrats is to explain how to either handle or avoid such paradoxical cases.

Contributions

In his paper 'Substantive and Meta-Agreement', Christian List first notes that the paradoxical cases of aggregation are ones where there is a great degree of diversity among the preferences or views of different individuals. If that diversity can be sufficiently reduced, the paradoxes disappear. This raises the question of whether the transformative aspect of deliberation can be of any help here. In particular, can group deliberation reduce the level of conflict between the preferences or views of different individuals in such a way as to avoid the paradoxical cases?

Deliberative democrats have often emphasized the idea of deliberation-induced consensus, or what List calls 'agreement at a substantive level'. If deliberation were to produce consensus, this would obviously make aggregation obsolete. There would be no longer any conflict to resolve. This idea shifts all the work to deliberation's capacity to *transform* individual preferences or views, and defines away the problem of *aggregation*. If successful, this strategy would provide a powerful response to the paradoxes of aggregation. But it is overly optimistic to expect deliberation to produce unanimity in all cases, and we have no empirical support for this expectation.

However, List points out that, even if deliberation fails to bring about a perfect consensus, such a strong form of agreement – i.e. 'agreement at a substantive level' – is not necessary for the avoidance of the paradoxes of aggregation. Rather, a less demanding form of agreement, 'agreement at a meta-level', is already sufficient for avoiding them. Informally, a group of individuals are said to agree at a meta-level if they all conceptualize the issue in terms of the same shared issue-dimension. List explores some social-choice-theoretic formalizations of this idea, inspired by Duncan Black's concept of *single-peaked* preferences.

The bulk of List's paper is devoted to a discussion of the escape-routes from the paradoxes of social choice that are opened up by 'agreement at a meta-level'. Following earlier work by Miller (1992), List discusses the hypothesis that group deliberation can bring about agreement at a meta-level, thereby enabling consistent aggregation. Although the familiar problem of preference aggregation is the starting point for List's discussion, he shows that the concept of 'agreement at a meta-level' can also be applied to the problem of aggregation over multiple propositions.

Philip Pettit's paper, 'A Dilemma for Deliberative Democrats', focuses on the problem of aggregation over multiple propositions and asks how much of a problem the 'doctrinal paradox' – or 'discursive dilemma', as he prefers to call it – poses for deliberative democracy. Pettit begins his discussion by presenting three constraints on public decision-making that he takes to be characteristic of a deliberative conception of democracy. According to the *inclusive constraint*, all members of a group should have an equal entitlement to vote on the resolution of certain collective issues. According to the *judgmental constraint*, the individuals should deliberate on the basis of common concerns prior to voting. According to the *dialogical constraint*, the deliberation should be conducted in a dialogue that is open and free from coercion.

Pettit argues that the three constraints still leave open the question of what decision procedure should be adopted, and how votes should be aggregated. To illustrate this point, he introduces the 'discursive dilemma', a version of the 'doctrinal paradox' explained above. The dilemma shows that there is a tension between two plausible demands: between the demand that a group be responsive to the views of the individuals on every proposition, and the demand that the group be rational in the set of views it collectively endorses. How can that tension be resolved? Which of the two demands is the more important one in a deliberative democracy?

Pettit reviews several arguments that have been advanced in the literature on deliberative democracy, and argues that they are all unclear on the question of whether the ideal of deliberative democracy should be taken to privilege the demand of responsiveness or the demand of rationality. He then turns to what he calls the republican argument, suggesting that that argument points towards a solution.

Republican theory can be characterized in terms of the importance it places on people's enjoying freedom as non-domination. In the political sphere, Pettit argues, republican freedom requires the contestability of collective decisions by the individuals who are affected by them. Particularly, if individuals are to be able to judge or contest the decisions of a group in relation to alleged reasons, then that group must be answerable to those reasons; it must be 'conversable', as Pettit calls it. Applied to the 'discursive dilemma', he holds that a group that privileges rationality will be conversable in this fashion, whereas a group that fails to ensure collective rationality – whether it is for the sake of responsiveness or for some other reason – will fail to be conversable. Therefore, to ensure the contestability of its decisions, a group must secure collective rationality. Pettit concludes that republican theory thus provides an argument for solving the 'discursive dilemma' by privileging the demand of rationality.

While Pettit's paper can be seen as a discussion of how to solve the 'doctrinal paradox' from a procedural perspective, the paper by Bovens and Rabinowicz addresses the aggregation problem that may lead to that paradox from an epistemic perspective, i.e. from the perspective of *truth-tracking*. Bovens and Rabinowicz first introduce a complex social decision. The setup is very similar to the one in the example of the three-member court above. A group of individuals has to decide whether a conclusion (e.g. proposition R) is true on the basis of two premises (e.g. propositions P and Q). The conclusion is to be accepted if and only if the two premises are judged to be true, i.e. ($R \leftrightarrow (P \wedge Q)$). As we have seen, simultaneous majority voting on all the propositions may lead to the 'doctrinal paradox' or 'discursive dilemma'.

Bovens and Rabinowicz distinguish two decision procedures that might be used to solve that dilemma. On the *premise-based procedure*, the group applies majority voting on each of the premises (i.e. propositions P and Q), but not on the conclusion (i.e. proposition R), and lets the force of logic (i.e. the inference rule ($R \leftrightarrow (P \wedge Q)$)) dictate the collective judgment on the conclusion (i.e. R), effectively ignoring the majority verdict on it. Given the individual judgments in Table 1, the premise-based procedure leads to the collective acceptance of the conclusion (i.e. the defendant is liable). On the *conclusion-based* procedure, the group applies majority voting only on the conclusion (i.e. R), but not on the premises (i.e. P and Q), thereby effectively ignoring the majority verdicts on them. Given the individual judgments in Table 1, the conclusion-based procedure leads to the collective rejection of the conclusion (i.e. the defendant is not liable). Thus the premise-based and conclusion-based procedures may produce divergent outcomes.

The main part of the paper by Bovens and Rabinowicz compares the relative advantages and disadvantages of the two decision procedures from the perspective of truth-tracking. Suppose that there is an independent truth of the matter on whether or not each premise is true, and by implication on whether or not the conclusion is true. Suppose further that each individual group member has a certain probability (*competence*) of making a correct judgment on each premise, where, roughly speaking, each individual is better than random at tracking the truth, but nonetheless fallible. We can then ask which of the two decision procedures, the premise-based one or the conclusion-based one, is more likely to reach a correct decision on the conclusion. Bovens and Rabinowicz give a detailed account of the conditions under which the premise-based procedure is the better truth-tracker and the conditions under which the conclusion-based procedure is the better truth-tracker.

Under a large class of conditions, the premise-based procedure reaches the correct decision on the conclusion with a higher probability than the conclusion-based procedure. Exceptions are, however, situations where the number of group-members is small, or where their competence is low, or where the conclusion is unlikely to be true. Bovens and Rabinowicz explain that the reason for this is that the conclusion-based procedure performs better when it comes to reaching the correct decision by mistake.

What does it mean to reach the correct decision by mistake? Suppose *P* is true, *Q* is false, and consequently *R* is also false. Now suppose that a majority of individuals come to reject *R*. But their reason for rejecting *R* is *not* that they have found *P* to be true and *Q* to be false, but rather that they believe *P* to be false and *Q* to be true. Then the majority judgment on the conclusion is correct, but the group has reached this judgment as a result of incorrect judgments on each of the premises. In principle, both the premise-based procedure and the conclusion-based procedure admit the possibility of reaching a correct decision on the conclusion by mistake. But, as Bovens and Rabinowicz show, this happens more often under the conclusion-based procedure than under the premise-based procedure.

The issue of whether or not a correct decision is reached by mistake is not only of technical interest, but it is also of great relevance for the context of a deliberative democracy. Deliberative democrats will typically care not only about the *decision* a group makes, but also about the *reasons* for which the group makes that decision. In cases where there is a truth to be tracked, deliberative democrats may thus care not only about whether a collective decision tracks the truth, but also about whether it tracks it *for the right reasons*.

In a bold departure from the classical notion of truth-tracking in the social-choice-theoretic literature, Bovens and Rabinowicz introduce the concept of *reaching the truth for the right reasons*, distinguishing it from the concept of *reaching the truth for whatever reason*. This conceptual innovation opens up a new way of linking truth-tracking considerations with the debate on deliberative democracy. Bovens and Rabinowicz show that the premise-based procedure is always better than the conclusion-based procedure at *reaching the truth for the right reasons*.

In conclusion, the three papers in this part of the volume together make a strong case for the meaningfulness of *aggregation* within a *deliberative* conception of democracy. While the paper by List discusses deliberation's potential to transform individual preferences or views *prior* to the aggregation, the papers by Pettit and

Bovens and Rabinowicz address the question of what aggregation procedure to adopt within a deliberative democracy. Pettit addresses this question from a procedural perspective, whereas Bovens and Rabinowicz's perspective is an epistemic one. Despite these different perspectives, the two papers support a strikingly similar conclusion. In complex decisions over multiple propositions groups should adopt the premise-based procedure: that procedure not only respects the demand of rationality, but it is also good at tracking the truth for the right reasons.

References

Arrow, K. (1951) *Social Choice and Individual Values*, New York (Wiley).

Chapman, B. (1998) "More Easily Done than Said: Rules, Reason and Rational Social Choice", *Oxford Journal of Legal Studies* 18, 293-329.

Kornhauser, L. A. (1992) "Modelling Collegial Courts. I. Path-Dependence", *International Review of Law and Economics* 12, 169-185.

List, C. and P. Pettit (2002) "Aggregating Sets of Judgments: An Impossibility Result", *Economics and Philosophy* 18, 89-110.

Miller, D. (1992) "Deliberative Democracy and Social Choice", *Political Studies* 40 (special issue), 54-67.

Riker, W. H. (1982) *Liberalism Against Populism*, San Francisco (W. H. Freeman).

Deliberation and Social Order – Introduction to Part III

Christoph Luetge

General Remarks

The final part of this volume is mainly concerned with questions of how deliberation and stability of the social order go together. To put it in another way: How can reforms and arrangements proposed by theorists of deliberative democracy be implemented while taking into account the 'realities' of social systems?

This is not to say that the contributions to this section go into details with regard to actual political processes of implementation. Rather, they focus on problems of maintaining the social order to a particular extent. Critics of discourse ethics, on which the theory of deliberative democracy builds, have for a long time regarded this point as an important weakness of the discourse approach. The idea of unforced communication, of 'uncoerced discourse', seemed to belong rather to a 'Kantian limbo' (Binmore, 1994-1998).

For social theorists like F. A. von Hayek and J. M. Buchanan, on the other hand, the 'problem of social order' has been the central focus of attention. Constitutional economics (cf. Brennan and Buchanan, 1985), naturalistic game theory (cf. Binmore, 1994-1998) and institutional ethics (cf. Homann, 2002) all consider problems of implementation as the systematic starting point of their approaches.

The question is whether deliberative democracy has inherited the problems of its 'ancestor' or whether its proponents have more adequately taken into account the feasibility of their proposed reforms and (institutional) arrangements. And might it be that implementing more processes of deliberation even leads to a more stable social order? These questions are addressed in this section.

Contributions

In his paper 'What is Meant by Consent?', Andreas Suchanek's intention is to clarify the concept of consent. He does so by distinguishing between two approaches which differ in their ideas on the self-enforcement of consent: The first one, justificationism, relies on normativistic postulates without stating an explicit way of making consent self-enforcing. The economic approach, on the other hand, points in the right direction by providing a fruitful heuristics: 'Look for mutual advantages!' might be called its battle-cry. Suchanek then goes into more detail on how consent provides the basis for social order. Distinguishing between three aspects of consent, he maintains that the cost of enforcing rules may increase or decrease, depending on the scope of, especially implicit, consent. Therefore securing consent is an essential investment in the stability of the social order, and consent theory is a most valuable theoretical enterprise for the functioning of modern societies.

While Martin Rechenauer's comment is largely affirmative, though pointing to some possibilities for elaborating the concept of consent further, and trying to reestablish the concept of reason, Jurgen De Wispelaere is rather critical of Suchanek. According to Wispelaere, justificationism might be given a better standing, taking into account empirical considerations.

Stefan Voigt's paper 'The Consequences of Popular Participation in Constitutional Choice – Towards A Comparative Analysis' takes an empirical turn, too. His theoretical basis is the research program of positive (as opposed to the more traditional normative) constitutional economics. Voigt aims at developing empirically testable hypotheses with regard to constitutions. These hypotheses take into account matters of discourse, and explore the ways in which discourse affects the content and/or the success of constitutional rules.

Both comments take a somewhat critical view: Michaela Haase does not see the necessity of establishing positive constitutional economics as a third way between discourse ethics/deliberation theory on the one hand and (normative) constitutional economics on the other. Moreover, Horst Hegmann points to limitations of Voigt's project, favoring an approach based more strongly on 'genuine deliberation'.

The final paper by Robert Goodin and Geoffrey Brennan, 'Bargaining over Beliefs', sets out to explore uncovered ground in between the domains of economics and deliberative theory broadly speaking. Goodin and Brennan, taking up an epistemic perspective, aim at extending the concept of bargaining to beliefs. In 'ordinary' economics, distributions are the object of bargaining. But it seems possible to extend the notion of bargaining to cases where different agents have identical interests *but* different perceptions of the situation. In these situations, arguments are exchanged, and much of the standard logic of bargaining can be reconstructed. There are conflicts, but also possibilities for compromise: Some perceptions may be considered 'as if true' by all parties involved, in a preliminary way, and only for specific purposes and problem situations. If these perceptions turn out not to be successful in the end, their 'inventors' will be held responsible and be blamed for them.

Goodin and Brennan go on to develop an elaborate model for such situations. They defend it against possible critiques from bargaining theory as well as from philosophy of science: A 'principle of charity' considered by philosophers of science fulfils a similar function as the bargaining over beliefs argued in this paper.

Generally speaking, bargaining and 'non-bargaining' can no longer be seen as strictly separated, a result that is especially relevant for the discussion between deliberation and decision in this volume.

Thus it seems that a promising agenda for bridging the apparent 'gap' between deliberation and decision, between the theory of deliberative democracy and economic bargaining theory, might be provided by systematically integrating the concepts of one theory into the other not just 'importing' them without change. This is done by Suchanek in showing that and how order can be enforced, implemented, and better implemented through deliberation. Voigt similarly tries to integrate deliberative concepts into positive constitutional economics. Goodin and Brennan, finally, extend the economic concept of bargaining to questions of belief. But in all three cases, the economic concepts themselves are altered to some extent. So we end up with a positive result: Within the theoretical framework of bargaining and decision, deliberation can be conceptualized as contributing to the stability of the social order.

References

Binmore, K. (1994-1998) *Game Theory and the Social Contract*, 2 vols., Cambridge, Mass. (MIT Press).

Brennan, G. and J. M. Buchanan (1985) *The Reason of Rules: Constitutional Political Economy*, Cambridge (Cambridge University Press).

Homann, K. (2002) *Vorteile und Anreize: Zur Grundlegung einer Ethik der Zukunft*, ed. C. Luetge, Tübingen (Mohr Siebeck).

PART I

DELIBERATION AND CONSTITUTIONAL THEORY

Chapter 1

Deliberative Institutional Economics, or Does Homo Oeconomicus Argue?[1] A Proposal for Combining New Institutional Economics with Discourse Theory

Anne van Aaken

Abstract

Institutional Economics and Discourse Theory stand unconnected to each other, although they are both theories concerning the legitimacy of institutions (normative) and the functioning and effectiveness of institutions (positive). Both use as theoretical constructions rational individuals and the concept of consensus for legitimacy. Discourse theory emphasizes the conditions of a legitimate consensus. It could thus enable institutional economics to escape the infinite regress of judging a consensus legitimate. Institutional economics uses an empirically testable social science paradigm (rational choice) of explaining and predicting the functioning of institutions. The paper outlines a theoretical synthesis of the two theories by finding points in common and possibilities of fruitful combinations concerning the problems of legitimacy, institutional design and effectiveness of legal norms.

Introduction

Individuals may make collective decisions through a number of mechanisms such as deliberation, negotiation and choice,[2] which may in turn be judged by different criteria – efficiency, fairness, acceptance, and legitimacy. The theoretical thinking on deliberative democracy is normally subsumed under Discourse Theory,[3] where

---

[1] Reprinted with permission of Sage Publication Ltd from Anne van Aaken, Deliberative Institutional Economics, in Philosophy & Social Criticism 28 (4), 2002. I would like to thank Horst Hegmann, Christian Kirchner, Matthias Meyer, Philip Pettit, Stefan Voigt, Michael Wohlgemuth for valuable comments.

[2] As in Elster (1998b), p. 5.

[3] See Sabel (1995), pp. 1, 4ff. for an overview and for fundamentals Habermas (1962; 1988; 1992). Also Rawls (1990) is cited as a theoretical precursor due to the concept of reflective equilibrium (pp. 38ff.). For application of Discourse Theory in legal theory see Alexy (1996b; 1996a).

arguing and/or deliberation are regarded as means of achieving social coordination and legitimacy. This is in contrast to Institutional and Constitutional Economics, which emphasizes bargaining and, particularly, the rational decision following it. The underlying approach is *not* primarily political or ideological but derives from different assumptions regarding the circumstances in which people act for what reasons and in what manner. It therefore leads to different methods. In the methodological discussion that is of interest here, *homo oeconomicus* occupies a central position. Does he argue? And if so, what is the effect on his preference, cognition[4] and resulting decisions? How do the *conditions* for decision-making (normative and positive) affect the result, its acceptance and/or legitimacy, and the legitimacy of rules and laws?

The aim of this article is to find points of contact, and features that are common to both Discourse Theory and the New Institutional/Constitutional Economics.[5] These could encourage further research, particularly into the shaping of decision-making processes such as legal or democratic procedures, and including business organization theory.[6] Court hearings, for example, are built around a deliberative process that not only gives the parties the right to argue their case but also calls for deliberation and impartiality on the part of the judge and requires the court to substantiate its findings (principle of fair trial). These institutional facilities function in conditions that come close to those formulated by Discourse Theory and help to make legal rulings more legitimate and, thus, better accepted. Similar structures can be found in administrative proceedings.

A paradigmatic representation of the two outlooks is followed by a search for points of contact, with particular reference to the contribution Discourse Theory can make to the New Institutional Economics, and an attempt at theoretical synthesis. I shall then deal with the explicative and normative content of what I call 'Deliberative Institutional Economics'. My thesis is that it can better *explain* existing institutions. I also suggest that those thinking in terms of *normative* Institutional Economics can better assess institutional alternatives if their analysis allows for the *discursive conditions* that affect not only cognition but also the preferences of individuals involved in processes of social coordination such as court hearings, democratic procedures, and administrative action.[7] Deliberative procedures are de

---

[4] The connection between cognition and preferences is unclear. As far as the influence of the perception of a situation on the following decision is concerned experimental and behavioral economics deals with it. The influence of preferences in cognition is mainly a domain of motivational research.

[5] For the purpose of this paper it is not necessary to distinguish between Constitutional Economics (Public Choice) and New Institutional Economics and the differences within. Nevertheless it can be said that Constitutional Economics focuses rather on normative questions whereas New Institutional Economics is mostly occupied with positive research. If there are relevant differences, it will be mentioned in the text.

[6] See also Dryzek (1990) for examples, especially alternative dispute resolution, of the application of 'discursive design'.

[7] For the latter see also Sabel and Cohen (2001); Sabel and Gerstenberg (2001). See Dryzek (1990) for application of Discourse Theory to Alternative Dispute Resolution and Stark and Bruszt (1998) for the application to network structures in society.

facto already incorporated in most of the institutions governing the three state powers.[8]

Several implications of incorporating deliberation into economics will therefore be discussed, i.e. (1) the possibility to reach consensus through deliberation (positive); (2) the legitimacy of such a consensus (positive and normative); (3) the utility to be derived from the deliberation process as such (process versus decision utility) (positive), and (4) the effect on the individuals' interest in rule-following as a result of acceptance of the rule-making process (positive).

New Institutional Economics

New Institutional Economics is indebted to methodological individualism in its positive analysis and assumes that a person having (bounded[9]) rationality and constant preferences will seek to maximize (individual) utility when making decisions in conditions of scarcity. Rather than relying on empirical behavioral analyses, it uses what is known as the REMM[10] hypothesis to derive adjustment reactions expected after institutional changes. Important factors that are presupposed are stable preferences, and a well-defined utility function of human beings whose actions are therefore result-oriented. Normally, the concept of utility in economics and decision theory nowadays is defined as a positivist version of desirability, making it a theoretical construct with a concrete content derived from 'revealed preferences'.[11] The model, no longer limited to economic issues in a narrower sense, now also serves to analyze political and general institutional contexts and does not question the presupposed constant preferences and their origin or ethical assessment. The underlying concept is that of the responsible citizen who is aware

8 See also Benhabib (1994), p. 42: '(T)he deliberative theory of democracy is not a theory in search of practice, rather it is a theory which claims to elucidate some aspects of the logic of existing democratic practices better than others.'

9 The concept of bounded rationality is more and more widely used in economics, especially in Institutional Economics. For the groundbreaking work, see Simon (1957; 1993), for application of bounded rationality in law and economics see Jolls, Sunstein and Thaler (1998).

10 **R**esourceful, **E**valuating, **M**aximizing **M**an. The REMM model (for basic information see Meckling (1976)) is an improvement on *homo oeconomicus* insofar as the actor thus modeled chooses between 'given' alternatives. By contrast, the 'resourceful' in REMM emphasizes that the alternatives are by no means given but often have to be found and developed through creative human action. The model, while permitting any type of aim an individual may adopt, abandons the assumption of complete information and no transaction costs. See also Tietzel (1981), p. 125. REMM was broadened to **R**esourceful, **R**estricted, **E**xpecting, **E**valuating, **M**aximizing **M**an (RREEMM) by Lindenberg (1985).

11 For a simplified outline of the theory of revealed preferences see Samuelson (1948). For a summary of various forms and a critique see Hausman (2000). For the problem of applying this theory to law and a different concept of preferences see Sunstein (1996), particularly pp. 931ff.

of his interests and preferences.[12] The strict analytical separation between stable preferences and restrictions thus permits the empirical examination of behavioral changes with no need to discuss a change of preferences. In short, a formal concept of rationality[13] assumes a system of given subjective preferences and neglects both their origin and content.[14]

Reaching Consensus

Starting from given preferences, the New Institutional (and particularly Constitutional) Economics deals with the effectiveness and legitimacy of institutions and, through a suitable blend of coordination procedures performed by the state and the market, looks for rules producing results that best suit these preferences. It normally[15] proposes to use consensus as a criterion for assessing the substantive rightness of institutions,[16] a concept with a procedural understanding of rationality[17] derived primarily from Constitutional Economics, on which we may therefore focus in the following.

In seeking consensus, an individual weighs advantages and disadvantages (not necessarily limited to financial and material ones), an advantage being anything he regards as such. It is assumed that nobody would accept a worsening of his personal situation caused by rules, and that rules thought to improve it are considered efficient *if* and *because* they can produce *unanimity*. There is an assumed harmony of individual utility maximization and supra-individual substantive rightness.[18] Economics in this connection is concerned with individual decision-making and disregards the possibility of previous deliberation and institutions established for this purpose.

---

[12] As in Frey and Kirchgässner (1993), p. 134. Hayek (1991), p. 133, with reference to Alexis de Tocqueville, identifies the advantage of a democracy primarily in the *process of opinion forming*.

[13] Formal rationality in this context means that individuals have a capacity for the *reflexive, complete, transitive, consistent (in time)* and *continuous* organization of their preferences. This applies to decisions made under conditions of certainty and uncertainty. For more of an overview and details regarding forms of rationality in economics see Tietzel (1981).

[14] See also Sen (1977; 1993) who criticizes this focus on the consistency criterion.

[15] As formulated by Richter and Furubotn (1996), pp. 477, 493ff., Institutional Economics lacks a normative standard because of problems relating to allocative efficiency.

[16] Erlei, Leschke and Sauerland (1999), p. 54, and Homann and Kirchner (1995), p. 192, criticize the normative deficit of the New Institutional Economics and propose (hypothetical) consensus.

[17] For general information on procedural concepts of rationality in social philosophy see Tschentscher (2000).

[18] As in Tschentscher (2000), p. 170 who supposes *egoistic* utility maximization which is, however, not implied as the content of the utility functions is unknown and any content, egoistic or altruistic, is possible and permissible.

There are, however, approaches in Constitutional Economics that no longer assume given preferences at a *constitutional* level.[19] Vanberg and Buchanan[20] (analytically) single out theories and interests as components of constitutional preferences, the former being a cognitive and factual element in the (subjective) forecast of how different rules affect results, the latter involving the subjective assessment of results expected from rules, making it a pure value judgment.[21] The two components may cause differences of opinion and prevent agreement. To avoid disagreement between individuals and bring the theory components closer together, one can provide more information (e.g. from experts) or have a discourse.[22] The interest components of preferences are thought to remain constant, however, which would exclude modification through discourse, and the question of *why* or *due to what processes* the interest component of people might change is disregarded. This gap can be filled by deliberative theories emphasizing discourse as a means of considering and exchanging arguments to reach agreement.[23]

Legitimacy of Consensus

In Constitutional Economics, rules are assumed to be legitimate if rational individuals seeking to maximize utility (can) unanimously agree to them. Constitutional Economics in particular opposes the 'maximization concept' of welfare economics[24] by saying that, in contrast to approaches taken by welfare economics (and utilitarianism), efficiency cannot be defined *regardless of individual*

---

19 But see also differently Buchanan (1959), pp. 136f.: 'The purpose of political discussion is precisely that of changing "tastes" among social alternatives. The economist ... must try to incorporate the predicted preferences of individuals, not as they exist at a given moment, but as they will be modified after responsible discussion' and Buchanan (1986), pp. 89f: 'Auf einer zweiten oder "konstitutionellen" Ebene des Diskurses müssen aber vorhandene Sets von Präferenzen nicht als gegeben akzeptiert werden, und eines der Ziele eines solche Diskurses ist ja in der Tat eine wirksame Kritik solcher Präferenzen, die auf eine Verbesserung durch angemessenen institutionellen Wandel abzielt. Präferenzen für Kitsch sind auf dieser Ebene nicht so gut wie Präferenzen für Dichtung, und eine der Hauptaufgaben des Sozialphilosophen und Wissenschaftlers ist die Gestaltung einer konstitutionell-institutionellen Struktur, welche die Hervorbringung "besserer" Präferenzen (z.B. Dichtung) fördert'.

20 As regards the following see Vanberg (1994), chapters 10 and 11; see also Hegmann (1998).

21 Vanberg (1994), chapter 10 and particularly p. 169.

22 Combining Discourse Theory with Constitutional Economics is limited to the theory component here; for a different approach see Frey and Kirchgässner (1993) who consider the discourse as proceeding the decision.

23 See Aufderheide (1996), p. 187 for a graphical overview of the different understandings of consensus including the interest and theory components.

24 Buchanan (1988), p. 135: 'This shift in the focus of positive inquiry carries normative implications. Conceptions such as aggregate efficiency in the allocation of resources become, at best, examples of functionalist error, along with the more explicitly normative variants of the social welfare functions'.

choices.[25] This is because Constitutional Economics assumes that preferences and their intensities cannot be observed and thus are not comparable on an interpersonal basis. 'Objectivistic' approaches in welfare economics are therefore denied. For the comparison of given preferences relating to the desirability of certain goods or rules there is no superordinate standard enabling the definition of a social welfare function which could then be optimized.[26] This means that 'the legitimacy of ethics ... in theory requires the consent of those involved to the rules ... .[27] A normative effect can only come from the intentions of those concerned'.[28]

Other issues discussed include the voluntary character of the agreement and the type of exchange taking place, in other words, *the conditions for the validity of the consensus.* Here we find differences in Constitutional Economics, with Brennan and Buchanan considering an agreement *non*-legitimate only if it was 'extracted by force or under conditions of total duplicity by one of the parties'.[29] They are satisfied if 'individuals are observed to be responding freely within the minimally required conditions of mutual tolerance and respect...'.[30] No further elaboration is, however, given on the minimal conditions of tolerance and respect. Inequalities concerning income or the ability to express oneself are explicitly neglected, as is the issue of whether the situation prevailing before the conclusion of the contract (the status quo) was fair.[31]

Vanberg, by contrast, deals more thoroughly with the voluntary character and looks at the type of restrictions under which the exchange or consensus take place because '... in order to specify what is meant by "voluntary choice" and "voluntary exchange", one has to somehow qualify the conditions under which the respective choices are made'.[32] The question then is how to define coercion.[33] Although coercion might already be assumed if individual choice comes up against limiting factors (budgetary or physical), such restrictions are simple facts of life because the phenomenon of scarcity will invariably force individuals to abandon one alternative if they choose the other (opportunity costs). Such a definition is useless, as is

---

[25] This is where we find a conflict with the Pareto efficiency in terms of welfare economics. In the words of Coleman (1990), p. 143, 'If, on grounds of utility or welfare, P is preferable to R, then we might expect people to choose P over R. If however, for whatever reason, they choose R over P then that is the end of it; R, not P is efficient'. This contrasts with welfare economics, where Pareto efficiency could be technically determined.

[26] See also Alessi (1992), particularly p. 329. For new 'objectivist' approaches in welfare economics, see Sen (1979; 1997a; 1997b).

[27] Homann (1997), p. 16.

[28] Homann (1997), p. 25.

[29] Brennan and Buchanan (1986), p. 102.

[30] Buchanan (1984), p. 6.

[31] See also Coleman (1990), pp. 146f.: 'Buchanan takes the status quo as the appropriate point of departure for social contract theory. This is a very different approach than one might be inclined to take since there is no reason to suppose that the status quo reflects a particularly fair distribution of holdings. ... This is simply status quoism of the worst kind. For its central claim, if true, is true regardless of the morality of the holdings'.

[32] Vanberg (1994), pp. 211f.

[33] See Hayek (1991), chapter 9.

the criterion of coercion through 'natural conditions' or human action, because the two are inevitably linked. An owner of water in the desert withholding this vital resource from another person may be acting exactly as someone in our part of the world, but it would still not be the same.

Another criterion Vanberg discusses is the infringement of absolute rights. This would represent coercion and thus make the consensus involuntary. The next question would be what exactly 'rights' means, and might lead one to consider two types: one a class of pre-positive rights applied regardless of the ones defined in the legal system, the other limited to positive rights applied in the respective society. The first type is clearly incompatible with the theory of Constitutional Economics as it assumes an external criterion, the second one is contingent because coercion is defined by the rules and laws of a society. This version is opposed by Vanberg[34] because even rules applying in totalitarian states would then have to be accepted as involving no coercion. Constitutional Economics would get into a never-ending regress if it cannot resolve the following problem:

> (O)ne cannot give normative content to the notion of voluntary choice without introducing at some point in the chain of procedural argument, some substantive criterion of 'goodness', a criterion that is more than a reiteration of the argument that the process is good to the extent that it is in accordance with rules that are the outcome of a 'good process'.[35]

As a first step, Vanberg proposes a value judgment of the following kind: 'To the extent that social processes are good, measured against some criterion X, the outcomes of those processes qualify as good'.[36]

The problem then is how to specify X. If it were found, it could be used (simultaneously) at all levels of seeking agreement because, according to Vanberg, looking only at 'in-period choices' would be inadequate[37] for qualifying voluntary consensus. He therefore looks for a substantial criterion[38] that may link up to a procedural one. The former is known as the *cost avoidance* criterion. It says that the costs of choosing to refuse consensus *must not be prohibitively high and man-made*. For example, the costs of someone given the choice 'your money or your life' would be prohibitive and his consent could not be called voluntary. The more alternatives individuals have, the more voluntary their choice, which incidentally favors the market as a mechanism of coordination in many cases. But even assuming the necessity of a state is a perspective that leaves room for the question if, and how, alternative coercion-reducing institutional arrangements can be found in the

34 Vanberg (1994), pp. 212f.
35 Vanberg (1994), p. 214.
36 Vanberg (1994), p. 214.
37 Vanberg (1994), p. 215.
38 Vanberg (1994), p. 215: 'This third criterion is based in an argument that is apparently behind the idea that a voluntary exchange transaction reliably indicates what both parties "really prefer", while a coerced transaction does not.'

public sphere.[39] Such considerations, and particularly ways of giving people a 'voice', are often neglected even though they are the only alternative to a normally costly 'exit'.[40]

Vanberg does not give us a clear qualitative criterion for demarcation here but at least makes it possible to discuss 'quantitative' trends. Nevertheless, what Michelman calls 'paradox of democracy',[41] i.e. the problem that there is neither a procedural independent finding of the 'good' nor a purely procedural solution to the paradox, can only be solved if there are some substantive elements to escape the infinite regress of legitimacy.[42] At this point of the argument, I would suggest a link with Discourse Theory because it seeks to guarantee the conditions and voluntary character of a consensus in terms of a (non-authoritarian) discourse. In other words, the conditions of Discourse Theory are positive criteria that must be met if a discourse is to be legitimate, whereas Constitutional Economics defines negative standards beyond which consensus is not legitimate. From a discursive viewpoint, the requirements specified by Constitutional Economics are necessary but not sufficient to legitimize agreement and need to be stricter. The conditions of Discourse Theory could, in my opinion, be a possible candidate for Vanbergs' criterion X to escape the infinite regress of Constitutional Economics.

Procedural versus Decision Utility

Similar to economics as a whole, the New Institutional (and Constitutional) Economics looks only at the *outcome utility* of decisions.[43] New Institutional

---

[39] A citizen facing alternatives may see a difference, for example, between entering into a contract under public law pursuant to §§ 54ff. VwVfG (German administrative procedural law) with an administrative department, or simply being submitted to an administrative order, which might be right-infringing.

[40] For the notions of exit, voice and loyalty see Hirschman (1970).

[41] As Michelman (1999), p. 34 calls it. See also for this problem Sabel and Gerstenberg (2001), p. 35.

[42] See also Cohen (1991), p. 26: 'Neither the commitment nor the capacity for arriving at deliberative decisions is something we can simply assume to obtain independent from the proper ordering of institutions. The institutions themselves must provide the framework for the formation of the will; they determine whether there is equality, whether deliberation is free and reasoned, whether there is autonomy, and so on'.

[43] The utility concept may, according to Bentham, either be defined by the hedonistic *experience* of the decision result, or by the preference or *desire* for such a result, i.e. its wantability. It is then clear that the relation between preferences and the hedonistic consequences of a choice is asserted rather than examined. The theory of rational decision simply assumes that the two concepts correspond. Related studies, see Kahneman (1997), have shown that there is no simple relation, and a distinction should therefore be made between two utility concepts. One of these is the (ex post) *experienced utility* as a measure of the hedonistic experience, the other is the *decision utility* which serves to weight the result (ex ante). This not only makes it possible to inquire about the (formal) consistency of a decision, but one may also ask if the decision maximizes the *expectation of experienced utility*. Rabin (1998) makes the following comment on p. 33: 'The realization that decision and experienced utility may be systematically different cuts to the core of our

Economics to a large extent still uses the concept of a fully rational individual. Constitutional Economics and other parts of New Institutional Economics use a concept of bounded rationality. This line of research finds its most elaborated studies undertaken in a field known as experimental or behavioral economics[44] (based mainly on cognitive psychology). These studies have dealt with the specific conditions (especially cognitive ones) in which individual decisions are made. There are also approaches that distinguish outcome from procedural utility and try to measure the latter.[45] There, utility is assumed to be measurable by individuals' subjective reported well-being. But even if those so-called anomalies are taken into account, the learning process by communication to weaken these – for the individual normally costly – anomalies is ignored.

Of particular interest in the research of behavioral economics are findings relating to reference points. The standard model in economics assumes that preferences are independent of the situation in which they are revealed so that the description and presentation of alternatives will have no effect on decision-making.[46] However, utility for individuals depends not only on ultimate net worth as an absolute quantity (as the standard model assumes), but also on what are called '*reference points*'.[47] To give an everyday example: the same temperature is felt differently depending on whether a person is used to warm or cold temperatures. This is not just a physical but also a mental phenomenon found in all spheres of life, and it means that the *primary agents of utility are not states but events in a dynamic process*. Utility thus becomes a profit or loss in relation to a reference point, which is often the status quo but of course may be subject to outside factors. If there are no exogenous fixed reference points, it is possible to frame the situation in a way which influences the decision heavily (so-called 'framing').

The choice of the reference point is particularly crucial in negotiations and when seeking a consensus. People tend to see things in a light that favors their own purpose, i.e. they are likely to regard reference points as 'fair' if they serve their interests ('*self-serving bias*').[48] Even those who consider 'fairness' important will interpret the facts for their own advantage. The question arises, of course, what 'fair' means. Conversely, perceptions of 'unfair' behavior or rules will again depend on a reference point.[49] These distorted 'fair' reference points are of interest in

---

model of choice'. This approach, while going further than the theory of revealed preferences, still leaves out considerations preceding the decision, and the communicative processes. The individual making the decision is still an enlightened Robinson Crusoe.

44 For a survey of findings, documentation of experiments and implications for institutional design see Eichenberger (1992) and more specifically for law, Jolls, Sunstein and Thaler (1998).

45 Frey and Stutzer (2001).

46 Eichenberger (1992), p. 28.

47 Kahneman and Tversky (1979). Formally speaking, the utility function depends not only on consumption at the time t;$U(c_t)$, but also on the reference point $U(c_t, r_t)$.

48 Dahl and Ransom (1999), p. 703: 'A self-serving bias occurs when individuals subconsciously alter their fundamental view about what is fair or right in a way that benefits their interests'.

49 See also Hoffman and Spitzer (1993).

all arbitration procedures such as salary negotiations, and often prevent the parties from reaching agreement.[50] This provides another point of contact with deliberative approaches because reference points may also be altered and identified by way of deliberation. Schelling's[51] *focal point* may be interpreted in the same manner as deliberation makes it possible to find or, possibly, fix such a point. Another major anomaly that may be alleviated by deliberative processes is the '*availability bias*', which captures the tendency of individuals of overestimating the probability of events or using information that is more impressive. This anomaly may also be altered by deliberative learning processes.[52]

These and other anomalies cause costs for the individuals,[53] which creates an incentive to reduce these anomalies (learning effects[54]). As these learning effects can be observed in repeated games, it can safely be assumed that anomalies are not fixed, but depend on specific circumstances (situations and restrictions). It is plausible to assume that deliberation may also be a means to promote learning effects and thus reduce individual costs. If deliberative processes could enhance the alleviation of anomalies, institutions should be so designed to allow for these processes.

Effectiveness of and Compliance with Rules

Constitutional economists strictly differentiate between actions and rules and, thus, a constitutional interest and an interest to act,[55] or between constitutional and operative levels (similar to rule-utilitarianism and act-utilitarianism). This distinction applies both to the effectiveness of legal rules and the issue of justice and, thus, to the legitimacy of rules and their content. Constitutional Economics links up the two problems by assuming that the persons involved will more probably agree to rules which are incentive-compatible, as they are less costly. While a lack of interest in *rule-following* detracts from the *effectiveness of legal norms*, a lack of *interest in the validity* of rules (or the acceptance of legal norms) jeopardizes the stabil-

[50] For an experiment regarding a claim for damages based on tort see Jolls, Sunstein and Thaler (1998), p. 1532. If a defendant or claimant is asked to forecast the 'impartial' decision of the judge, then the persons involved in the test as claimants significantly overestimated the amount of damages while it was exactly the other way round when they were in the position of the defendant.

[51] Schelling (1960), pp. 57ff.

[52] For the experiments with deliberative opinion polling see List, McLean, Fishkin and Luskin (2000).

[53] See Eichenberger (1992); Eichenberger and Frey (1993), p. 61, for the lower utility level if individuals do not follow the Neumann-Morgenstern-axiom, as, for example, they do not perceive all winning possibilities and may be exploited by others.

[54] Eichenberger and Frey (1993), p. 57, talk primarily of *individual* incentives to reduce anomalies. This presupposes that individuals are aware of the anomaly.

[55] Brennan and Buchanan (1993), p. 129, see also Vanberg (1997), chapter I and Vanberg (1999a), p. 43.

ity of legal systems[56] because of constant pressure to change the legal rules.[57] Homann therefore recommends that

> rules be so designed as to reliably stimulate the compliance of individuals, thus enabling Constitutional Economics to adopt an idea which Kant, and many of his successors in modern philosophical ethics, have been unable to think, namely that the binding force of ethical rules is contingent: rules are binding with regard to actions and assert themselves because they are incentive-compatible (at least in ideal circumstances; A.v.A.), but contingent and in need of substantiation with regard to alternative rules.[58]

On the effectiveness of moral or legal norms, I would not agree with Homann that the incentive-method is the *only* capable method for securing effectiveness.[59] I would agree though that the economic method of rational choice and especially the thinking in dilemma-structures is in principle more promising concerning the effectiveness of rules. Herein lies a huge potential for economic analysis of law, as incentive compatible rules are more effective and less costly than those rules which need to be sanctioned. Nevertheless it is important to look at other determinations of rule-following, which will be done when I discuss Discourse Theory.

---

[56] As stated by Vanberg (1999a), p. 46 with reference to Rawls' *modus vivendi* and *overlapping consensus*; for related concepts see Rawls (1994), pp. 293ff and particularly pp. 306ff. The long-term stability of a legal system and its resistance to external changes can only be guaranteed by general consensus. With reference to this problem and Kant see Alexy (1996b), p. 420.

[57] The difference is made clear in an example given by Vanberg (1999a): Whereas a thief is not interested in rule-following but certainly in the validity of rules, a revolutionary is not interested in the latter.

[58] Homann (1997), p. 14, see also Homann and Kirchner (1995), p. 197: 'Economics is ethics with other means'; Homann (1997), p. 27: 'Incentive ethics is regarded as the ethics which is adequate to the modern world'. This also means that the morality of a society is reflected in its conditions for action, i.e. its rules, and no longer in the personal ethics of the individual.

[59] Homann (1997), p. 14. Correctly it should be formulated that incentive compatible rules are more likely to be consented to as they are less costly concerning surveillance and compliance. Incentive-compatibility is thus only a necessary but not a sufficient condition for consensus. An interest in the validity of rules exists only if the expected utility of the rules exceeds the expected costs of sanctions for the rules.
The critic of the New Institutional Economics by the old Institutional Economics, which treats the changeability of preferences through institutions, and also of legal sociology which considers the changeability of preferences through legal norms so important may also be mentioned.

Discourse Ethics and Deliberation

Deliberative theories, particularly as they relate to deliberative democracy,[60] see themselves as successors to Discourse Theory, and the theory of justice developed by Rawls (concept of reflective equilibrium).[61] Discourse Theory regards human communication as something more than just an anthropologic feature and, in their assessment of actions and society, concentrate on communicative and/or discursive rationality.[62] Unlike economics or, more generally, the rational choice paradigm, Discourse Theory is not concerned with the *aggregation* but rather the *transformation of preferences* through deliberative processes. This means that individuals basically are willing to change their preferences and/or interests.[63] One main characteristic of the process of deliberation is the need to give reasons.

Reaching Consensus

Deliberation is defined in somewhat varying terms,[64] depending on whether the orientation toward the result[65] or process prevails.[66] What the deliberative theories

---

[60] For a short survey see Cohen (1991), p. 17 with the following definition: 'By a deliberative democracy I shall mean, roughly, an association whose affairs are governed by the public deliberation of its members'. And again on p. 21: 'The notion of a deliberative democracy is rooted in the intuitive ideal of a democratic association in which the justification of the terms and conditions of associations proceeds through public argument and reasoning among equals'. See also Dryzek (1990); Elster (1998a); Dryzek (2000b; 2000a).

[61] See Rawls (1990), pp. 38ff. There are of course important differences between deliberative theories and Discourse Theory and I would suggest that the connection between deliberative theories and Constitutional Economics is more easily made than between Discourse Theory and Constitutional Economics. Nevertheless, Discourse Theory provides the theoretical basis for deliberative theories, see also Habermas (1999), who himself suggests a model of deliberative politics.
For a (critical) discussion of Rawls, see Cohen (1991), pp. 18ff.; Benhabib (1994), pp. 35ff. For a (critical) discussion of Habermas (1992), see Sabel and Gerstenberg (2001), pp. 31ff. and Sabel and Cohen (2001), pp. 11f.

[62] For an outline see Habermas (1988), particularly vol. 1, and Habermas (1992).

[63] Ferejohn and Pasquino (2000), p. 2: 'But whether goals or purposes change as a result of deliberation or whether they merely remain open to revision, the way that deliberation changes or reinforces goals or purposes is by giving reasons or arguments. Deliberation in this sense is participating in the process of reasoning about public action. This entails being open to reasons, willing to alter your preferences, beliefs or actions if convincing reasons are offered to do so – and being willing to base attempts to persuade others in giving reasons rather than threatening coercion or duplicity.'

[64] For details see contributions in Elster (1998a).

[65] In the result-oriented definition of Stokes (1998), deliberation is 'the endogenous change of preferences resulting from communication'.

[66] Cohen (1991), p. 23, Benhabib (1994), fn. 13, and Gambetta (1998) by contrast focus on the process itself by saying that all it takes for deliberation is a conversation whereby individuals speak and listen sequentially before making a collective decision. As the ration-

have in common, however, is that (as in Constitutional Economics) all those concerned are involved in the collective decision (democratic element) which is made after hearing and accepting arguments, and that participants in the discourse (at least officially)[67] feel committed to rationality and impartiality (deliberative part). This deliberative part concerning the interest component of preferences distinguishes Discourse Theory from Constitutional Economics. This makes it possible (but not necessary) to influence not only the theoretical component of preferences but also the one relating to interests. This is done through learning processes that may alter both interests *and* theories, the assumption being that people have a private and a public autonomy which supplement each other. While the former has to do with individual choices and implementing a personal concept of what is good, the latter revolves around choices to be made together with others and putting into practice a political concept of what is fair or good.[68] The latter is especially interesting for the definition of the public good, which is in principle open, i.e. no definition of the public good is given ex ante, but is left to the constantly reversible deliberative process.[69]

Learning processes have several components. First, the deliberative forum can gather dispersed information and dispersed intelligence. Second, the arguments given need to make sense to everybody. But even if there is consensus about the theories concerned, there must still be a weighing between the different affected interests. This weighing may be structured by giving some reasons more weight than others. Those reasons may be constitutional arguments or those concerning basic rights, which should a get a higher weight than all others.[70]

Legitimacy of Consensus

Discourse Theory does not distinguish between the level of actions and rules as Constitutional Economics does. Discourse Theory is primarily a theory of reasoning and accepts rules and value statements as correct and legitimate if consensus

---

ality concept of Discourse Theory is generally procedural, only the process-oriented approach will be discussed in the following. In other words, preferences may, but do not necessarily have to, change in the discursive process.

[67] According to Alexy (1995), pp. 133, 142ff., elites and tyrants see an individual utility in justifying social systems as, in the long term, legitimacy is less costly and more stable than pure force. Legitimacy is established where elites make allowance for people's interest in substantive rightness (even if this is only alleged). The rules of the discourse can then be justified by stability interests (advantageous in the long term). Even if the interest in the rules of the discourse was not subjectively there, or just a (Machiavellian) pretext, that does not detract from at least the objective and/or institutional validity of the rules.

[68] This differentiation follows Alexy (1995), p. 127 and the analysis of concepts in the history of ideas made by Habermas (1992), pp. 112ff.

[69] See extensively Engel (2000). See also Sabel and Cohen (2001), p. 4: '(T)he deliberate conception of collective decision making extends the idea of treating people with respect from rights and procedures to justifications themselves.'

[70] See Sabel and Cohen (2001), pp. 6f. However, this does not predetermine the weighing of the conflicting interests itself.

can be reached by following certain discourse rules (which make a discourse 'non-authoritarian'), i.e. through an ideal speech situation. These rules make some general demands on rational and practical argumentation, are vital for the substantive rightness of the discourse and apply also to monologues. Requirements include freedom from contradiction, a capacity for universalization by using language consistently, clear terms and diction, empirical truth, taking consequences into account, and weighing up things. Specific rules are to guarantee that a discourse (of several people) is impartial. Presenting the whole Discourse Theory here would go too far, and a few brief notes should suffice. To cite the discourse rules in the words of Alexy:[71]

> 1. Anyone who can speak may take part;
> 2.(a) Anyone may question any statement made;
> 2.(b) Anyone may introduce any statement into the discourse;
> 2.(c) Anyone may express their attitudes, desires and needs;
> 3. No speaker may be prevented from exercising the rights listed in 1. and 2. by coercion applied within or outside the discourse.

If the rules of the discourse apply, then the following condition of universal agreement and substantive rightness applies:

> A norm may find universal consent in a discourse only if the consequences of general compliance for satisfying the interests of each individual can be accepted by all. ...Exactly those norms are correct and valid which are judged correct by everyone in an ideal discourse.[72]

No claim to ultimate reasons[73] need to be made in demanding that actual and practical discourses on norms or results should comply with discourse rules as far as possible.[74] While the ideal of the non-authoritarian discourse is certainly unachievable, Alexy notes[75] that one could very well pursue an ideal that may never be attained.[76] Seeking to approach the ideal of the Discourse Theory can nonetheless be quite interesting particularly for institutional design and, just as the consensus in Constitutional Economics, would make the ideal discourse *an enlarged regulatory idea for shaping institutions.*[77]

---

[71] Alexy (1995), p. 130.

[72] Alexy (1995), p. 131, where Alexy quotes the relevant rules established by Habermas and Kant.

[73] For the abandonment of ultimate reasoning in Discourse Theory see Habermas (1983).

[74] As in Frey and Kirchgässner (1993), p. 131.

[75] Alexy (1996b), pp. 158f.

[76] It is conceded here that the ideal character of a discourse may be problematic if it actually involves the legitimacy and acceptance of institutions, but empirical studies have shown that better agreement on rules makes a difference as regards both their acceptance and observance. See also Tyler (1990; 1994).

[77] This becomes interesting, if one asks for institutional efficiency rather than for allocative efficiency as welfare economics and most parts of the law and economics movement does.

Discursive Theory does not limit deliberation to constitutional processes but regards it as ubiquitous on all levels, meaning that it is a deliberative process suitable and advisable not only on the constitutional level but also for all levels of institutions. It might be applied not only to democratic procedures in a strict sense but also to administrative procedures especially when they interfere with citizens' rights.

What makes Discourse Ethics problematic, however, is that it does not make sufficient allowance for the phenomenon of scarcity and the related opportunity costs,[78] which is eminent from a legal viewpoint. The argument that a discourse and the consensus reached by it, is fulfilling the discourse criteria is not quite valid if the legitimacy of the results has to be judged in reality where discourses have to be restricted or even broken off due to the actual scarcity problem. Legitimacy then depends on whether the discourse is accepted as such by the participants, and the question will have to be answered empirically in the end. The theories of deliberative democracy assume though that the crucial criterion for legitimacy is not the consensus (even if it may stay the goal). Also results reached by majority rule are legitimate if and only if they are the decisions on different alternatives reached in a discourse of free and equals. Even if majority rules are a means of aggregating of preferences, the difference to non-deliberatively aggregated preferences and to Constitutional Economics is stressed.[79]

Procedural versus Decision Utility

Discourse Theory does not explicitly account for procedural utility of deliberation as utility is not a concept used in Discourse Theory. We may therefore regard the approaches in economics which explicitly now take into account procedural utility.[80] Procedural utility refers to the utility that people gain from the decision making process itself quite irrespective of the outcome of the decision. It was possible to identify empirically the utility derived from processes in political decision-making, esp. the utility of actual and potential participation in political decision-making processes. Frey and Stutzer considered participatory decision-making in politics a possible source for procedural utility, especially rights to directly participate in the democratic process, which are supposed to give citizens a feeling and a cognitive understanding that their preferences are seriously taken into account in a fair political process. Even though this study does not look at the details of the deliberative process of participation, it nevertheless takes the first step according to which having the possibility of taking part in deliberative processes does enhance individual well-being.

---

[78] See also Avio (1999), pp. 528f. Opportunity costs of some participants may be higher than those of others which might lead to inequality.

[79] Cohen (1991), p. 23.

[80] See Frey and Stutzer (2001).

The thinking behind Discourse Theory has been supported by experiments, one undertaken by Tyler[81] in Chicago in which he empirically studied the motives for complying with rules and established a link with legitimacy. For rule-following and the acceptance of government decisions, particularly those made by law courts and (rights-infringing, interventionist) administrative acts, he found both a normative and an instrumental perspective of rule-following. The latter is based on the economic analysis of law and assumes that people comply with rules because of *external incentives*. The sociological model of social control also fits this instrumental perspective, as it is result-oriented and not concerned with *rule application*. It is supposed that the results of legal proceedings, for example, are accepted only if they are thought to be beneficial in result. A specific problem arising in connection with institutional propositions that rely merely on sanctions is the high cost of monitoring.

What Tylor calls the normative perspective, by contrast, would study the effect a person's views on fairness of procedures of government action and the generation of rules has on compliance. This implies intrinsic motives for rule-following which are independent of external incentives. One may further differentiate between individuals motivated to comply with rules by ethics that they have internalized (so that they might even break rules found legitimate but inconsistent with their ethics), and others who comply because they consider rules and government authorities legitimate. The latter is most interesting here, i.e. the conditions in which people are willing to follow rules because they consider them, or their application by authorities, to be legitimate. According to Tyler's empirical study, these conditions include aspects of a fair procedure, i.e. 'neutrality, impartiality, lack of bias (or self-interest on the part of the authority, A.v.A.), honesty, efforts to be fair, politeness, and respect for citizens rights'.[82] People 'settle issues of loyalty and obedience to organizational rules and authorities by focusing on the procedure by which the authorities make decisions'.[83]

This procedural justice may be further subdivided into process control and decision control. Process control allows those concerned to frankly present their arguments or opinions that need not necessarily affect the result. Process control affects satisfaction and the perceived fairness of a procedure in a way that is independent from decision control.[84] Here process utility supplements decision utility, which of course remains in force, particularly if the result does not relate to 'low cost decisions'. According to Tyler, 'interaction is a game of mixed motives'.[85] His model, in the end, also relies on selfishness but differentiates between short-term and long-term interests. Individuals considering the legitimacy of legal authorities will focus on procedural justice. Where this is not perceived, rule-following suf-

[81] Tyler (1990) who also refers to similar studies.
[82] Tyler (1990), p. 7.
[83] Tyler (1990), p. 172. See also Frey and Stutzer (2001), p. 3, for further literature.
[84] See Tyler (1990), p. 116 for further literature and Sabel and Gerstenberg (2001), p. 34.
[85] Tyler (1990), p. 171. Tyler does not use the notion of 'game' in a game-theoretical sense.

fers. *In short, 'not experiencing fair procedures undermines legitimacy'*[86] *and lack of legitimacy undermines in turn compliance.*

Deliberative Institutional Economics

This approach of Deliberative Institutional Economics can only be briefly summarized in the following,[87] but at least some points regarding the need to combine Discourse Theory with Institutional Economics can be identified. Problems and possibilities of discursive institutional design will be mentioned. Further research is certainly needed.

Theoretical Combination

To put it in a nutshell, Institutional Economics is concerned with a *homo oeconomicus* who optimizes given preferences by negotiating and interacting with others and seeking to influence them with the 'carrot and the stick' (external incentives). From a normative angle, Constitutional and New Institutional Economics looks for institutions and/or decision-making rules (institutional comparison) that best help citizens to achieve their (given) interests. Discourse Theory, by contrast, is built around a *homo communicans* who makes a claim to substantive rightness by presenting arguments in public, and seeks a dialogue with partners whose preferences he hopes to alter by offering better reasons. Positions of power or coercion must not be used, and the discourse is subject to rules designed to make it legitimate.

While neither approach may claim exclusivity, combining them can be quite productive. For every *homo oeconomicus* there is, in the background, a *homo communicans* who in turn also has to make rational decisions. People normally use both strategies and thus there is the need of a behavioral model of action bringing both approaches together – a *homo rationalis communicans*. What is helpful here is that the two paradigms do not contradict each other and merely use different perspectives, creating several points of contact between New Institutional Economics and Discourse Theory.

[86] Tyler (1990), p. 172.

[87] Note the difference in the link established between institutional economics and Discourse Ethics by Avio (1999) who sees his approach as following the tradition of the old institutional economics represented by Veblen and Commons, and explicitly remote from the New Institutional Economics with its neo-classical model of homo oeconomicus which he opposes. The latter is no longer much used, however, and Avio's criticism is therefore misleading even though it still applies to the economical analysis of law in the succession of Posner, see also Posner (1998) and Posner (1993).

Reaching Consensus

Let us first look at the possibility of reaching agreement by way of deliberation. Constitutional Economics assumes given preferences, and the adoption of rules in a consensus reached by individuals considering their own interests. If the parties dissent, the status quo prevails as legitimate since it has been proven to be Pareto-optimal. A discourse on the theoretical component of preferences is, however, possible at constitutional level and may involve extra information provided by experts, or a discourse on the actual consequences of rules which are at issue. What is neglected in this context is a possible change also of the interest component of preferences through deliberation. It is also conceivable that public pressure to give reasons (under the rules of the discourse) could alter people's positions in cases where they cannot easily present selfish views, which would at least restrict their strategic or opportunist behavior.[88] Another question is whether people are always aware of their own interests and/or purposes. Frey and Kirchgässner as economists in this connection refer to meta-preferences, i.e. the preferred views of an individual on what his or her (actual) preferences should be (preferences regarding preferences).[89] These are more likely to be discovered or emphasized in a process of deliberation.

Constitutional Economics supposes that people faced with a public decision would rather deliberate on their own and then just decide (in a way a Kantian idea). This may be costly to the individual as the pros and cons need to be searched individually. Deliberation may reduce these costs, as the different arguments (including ex ante dispersed information) can be expected to be delivered through the discourse.[90]

On a sub-constitutional plane, Constitutional Economics continues to keep the theoretical component of preferences constant. Discourse Theory, by contrast, tolerates changes in components relating both to interests and theory, and does so at all stages of the normative hierarchy. Admitting deliberation at all levels appears appropriate in this light because of the conflicts, and collective action, required in all conceivable situations and at all levels of norms. This implies that deliberative procedures have to be regarded not only in democratic procedures (e.g. direct democratic institutions) but also within the executive power, i.e. in situations between state and citizen, especially administrative procedures. In other words, deliberative institutions can be used in general-abstract constellations (making of norms) as well as in individual-concrete constellations (applying the norm to particular cases).

---

[88] See also Benhabib (1994), Cohen (1991), and Elster (1998b). Conversely, the distortion of preferences through public discourse is described by Kuran (1997).

[89] For a basic comparison see Harsanyi (1955) and particularly p. 315 where a difference is made between subjective and ethical preferences, the former being of a personal, the latter of a social nature, and Sen (1977), pp. 99ff. who speaks of 'rankings of preference rankings'.

[90] I thank Stefan Voigt for this argument.

As is well known, a purely formal look at the theory of social choice and the aggregation of preferences results in Arrow's (im-)possibility theorem,[91] which has been argued to have severe implications for the normative theory of democracy. Dryzek and List[92] therefore propose incorporating deliberative processes into the theoretical analysis to cover preference structures.

> (D)eliberative democracy is an account of how communication processes can change, and possibly structure, people's preferences and dispositions toward collective decision making. Social choice theory, in turn, can inform us on what input-output relations are available in collective decision making.[93]

Deliberation could, for example, reduce the 'unrestricted domain' of admissible preferences, and it could also structure preferences. Where these are 'single peaked', which may be promoted through deliberation, it will be possible to find social choice procedures that are not subject to the impossibility theorem.

Legitimacy of Consensus

New Institutional Economics and Discourse Theory concern themselves with procedural rationality and, on a social plane, are basically open as regards their outcome.[94] Both theories are cognitivistic insofar as they suppose that those moral

---

[91] For an outline see Arrow (1951). The theory of collective decisions (or social choice) deals with problems resulting from the *search* of numerous individuals for joint decisions (aggregation). Under Arrow's impossibility theorem, it may be possible that no reasonable and consistent decision process enabling choices from a number of alternatives can be found for a society. He basically requires of such a procedure that (1) all systems including the social order must be transitive, (2) all preferences are admissible ('unrestricted/universal domain'), (3) society must prefer alternative A over alternative B if each individual does so (Pareto principle), (4) where a choice is made between two alternatives, only the preferences of individuals with regard to these alternatives need be considered (independence from irrelevant alternatives), (5) no-one must be a dictator.
This is an urgent problem in all types of collective decision-making, as in bodies of judges or parliaments. Regarding the importance of the theory of social choice and Arrow's impossibility theorem see Höffe (1980), pp. 30ff. For general information on attempts to solve the impossibility theorem see Heller, Starr and Starrett (1986).

[92] Dryzek and List (2003), see also experiments with 'deliberative polls' for an empirical backup of the theoretical approach: List, McLean, Fishkin and Luskin (2000).

[93] Dryzek and List (2003), quoted from an earlier version.

[94] This means that Constitutional Economics, on an individual level, is consequentialist as 'opting for consequentialism ... does not concern the substantive rightness of a philosophical position, but ... feeds back to the thesis that individual actors will, at least in most of their decisions, make some allowance for their consequences'. Kirchner (1997), p. 17. The individualist/consequentialist approach is linked here to the position of normative individualism and thus, on the social plane, leads to a procedural (and therefore preference-dependent) deontological position of indeterminate content. See also Brennan and Buchanan (1986), p. 45: 'The contractarian-constitutionalist position is almost necessarily nonconsequentialist and deontological. Evaluative criteria must be applied to rules or

judgments and norms may claim validity, which are reasonable to everybody concerned and therefore are based on commonly agreeable reasons. Another common feature is that, in a consensus on rules, both assume that the consensus is only composed of interests that are capable of generalization.[95] While not necessarily excluding a close look at decision-making processes, Constitutional Economics, with its incentive ethics neglects such considerations, being focused on results. However, the requirements for legitimizing a consensus cannot be further specified if, in normative terms, the conditions of the decision-making process are largely neglected and no close examination is made particularly of the institutional facilities enabling decision processes. As regards the legitimacy of institutions, acceptance is greater if a procedural approach is used allowing individuals to express their opinions and interests in a discourse, and if everybody is forced to give reasons for their opinions.[96] This calls for opportunities to express one's views and, not least, institutional pressure to give reasons for them.

Whereas Discourse Theory mainly discusses requirements that must be met if individuals are to recognize universalistic interests, economic approaches come in later to look at the decision proper and its (formal decision) rules, the scarcity conditions, opportunity costs, and strategic interests. It is plain to see that here, too, decisions are invariably preceded by discourses which may change individual attitudes and, therefore, the resulting decisions. And there is no doubt that these discursive processes must also be (and are, in fact,) controlled by institutions which in turn make allowance for scarcity conditions in society and individual opportunity costs. In other words, discursive rules give positive criteria that have to be fulfilled if a consensus is to be judged legitimate, whereas Constitutional Economics formulates negative criteria beyond which a consensus is deemed illegitimate. From the viewpoint of Discourse Theory the conditions of Constitutional Economics are necessary but not sufficient conditions for a legitimate consensus – the former apply substantially stricter conditions as the latter. Those conditions may give a substantive criterion X in the sense of Vanberg to end the infinite regress in Constitutional Economics, caused by the purely procedural understanding of a freely agreed consensus.

This leads to the question of 'optimal deliberation'.[97] Constitutional Economics basically should have no problems accepting the fact that institutional design should match the rules of the discourse. First, this is because it, too, wants to give

---

processes rather than to end states or results.... As such, there is no means of evaluating any end state, because there is no external standard or scale through which end states can be "valued"'. Also in Buchanan (1988), p. 136: 'Any teleological conception of the law, and of the constitution and of the role of the judiciary, is simply out of bounds under any contractarian or exchange conceptualization of social order'.

[95] Of interest in this connection is Vanberg (1999b), p. 9 who refers to the Discourse Theories of Apel and Habermas and makes a comparison between 'constitutional interests capable of consensus' as a criterion of the substantive rightness of (constitutional) contents, and the criteria for the rules of a discourse requiring a capacity for universalization, and impartiality.

[96] See also Dryzek (2000b).

[97] For details see Shapiro (2000).

individuals an opportunity to express their preferences in an *enlightened* manner. Secondly, it wants them to follow rules, which is more likely if they recognize rules as legitimate. Deliberative procedures and mandatory reason-giving by state institutions are a substitute or a complement to (direct) democratic legitimacy. They are, to a certain extent functionally equivalent. After all, disclosing authoritative decisions and offering arguments in their favor is a necessity if principals are to exercise control over their agents, no matter if the relationship politicians/citizen, administrative agencies/citizen or jurisdiction/citizen is concerned. The theoretical deficit in Constitutional Economics was diagnosed in the fact that it presupposes the enlightened manner of individuals in choosing rules, and does therefore not account for the institutional necessities enabling the individuals to do so in reality. Here, Discourse Theory can help to enhance legitimacy of consensus.

Procedural versus Decision Utility

It is also possible that New Institutional Economics, with its focus on decision utility rather than process utility, does not cover all components of acceptance and rule-following. Where process utility is important, institutions should be designed accordingly, particularly if there is a commitment to normative individualism, which takes these 'utility potentials' into account.

Economics is primarily a social science that seeks to explain and predict. A precondition for that is a model of human behavior as explanatory model. Rational-Choice theory certainly is a very successful theory, to which there is no other, better paradigm in sight, especially with regard to the need of predictions and norm impact analysis. Nevertheless in my view the paradigm is in need of a complement, especially if institutional design beyond the market is analysed. Discourse Theory lacks its own social science paradigm that would enable it to make explanations or predictions. Nevertheless, *homo communicans* is a rational, unemotional individual and therefore in principle compatible with *homo oeconomicus.* If the potential of explanation and prediction of *homo oeconomicus* is to be strengthened, it is advisable to integrate the communicative aspect of human behavior and use a *homo rationalis communicans.* The analytic stringency of economics is then admittedly partly abandoned, and the accent shifts instead to social mechanisms that may be vital.

Effectiveness of and Compliance with Rules

The acceptance of rules and decisions is a key element of rule-following and vital for political and legal science of institutional design. Even in cases where unanimous decisions are not obtained, rules presumably become more acceptable if decision-making processes are perceived to be fair and just. A Deliberative Institutional approach does not detract from the individualist approach of New Institutional Economics with its orientation toward self-interest, but rather expands it. A particularly important factor in the effectiveness of institutions is the promotion not only of extrinsic, but also of intrinsic motives for an individual's compliance with rules. This is the case if procedures are regarded as fair, meaning that a person may not only expect a fair result but can express opinions and is given good and impartial reasons for a decision. The participants of the discourse will – according to Discourse Theory – regard the fact that the discourse conditions are adhered to as a sufficient condition of compliance with a rule.[98] This certainly may be put in doubt, but again we find a possible complement of Institutional Economics. If the latter trusts mainly in incentive-compatible rules (self-interest) for compliance, the former focuses on the acceptance of the decision through reason-giving. These concepts seem complementary. If democracy is more than a mere aggregation of preferences at all levels, then the discursive element of law is vital in claiming legitimacy, which in turn affects rule-following and therefore the effectiveness of the law. Thus, for institutional design it seems plausible to test not only for incentive-compatibility but also for discourse-compatibility.[99] Institutions may then also be criticized on the ground that they are discourse-incompatible.

Applications

When it comes to decision-making, implementation and monitoring, deliberative procedures can play a role in collective action, and particularly in exercising government power. The following examples are far from telling the whole story but should demonstrate that deliberation, however imperfect, is ubiquitous in democratic states. I will look at the possibilities and practices of deliberative procedures in all the three state powers separately, starting with the legislative power, then the executive power and finally the judiciary.

Let us first consider democratic decision-making processes. What Frey and Kirchgässner criticize about Discourse Theory is that, except for Habermas,[100] it makes no practical suggestions for the institutional design of democratic processes[101] or, when it does, mostly refers to representative procedures. The two authors, by contrast, explicitly refer to discursive ethics in order to show the purpose of direct democratic procedures from the viewpoint of New Institutional Economics.[102] In discussing institutions such as popular (constitutional) initiatives and mandatory/optional plebiscites which are part of Switzerland's semi-direct democracy, they find that some, but clearly not the majority, of all plebiscites went against the recommendations of representatives (between 1848 and 1990, 61% of optional plebiscites were adopted as proposed by parliament). This means, on the one hand, that the preferences of representatives and those represented may differ, which is quite in keeping with the assumptions of New Institutional Economics. On the other hand, Frey and Kirchgässner want to show that it is the institutions of direct democracy which enable a discourse not only among political circles but

98 See Cohen (1991), p. 22: '(T)he participants suppose that they can act from the results, taking the fact that a certain decision is arrived at through their deliberation as a sufficient reason for complying with it'.
99 I would like to thank Philip Pettit for this hint.
100 See Habermas (1992).
101 Frey and Kirchgässner (1993), pp. 132f.
102 Similar to Saward (2000).

also for society as a whole in the first place (or the 'principal' in terms of New Institutional Economics).

This discourse has the following characteristics:[103] 1) Bills are always discussed in comparison with alternatives; 2) The more important the bill (depending on the unit of governmental jurisdiction), the more intensive the debate; 3) The discourse often starts from the bottom, particularly by way of a legislative initiative; 4) Political parties, interest groups and individuals from all social strata take part. These institutions, naturally, do not conform to the rules of the discourse, but are closer to the ideal compared with purely representative democracy. And while strategic arguments may well be expected from participants, with opportunity costs (particularly those of individuals) coming into play, this is at least a discourse where each party can more or less enter its arguments (albeit at different opportunity costs). There is a powerful stimulus for those representing opposite positions to criticize the other side and force it to disclose its arguments, creating exactly the type of discourse in which each side has to give reasons for its claims. While this also applies to cases where no agreement is reached because the sides still have diverging interests or theories, what we may expect according to Frey and Kirchgässner is better information for voters who can be observed to 'behave in more altruistic ways than in other, and particularly economic, decisions'.[104] This would give the so-called meta-preferences a greater decision-making role in votes involving discursive processes[105] but does not, of course, mean that individuals disregard their own interests. These may, however, be modified by providing more information – changing the theoretical component according to Buchanan and Vanberg – or by altering the interest component with regard to meta-preferences.

Other proposals have come from Ackerman and Fishkin who suggest giving people a day off ('deliberation day') for gathering and exchanging views and information prior to important votes and elections.[106]

A deliberative application for government administration has been proposed by Mastronardi[107] who examined the potential for communicative rationality in the Swiss administrative process using the example of audit commissions.[108] This he describes as a democratic procedure for supervising the administration, which becomes all the more important (with government bodies having to give reasons for their actions and disclose their arguments) the less democratic monitoring there

---

103 Frey and Kirchgässner (1993), pp. 139f.

104 Frey and Kirchgässner (1993), p. 141.

105 Frey and Kirchgässner (1993), p. 141.

106 Ackerman and Fishkin (2000), p. 1: 'Deliberation Day – a new national holiday. It will be held one week before major national elections. Registered voters will be called together in neighborhood meeting places, in small groups of 15, and larger groups of 500, to discuss the central issues raised by the campaign. Each deliberator will be paid $150 for the day's work of citizenship, on condition that he or she shows up at the polls the next week. All other work, except the most essential, will be prohibited by law.'

107 Mastronardi (1991/1992).

108 These are organs for parliamentary supervision of the administrative system and the administration of justice in Switzerland, with government bodies being monitored by other state agencies rather than citizens.

is. While administrative supervision by other government agencies is just monitoring within the state itself, the approach would seem to be of general importance for administrative practices that affect individuals. Such external monitoring[109] may apply to procedures involving one person, or many as in public enquiries (public works planning procedures).[110] In both cases, those concerned will be heard and may object in a legally effective way. Even more important is the fact that administrative decisions may only be supervised if reasons have to be given which the authority then needs to present in detail before legal action is taken, or in a lawcourt. There is a trend, in Germany at least, toward requiring authorities to give more reasons when taking discretionary action. This supervision of decisions is, however, primarily geared to legality rather than expedience, leaving a wide area exempt from the need of reason-giving and judicial overview. These questions may be discussed in detail only if the need for deliberation and reaching agreement is included in the analysis.

Another possibility are direct-deliberative polyarchies, in which the local/and/or regional entities are governed through central supervision and (possibly) central intervention but are competing through direct-democratic local autonomy to find the best regulative practices (democratic experimentalism).[111] This model is understood as an alternative between market and state. The only prerequisite for this practice is a prescribed objective of the central state towards the toleration of constitutional boundaries. The exchange of information is to be guaranteed by the central state. This suggestion shifts the decision competence from the administrative agency of local entities to the citizens, which may exercise their quasi-legislative competencies within the limits of the former competencies of the agencies.

At this junction, let us briefly discuss implications for the judicial system. Studies made by Tyler[112] have shown that, in court proceedings, people assess not only the results of judgment but, at least to the same extent, the procedure itself. They attach particular importance to the way the parties are treated by the judge: whether he listened and heard all arguments, and whether he appeared neutral and gave good and exhaustive reasons for his judgment. Democratic systems have rules for legal procedures that give the parties an opportunity to present their arguments both in administrative and civil cases, and with even more details specified in the law of criminal procedure. The courts are then forced to weigh the arguments in their findings and substantiate their decision.

---

[109] See also the instrument of mass suits, such as citizen suits or class action Aaken (2003).

[110] Public enquiries are formal planning procedures for large projects (airports, waste disposal plants, etc.) – see §§ 72ff VwVfG (German administrative procedural law) – requiring hearings and oral procedures in which all objections are to be discussed.

[111] See Sabel and Cohen (2001); Sabel and Gerstenberg (2001). Sabel and Cohen (2001), p. 8, cite some examples: 'Urban poverty, local economic development, and effective social service delivery... . Solving them requires cooperation across quite different institutions and groups – for example lending institutions, health care providers, technology diffusers, education and training establishments, housing authorities, community development corporations, neighborhood associations'.

[112] Tyler (1990).

Ferejohn and Pasquino,[113] in studying deliberative expectations with regard to constitutional courts and comparing the U.S. with Europe, have found two types of deliberative action. On the one hand, these courts state reasons which may make those subject to the law change their mind so that social consensus is achieved. On the other, there are discursive processes taking place within the courts. Leaving details and differences aside, the important thing here is that constitutional courts invariably have to substantiate their judgment in order to gain acceptance and change preferences.[114] This applies in particular when it is assumed that the findings of constitutional courts fundamentally affect other hypothetic or real cases. The requirement to give reasons means that arguments are made public, which in turn may improve effectiveness because those subject to the law can better assess their expectations. Constitutional courts cannot simply publish their rulings but are bound to state reasons in all democratic countries.[115]

Conclusion

Economics focuses on explanation and prognosis of social phenomena, whereas Discourse Theory can be considered in the first place to be a normative theory of society, which lacks an elaborate social science paradigm. Economics may therefore deliver a paradigm to Discourse Theory, which, if it does not neglect the communicative aspects of human behavior, promises to be very fruitful for positive and normative questions.

New Institutional Economics/Constitutional Economics and Discourse Theory differ in their normative standpoints and their normative focus, even though both are procedural theories of rational decision. Discourse Theory is concerned with the conditions of decision procedures and their relevance for the individual. This has implications for the procedure of finding consensus and the acceptance and legitimacy not only for rules and norms but also for single (legal/administrative) cases. To neglect these conditions bears the danger of not being able to sketch an adequate institutional design. As Deliberative Institutional Economics suggests, norms need to be incentive-compatible and discourse-compatible.

---

113 Ferejohn and Pasquino (2000).

114 The reader is again reminded of the U.S. Supreme Court judgment in Brown vs. Board of Education, 347 U.S. 483 (1954) against racial segregation in schools.

115 There is, however, a wide range in the scope of reasoning and, often, the extent to which dissenting opinions may be published.

References

Aaken, A. van (2003) "Massenklagen im öffentlichen Recht aus institutionenökonomischer Sicht: Eine Art der direkten Volksrechte", *Kritische Vierteljahresschrift für Gesetzgebung und Rechtswissenschaft*, Heft 1, 44-75.

Ackerman, B.A. and J. Fishkin (2000) *Deliberation Day: Deliberating about Deliberative Democracy*, Austin/Texas, http://www.la.utexas.edu/conf2000/papers.html.

Alessi, L. de (1992) "Efficiency Criteria for Optimal Laws: Objective Standards of Value Jugdements?", *Constitutional Political Economy* 3, 321-342.

Alexy, R. (1995) "Diskurstheorie und Menschenrechte", in Alexy, R. (ed.) *Recht, Vernunft, Diskurs: Studien zur Rechtsphilosophie*, Frankfurt a. M. (Suhrkamp), 127-164.

Alexy, R. (1996a) *Theorie der Grundrechte*, Frankfurt a.M. (Suhrkamp).

Alexy, R. (1996b) *Theorie der juristischen Argumentation: Die Theorie des rationalen Diskurses der juristischen Begründung*, Frankfurt a.M. (Suhrkamp).

Arrow, K. J. (1951) *Social Choice and Individual Values*, New York et al. (John Wiley).

Aufderheide, D. (1996) "Konstitutionelle Ökonomik versus Theorie der Wirtschaftspolitik: Herausforderung des Herausforderers? Kommentar zu Stefan Voigt", in Pies, I. and M. Leschke (eds.) *James Buchanans konstitutionelle Ökonomik*, Tübingen (Mohr), 184-192.

Avio, K. L. (1999) "Habermasian Ethics and Institutional Law and Economics", *Kyklos* 52, 511-535.

Benhabib, S. (1994) "Deliberative Rationality and Models of Democratic Legitimacy", *Constellations: An International Journal of Critical and Democratic Theory* 1, 1-50.

Brennan, G. and J. M. Buchanan (1986) *The Reason of Rules: Constitutional Political Economy*, Cambridge (Cambridge University Press).

Brennan, G. and J. M. Buchanan (1993) *Die Begründung von Regeln: konstitutionelle politische Ökonomie*, Tübingen (Mohr).

Buchanan, J. M. (1959) "Positive Economics, Welfare Economics, and Political Economy", *Journal of Law and Economics* 2, 124-138.

Buchanan, J. M. (1984) *Die Grenzen der Freiheit: zwischen Anarchie und Leviathan*, Tübingen (Mohr).

Buchanan, J. M. (1986) "Kommentar", in Koslowski, P. (ed.) *Ethik des Kapitalismus*, Tübingen (Mohr), 81-92.

Buchanan, J. M. (1988) "Contractarian Political Economy and Constitutional Interpretation", *AEA Papers and Proceedings*, Mai 1988, 135-139.

Cohen, J. (1991) "Deliberation and Democratic Legitimacy", in Hamilton, A. and P. Pettit (eds.) *The Good Polity*, Oxford (Oxford University Press), 17-34.

Coleman, J. L. (1990) "Constitutional Contractarianism", *Constitutional Political Economy* 2, 135-148.

Dahl, G. B. and M. R. Ransom (1999) "Does Where You Stand Depend on Where You Sit? Tithing Donations and Self-Serving Bias", *American Economic Review* 89, 703-727.

Dryzek, J. S. (1990) *Discursive Democracy: Politics, Policy, and Political Science*, Cambridge (Cambridge University Press).

Dryzek, J. S. (2000a) *Deliberative Democracy and Beyond: Liberals, Critics, Contestations*, Oxford, New York (Oxford University Press).

Dryzek, J. S. (2000b) *Deliberative Democracy and Discoursive Legitimacy: Deliberating about Deliberative Democracy*, Austin/Texas, http://www.la.utexas.edu/conf2000/papers.html.

Dryzek, J. S. and C. List (2003) "Social Choice Theory and Deliberative Democracy", *British Journal of Political Science*, forthcoming.

Eichenberger, R. (1992) *Verhaltensanomalien und Wirtschaftswissenschaft: Herausforderungen, Reaktionen, Perspektiven*, Wiesbaden (Deutscher Universitätsverlag).

Eichenberger, R. and B. S. Frey (1993) "'Superrationalität' oder: Vom rationalen Umgang mit dem Irrationalen," in Herder-Dorneich, P., K.-E. Schenk and D. Schmidtchen (eds.) *Jahrbuch für Neue Politische Ökonomie* 12, 50-84.

Elster, J. (ed.) (1998a) *Deliberative Democracy*, Cambridge (Cambridge University Press).

Elster, J. (1998b) "Introduction", in Elster, J. (ed.) *Deliberative Democracy*, Cambridge (Cambridge University Press), 1-18.

Engel, C. (2000) *Offene Gemeinwohldefinitionen*, Preprints aus der Max-Planck-Projektgruppe Rechts der Gemeinschaftsgüter Bonn 2000/16, http://www.mpp-rdg.mpg.de/pdf_dat/00016.pdf.

Erlei, M., M. Leschke and D. Sauerland (1999) *Neue Institutionenökonomik*, Stuttgart (Schäffer-Poeschel Verlag).

Ferejohn, J. A. and P. Pasquino (2000) *Deliberative Institutions*, Working Paper.

Frey, B. S. and G. Kirchgässner (1993) "Diskursethik, Politische Ökonomie und Volksabstimmungen", *Analyse & Kritik* 15, 129-149.

Frey, B. S. and A. Stutzer (2001) *Beyond Bentham – Measuring Procedural Utility*, Working Paper, University of Zurich, Institute for Empirical Research in Economics.

Gambetta, D. (1998) "'Claro!': An Essay on Discursive Machismo", in Elster J. (ed.) *Deliberative Democracy*, Cambridge (Cambridge University Press), 19-43.

Habermas, J. (1962) *Strukturwandel der Öffentlichkeit: Untersuchungen zu einer Kategorie der bürgerlichen Gesellschaft*, Neuwied am Rhein (Luchterhand).

Habermas, J. (1983) "Diskursethik – Notizen zu einem Begründungsprogramm", in Habermas, J. (ed.) *Moralbewußtsein und kommunikatives Handeln*, Frankfurt a.M. (Suhrkamp), 53-125.

Habermas, J. (1988) *Theorie des kommunikativen Handelns*, Frankfurt a.M. (Suhrkamp).

Habermas, J. (1992) *Faktizität und Geltung: Beiträge zur Diskurstheorie des Rechts und des demokratischen Rechtsstaates*, Frankfurt a.M. (Suhrkamp).

Habermas, J. (1999) "Drei normative Modelle der Demokratie", in Habermas, J. (ed.) *Die Einbeziehung des Anderen: Studien zur politischen Theorie*, Frankfurt a.M. (Suhrkamp), 277-292.

Harsanyi, J. C. (1955) "Cardinal Welfare, Individualistic Ethics, and Interpersonal Comparisons of Utility", *Journal of Political Economy* 63, 309-321.

Hausman, D. M. (2000) "Revealed Preference, Belief, and Game Theory", *Economics and Philosophy* 16, 99-115.

Hayek, F. A. v. (1991) *Die Verfassung der Freiheit*, Tübingen (Mohr).

Hegmann, H. (1998) "Wissenssoziologische Aspekte der Verfassungsökonomik – Das Beispiel der Nachhaltigkeitsdebatte", in Renner, A. and F. Hinterberger (eds.) *Zukunftsfähigkeit und Neoliberalismus: Zur Vereinbarkeit von Umweltschutz und Wettbewerbswirtschaft*, Baden-Baden (Nomos), 175-195.

Heller, W. P., R. M. Starr and D. A. Starrett (1986) *Social Choice and Public Decision Making: Essays in Honor of Kenneth J. Arrow*, Cambridge (Cambridge University Press).

Hirschman, A. O. (1970) *Exit, Voice and Loyalty*, Cambridge/Mass. (Cambridge University Press).

Höffe, O. (1980) "Entscheidungstheoretische Denkfiguren und die Begründung", *Archiv für Rechts- und Sozialphilosophie*, Beiheft N. F., Nr. 14 (Argumentation und Recht), 21-58.

Hoffman, E. and M.L. Spitzer (1993) "Willingness to Pay vs. Willingness to Accept: Legal and Economic Implications", *Washington University Law Quarterly* 71, 59-114.

Homann, K. (1997). "Sinn und Grenze der ökonomischen Methode in der Wirtschaftsethik", in Aufderheide, D. and M. Dabrowski (eds.) *Wirtschaftsethik und Moralökonomik*, Berlin (Duncker & Humblot), 11-42.

Homann, K. and C. Kirchner (1995) "Ordnungsethik", in Herder-Dorneich, P., K.-E. Schenk and D. Schmidtchen (eds.) *Jahrbuch für Neue Politische Ökonomie* 14, Tübingen (Mohr), 189-211.

Jolls, C., C. R. Sunstein and R. H. Thaler (1998) "A Behavioral Approach to Law and Economics", *Stanford Law Review* 50, 1471-1548.

Kahneman, D. (1997) "New Challenges to the Rationality Assumption", *Legal Theory* 3, 105-124.

Kahneman, D. and A. Tversky (1979) "Prospect Theory: An Analysis of Decisions under Risk", *Econometrica* 47, 312-327.

Kirchner, C. (1997) *Ökonomische Theorie des Rechts*, Berlin et al. (Walter de Gruyter).

Kuran, T. (1997) *Leben in Lüge: Präferenzverfälschungen und ihre gesellschaftlichen Folgen*, Tübingen (Mohr Siebeck).

Lindenberg, S. (1985) "An Assessment of the New Political Economy: its Potential for the Social Science and for Sociology in Particular", *Sociological Theory* 3, 99-114.

List, C., I. McLean, J. Fishkin and R. Luskin (2000) *Can Deliberation Induce Greater Preference Structuration? Evidence from Deliberative Opinion Polls*, Paper presented at the Annual Meeting of the American Political Science Association, Washington DC.

Mastronardi, P. (1991/1992) "Die Praxis demokratischer Verwaltungskontrolle in der Schweiz. Chancen diskursiver Rationalität?", in Häberle, P. (ed.) *Jahrbuch des öffentlichen Rechts der Gegenwart*, Tübingen (Mohr), Neue Folge, Bd. 40, 131-147.

Meckling, W. H. (1976) "Values and the Choice of the Model of the Individual in the Social Science", *Schweizerische Zeitschrift für Volkswirtschaft und Statistik* 112, 545-560.

Michelman, F.I. (1999) *Brennan and Democracy*, Princeton (Princeton University Press).

Posner, R. A. (1993) "The New Institutional Economics Meets Law and Economics", *Journal of Institutional and Theoretical Economics* 149, 73-87.

Posner, R. A. (1998) *Economic Analysis of Law*, New York (Aspen Law & Business).

Rabin, M. (1998) "Psychology and Economics", *Journal of Economic Literature* 36, 11-46.

Rawls, J. (1990) *Eine Theorie der Gerechtigkeit*, Frankfurt a.M. (Suhrkamp).

Rawls, J. (1994) *Die Idee des politischen Liberalismus: Aufsätze 1978-1989*, Frankfurt a.M. (Suhrkamp).

Richter, R. and E. Furubotn (1996) *Neue Institutionenökonomik: eine Einführung und kritische Würdigung*, Tübingen (Mohr).

Sabel, C. (1995). *Design, Deliberation, and Democracy: On the New Pragmatism of Firms and Public Institutions*, http://www.law.columbia.edu/sabel /papers/Design.html.

Sabel, C. F. and J. Cohen (2001) *Directly Deliberative Polyarchy*, http://www.law.columbia.edu/sabel/papers/DDP.html.

Sabel, C. F. and O. Gerstenberg (2001) *Directly-Deliberative Polyarchy: An Institutional Ideal for Europe?*, http://www.law.columbia.edu/sabel/ papers.htm.

Samuelson, P. A. (1948) "Consumption Theory in Terms of Revealed Preferences", *Economica* 15, 234-266.

Saward, M. (2000) *Direct and Deliberative Democracy: Deliberating about Deliberative Democracy*, Austin/Texas, http://www.la.utexas.edu/conf2000/ papers.html.

Schelling, T. C. (1960) *The Strategy of Conflict*, Cambridge/Mass. (Harvard University Press).

Sen, A. K. (1977) "Rational Fools: A Critique of the Behavioral Foundations of Economic Theory", *Philosophy and Public Affairs* 6, 317-344.

Sen, A. K. (1979) "Personal Utilities and Public Judgement: Or What's Wrong with Welfare Economics?", *Economic Journal*, 537-558.
Sen, A. K. (1993) "Internal Consistency of Choice", *Econometrica* 61, 495-521.
Sen, A. K., (ed.) (1997a) *Choice, Welfare and Measurement*, Cambridge/Mass. (Harvard University Press). First published: Oxford (Blackwell) (1982).
Sen, A. K. (1997b) *On Ethics and Economics*, Oxford et al. (Blackwell).
Shapiro, I. (2000) *Optimal Deliberation: Deliberating about Deliberative Democracy*, Austin/Texas, http://www.la.utexas.edu/conf2000/papers.html.
Simon, H. A. (1957) *Models of Man*, London et al. (J. Wiley).
Simon, H. A. (1993) *Homo Rationalis*, Frankfurt a.M. et al. (Campus Verlag).
Stark, D. and L. Bruszt (1998) *Postsocialist Pathways: Transforming Politics and Property in East Central Europe*, Cambridge (Cambridge University Press).
Stokes, S. (1998) "Pathologies of Deliberation", in Elster, J. (ed.) *Deliberative Democracy*, Cambridge (Cambridge University Press), 123-139.
Sunstein, C. R. (1996) "Social Norms and Social Roles", *Columbia Law Review* 96, 903-968.
Tietzel, M. (1981) "Die Rationalitätsannahme in den Wirtschaftswissenschaften oder der homo oeconomicus und seine Verwandten", in Jürgensen, H., K. Littmann and K. Rose (eds.) *Jahrbuch für Sozialwissenschaften* 32, Göttingen (Vandenhoeck & Ruprecht), 115-138.
Tschentscher, A. (2000). *Prozedurale Theorien der Gerechtigkeit: Rationales Entscheiden, Diskursethik und prozedurales Recht*, Baden-Baden (Nomos).
Tyler, T. R. (1990). *Why People Obey the Law*, New Haven et al. (Yale University Press).
Tyler, T. R. (1994) *The Psychology of Legitimacy*, Chicago (American Bar Foundation).
Vanberg, V. (1994) *Rules and Choice in Economics*, London et al. (Routledge).
Vanberg, V. (1997) *Rule-Following: Abandoning the Hypothesis of Omniscience in Economics: What are the Implications?*, Working Paper, Fribourg/Switzerland.
Vanberg, V. (1999a) "Die Akzeptanz von Institutionen", in Korff, W. et al. (eds.) *Handbuch der Wirtschaftsethik*, Gütersloh (Gütersloher Verlagshaus), Bd. 2, 38-50.
Vanberg, V. (1999b) *Ordnungsökonomik und Ethik*, Freiburger Diskussionspapier zur Ordnungsökonomik 99/2, Freiburg i.B.

Deliberative Institutional Economics: Mind the Gap! Comment on Anne van Aaken

Michael Wohlgemuth

Given the scope and originality of Anne van Aaken's paper, it has to remain largely suggestive and by no means exhaustive. Its aim is to open new vistas rather than to present a clear-cut model of the political process. And it does so very well. Since I am sympathetic to van Aaken's general approach, I will not offer much in terms of differing judgements. Instead, I suggest additional theories that might strengthen her concept of Deliberative Institutional Economics. I use two simple diagrams to illustrate some of van Aaken's arguments and my own comments.

A Methodological Playing Field

Figure 1 shows a methodological playing field which I will use to locate van Aaken's research programme and my own proposals.

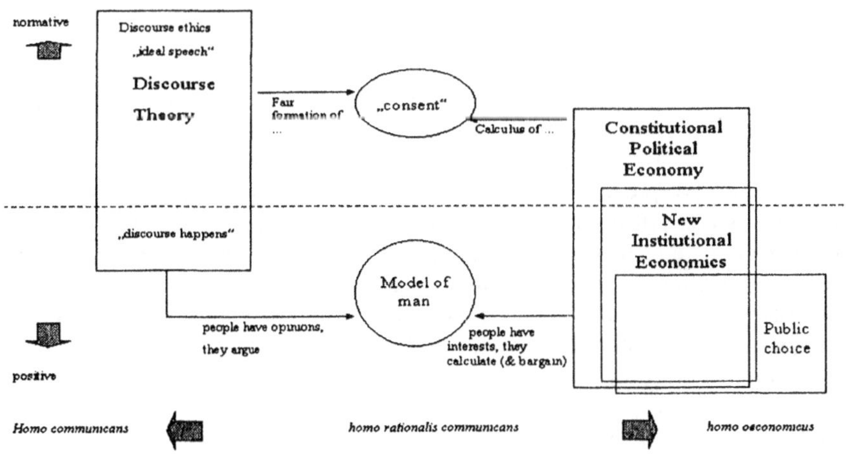

Figure 1: A methodological playing field for the creation of Deliberative Institutional Economics

Various sub-disciplines of economics can be confronted, and, as van Aaken argues, combined, with discourse theory. She highlights two methodological variables that can be used to define theoretical building blocks for constructing Deliberative Institutional Economics:

(1) the audacity with which they enter normative territory, and
(2) the rigidity with which they adhere to hard core *homo oeconomicus* assumptions.

Positive Economics and Normative Discourse Ethics

The line between 'normative' and 'positive' is not easy to draw. The dotted line in Figure 1 is only a suggestion. The reader should feel free to adjust the line according to his or her methodological instincts. Obviously, Discourse Theory (DT) covers more normative ground and is less concerned with positive theory than mainstream economics. In both areas, however, van Aaken argues (and I agree) that Discourse Theory and NIE can learn from each other, with the most relevant contributions relying on their respective comparative advantage or comparative focus. DT can help clarify the concept of 'voluntary consent' which is prominent in Constitutional Political Economy (CPE) by providing criteria and conditions of a consent's fair and equitable formation. Economics, especially New Institutional Economics (NIE) and Public Choice Theory, can help clarify conditions of *real* speech situations by providing a more sober model of man, of his or her incentives, opportunity costs and constraints.

The Logic and Creation of Consent

Let me make a few more remarks on consent, which has aptly been called an 'elusive concept'. For all its elusiveness it remains of fundamental normative concern for both CPE and DT. But there are important differences. DT is concerned with the communicative process that leads to agreement – which need not be unanimous. CPE is concerned with the logic or calculus of consent, and unanimity remains the ultimate standard of normative individualism. CPE derives consent as the basic norm from our market model of exchange and the logic of choice. This model assumes individuals who, by exchanging property rights, reveal preferences that require no justification or explanation. In CPE, voluntary consent results from the revelation and aggregation of (mostly) given preferences as expressed in individual choices. In DT, agreement is a possible (but not necessary) result of communication that is organised with the aim to create and change preferences and beliefs.

The link between the two paradigms suggested by van Aaken may not be the only possible one. But it is a good one. CPE should be able to strengthen its normative position if it relates the voluntariness of consent to the discursive quality of deliberation. But to make this link convincing, it is insufficient to fix it only in the lofty space of normative (wishful) thinking. One would have to add stronger ties on more solid grounds of positive theory. Aware of this need, van Aaken proposes a model of man as *homo rationalis communicans*. This leads to a discussion of the horizontal distinction in Figure 1.

Mind the Gap: Models of Man

DT, as van Aaken argues, does not provide much of a positive theory or explanatory model of man. Economics, with its logic of choice, claims to provide just that. Still, in terms of implicit or explicit understandings of human action, both theories provide enough content that allows us to discover important differences or to suggest useful combinations. Van Aaken opts for the combination, thus creating *homo rationalis communicans*. This conception borrows from discourse theory the indisputable fact that people have opinions, world views or beliefs, which are shaped from experience and communication with others. People argue; in fact they love to argue. Economics, in turn, provides assessments of interests and incentives, which, combined with scarcity constraints and opportunity costs, could give us an idea of when and how people can be expected to argue or bargain.

Personally, I am more impressed by the differences between the model of man in DT and that of mainstream economics; I am not convinced that taking the skeleton of *homo oeconomicus* and adding the meagre flesh of discourse theory would create a vital and sanguine communicating and acting human being.

'Given Preferences'

The assumption of 'given preferences', which lies at the centre of the economic logic of choice, may be the major barrier to bridging the gap between DT and any kind of mainstream economics. At the same time it is hard to identify the width of the gap. Economists (with some good reason) claim that 'given preferences' are necessary for their models to work, to avoid tautological reasoning and cheap excuses ('why, preferences must have changed ...'). But what exactly do we mean by 'given preferences'?

(1) What is meant by 'given': known, fixed, or stable? For how long, for whom?
(2) What is meant by 'preferences': goals, evaluations, tastes, complete and consistent value orderings, beliefs, interests, or interests and theories?

The width of the gap between discourse theory and economics depends on how we answer these two questions. When modelling the preferences of actors, economists often assume that all alternatives are given, that these are ranked according to their propensity to yield utility, and that the relevant amounts of utility are known. Further, they assume that all this is 'given' and 'fixed' once and for all. On this account of preferences, economics cannot provide a workable micro-foundation for a *Deliberative* Institutional Economics, and it seems clear to me that there is a gap that could hardly be bridged. Figure 2 tries to illustrate this foundation in positive social science.

Bridging the Gap

Van Aaken sketches some building blocks for bridging the gap between DT and economics. Most are derived from a somewhat broadened (institutional) economics perspective. I am confident that these theories can help to support Deliberative Institutional Economics (DIE). But I am not convinced that they are solid enough to build a bridge on which, say, Habermas and Buchanan would meet and hug.

Let me propose seven potential building blocks that may help to solidify DIE. One might reject this as 'pure eclecticism' (Voigt, 1996). Perhaps some of these blocks are not needed after all. But I have doubts about the comparative advantage of the alternative strategy, which would be to reinterpret and broaden NIE and DT almost beyond recognition just in order to find points of contact. There is some respectable positive social science out there which can provide valuable material for the task at hand.

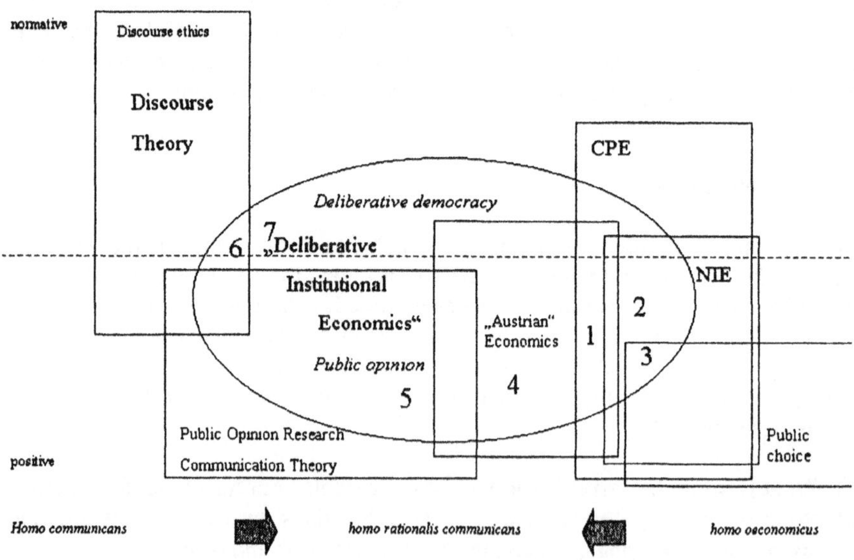

Figure 2: Building blocks for bridging the gap between economics and discourse theory

With regard to intersections (1), (2) and (6) – the building blocks of DIE very well described by van Aaken – I will confine myself to only mentioning some relevant messages and their known labels. I will be a little more explicit about what I propose to consider in field (3) and add to fields (4) and (5). I conclude with some speculations about potential contents in the (theoretically not well-covered) area (7).

(1) Constitutional Political Economy (CPE) elements: people's constitutional preferences reflect interests and theories (Vanberg and Buchanan, 1989). Rules should reflect voluntary consent, as far as possible (Vanberg, 1994, ch. 13).

(2) New Institutional Economics (NIE) elements: (only) by assuming bounded rationality, the value of rules that stabilise expectations can be assessed. Other relevant aspects of NIE relate to the incentive-compatibility of institutions, the costs of co-ordination and the opportunity costs of non-decision, or the meaning of shared mental models (e.g. Denzau and North, 1994; Hayek, 1967).

(3) Public Choice Theory elements: the homo politico-oeconomicus has little incentives to act as an active, informed, unbiased participant in political discourse. He or she is 'rationally ignorant' and/or a 'rational non-participator' (Downs, 1957); our citizen-voter may even be 'rationally irrational' in collective action (Caplan, 2001) with large numbers and small costs (Brennan and Lomasky, 1993).

I include two additional intersections because I believe that some important links between DT and mainstream economics can be created by referring to (careful selections of) an 'Austrian' economics of the social order (4) and of theories of public opinion formation and political communication (5) that seem complementary to the economic and deliberative approaches.

Austrian Economics

(4) It may seem surprising to find 'Austrian economics' suggested as a building block for Deliberative Institutional Economics. Indeed, the block is not yet well trimmed since Austrians have not contributed much to a positive economics of politics so far (but see Wohlgemuth, 2002a; 2002b). Hayek's view of democracy as a process of opinion formation provides a starting point. There are other relevant 'Austrian' or 'evolutionary' concepts of the social order: cognition as theory formation; the discovery and use of non-centralisable dispersed knowledge (social division of knowledge); the value of freedom, decentralisation and experimentation for the discovery of social problem solutions; the importance of political entrepreneurship and opinion leadership (Schumpeter).

There remains the task to free these Austrian or evolutionary theories from their occasional ideological connotations and from their preoccupation (as positive theories) with market processes. It should then be possible to apply such theories of knowledge-creation, co-ordination and communication to political processes. And if analogies (to spontaneous market processes) fail, this should reveal important differences and thus new dimensions to a comparative institutional analysis. In addition, modern findings of the New Institutional Economics and other Social and Political Sciences only wait to be interpreted in an 'Austrian' spirit (hence the areas of overlap with (5), (1) and (2)). Such combinations could produce positive and normative assessments of deliberative democracy (under the rule of law) as something like a Hayekian 'discovery procedure' (Wohlgemuth, 1999).

Other Related Theories

(5) Between (and often beyond) economics and DT one finds many theories that are relevant for our task at hand. The social and behavioural sciences tell us a lot about deliberation, its institutions and the way these institutions (formal and informal) shape processes of political communication. If deliberative democracy is the normative focus, public opinion formation should, I think, be an essential object of its positive theory component. People do not and cannot act on the basis of 'given preferences'. They act on the basis of preliminary opinions (theories). Preferences 'do not usually have the courtesy to parade themselves in rank on the drill ground of the imagination' (Boulding 1956, p. 84); they are the results of a 'highly learned process of interpretation and acceptance' (ibid., p. 14). In addition, people often do not express their true opinions but those they believe to be generally held, politically correct, or strategically convenient ('preference falsification', Kuran, 1995). Finally, public opinion has a limited carrying capacity because of a constitutional scarcity of people's attention (Luhmann, 1975). Political entrepreneurs and mass media enter the stage precisely when opinions and 'issue spaces' are neither complete nor given. They create issues and change opinions by offering (self-serving) reference points (framing), exploiting anomalies, etc. (Quattrone and Tversky, 1988).

Discourse and Deliberative Institutional Economics

One could argue that the building blocks proposed so far can also be stumbling blocks if we really want to reach far into the fields of discourse ethics. Economics, by holding on to *homo oeconomicus* in a strict sense is hardly able to even grasp the idea that people argue and that discourse happens. Public opinion research and Austrian economists acknowledge the importance of opinion formation; but at the same time they show that real processes of political communication are far from any notions of an 'ideal speech situation'. Still, van Aaken is right to take some basic ideas of discourse theory on board.

(6) As already argued, the stronger elements of Discourse Theory would include a refinement of the regulating idea of voluntary consent or legitimate majority decision. DT tells us that collective decisions should be based on inclusion, fairness (of the process *and* the status quo), and openness of deliberation. Actors need to give reasons. Deliberative democracy is not about the aggregation of given preferences (tastes), as social choice theory à la Arrow or spatial voting theory à la Downs see it. It is about the formation of opinions and shared perceptions. This offers an interesting link to the (normative) aspirations of CPE. Inclusive deliberation may create shared judgements that reflect more informed and universalisable beliefs. These, in turn, may support constitutional preferences for isonomia and the rule of law.

Uncovered Ground

Our discussion has so far focused on 'positive' issues and theories that relate to van Aaken's conceptions of *homo rationalis communicans*. As Figure 2 suggests, our building blocks may not sufficiently reach out to normative territory.

(7) In terms of normative conclusions, van Aaken (and I) have not covered much ground. But a combined view of elements 1 to 6 suggests some normative ideas. Deliberation as an integral part of the democratic process should support 'knowledge falsification', i.e. the discovery of false beliefs. At the same time it should discourage 'preference falsification', understood as the strategic misrepresentation of true preferences. For a combined effect of socially productive 'opinion falsification' enhancing the quality of public opinion (Wohlgemuth, 2002b), several constitutional arrangements seem critical:

(a) an open democracy that offers and creates alternatives; thus supporting cost-avoidance in collective choices and at the same time informing political processes of discovery and learning;
(b) a limited democracy (rule of law) that safeguards individual freedom to act and to argue, and that at the same time provides limits and orientations for political discourse – thus supporting manageable communication and universalisable rules;
(c) a combination of representative and direct democracy that allows for popular initiatives, thus breaking the agenda-setting monopoly of the political class, and at the same time focusing popular discussion and public opinion on practical alternatives.

I think that many proponents from the different fields of social science discussed here – from a hard-core Chicago Public Choice economist to an ideal speech philosopher – could in principle agree on such basic normative conclusions, albeit for different reasons based on different theories about man and society.

References

Aaken, A. van (2004) "Deliberative Institutional Economics, or Does Homo Oeconomicus Argue? A Proposal for Combining New Institutional Economics with Discourse Theory", in this volume.

Boulding, K. E. (1956) *The Image. Knowledge in life and society*, Ann Arbor (University of Michigan Press).

Brennan, G. and J. M. Buchanan (1986) *The Reason of Rules: Constitutional Political Economy*, Cambridge (Cambridge University Press).

Brennan, G. and L. E. Lomasky (1993) *Democracy and Decision. The Pure Theory of Electoral Preference*, Cambridge (Cambridge University Press).

Buchanan, J. M. (1975) *The Limits of Liberty – Between Anarchy and Leviathan*, Chicago (University of Chicago Press).

Caplan, B. (2001) "Rational Ignorance vs. Rational Irrationality", *Kyklos* 54 (1), 3-26.

Denzau, A. T. and D. C. North (1994) "Shared Mental Models: Ideologies and Institutions", *Kyklos* 47, 3-31.

Downs, A. (1957) *An Economic Theory of Democracy*, New York (Harper & Row).

Hayek, F. A. (1967) "Rules, Perception and Intelligibility", in *Studies in Philosophy, Politics and Economics*, Chicago (University of Chicago Press), 43-65

Kuran, T. (1995) *Private Truths, Public Lies. The Social Consequences of Preference Falsification*, Cambridge (Harvard University Press).

Luhmann, N. (1975) "Öffentliche Meinung", in *Politische Planung. Aufsätze zur Soziologie von Politik und Verwaltung*, Opladen (Westdeutscher Verlag), 9-34.

Quattrone, G. A. and A. Tversky (1988) "Contrasting Rational and Psychological Analysis of Political Choice", *American Political Science Review* 82, 719-736.

Vanberg, V. (1994) *Rules and Choice in Economics*, London (Routledge).

Vanberg, V. and J. M. Buchanan (1989) "Interests and Theories in Constitutional Choice", *Journal of Theoretical Economics* 1, 49-63.

Voigt, St. (1996) "Pure Eclecticism – The Tool Kit of the Constitutional Economist", *Constitutional Political Economy* 7, 177-96.

Wohlgemuth, M. (1999) "Democracy as a Discovery Procedure. Toward an Austrian Economics of the Political Process", *Max-Planck-Institute for Research into Economic Systems, Jena*, Discussion Paper 17/99.

Wohlgemuth, M. (2002a) "Evolutionary Approaches to Politics", *Kyklos* 55 (2), 269-292.

Wohlgemuth, M. (2002b) "Democracy and Opinion Falsification. Towards an 'Austrian' Economics of the Political Process", *Constitutional Political Economy* 13 (3), 223-246.

What Do We Learn by Asking Whether Homo Oeconomicus Argues? Comment on Anne van Aaken

Matthias Meyer

1 General Remarks

I was pleased when I learnt about the topic of Anne van Aaken's paper. Whenever I come across the issue addressed in her paper, I feel, as she does, that, although both strands of theories stand almost unconnected to each other, there might be some potential for mutual learning.

Van Aaken correctly points out that both approaches address the legitimacy of institutions.[1] Moreover, she thinks that each approach has a comparative advantage. Economics – as a *positive* theory – can offer a tested social science paradigm. The strength of discourse theory seems to lie in its *normative* aspect. In particular, it addresses more explicitly the conditions of a legitimate consensus. Subsequently she takes these observations as a starting point to outline 'a proposal for combining New Institutional Economics with discourse theory'.[2]

However, the question is what such an attempt of integration – or less ambitious: mutual learning – could look like. As we know from experience, this kind of discourse between paradigms is often far from (an) ideal (speech situation). One of the main reasons why such a discourse may fail is that theories and their concepts are taken too literally. Particularly for outsiders unfamiliar with economic thinking there is a danger that theoretical constructs like the concepts of *homo oeconomicus* or revealed preferences are taken too literally as a description of reality.

2 Problem-Dependence of Theories and Interdisciplinary Discourse

Philosophers of science have emphasized the *problem-dependence* of theories. Theories refer not only to *reality* but also to a *problem*.[3] When discussing theories and their concepts we have to think of them in terms of a three-place relation: problem-theory-reality. In consequence, different theoretical concepts get their meaning from their application to a particular problem and not only from their

[1] Further, she observes that both strands seem to use similar concepts such as rationality and consensus as the final basis for legitimacy norms.

[2] Van Aaken, 2004, p. 3.

'external' reference.[4] Therefore, one has to understand and judge the function of these often abstract and sometimes 'unrealistic' concepts from the perspective of the problem at hand.

For an interdisciplinary discourse – which has been attempted in van Aaken's paper – this has important consequences. As a first step, one must first identify the basic research questions addressed by the theories under discussion. This basic problem is the starting point for reconstructing each respective research program. Then, in a second step, one can translate from one discourse into the other. Here again the point of reference is the problem of the approach, not *reality*.

Although I can identify certain passages in van Aaken's paper which clearly show an awareness of this issue,[5] I miss it at other crucial points. Especially at the core of the interdisciplinary discourse I got the impression that she lost sight of it.[6] Her primary point of reference and hence of intertheoretical integration seems to be reality. As a strong indicator for this thesis I take, first, the frequent appeal to results from experimental economics and, second, van Aaken's suggestion of a new model of man: the 'homo rationalis communicans', which is constructed as a cross-breeding of homo oeconomicus and homo communicans. Or to summarize in her own words: 'there is the need of a behavioral model of action bringing both approaches together: a *homo rationalis communicans*.'[7]

This seems to me exactly the main shortcoming of the paper. In my opinion, the construction of another, more 'empirically correct', model of man is not the adequate point of departure. The research question comes first: either to fruitfully integrate ideas and insights of one program into the other or for the even more ambitious aim to develop a new research program. This rather general point could be illustrated by discussing different suggestions which are made by van Aaken.[8] In the following, I will concentrate on the issue of constant preferences which is given a prominent role in the paper.

---

[3] E.g. Popper: '*Yet science starts only with problems.* ... The conscious task before the scientist is always the solution of a problem through the construction of a theory which solves the problem', (Popper, 1963/1996, p. 222). For economics this idea has been systematically developed by Suchanek 1994.

[4] The later Wittgenstein emphasized this point concerning language in general.

[5] For example, when she talks of 'theoretical constructions', Van Aaken, 2004, p. 3.

[6] This shortcoming is reflected in another problematic aspect of van Aaken's paper. In my opinion, she does not put enough effort into differentiating between the different approaches within each strand. Both – New Institutional Economics and Constitutional Economics on the one hand and Discourse Ethics and Deliberative Democracy on the other – are referred to simultaneously, although there are relevant differences in these different approaches beside their common direction. It would be desirable to draw sharper distinctions between them.

[7] Van Aaken, 2004, p. 19.

[8] As I do not feel competent enough in the area of Discourse Theory, my remarks will mainly focus on the suggestions which are made concerning the economic strand and Constitutional Economics in particular.

3 Are Preferences Constant – Yes, Concerning the Problem of Social Order They Are

I take the basic problem of Constitutional Economics and its close relative New Institutional Economics to be the *problem of social order*, which is the definition and implementation of rules for enhancing social cooperation.[9] In essence, Constitutional Economics is a normative theory about institutions. In the language of Brennan and Buchanan, it is concerned with the *reason of rules*. The function of *homo oeconomicus* in this research program can be described as follows: It is a theoretical construct to enable the derivation of adjustment reactions to changes of rules, not a description of how rules are factually chosen.

What do we gain from asking whether homo oeconomicus argues? I agree with van Aaken – and with many others – that democracy is 'more than an aggregation of preferences'. More precisely, I think one of the major contributions of Deliberative Democracy is its emphasis on the importance of discourse and deliberation processes for modern societies. I also agree that these can enhance the understanding and acceptance of institutions, whether new or old.

The point of departure is – again – how both of us would account for these phenomena. Van Aaken accounts for them by referring to the *homo rationalis communicans*, who seems to have the attractive feature – among others – that he can be convinced by *good reasons*. Along these lines she wants to incorporate one of the central features of discourse theory, 'the transformation of preferences through deliberative processes'.[10]

Prima facie this seems to be the case: People may change their behavior after discussion. But with regard to the problem of social order I would favor a different approach. I would refer to the distinction made by Vanberg and Buchanan between an interest and a theory component of preferences.[11] Building on this distinction one can take the following position on the effects of deliberative processes. Discourse affects the theory component; the interest component remains unchanged. This strategy has several advantages:

Firstly, it takes the wants of all people seriously. It does not take the line of discourse theory of discrediting some of them *ex ante* as being strategic or self-interested. Moreover, it addresses the problem of social order with all the clarity needed and does not already incorporate the solution in the exposition of the problem. Instead, this approach to the problem forces the scientist to search for rules which can be accepted by all. As a consequence people only have to endorse the rules, not some common good. As Hayek puts it: Modern societies are rule-integrated, not goal-integrated.

At the same time, the role of the scientist is precisely defined. He is not a preacher or a philosopher-king with the task of convincing people to have certain preferences. Instead he has to identify and explain the function and beneficial effects of the respective rules – a purely scientific endeavour *within* a normative

[9] See Suchanek, 2004.

[10] Van Aaken, 2001, p. 14; italics omitted.

[11] See Vanberg and Buchanan, 1989/1994.

program. By explaining the 'reasons of rules' he confines his contribution to the theory component. Finally, the rather vague notion of 'good reasons' in discourse theory can now be translated into the more precise notion of 'reason of rules' in Constitutional Economics.

From this perspective, the comparative advantage on the *normative* side of an economic analysis of rules becomes visible. *Homo oeconomicus* can be convinced, but only by reasons concerning institutions, not by referring to such crypto-normative concepts as a 'common good'. Especially in our modern individualistic and pluralistic societies, I consider it to be one of the main advantages of such an approach. By abandoning the assumption of constant preferences, we would also give up this enormous strength of economics to generate valuable contributions to the public discourse.

4 Conclusion

In my view, there is more lost than gained by following the path outlined by van Aaken. In particular, Constitutional Economics loses its strength as a normative theory. By this I do not deny the existence of any potential for mutual learning between both strands, which suggests a continuation of the efforts undertaken in the paper. But it may be useful to remember Einstein's famous remark that God is the only one in the position to integrate *empirically*. As a consequence, man has to come up with an adequate *theoretical* integration.

References

Aaken, A. van (2004) "Deliberative Institutional Economics, or Does Homo Oeconomicus argue", in this volume.

Popper, K. R. (1963/1996) "Why are the Calculi of Logic and Arithmetic Applicable to Reality", in *Conjectures and Refutations: The Growth of Scientific Knowledge*, London (Routledge & Kegan Paul), 201-214.

Suchanek, A. (1994) *Ökonomischer Ansatz und theoretische Integration*, Tübingen (Mohr).

Suchanek, A. (2004) "What is Meant by Consent?", in this volume.

Vanberg, V. and J. M. Buchanan (1989/1994) "Interests and Theories in Constitutional Choice", in V. Vanberg: *Rules and Choice in Economics*, London (Routledge).

Chapter 2

Constitutionalism and its Alternatives

John S. Dryzek

Abstract

It is often held that, among different possible sources of political and economic order, constitutions are the only ones on which we have any systematic influence. That is, we can within limits design and modify them, whereas the alternatives are recalcitrant. The aim of this paper is to identify some alternatives and to show that there are some that can be the target of informed reconstruction in the interests of better politics and better outcomes. I will particularly focus on the role that can be played by discourses and deliberation. These alternatives point to a discursive democracy that in key ways eludes constitutions and constitutionalism.

Constitutions are not alone in their capacity to order political and economic affairs. A hyper-constitutionalist such as Viktor Vanberg might accept the existence of alternative sources of order, yet still argue for the primacy of constitutional analysis and design on the grounds that, among these alternatives, constitutions are the only ones on which we have any purchase. That is, we can within limits design and modify them, whereas the alternatives are recalcitrant. Here I will identify some alternatives and show that there are in fact some that can be the target of informed reconstruction in the interests of better politics and better outcomes. In particular, I will emphasize the parts that can be played by discourses (in the sense of shared sets of constrained understandings that facilitate communication) and deliberation (in the sense of communication that is relatively unconstrained). These alternatives point to a discursive democracy that in key ways eludes constitutions and constitutionalism.

The Relevance of Constitutions

In a recent work I used the expression 'the constitutional surface of the liberal state' Dryzek (2000, p. 2). That was mainly just a piece of rhetoric designed to open the door to a non-constitutionalist account of deliberative democracy. Constitutions do of course matter. In the 1990s we saw just how catastrophic bad constitutions could be. The federal constitution of Yugoslavia was fatally flawed because it defined republics on an ethnic rather than regional basis, and appeared to give them primacy over the federal center. This arrangement could only work so long as a strong communist party could coordinate the actions of federal and republic leaders (Bunce, 1999). Similarly the constitution of Czechoslovakia left over from the communist era was partly responsible for the 'velvet divorce' because it gave the Czech and Slovak prime ministers a mutual veto. When the two prime ministers were at loggerheads ideologically, it made sense for both to seek the divorce – even though most of their citizens opposed it.

The question is, how much do constitutions matter in comparison to their alternatives?

Empirical evidence can be brought to bear, not all of which would be welcomed by the constitutionalist. First, it seems that we can get similar outcomes across constitutionalized and non-constitutionalized situations. For example, Janet McLean (2001) points out that though New Zealand has only a non-constitutional Bill of Rights with no provision for judicial review of legislation, the rights culture in law and politics is just as vital as in the United States and Canada. Second, it is clear that similar constitutions produce radically different results in different contexts. For example, when Westminster-style parliamentary systems were adopted by newly independent British ex-colonies in Africa and elsewhere, they soon proved mere parodies of the original.

More recently, many post-communist countries have adopted liberal constitutions designed to protect and promote a market system along Western lines. While in some cases the results have been more or less as desired, in other cases (notably Russia) the result has been mafia capitalism. The Russian case highlights the limits of constitutionalism, because it seems that some alternative source of order is necessary to make the constitution itself work as intended. Candidates include coercion, discourse, and deliberation, on each of which I will have more to say shortly.[1] Let me suggest that to the extent that they do not recognize the ordering force of discourse, and deliberation, liberal constitutionalists will have to fall back on coercion. Now, there is no reason why liberal constitutionalism cannot recognize these alternative sources of order, but to do so it must be expansive in its view of how the world works, and, in particular, to move beyond any universalistic assumptions about behavioral motivation (of the sort that characterize more formal analysis).

---

[1] Two sorts of ordering force I will pay no attention to here are material and cultural. The reason is that neither provides any purchase for anyone interested in changing or improving states of affairs. Marxists once argued that material forces – capitalism and its class structure – were the underlying reality of liberal societies, such that liberal democratic constitutions were mostly window-dressing. While I think that materialism remains important despite the demise of Marxism, especially in light of constraints emanating from the structure of the transnational capitalist political economy, it does not allow for much in the way of leverage, except for the identification of locations beyond its causal reach (Dryzek, 1996a). I am more skeptical of cultural explanation, perhaps because I have in mind a cultural determinism only too happy to consign particular parts of the world to war and poverty. Culture may sometimes have independent causal force, though in my judgment 'cultural explanation' normally mistakes effect for cause. The aspects of culture that can be changed I would subsume under the heading of 'discourses', which I will discuss shortly.

Coercive Constitutionalism

Without such expansiveness, liberal constitutional political economy is prone to the coercive temptation. The standard constitutionalist reply when it comes to cases like Russia is that of course liberal capitalist constitutions require effective enforcement of property rights if they are to produce the desired results. Now, in Russia there is an agency that enforces property rights: but it is the mafia, not the state (Varese, 2001). The mafia supplies protection precisely because the state cannot. The liberal constitutionalist position here therefore requires a strong state to displace the mafia from this role. The problem is that the precise strength of the state cannot be both specified and limited through purely constitutional means (because it is inadequacy in constitutional specification that leads to the need for the strong state to begin with).

Without any clear limits, there is a temptation to resort to ever more authoritarian measures. Here we can remember the strictures of Karl Popper about the inevitable authoritarianism that accompanies attempts at holistic social engineering – and when the situation is as far from a functioning liberal market as the Russian economy is, a holistic transformation is indeed required. Given the imperfections of human knowledge of the social world, implementation of the blueprint always falls short of expectations. There is an ever-present incentive to apply just a little more coercion in the hope that a recalcitrant society will fall into line. Here the authoritarian face of liberalism is revealed. Reflecting on a previous generation of liberal constitutionalist holistic social engineers, Edmund Burke commented that 'in the groves of their academy, at the end of every vista you see nothing but the gallows'. Lest we think this is a problem only for transitional societies seeking to introduce liberalism for the first time, a glance at 1980s Britain shows how authoritarian liberalism can work in more developed societies. Free market reforms were secured by a stronger, more prescriptive, and more coercive state (Gamble, 1988).

From Coercion to Metaconstitutionalism to Deliberation

What can save us from liberal constitutionalism's authoritarian danger? To their credit, Vanberg and Buchanan (1996) recognize the need to constrain constitutional engineers. Their solution to the problem is a 'metaconstitution' that encourages a market in constitutions, such that those subject to bad constitutions can exit from them. In practice, this reduces to promotion of the 'free movement of persons, resources, and ideas' across boundaries (p. 54). Part of the justification for this market is drawn from Hayek (and so resonates with the Popperian point I just made): imperfections in our knowledge about how particular constitutional devices will work in practice means that we must allow for experimentation with, and competition across, alternatives (p. 51). So now our list of extra-constitutional sources of order stands at two: coercion and markets. However, as the Vanberg and Buchanan specification of the metaconstitution implies, markets themselves have to be regulated by constitutional means.

There are a few practical difficulties in implementing a market in constitutions in a world increasingly hostile to asylum seekers, and, of course, exit is very costly to the individuals contemplating it. Moreover, it is not clear that massive exit will necessarily lead a regime to rethink its constitution, especially if those leaving are the regime's critics.

Vanberg and Buchanan look only to exit for individuals to express their dissatisfaction with a prevailing constitution. In terms of Hirschman's (1970) categories, dissatisfaction might also be expressed in terms of voice (which Vanberg and Buchanan, p. 52, recognize only as a poor alternative to exit whose inferiority does not even require justification). Here I want to stress voice as a source of order, not just complaint – adding a third item, deliberation, to the extra-constitutional list of sources of order. There are mechanisms endogenous to deliberation that can make collective choices more tractable by structuring preferences (Dryzek and List, forthcoming). However, here I want to stress the role of deliberation in creating new states of affairs (which may or may not then take constitutional form). This involves 'movement' as well as 'order' – though of course even the most well-ordered society requires some capacity for movement.

This introduction of deliberation is consistent with one strand in liberal constitutionalist thinking that has recently joined forces with the theory of deliberative democracy. According to theorists such as Rawls (1993), and Ackerman (1991), scarce deliberative capacities ought not be wasted on ordinary, day to day policy making. Rather, they should be reserved for special, constitution-making occasions (and what Rawls calls matters of 'basic justice' – equality of opportunity and the distribution of material goods). On such occasions it is deliberation that is decisive, and that deliberation takes place free from the constraint of constitutional (or even meta-constitutional) rules. This is I think clearest in Ackerman's interpretation of American constitutional history. Ackerman points to rare great crises of the state (the founding, civil war amendments, and Great Depression) when what he calls the people as a whole begin deliberating about the shape of a changed institutional order. This does not mean that every American joins the deliberation, simply that every institution is involved, and participation is expanded beyond its normal bounds. Equally important, the content of political interaction becomes more profound and less narrowly partisan. And existing constraints on politics – including constitutional constraints – are temporarily suspended. This points to a limit to constitutions as sources of order: they cannot cope with great crises.

Deliberative Democracy Under the Constitution – and Beyond

Now, liberal constitutionalist deliberative democrats do allow that deliberation can occur within constitutional parameters. Bessette's (1980) deliberative interpretation of the US constitution emphasizes the role of Congress. Uhr (1998) emphasizes parliament. Rawls (1993, p. 231) stresses deliberation in the legal system, especially the Supreme Court. However, these accounts of constrained deliberation place little stress on deliberation as an extra-constitutional ordering device. Let me look now at thinkers for whom the most important deliberative aspect of constitutions is to be found in the realm they protect outside the formal institutions of the state.

For Habermas (1996), the public sphere (defined as an arena of association concerned with public affairs but not possessing any formal share of state power) is one of the most important sites of deliberation. The public sphere is the source of authentic public opinion formed in communicative action, which can then influence legislation. While Habermas has by this time moved quite far in a liberal direction, this continued emphasis on the public sphere represents continuity with the pre-liberal Habermas. Similarly, on Walzer's (1991) republican interpretation, the U.S. Bill of Rights exists to protect a broad public realm of deliberation in civil society. This account is very different from the standard liberal interpretation of the Bill of Rights as protecting a private realm of individual pursuit of interests beyond the grasp of government.

For both Walzer and Habermas, constitutions protect but do not design a public realm, governed by principles of movement and order that cannot themselves be specified by constitutional means. In a sense, what they seek is a bit like the kind of deliberation Ackerman wants on great occasions, unconstrained by institutional rules; but they want it to be a more permanent feature of the polity. Historically, the most momentous shifts in the character of the modern state have their origins in the public sphere. The creation of the liberal capitalist state was preceded by a bourgeois public sphere, an arena of debate excluded from any formal share in power by monarchy, aristocracy, and theocracy (Habermas, 1989). The creation of the Keynesian welfare state was preceded by a working class public sphere excluded from state power. (Of course, welfare state innovations preceded the entry of the organized working class into the state, especially in Germany; but those early innovations were themselves responses to the perceived threat from the working class public sphere.)

It is important to note that these two historical examples of public spheres flourished not because of constitutions that protected their members, but rather because of their members' exclusion from access to the state, exclusion that was enforced by both constitutional and extra-constitutional means. I have argued that the kind of state most conducive to deliberative authenticity in the public sphere is a passively exclusive one, one that provides few points of access but otherwise leaves civil society alone (Dryzek, 1996b). This argument holds for recent as well as deeper history. For example, the reason Germany had such a flourishing green public sphere in the 1970s and 1980s was the passively exclusive character of the state. This was a matter of legal corporatism buttressed by an administrative tradition that sees state and society as an organic whole, the public interest as unitary, such that opposition to policy is interpreted by administrators as obstruction. The consequences are profound, not just for the democratic vitality of the public sphere, but also eventually for the character of the state itself. Germany now has environmental policies that are among the world's most progressive and is among the greenest of states precisely because of this legacy of a green public sphere and the passive exclusion that inadvertently sustained it (Dryzek et al., forthcoming). Passive exclusion happened, but it could not have been designed by constitutional means, because its consequences are so counter-intuitive. Indeed, well-meaning constitutional redesign would probably have made matters worse from the point of view of democratic vitality by drawing off energy from the public sphere into the state.

The public sphere is a political location oriented toward, but distinct from the state. Politics within the state is far more easily regulated by constitutional means than politics within the public sphere. What I will now do is historicize this point to argue that the state capable of being regulated by constitutional means is becoming less important in relation to other sorts of politics.

Discourses as Ordering Devices

Aside from deliberation, politics in the public sphere and the state can be subject to the influence of discourses. The term 'discourse' can take on quite different meanings, including one that is synonymous with authentic deliberation (as, for example, in Habermas). The meaning I have in mind here is more constrained: a way of making sense of the world, based on a shared set of assumptions, judgments, contentions, capabilities, and dispositions. A discourse therefore provides those who engage it with a point of reference that facilitates their communication. Thus it can be added to the list as a fourth extra-constitutional source of order (along with coercion, markets, and deliberation). The most powerful contemporary global discourse is arguably market liberalism, a shared set of understandings that orders the interactions of policy makers, opinion formers, and corporations worldwide. In global environmental affairs, the dominant discourse since the mid-1980s has been that of sustainable development, which displaced an earlier discourse of survival in the face of ecological limits. In Northern Europe, the dominant environmental discourse is that of ecological modernization, which shares some features with sustainable development.

Discourses pervade the understandings of public officials and others involved in the conventional politics of the state, and so are not confined to the public sphere. However, the public sphere is a realm of relative freedom in experimentation with the interplay of different discourses – and it is the likely source of challenges to dominant discourses. Historical examples here would include the rise of liberalism (in the early bourgeois public sphere), socialism, feminism in the 1970s, even the revival of market liberalism in right-wing think-tanks in the 1970s.

Discourses as sources of order (and movement) become more important to the degree other ordering devices are weak. This is why they are especially powerful in the international system, whose authoritative institutions are of course much weaker than their analogues within the state (Dryzek, 2000, pp. 115-39). But their historical importance in ordering collective life has always been substantial, if not always recognized (especially by those subject to particular discourses). The only way to demonstrate this importance is to write histories. As written by Michel Foucault and his followers, such histories mostly recount oppression, more insidious because it is internalized and enforced by the oppressed. Thus any emphasis on discourses as extra-constitutional sources of order would be normatively unattractive – even if anyone could manipulate their content, which in the Foucauldian world is problematic (though this world does allow resistance to dominant discourses).

For all their differences, Foucauldians and liberal constitutionalists have in common the fact that they are rooted in a very familiar world that arose and was consolidated with modernity. Foucauldian genealogies only *continue* to make sense to the degree discourses (about sexuality, health, sanity, governmentality, and so forth) still have overwhelming causal force upon those subject to them. Liberal constitutionalism for its part has a very mechanistic view of the world: designing a constitution is a bit like designing a machine, with the parts supposed to behave in reasonably constant and predictable ways. Constitutional political economists are fond of drawing a distinction between 'constitutional' and 'in-period' collective choices. The implication is that the latter people behave in predictable and consistent fashion. To the degree they do not, then constitutional designs will not have stable or predictable outcomes.

Reflexive Modernization

However, the world may be changing in a direction that undermines any such paradigms with a stake in the predictability and fixedness of social and political life. Here I will introduce the idea of a reflexive modernity as advanced by, among others, Ulrich Beck and Anthony Giddens (Beck, 1992; Beck, Giddens and Lash, 1994). I do not wish to endorse all their claims about how the world is changing, lacking the space to give them the scrutiny they deserve. Some of these claims have only tenuous empirical referents. So my argument has an 'if...then' form; that is, to the extent that reflexive modernization does indeed occur, then an emphasis on discursive sources of order as opposed to constitutions, markets, and coercion becomes more compelling.

The defining feature of a reflexive modernity is that significant numbers of people no longer accept without question the traditions in which they have been socialized. The traditions in question might be pre-modern cultures or religions, or modern acceptance of the need to adjust to economic growth and technological change. In what Beck calls 'semi-modernity' economic growth and technological progress were taken for granted. Even as some negative side effects were recognized, the idea was mainly to adjust to whatever these forces brought.

In these terms, liberal constitutionalism is most at home in semi-modernity. Liberal constitutions are, of course, modern phenomena. But, as I have already argued, they require a substantial degree of predictability in the way people behave. Moreover, effective constitutions require that in their interactions, individuals accept and take for granted the rules, as being part of the (quasi) natural order of things.[2] In short, prevailing constitutional arrangements work because they have

[2] Constitutional history does feature periods of instability where the constitution itself is controversial and not accepted by a large part of the population. The last 200 years of French history is mostly like this. But such instability is rarely seen by any party as a matter

a supportive discourse. Reflexive modernization means that the ratio of rule questioning to rule obedience increases.

In a reflexive modernity, rules and discourses alike become less total in their reach, targets of reflection, informed scrutiny, and reconstruction, at least at the margins. Indeed, the very existence of Michel Foucault and his followers can be explained in these terms. These people are the products of a reflexive modernity because they are capable of identifying and reflecting upon discourses to which they and others have been subject.

Democratic politics has to be committed to the autonomy of citizens. In light of these new opportunities for expanding autonomy, one of the main tasks of democratic theory and democratic practice is to promote reflection upon discourses and the way they can distort preferences and behavior. Here we are operating in a realm where both preference distortion and escape from this distortion are extra-constitutional matters. Constitutional political economists who hail from the semi-modernity where preferences do not behave so badly may find this realm a difficult place.

If we recognize both the importance of discursive sources of order and the possibility of their reflexive reconstruction, what levers for change are there comparable to the more formal design process that constitutional political economists can recommend? To begin, problem diagnosis can be a bit different. To return to the case of the Russian political economy, the diagnosis of its failings would emphasize that the constitutional hardware that has been introduced lacks the supportive discourse necessary to make it work. The solution is therefore less likely to involve the coercive enforcement of property rights, and more likely to stress measures that would affect the discourse. This is not a matter of discursive engineers imposing a blueprint. Any reflexive and democratic commitments here would require that discursive reconstruction itself be controlled by the agents who will be subject to the institutions and discourses at issue. Thus there is an implicit commitment to the promotion of the full autonomy of these individuals (Dryzek, 1996c pp. 69-70). If this sounds like the slow boring of hard boards, so be it; but the alternative quick fix has manifestly failed to work.

Constitutive Reasoning

Discursive reconstruction has few decisive moments analogous to the drama of constitutional adoption or amendment. Interventions large and small can help reconstruct discourses. The key, though, is that when contemplating interventions one reasons constitutively rather than instrumentally, to use the categories of Tribe (1973). Reasoning constitutively, an actor goes beyond the instrumental question of whether an action will help achieve some set of goals. The actor also asks whether or not the action helps constitute or undermine a desirable world or situation. Elsewhere

---

of the waning relevance of constitutions; it is in fact precisely the opposite, a recognition of just how important the constitution is, the solution just being that of identifying the right constitution.

(Dryzek, 1996d) I develop an example at length of constitutive reasoning in environmental policy choice between regulatory and incentive-based mechanisms. In instrumental terms, incentive-based instruments may indeed be as superior as microeconomic policy analysts tell us. But constitutively, they draw on and reinforce a discourse which has insidious effects. This discourse does not stigmatize pollution as morally wrong, and it involves government selling rights to something which in truth it does not own.[3] More generally, it is the task of analysis to identify and elucidate the discourses that are drawn upon, reinforced, or undermined by particular policies, constitutional proposals, evaluations, and other contributions to the conversation of public affairs. In a world of consequential and competing discourses, intelligent action concerned with system-level outcomes just has to be reflexive action.

This conclusion is especially applicable when constitutional sources of order are weak. The best illustration here is the international system, where interactions between NGOs, corporations, state agencies, and others are largely ordered by discourses, unregulated by constitutional rules (Berejikian and Dryzek, 2000). Opportunities for reflexive international action expanded with the end of the Cold War, which had provided some relatively fixed parameters for action. The tragedy of current international affairs is the inability of key policy makers in the George W. Bush White House to recognize the possibilities for intelligent reflexive action. Their formalistic, realist view of the world sees intelligent action in very narrowly instrumental terms; seemingly they care little or nothing about the constitutive effects of their actions. In acting in such blinkered fashion, they are inadvertently reproducing exactly those aspects of the world (visceral hostility to the United States and its interests) they presumably would like to change.

Seemingly limited decisions can have major consequences, especially if they signal a change in identity of the actor in question. In an earlier era, withdrawal from Afghanistan signaled a change in Soviet identity, that it was no longer uncompromising in its defense of the territory of its ideological bloc. Many actions of the George W. Bush administration signal hostility to multilateral ordering of world affairs – a case of overkill – but a small subset would be enough to signal the change, and lead other actors to adjust accordingly.

The international system may be an extreme case, but discourses help to order collective affairs in more constitutionalized settings too – partly because functioning constitutions require a supportive discourse in order to work. Formalist constitutional analysts ignore the discursive realm at their peril: their interventions may have wholly unintended consequences of the sort seen in the Russian economy.

Constitutive reasoning and reflexive analysis are on the face of it a lot more demanding, complicated, and elusive than the more formal analysis that constitutional political economists can deploy. However, reflexive action does have one feature that makes it easier to contemplate than constitutional redesign. For this

---

[3] Given the Wittenberg associations of this paper, it is appropriate to point to a parallel with Martin Luther here. One of Luther's main targets was the selling of indulgences by the church; just as the church has no right to sell indulgences, so the government has no right to sell licenses to pollute. See Goodin, 1994.

kind of action can help bring about different situations without any coordinated collective action. All that is needed is for actors to think through the consequences of their individual actions. Reflexive behavior and constitutive action by some critical mass of actors then becomes the key to more systemic change.

The idea that intelligent action must often be constitutive action is eventually recognized by, of all people, James Buchanan. Bemoaning the decline in constitutional sensibility in the United States, Buchanan (1989, p. 26) argues that 'each one of us, as a citizen, has an ethical obligation to enter directly and/or indirectly into an ongoing and continuing constitutional dialogue that is distinct from, but parallel to, the patterns of ordinary activity carried on within those rules that define the existing regime'. Further, 'participating in the discussion of constitutional rules must reflect the presence of some ethical precept that transcends rational interest for the individual' (p. 29). Implicitly advocating constitutive reasoning, Buchanan goes on to bemoan 'a politics that is almost exclusively dominated by and derivative from the strategic choices made by competing interests in disregard of the effects on political structure' (p. 31). So Buchanan here overthrows both the behavioral assumption of public choice and the distinction between constitutional and in-period collective choice. While welcoming his emphasis on constitutive reasoning, I would point out that such reasoning need not be directed just at the constitution: it can also be directed at other sources of order.[4]

Reactions to a Constitutional Void

One common reaction to a void of the sort illustrated by the international system is to try to constitutionalize it. This tendency is exemplified by the work on cosmopolitan democracy by David Held (1995) and his associates, who have specified in great detail reforms such as cosmopolitan law, a global legal system, and a global parliament to which all global agencies would be accountable. While Held's vision of a humane and social democratic global polity is in some ways quite compelling, it is very distant from the contemporary realities of the international system.

A very different kind of response would try to navigate rather than abolish constitutional voids, of which the international system is just one example. Plenty of problem solving goes on in locations scarcely reached by constitutions. It takes place not within legislatures, administrative agencies, courts, or corporate boardrooms, but in networks that transcend the boundaries of both organizations and political units. Much of this activity can be called 'paragovernmental' (Jänicke, 1996). It might involve companies renouncing misbehavior in the face of a consumer boycott; or collaborative problem solving involving community groups and corporations. Problem-solving networks can involve governmental actors – but generally as participants in the network, not with any special authority (Sabel, Fung, and Karkkainen, 2000). Moreover,

[4] Buchanan does not give a single example of the kind of ethical reasoning and action he has in mind.

the problem solving in question need not at any point involve any legislative input or oversight.

Establishing the incidence of this sort of problem-solving interaction, and its relative importance in comparison to more traditional (constitutionalized) sorts is not easy, so again the argument here must have a conditional aspect. But to the degree that this kind of 'network society' problem solving is important, then constitutions decrease in their relevance as sources of order in comparison to discourses and deliberation (Hajer and Wagenaar, 2003). And again the appropriate kind of analysis and intervention suited to such a society is reflexive and constitutive, as opposed to formal and instrumental.

Discursive Democracy

Constitutions and their alternatives both matter. In the end, the relative importance of different sources of order (and movement) cannot be legislated or left to theorists to debate endlessly. Empirically, it is a matter for comparative and historical inquiry to sort out. When it comes to democratic theory, I believe that the future of the pursuit of democratic authenticity (the key to the deliberative turn in democratic theory) can be sought not in getting the constitution right, but in attending to the contestation of discourses. The essence of discursive democracy can be found in dispersed and competent control over the contestation of discourses in the public sphere (Dryzek, 2000). While it is possible for states to adopt constitutions that provide some protection for this sphere, there are also times when it is beyond the reach of state protection – especially when it comes to transnational politics. Further, the wellbeing depends as much on the informal and so non-constitutional aspects of state structure as on constitutional specification. That wellbeing also depends, reflexively, on the actions of those who engage contestation. Participation in deliberation is likely to induce those involved to call to mind interests other than their own, making the bearers of those interests less in need of constitutional rights to protect them. At any rate, the project of discursive democratization has to both uncover and counteract extra-constitutional agents of distortion; and to do this, it needs extra-constitutional devices at its disposal.

References

Ackerman, B. (1991) *We the People I: Foundations*, Cambridge, MA (Harvard University Press).

Beck, U. (1992) *Risk Society: Towards a New Modernity*, London (Sage).

Beck, U., A. Giddens, and S. Lash (1994) *Reflexive Modernization: Politics, Tradition and Aesthetics in the Modern Social Order*, Cambridge (Polity).

Berejikian, J. and J. S. Dryzek (2000) "Reflexive Action in International Politics", *British Journal of Political Science* 30, 193-216.

Bessette, J. M. (1980) "Deliberative Democracy: The Majoritarian Principle in

Republican Government," in Goldwin R. A. and W. A. Shambra (eds.) *How Democratic is the Constitution?* Washington, DC (American Enterprise Institute), 102-116.

Buchanan, J. M. (1989) "The Ethics of Constitutional Order," in *Essays on the Political Economy*, Honolulu (University of Hawaii Press), 25-31.

Bunce, V. (1999) *Subversive Institutions: The Design and Destruction of Socialism and the State*, Cambridge (Cambridge University Press).

Dryzek, J. S. (1996a) *Democracy in Capitalist Times: Ideals, Limits, and Struggles*, New York (Oxford University Press).

Dryzek, J. S. (1996b) "Political Inclusion and the Dynamics of Democratization", *American Political Science Review* 90, 475-87.

Dryzek, J. S. (1996c) "From Irrationality to Autonomy: Two Sciences of Institutional Design", in Sołtan, K. S. and S. L. Elkin (eds.) *The Constitution of Good Societies.* University Park (Pennsylvania State University Press), 57-75.

Dryzek, J. S. (1996d) "The Informal Logic of Institutional Design", in Goodin, R.E. (ed.) *Theories of Institutional Design*, Cambridge (Cambridge University Press) 103-125.

Dryzek, J. S. (2000) *Deliberative Democracy and Beyond: Liberals, Critics, Contestations*, Oxford (Oxford University Press).

Dryzek, J. S., D. Downes, C. Hunold, and D. Schlosberg, with H.-K. Hernes (Forthcoming) *Green States and Social Movements: Environmentalism in the United States, United Kingdom, Germany, and Norway*, Oxford (Oxford University Press).

Dryzek, J. S. and C. List (Forthcoming) "Social Choice Theory and Deliberative Democracy: A Reconciliation", *British Journal of Political Science.*

Gamble, A. (1988), *The Free Economy and the Strong State*, Basingstoke (Macmillan).

Goodin, R. E. (1994) "Selling Environmental Indulgences", *Kyklos* 47, 573-95.

Habermas, J. (1989) *Structural Transformation of the Public Sphere: An Inquiry into a Category of Bourgeois Society*, Cambridge (MIT Press).

Habermas, J. (1996) *Between Facts and Norms: Contributions to a Discourse Theory of Law and Democracy*, Cambridge (MIT Press).

Hajer, M. and H. Wagenaar (2003) (eds.) *Deliberative Policy Analysis: Understanding Governance in the Network Society*, Cambridge (Cambridge University Press).

Held, D. (1995) *Democracy and the Global Order: From the Nation State to Cosmopolitan Governance*, Cambridge (Polity).

Hirschman, A. O. (1970) *Exit, Voice, and Loyalty*, Cambridge (Harvard University Press).

Jänicke, M. (1996) "Democracy as a Condition for Environmental Policy Success: The Importance of Non-Institutional Factors", in Lafferty, W. M. and J. Meadowcroft (eds.) *Democracy and the Environment: Problems and Prospects*, Cheltenham (Edward Elgar), 71-85.

McLean, J. (2001) "Legislative Invalidation, Human Rights Protection, and Section 4 of the New Zealand Bill of Rights Act", *New Zealand Law Review*, 421-48.
Rawls, J. (1993) *Political Liberalism*, New York (Columbia University Press).
Sabel, C., A. Fung, and B. Karkkainen (2000) Beyond Backyard Environmentalism, *Boston Review*, http://bostonreview.mit.edu/BR24.5/sabel.html.
Tribe, L. H. (1973) "Technology Assessment and the Fourth Discontinuity: The Limits of Instrumental Rationality", *Southern California Law Review* 46, 617-60.
Uhr, J. (1998) *Deliberative Democracy in Australia*, Melbourne (Cambridge University Press).
Vanberg, V. J. and J. M. Buchanan (1996) "Constitutional Choice, Rational Ignorance, and the Limits of Reason", in K. E. Sołtan and S. L. Elkin (eds.) *The Constitution of Good Societies*, University Park (Pennsylvania State University Press), 39-56.
Varese, F. (2001) *The Russian Mafia*, Oxford (Oxford University Press).
Walzer, M. (1991) "Constitutional Rights and the Shape of Civil Society", in Robert E. Calvert (ed.) *The Constitution of the People: Reflections on Citizens and Civil Society*, Lawrence (University Press of Kansas).

Democracy, Discourse and Constitutional Economics: Comment on John S. Dryzek

Viktor J. Vanberg

Introduction

John Dryzek's essay touches upon a variety of issues and it contains – explicitly and implicitly – a number of claims, many of which invite a critical response. Within the space limits appropriate for a comment, though, a selection must be made. I want to focus my remarks on the issue that, as indicated in its title, is not only central to his present paper but that, to my reading, concerns a principal claim that he has made in some other recent contributions (cf. Dryzek, 2000; 2001) as well, namely his emphasis on discourse and deliberation as 'alternative sources of order', by contrast to constitutions and rules as ordering devices, and his suggestion that 'deliberative democracy' represents a superior alternative to 'liberal constitutionalism'.

Since Dryzek advances his arguments for deliberative democracy partly in terms of a critique of the research program that I myself subscribe to, namely constitutional political economy, and since he appears to essentially equate the constitutional economics perspective with that of liberal constitutionalism, I shall begin my comment with a short summary of some of the essential tenets of constitutional political economy and, indeed, of liberal constitutionalism.[1]

It should be noted at the outset that discourse theorists and constitutional economists share, quite apparently, an important common interest, namely their interest in the issue of legitimacy in collective choice in general, and of democratic legitimacy in particular. They also start, it seems, from some important common understanding of the ultimate source of such legitimacy. Constitutional economists can readily agree with Dryzek's assertion: 'Democratic politics has to be committed to the autonomy of citizens' (p. 54).[2] And they have no reason to object to the notion that 'claims for or against collective decisions need to be justified to those subject to these decisions in terms that, given the chance to reflect, these individuals can accept' Dryzek (2001, p. 643).[3] Constitutional economists will, however, have some disagreement with the claim that Dryzek cites as the core claim of the

[1] For a more detailed discussion see Vanberg, 1999.

[2] Quotations identified with page numbers only are from J. Dryzek's contribution to this volume.

[3] For a similar statement see Dryzek, 2000, p. 1.

theory of deliberative democracy, namely 'that outcomes are legitimate to the extent they receive reflective assent through participation in authentic deliberation by all those subject to the decision in question' (ibid.).[4] And they will especially disagree with Dryzek's conclusion that the 'essence of democracy itself is ... deliberation, as opposed to voting, interest aggregation, constitutional rights, or even self-government' Dryzek (2000, p. 1). The following discussion should make clear why constitutional economists find it necessary to draw a critical distinction between the two kinds of statements quoted above.

Central Tenets of Constitutional Economics

When constitutional economists subscribe to the notion that legitimacy in democratic politics derives from the voluntary and informed agreement among citizens, it is because they look at a democratic polity, in the words of John Rawls (1971, p. 84), 'as a cooperative venture for mutual advantage'. In other words, the 'essence of democracy' is seen in the fact that democratic polities are *citizens' cooperatives*. Not different from ordinary business cooperatives their purpose is to realise common benefits for their members, even if democratic polities are cooperatives of a very special kind. Their purpose is to provide their members-citizens with common benefits that they could not, or not as effectively, achieve through other avenues of social cooperation. Mutual advantage or common benefit means benefit for *all members*, and there is no other ultimate test for whether the interests of all are served than the voluntary and informed agreement of all.

As Buchanan has emphasised time and again, constitutional economics generalises the gains from trade paradigm – the paradigm that is at the heart of the economic theory of voluntary exchange as a mutually beneficial transaction and of markets as arenas for voluntary exchange – to collective action in general and politics in particular. Just as in ordinary (market-) exchange both parties benefit, collective action, including political organisation, is seen as a means through which a multitude of participants can realise common gains, be it through complex multilateral exchange which underlies collective goods production (where by pooling their individual contributions the participants achieve an outcome that promises benefits to everybody in excess of the sacrifice made), or be it through their joint commitment to rules which allow for a 'better game', where the gains from joint commitment for everybody involved exceed the sacrifice involved in submitting to the respective constraints. And just as in ordinary exchange voluntary agreement among the parties involved provides the only conclusive evidence that each of them considers the transaction beneficial in his own judgement, voluntary agreement among all participants in collective action provides the only conclusive evidence that each and everybody judges the complex exchange or the joint commitment beneficial in his own terms.

---

[4] Dryzek (2001, p. 643) credits Joshua Cohen (1989) with this 'classic formulation' that 'is still the claim at the theory's core'.

The specific focus of constitutional economics is on the *mutual gains from joint commitment*, i.e. on the common gains that the participants can realise by agreeing to submit, in their dealings with each other, to suitable *rules of the game*, rules that – if effectively enforced – channel the actions and interactions of all involved in ways that are more attractive to everybody than would otherwise be the case. When constitutional economists talk about the effects that constitutions have in the sense of 'channelling' behaviour at the sub-constitutional level, they mean, of course, not merely constitutions written on paper but constitutions in the sense of institutional arrangements that include provisions that make the constitutionally enshrined rules of the game effective. That, in the absence of effective implementation, under similar 'formal constitutions' we may observe quite different political realities is an obvious truth not worth debating about.[5]

Its specific outlook makes constitutional economics an applied science in the sense that it can provide assistance to participants in co-operative ventures, – in the case of polities: to citizens as the members-constituents of the respective political communities – on how they might be able to achieve mutual gains by adopting better rules, i.e. rules that give the 'game' that they are involved in more attractive working properties, 'more attractive' in terms of their own judgement. A constitutional political economy that gives advice on how citizens of polities, or participants in other social settings, may jointly benefit from suitable changes in the rules of the game, has naturally as its ultimate addressee the individual citizens themselves. They are the ultimate judges on whether or not they consider in their own assessment as beneficial what the constitutional economist conjectures to be the advantages of proposed joint commitments. This imposes an effective constraint on what constitutional economists can conjecture about the desirability of alternative democratic practices. They cannot afford themselves the luxury of deducing proposals for democratic reform from some preconception of what 'the essence of democracy' is. Instead, they must provide arguments for why proposed reforms promise benefits to all citizens, and can, therefore, be assumed to be in their common interest. And they must, in principle, provide such argument to every single citizen who voices disagreement.

If we look, in the manner outlined above, at a democratic polity as a citizens' co-operative, i.e. as a co-operative enterprise that is supposed to create common benefits to its citizens or 'owners', the best way to understand what constitutional economics, and also liberal constitutionalism, are about, is to imagine oneself in the role of a constitutional adviser from whom the citizens of a polity, joined in a constitutional convention, would like to get advice on what they can do to enhance the prospects that their co-operative venture actually works out to their mutual

[5] In this sense it is not surprising that, as Dryzek (p. 48) points out, even though 'post-communist countries have adopted liberal constitutions', their political realities may be quite different from those of their western constitutional models. From this obvious fact one can, however, not conclude, as Dryzek (p. 48) suggests with reference to the example of Russian 'mafia capitalism' that the 'Russian case highlights the limits of constitutionalism'. It highlights no more than the noted obvious fact that constitutions on paper, and without appropriate institutional implementation, are not worth much.

advantage. Meaningful advice can, quite obviously, only concern things that the citizens can actually *choose* collectively, and it must, as noted before, meet the test that whatever is recommended can actually be shown to be in the common interest of all citizens involved. It is in light of the general perspective outlined above that I shall now take a closer look at John Dryzek's views on the role of deliberation in democratic process and on his concept of deliberative democracy.

Deliberative Democracy: An Alternative to Liberal Constitutionalism?

It is, as indicated above, one thing for an advocate of deliberative democracy to deduce from a preconception of what the 'essence of democracy' is that 'deliberative democracy' is a more genuine or authentic form of democracy than what liberal constitutionalism has to offer. It is quite a different thing for a discourse theorist to submit to the discipline of arguing to the citizens-members of a polity why it is in their common interest to follow his recommendations for how they should run their co-operative enterprise. This would require him, first, to show that what he recommends is something that the citizens are actually *able to choose* collectively and, second, to show why choosing what he recommends is actually in their *common interest.* As I shall argue below, if measured against that standard Dryzek's account of deliberative democracy appears to me to be wanting on both counts. This does not mean at all, however, that, from a constitutional economics perspective, deliberation and discourse would not have to play an important role in the democratic process. In the concluding part of this comment I shall explain in what sense constitutional political economists can join ranks with discourse theorists in their praise of the democratic virtues of discourse and deliberation.

It is an obvious truth that discourse and deliberation are important to any collective choice process and, in particular, to democratic politics. Where matters are to be decided for a group of individuals, and where such decisions are supposed to advance participants' common interests, the pondering of arguments on what potential choice alternatives exist and what their relative merits are must be viewed a natural part of the choice process. Yet, it is not this obvious truth that Dryzek has in mind with his concept of deliberative democracy. Such a view would, as he puts it, merely look at 'deliberation as an aspect of, rather than substitute for, conventional sorts of representative democracy' Dryzek (2001, p. 645). Dryzek's emphasis is on discourse and deliberation not as aspects of a constitutionally framed political process but *alternatives* to constitutions, as alternatives which 'point to a discursive democracy that in key ways eludes constitutions and constitutionalism' (p. 47). Constitutions, he reasons, 'are not alone in their capacity to order political and economic affairs' (p. 47). While acknowledging that '[c]onstitutions do of course matter' (p. 47), he speaks of 'discursive sources of order as opposed to constitutions' (p. 53) and he insists on the significance of discourse and deliberation as 'extra-constitutional sources of order' (pp. 49, 52), and as extra-constitutional 'ordering devices' (p. 52).[6] He stresses the 'importance of discursive sources of order' (p. 54) by contrast to 'the more formal design process that constitutional political economists can recommend' (p. 54), and he posits that 'democratic authenticity ... can be sought not in getting the constitution right, but in attending to the contestation of discourse' (p. 57).

Dryzek's remarks on discourse and deliberation as 'alternatives to constitutions' sound as if he had to offer valuable advice to citizens who want to know how they can improve the prospects for reaping mutual gains from their co-operative enterprise, advice that goes beyond the recommendations that constitutional political economists can make for how citizens, through suitable changes in the rules of the game, may come to play a better game, i.e. a game with more attractive working properties for everybody involved. In his contribution to this volume as well as in his thematically related earlier writings (cf. Dryzek, 2000; 2001) I was, however, unable to find any specific advice that would tell citizens what exactly they are supposed to do in order to reap the benefits of deliberative democracy.[7] To be sure, Dryzek points out that the kind of 'authentic deliberation' that he recommends is subject to the 'requirement that communication induce reflection upon preferences in non-coercive fashion' Dryzek (2000, p. 2), and he explains: 'This requirement in turn rules out domination via the exercise of power, manipulation, indoctrination, propaganda, deception, expression of mere self-interest, threats ..., and attempts to impose ideological conformity' (ibid.). Yet, such statements do no more than describe the desirable properties of a state of affairs that we may wish to achieve. They tell us nothing about what kinds of changes in the world as it is we can make, and ought to make, in order to get closer to that desired state of affairs.

As much as we may wish as citizens to live in polities in which only our commonly shared 'reflective preferences influence collective outcomes' (ibid.), free from manipulation, indoctrination, deception or threats, it is simply not in our power to choose such state of affairs *directly*. The only thing we can choose is to adopt certain procedures and to submit jointly to certain rules of the game, including mechanisms for their enforcement, of which we hope that they will make us deal with each other in ways that make our 'reflective preferences influence collective outcomes'. The Western constitutional debate including, in particular, the debates surrounding the framing of the American constitution, can be looked at from this perspective as a search for procedures, provisions and rules of the game that promise to improve, as much as is humanly possible, the prospects for democratic polities to function as true citizens' co-operatives, i.e. as co-operative enterprises that advance the common 'reflective preferences' of their members-citizens

---

[6] As Dryzek (p. 48) puts it: 'The question is, how much do constitutions matter in comparison to their alternatives?'.

[7] Dryzek's arguments for deliberative democracy may, of course, not be directed to the citizens themselves as the ultimate addressees who have to be convinced that the proposed scheme is in their interest. In that case the above critique would clearly be besides the point that Dryzek wants to make. But then the question arises as to whom he wants to convince of the superiority of deliberative democracy, and what consequences would follow if that effort in conviction were successful.

and that prevent policy choices to be distorted by manipulation, indoctrination, deception or threats. It may well be that the institutional solutions that have been found and have been implemented in modern democracies, even in their most workable and exemplary form, fall short from what might be achieved, and we should certainly act on the presumption that there is room for improvement.

Constitutional economists and liberal constitutionalists can surely agree with the call for more 'authentic democracy', for efforts to enhance 'the degree to which democratic control is substantive rather than symbolic, and engaged in by competent citizens' Dryzek (2000, p. 1), if by that is meant a kind of control that improves the prospects for citizens to ensure that the democratic cooperative enterprise is actually operated to further their common interests. What constitutional economists and liberal constitutionalists would like to know, however, is by what specific measures or provisions the 'deliberative turn' (ibid.) that Dryzek advocates is supposed to improve the prospects for 'substantive democratic control,' compared to the, if only modest, achievements of what Dryzek, in a derogatory tone, refers to as 'the constitutional surface of the liberal state' Dryzek (2000, p. 2).[8] The simple claim that discursive or deliberative democracy is a superior alternative to 'a model confined to politics in the vicinity of liberal constitutionalism' (ibid., p. 3) hardly qualifies as a sufficient answer to that question.

'Authentic Discourse' and Citizens' Interests

Implicit in Dryzek's concept of discursive or deliberative democracy is, quite apparently, the notion that 'deliberation' is a highly civilised and peaceful process of communication among persons who seek to convince each other by nothing other than the force of the better argument. This notion is, of course, reminiscent of Habermas' claim about the virtues of 'communicative action' – and it shares the weakness of Habermas' claim.[9] Habermas' claim can be interpreted in two ways. It can be meant, either, as the empirical or factual claim that whenever persons engage in verbal communication they are committed to achieving mutual understanding and to refrain from strategic, instrumental pursuit of their self-interest. A realistic outlook at everyday social life finds ample evidence that this conjecture is simply false. Alternatively, it can be meant as the definitional statement that as 'communicative action' we should classify those cases of communicative exchange in which the participants are committed to achieving mutual understanding, refraining from strategic, instrumental actions. In this case the statement tells us how we should use the term 'communicative action', but it does not tell us anything about whether and, if so, under what conditions we can expect to observe 'communica-

[8] Dryzek (2000, p. 4) speaks of 'an account of discursive democracy that refuses confinement to the constitutional surface of the liberal state'. In his contribution to the present volume Dryzek qualifies the phrase 'constitutional surface of the liberal state' as 'a piece of rhetoric' (p. 47).

[9] For an informative sympathetic critique of Habermas' theory of communicative action see Heath, 2001.

tive action' in the real world, or what we can do to assure that real-world communication exhibits the desirable properties of 'communicative action'. This is, however, what constitutional economists and liberal constitutionalists would like to know. They have no reason to disagree with the idea that the prospects for citizens to realise mutual gains through their democratic cooperative ventures are enhanced if they seek, in non-coercive and non-strategic communication, a mutual understanding of what their common interests are. The essential question is what specific measures citizens are supposed to take to come closer to this ideal, and how desirable these measures are to them if they consider their overall costs and benefits.

To be sure, Dryzek recognises that the kinds of discourse and deliberation that he has in mind are not simply the natural state of affairs, but that certain preconditions are needed for them to work as intended. Yet, he is not very specific about what these preconditions are and, more importantly, he gives us no hint for how citizens might create such conditions by means other than constitutional provisions. When, following Habermas, he describes the public sphere as 'one of the most important sites of deliberation' (p. 51) and notes that the 'public sphere is the source of authentic public opinion formed in communicative action' (p. 51), he explicitly acknowledges the role of constitutional provisions, such as the U.S. Bill of Rights, in protecting the public sphere as 'a realm of relative freedom in experimentation with the interplay of different discourses' (p. 52).[10] His apparent ambition, however, is to downplay the significance of constitutional provisions and to suggest that 'discursive democracy' has other, more important means at its avail to ensure that citizens may enjoy the benefits of a public sphere that encourages 'authentic deliberation'. What one would like to know is what exactly these other, non-constitutional means are supposed to be, i.e. what means other than submitting to suitable rule-constraints citizens might have at their disposal in order to secure an arena for 'authentic deliberation' and prevent such virtuous discourse from being replaced by, for instance, pure partisan strategic bargaining.

Even if we were told what citizens might do to secure an arena for 'authentic' discourse and deliberation, this would still not answer the further question of the extent to which, and the particular ways in which, citizens may want to employ the instrument of 'authentic discourse', if they consider, in economic parlance, its opportunity costs. As is true for all things in life, 'authentic discourse' will come at a cost, a fact that Dryzek does indeed recognise. Under the heading 'Deliberative Legitimacy and Large Scale' Dryzek (2001, pp. 644ff.) he discusses the problem that in large constituencies 'society-wide deliberation' may be too difficult an undertaking, and as potential remedy he considers two principal alternatives, namely, on the one hand, to restrict the number of occasions on which deliberation

[10] It may well be that, as Dryzek (p. 51) asserts, the 'republican interpretation', according to which 'the U.S. Bill of Rights exists to protect a broad realm of deliberation in civil society', is 'different from the standard liberal interpretation ... as protecting a private realm of individual pursuit of interest'. This does not, however, alter the fact that it is constitutional provisions, i.e. effectively enforced rules of the game, that allow the public sphere to function as an arena for non-coerced and free exchange of arguments on public matters.

is to take place and, on the other hand, 'somehow to restrict the number of people involved in deliberation' (ibid., p. 645).

What is surprising about Dryzek's discussion of this theme is that he does not seem to realise that these are exactly the kind of issues that 'liberal constitutionalism' has been labouring about for centuries, and that 'the constitutional surface of the liberal state' can be seen as an attempt to find, in face of the 'large scale'-problem, a reasonable balance between various kinds of interests that individuals harbour as participants in co-operative ventures.[11] Again, it may well be that better solutions than those provided by existing liberal constitutions can be found for the problem of securing democratic legitimacy under large-scale conditions. But those who think that they have better solutions to suggest would need to show why what they propose can actually be expected to work better than what we have – in light of what centuries of theory and practice of constitutional democracy have taught us. Dryzek's light-handed remark that in his 'own view ... it is deliberation on the part of representatives selected by lot that presents the fewest problems for democratic legitimacy' (ibid., p. 648), would carry more weight if it were placed in the context of the relevant arguments that have been made in the long-standing debate on the relative merits of alternative forms of democratic representation, including varieties of 'popular election' as well as 'random selection' (ibid., p. 645). Most importantly, with his arguments on the problem of democratic legitimacy under large-scale conditions Dryzek places himself, quite obviously, in the midst of a constitutional debate, in spite of his 'extra-constitutional' rhetoric and his claims to a 'non-constitutionalist account of deliberative democracy' (p. 47).

Discourse and Constitutional Economics

My arguments so far have focused on those aspects of Dryzek's concept of deliberative democracy that I find reason to object to. By contrast, in the remainder of my comment I want to draw attention to an understanding of the role of discourse and deliberation that can be readily endorsed by constitutional political economists and liberal constitutionalists. My disagreement, to repeat, primarily concerns Dryzek's claim that discourse and deliberation should be viewed as *alternatives* to constitutional devices, as well as his claim that the concept of deliberative democracy is an advance over liberal constitutionalism. As I shall detail in what follows, I have no difficulty in accepting those of Dryzek's arguments that emphasise the important supportive role that discourse can play in making constitutions work.[12]

[11] A paradigmatic example for the kind of reasoning that, with regard to these issues, constitutional economists engage in is, of course, J.M. Buchanan's and G. Tullock's (1962) classic contribution.

[12] I can agree with Dryzek's assertion that 'functioning constitutions require a supportive discourse in order to work' (p. 55), and I can also agree with the claim that one reason for the deficiencies of the Russian constitution is that it 'lacks the supportive discourse necessary to make it work' (p. 54), even if I would like to add that this is only one among a number of reasons, some of which are probably more important.

And, though I am quite willing to admit that 'formalist constitutional analysts' tend to 'ignore the discursive realm' (p. 55), I shall seek to show that there is no inherent reason for constitutional economists to do so.

As an applied science, a science that applies theoretical knowledge to the solution of practical problems, constitutional economics may assist citizens in solving the problem of how they might improve their prospects of realising mutual gains from joint commitment to suitable rules. The central issue in this regard is, how should processes of constitutional choice be organised in order to improve the prospects that the informed common constitutional interests of the persons involved are identified and implemented. To the extent that discourse can be expected to be conducive to this aim, it is something that constitutional economists will consider recommendable. There are, in particular, two kinds of problems that citizens have to overcome in order to identify their common constitutional interests, a knowledge problem and an interest problem. The question, therefore, is whether and how discourse and deliberation can help to solve these problems.

The knowledge problem concerns the fact that it is not rules per se that citizens are concerned about but the patterns of outcomes that rules tend to generate. Constitutional choice is motivated by the desire to improve the quality of the game that unfolds within the rules. Those rules are desirable that make for a desirable game, a game with working properties that serve the interests of the parties involved. How alternative rules work out in practice is, however, not always easy to recognise for citizens who have only imperfect constitutional knowledge, i.e. who are only imperfectly informed about the actual working properties of alternative rules. The capacity of citizens to make constitutional choices that work out to their common benefit is, therefore, dependent on their ability to base such choices on adequate constitutional knowledge. And discourse can help to improve their knowledge.

The interest problem concerns the fact that each participant's *immediate* constitutional interest is in rules that work out to his own advantage, not necessarily in rules that are in the common interest of all. Put differently, self-interested agents must be expected to have a natural interest in rules that are differentially advantageous to themselves, i.e. in *privileges*. To the extent, however, that the participant in the process through which rules are collectively chosen are motivated only to seek privileges for themselves, the unintended outcome may well be that their common constitutional interests remain undiscovered and the mutual gains that could be had from implementing these common interests remain unattainable. The capacity of citizens to realise mutual benefits from adopting rules that are in their common constitutional interests will depend, therefore, on their ability to reduce the incentives for privilege-seeking and to encourage efforts to identify rules that make for a better game for all involved. Discourse may be a means to do so.

From a constitutional economics perspective, discourse can be looked at as a procedure that helps participants in co-operative ventures, such as citizens of democratic polities, to find out what their common constitutional interests are, and to implement those interests. Apart from other strategies that citizens may employ to overcome the above noted knowledge and interest problems (cf. Vanberg and Buchanan, 1989; 1991), discourse and deliberation can provide a remedy for both.[13] Public discourse can be a suitable means to improve citizens' shared constitutional knowledge. And it can be an effective instrument for constraining privilege-seeking, not because participants are somehow made to be less interested in their own well-being, but because, in order to argue their cases successfully, they must do so in terms that are acceptable to other participants. It is not because of any motivational transformation, but because of these constraints that, as Dryzek supposes, 'participation in deliberation is likely to induce those involved to call to mind interests other than their own' (p. 57).[14]

It cannot be stressed enough that from the perspective of constitutional economics discourse can help citizens or members of co-operative enterprises to find out what their common (constitutional) interests are, i.e. the interests that they share. This is in fundamental contrast to a perspective that would view discourse as a means for discovering 'the common good', as something defined independently of the interests of the individual participants. For constitutional economists the 'common good' is nothing but that which is in the common interest of all concerned, and for them to claim that something is in the common interest of the citizens-members of a democratic polity is equivalent to claiming that it is something that all can agree on. On the other hand, notwithstanding their emphasis on participants' *interests*, constitutional economists can well agree with the notion that discourse is different from 'strategic bargaining' in the sense of a process in which everybody is concerned only with his own separate interest. If discourse is to assist citizens in identifying their common constitutional interests, it can only serve its purpose if participants are willing to communicate with each other in the spirit of searching for common ground. What is in their common interest is by no means always obvious for everyone to see, but is something that needs to be discovered. And the likelihood of it being discovered depends, of course, on efforts being made to discover it. If every participant is concerned only with his own separate interest, without considering what might be agreeable to other participants as well, and if nobody makes an effort to search for common ground, mutual benefits that could be had from joint commitment to rules that are in the common interests of all will not be realised. Stated differently, citizens will be the more able to succeed in realising gains from joint commitment the more they are able to carry on their constitutional discourse in the spirit of searching for common ground, as opposed to purely strategic bargaining. This means, in turn, that they share a common interest in

[13] Dryzek notes as an effect of discourse that 'the content of political interaction becomes more profound and less narrowly partisan' (p. 50).

[14] It is, however, doubtful whether, as Dryzek supposes, the fact that participants in discourse are induced to 'call to mind interests other than their own' makes 'the bearers of those interests less in need of constitutional rights to protect them' (p. 57). It is one thing to argue that the constraints of public discourse help people to identify their common constitutional interests, and it is a quite different thing to claim that discourse eliminates the need to enforce rules that are found to be in the common interest of all participants. The presence of referees in sports events is testimony to the fact that perfect agreement on the rules of the game does not per se secure compliance with the rules.

encouraging in each other a *constitutional ethics* in the sense of an obligation to actively participate in 'an ongoing and continuing constitutional dialogue' (p. 56) that aims at identifying common constitutional interests.

It is in the sense of the above interpretation that I read James M. Buchanan's comments on the need for a constitutional ethics. Even if Buchanan's wording[15] may invite Dryzek's censure of inconsistency, the notion of a constitutional ethics, at least if it is interpreted in the sense suggested above, can be consistently incorporated in a constitutional economics framework without overthrowing 'the behavioral assumption of public choice and the distinction between constitutional and in-period collective choice' (p. 56).

Conclusion

If, for advocates of discourse and deliberation, 'authentic democracy can be said to exist to the degree that reflective preferences influence collective outcomes' Dryzek (2000, p. 2), constitutional economists can readily agree with the plea for 'authentic democracy'. Yet, to insist, as constitutional economists and liberal constitutionalists would do no less than advocates of deliberative democracy, that only voluntary and informed agreement among all participants is what *ultimately* legitimises collective choices and social arrangements does not *directly* imply any specific requirement concerning the procedures that participants in co-operative ventures are to employ in administering their common affairs.

As Buchanan and Tullock (1962) have shown, unanimous agreement as legitimising principle is to be distinguished from unanimity as practical decision rule. The participants in co-operative enterprises may well, for reasons of expediency, voluntarily agree on carrying out their joint enterprise, on the sub-constitutional level, on the basis of rules that deviate more or less from a rule of unanimity, and they may even have good reasons to voluntarily agree on delegating decision making authority to representatives. Equally, what role the persons concerned may want to assign to discourse and deliberation, however these procedures may be specifically defined, cannot be deduced from a pre-defined concept of 'authentic democracy', but must be regarded as a matter that is subject to considerations of expediency. Considering the opportunity costs of discourse, persons may well voluntarily agree on limiting the role that they want discourse to play in carrying out their common affairs.

Whoever has recommendations to make on how 'democracy' can be improved, must have an addressee in mind to whom he directs his arguments. As noted above, when constitutional economists advance proposals for 'improving democracy' they consider as their ultimate addressee the citizens themselves, i.e. those who as members of democratic polities have to live with the consequences of whatever reforms are suggested. That is, constitutional economists submit their conjectures

[15] Dryzek (p. 56) cites Buchanan's statement that 'participating in the discussion of constitutional rules must reflect the presence of some ethical precept that transcends rational interest for the individual'.

about what reforms may count as improvements to the ultimate test that the suggested reforms must be judged as improvements by the citizens themselves. In other words, they submit to the discipline of having to convince the citizens themselves that they can expect to benefit, in their own judgement, from whatever constitutional recommendations are made. Advocates of deliberative democracy who are prepared to submit to the same discipline would need to argue to citizens what measures they should take in order to enhance discourse and deliberation, and why these measures promise to work out to their common benefit. And in order to substantiate the claim that deliberative democracy is a superior alternative to liberal constitutionalism, they would need to provide reasons for citizens why a regime of deliberative democracy promises more benefits to them than what liberal constitutionalism has to offer.

References

Buchanan, J. M. and G. Tullock (1962) *The Calculus of Consent – Logical Foundations of Constitutional Democracy*, Ann Arbor (The University of Michigan Press).

Cohen, J. (1989) "Deliberation and Democratic Legitimacy", in Hamlin, A. and P. Pettit *The Good Policy: Normative Analysis of the State*, Oxford, UK (Basil Blackwell), 17-34.

Dryzek, J. S. (2000) *Deliberative Democracy and Beyond: Liberals, Critics, Contestations*, Oxford (Oxford University Press).

Dryzek, J. S. (2001) "Legitimacy and Economy in Deliberative Democracy", *Political Theory* 29, 643-61.

Heath, J. (2001) *Communicative Action and Rational Choice*, Cambridge, Mass., and London (The MIT Press).

Rawls, J. (1971) *A Theory of Justice*, Cambridge, Mass. (Harvard University Press).

Vanberg, V. J. (1994) *Rules and Choice in Economics*, London and New York (Routledge).

Vanberg, V. J. (1999) "Markets and Regulation: the Contrast between Free-Market Liberalism and Constitutionalism", *Constitutional Political Economy* 10, 219-43; reprinted in Vanberg 2001, 17ff.

Vanberg, V. J. (2001) *The Constitution of Markets – Essays in Political Economy*, London and New York (Routledge).

Vanberg, V. J. and J. M. Buchanan (1989) "Interests and Theories in Constitutional Choice", *Journal of Theoretical Politics* 1, 49-62; reprinted as chpt. 10 in Vanberg 1994.

Vanberg, V. J. and J. M. Buchanan (1991): "Constitutional Choice, Rational Ignorance and the Limits of Reason", *Jahrbuch für Neue Politische Ökonomie* 10, 61-78; reprinted as chpt. 11 in Vanberg 1994.

Deliberation as a Discursive Feature of Contemporary Theories of Democracy: Comment on John S. Dryzek

Axel Tschentscher

1 Introduction

Observing a 'deliberative turn' within the debate about democracy means that diverse conceptions of democracy tend to be appraised in terms of their support or opposition to the notion of deliberative legitimacy – i.e., the notion that participation in genuine deliberation constitutes the core of democratic legitimacy.[1] It is questionable whether such a 'turn' really took place or if the current debate about deliberation is just another hype to disappear again in the near future. Irrespective of such reflections on the course of theory building, however, some questions raised by the debate are fundamental enough to be here to stay. They can be structured around the impact of deliberation on contemporary theories of democracy (section 2) and around the role discourse theory plays in this context (section 3).

2 Deliberation in Contemporary Theories of Democracy

Regarding the concept of deliberation in contemporary democratic theories, there are three major questions to be asked, namely: why might deliberation be supportive or constitutive of legitimacy (1), how does deliberation relate to discourse (2), and how does deliberation contribute to decision-making (3).

1) Deliberation as a Link Between Participation, Legitimacy and Legitimation

Does deliberation endorse legitimacy? Among Tom Tylor's observations about 'Why People Obey the Law'[2] there is the prominent thesis that giving 'voice' increases the chance of the outcome being perceived as legitimate irrespective of the decision taken. Accordingly, even parties who are defeated in court tend to accept the ruling if they had adequate opportunity to present their view. This observation neatly coincides with Niklas Luhmann's sociological definition of legitimacy as 'the generalized preparedness to accept, within a certain margin, a decision whose

[1] Cf. Dryzek (forthcoming), manuscript at p. 2f.
[2] Tylor, 1990.

content is not yet known'.[3] Generalizing, we can say that participation, at least to some extent, breeds legitimacy.

Granted, the *legitimacy* of sociological studies is nothing but empirical acceptance of something being legitimate. It is quite different from the normative notion of *legitimation*. From the normative perspective, people can simply be wrong in their perception. They can accept results as legitimate even though some necessary prerequisite of legitimation is missing. The benevolent dictator's rule, for example, does not achieve normative legitimation simply by his subjects' respect and loyal support.

With participation, however, legitimacy might at least work as a strong indicator of the form of legitimation we generally label as 'democratic'. If people believe that their voice is being adequately heard before a political decision is taken, they are not only very likely to actually accept the outcome, but the participation also strongly suggests that the final decision in some way expresses the will of the people, thereby fulfilling the most important *normative* criterion of legitimation in the democratic agenda. Simplifying again, we can summarize that participation breeds legitimacy *and* democratic legitimation.

The picture is still incomplete without considering the alternatives. Actual participation is only one among many procedures to ensure democratic legitimation. The more prominent 'classical' model heavily relies on formal representation rather than permanent participation. Such formality in the political process is inferior neither with regard to its actual acceptance by the people (legitimacy) nor with regard to its normative status (democratic legitimation). However, in the everlasting quest for the perfection of institutional settings, we might have to acknowledge that formal democracy is likely to go awry if the decision making by representatives gets removed from the actual will of the populace. The same is true whenever important decisions are taken with no prior deliberation at all, i.e., neither matched by public discussions nor by debate in the chambers of parliament. In such cases, linking popular deliberation to the process of lawmaking looks like one of the more promising improvements of the institutional setting. In addition to the formal procedures of democracy, deliberation thereby becomes a material safeguard for legitimacy and legitimation.

2) Deliberation and Discourse as Distinct Concepts

How does deliberation relate to discourse? This plain question gives rise to much confusion when discourse is simply equated with deliberation and thereby warped beyond recognition. Rather, deliberation and discourse are quite distinct concepts:

a) We can define *deliberation* – as used in 'deliberative democracy' – as public argument and reasoning among equal citizens prior to a decision.[4] This broad meaning of deliberation differs from the republican meaning ('deliberation within

---

[3] Luhmann, 1975, p. 28 ('eine generalisierte Bereitschaft, inhaltlich noch unbestimmte Entscheidungen innerhalb gewisser Toleranzen hinzunehmen').

[4] See Cohen, 1989, p. 21 – without explicitly mentioning that deliberation precedes decision. Cf. Fishkin, 1991, p. 35ff. – with reference to Habermas.

parliament') that used to be the focal point of attention before Cohen and Habermas redefined the issue. As late as 1985, Sunstein still relied on the republican concept of deliberation by Bessette who, in turn, considered deliberation outside of representative bodies – i.e., as a tool of direct democracy – the 'greatest threat' to the public interest.[5] Searching for the roots of such narrow understanding, we can follow the leads of both Sunstein and Bessette back to the Federalist Papers where deliberation merely figures as a 'medium' securing the superior orientation of representatives towards public interest ('Republic') as opposed to particular group interest ('pure Democracy').[6]

The broad sense of 'deliberation' that has been employed since the 1990s refers to public argument and reason. It thereby *prima facie* excludes secret discussions (no publicity) and strategic bargaining (no argumentation) even though both are readily acknowledged as pragmatic constraints within procedures that are still called 'deliberative'. While generally broad, the above definition also has a restrictive touch. It excludes arguments of those who are not affected by the decision at issue (no citizens).[7] The concept of deliberation thus centers around self-government. Accordingly, a dialogue about the matters of another state, community or family cannot be called 'deliberation' whereas it can (and must) be called 'discourse'. Also, whereas deliberation conceptually always precedes decision,[8] discourse has no such pragmatic goal: we can endlessly and meaningfully engage in (scientific, artistic, religious) discourse without any intent whatsoever of taking decisions. In short: deliberation is a democratically pre-formed 'sister' of discourse.

b) But what, exactly, defines discourse? Discourse is any dialogue that approximately satisfies the discourse rules.[9] Depending on the degree to which these rules are satisfied, there are two distinct sub-concepts of discourse: ideal and real discourse – each with a different relationship to deliberation.

An *ideal discourse* is a discourse that fully realizes the rules, i.e., a discourse 'under the conditions of infinite time, unlimited participation and complete absence of coercion by way of complete terminological precision, full empirical information, perfect ability and willingness to switch roles as well as complete absence of prejudice'.[10] This definition by Robert Alexy neatly illustrates that there can never be an ideal discourse in real life. And even if ideal discourse were possible, a consensus achieved at some time could not become binding in the sense of contractual agreement. Participants of an infinite discourse must accept any new argument

[5] See Sunstein, 1985, pp. 45f.; Bessette, 1980, pp. 112ff.

[6] Cf. Madison, 1787/1961, p. 62: '...refine and enlarge the public views by passing them through the medium of a chosen body of citizens'.

[7] Cf. Dryzek, 2001, p. 643 ('those subject to these decisions'; p. 652).

[8] Dryzek's suggestion that 'nonelectoral and nonvoting avenues of influence' avoid some problems of deliberations (Dryzek, 2001, p. 651) does not change the decision-centered nature of deliberation itself.

[9] For the content of discourse rules see Alexy, 1978, pp. 233ff.; cf. Tschentscher, 2000, pp. 222ff.

[10] Alexy, 1989/1995, p. 113.

coming up later on: in discourse, consensus is never final. Therefore, not only duress, but every definitive decision is a compromise between the discursive ideal and demands of reality. This kind of compromise seems to parallel deliberation where, similarly, 'consensus is ... neither possible nor desirable'.[11] But the reason for compromising is quite different in both cases: while deliberation omits consensus in order to fulfill its goal of subsequent decision-making, ideal discourse is averse to decision making itself. Considering deliberation's democratic pre-formation as a pragmatic tool of self-government, we can deduce that deliberation and ideal discourse are mutually exclusive.

c) Regarding *real discourse*, there is no agreement among discourse theorists where the line between ideal rules and pragmatic constraints should be drawn in order to define what still constitutes a real discourse as opposed to other forms of dialogue. In my opinion, a real discourse can be defined as a discourse under conditions that approximate ideal discourse (as far as it is adequate under the circumstances) and that at least entail that all participants abstain from intentional coercion by force or threats.[12] Vague as this definition may sound, it can at least distinguish between strategic and discursive rationality – a fundamental threshold that Habermas has not abolished during all the variations of his theory. Accordingly, *war* cannot be deemed some kind of 'military discourse' and *bargaining* does not constitute 'economic discourse'. Also, an electoral campaign, which is discourse as long as the positions are presented in terms of morality rather than mere self-interest of groups, is distinct from the non-discursive ballot. Equally, parliamentary debate is discourse, while the final vote is not.[13]

If we apply this definition, deliberation is at the same time narrower and wider than real discourse. It is narrower in that it is democratically pre-formed as a tool of self-government which excludes the voices of those people who are not affected and which also excludes those dialogues that are not geared towards decision making. It is wider wherever strategic or coercive elements are accepted as pragmatic constraints of deliberation, compromising the ideal of public argument and reason. Therefore, deliberation is neither a sub-class of real discourse nor a super-class; it is a similar, but still a quite distinct 'sister' concept. At most, deliberation can be called a *discursive feature* of contemporary theories of democracy.

3) Deliberation and Decision as Distinct Procedures

Perhaps the greatest similarity between deliberation and real discourse lies in their strict separation from the decision itself. As a procedure of argumentation (albeit pragmatically reduced as compared with real discourse) deliberation or real discourse necessarily end when any procedure of decision making is started. Deciding a case after legal proceedings, voting on a statute after debate in parliament, executing a decree after public discussion – all these are formal decision procedures

[11] Dryzek, 2001, p. 657.
[12] For details see Tschentscher, 2000, p. 219.
[13] Cf. Tschentscher, 2000, pp. 347ff.

distinct from the material procedure of deliberation preceding them. Deliberation and decision are related as mutually exclusive alternatives: one can either deliberate or decide, not both.

Where, then, lies the contribution of deliberation to decision-making? In the framework of deliberative theory, the decision inherits most of its legitimation from the preceding deliberation. When extensive deliberation has taken place, the decision, within a specific range of constitutionally admissible results, is legitimate no matter what the outcome might be. If, on the other hand, there has been no deliberation at all, the following decision procedure alone can only generate very limited democratic legitimation – if any at all. Therefore, the function of deliberation in the proceedings of democratic decision-making turns out to be that of background fairness as a prerequisite of procedural justice.[14]

3 The Impact of Discourse Theory on Contemporary Theories of Democracy

Regarding the impact of discourse theory on contemporary theories of democracy, one of the more obvious mistakes is the tacit understanding among some authors that discourse theory might be used as a tool to legitimize deliberative democracy while de-legitimizing other democratic approaches (1). Also, explicitly anti-deliberative measures like institutional fiat can be legitimate instruments of democratic organization (2). This leads to the question of whether real discourse has any place at all in contemporary models of deliberative democracy (3).

1) The Compatibility of Discourse Theory With Diverse Theories of Democracy

Classical theories of democracy, i.e., those formally reducing the legitimacy of collective decision making to voting procedures and personal representation, can also be defended by discourse theory as concepts of deliberative democracy. Discourse theory is quite compatible with non-discursive procedures for deliberation and decision. Therefore, it does not require that institutionalized democracy take some form of deliberative democracy.

Take the bargaining that leads to a binding contract enforceable by law: no discourse theorist would claim that contractors ought to be involved in non-strategic action in order to render the resulting instrument legitimate. Not even within the proceedings of parliament, discourse is always present or required by discourse theory: decision making without prior deliberation is, for example, often explicitly prescribed by the constitution whenever officials are to be elected. Regarding democratic legitimacy, discourse theory does not claim that institutionalized democracy must take some form of deliberative democracy.

---

[14] Cf. Tschentscher, 2000, p. 121 – with further references.

2) The Legitimation of Institutional Fiat in Theories of Democracy

Frequently, institutional fiat is acknowledged as a central decision procedure in democratic states. The president, for example, may have the final power to decide issues no matter what kind – if any – of public or parliamentary deliberation took place before. A court ruling is equally decisive no matter what the expectations of the parties might be. And even in lawmaking the majority decision about a statute is binding no matter how much deliberation took place beforehand.

Institutional fiat is a challenge to deliberative theories of democracy because it claims legitimation even where, according to deliberation theorists, there can be none. If only public argument and reasoning among equal citizens have the power to convey legitimation on subsequent decisions, instances of pure institutional fiat must be called 'illegitimate'. Such decision-making becomes the true anti-thesis of deliberation by insulating the formal decision itself from any material considerations preceding it.

Nevertheless, institutional fiat is one of the most important safeguards against decisive deadlock and therefore indispensable to an operative legal order. These pragmatic constraints cannot easily be captured by deliberative theories. Deliberation is only one among many concepts forming the institutional setting of democracies. In discourse theory, however, even non-deliberative procedures can be acknowledged as contributing to an overall picture of legitimate social order. Thus it is discourse theory, not deliberative theory that constitutes a comprehensive framework of democracy.

3) Real Discourse as an Element in Theories of Democracy

What, if anything, remains as the role of real discourse in a deliberative understanding of democracy? As a starting point, there will hardly be any doubt that real public discourse does exist both within democratic institutions and among those non-institutionalized interactions summed up in the term 'civil society'. But real discourse not only exists; it is also *valued* at least as a heuristic tool by all contemporary theories of democracy. No theorist assumes that citizens ought to 'sleep between elections'.[15] Taking the case of the current institutional arrangement of democracy in Germany as an example, we are looking at a classical representative framework accompanied by major supreme court decisions that effectively prevent deliberative experiments. Nevertheless, public discourse is considered indispensable for the democratic process, the media are frequently assigned the implicit role of a 'fourth power', and Ernst-Wolfgang Böckenförde, an influential scholar of German constitutional law, famously laments the dilemma of the state lacking the means to guarantee active democratic participation while at the same time essentially relying on that participation.[16]

---

[15] Cf. Dryzek, 2001, p. 655.
[16] Cf. Böckenförde, 1967, p. 93.

So what is the distinctive quality of classical *versus* deliberative democratic theory? It cannot be only the distinction between aggregative *versus* reflective aspects of decision making[17] since all democracies rely heavily on reflective processing of interests even within the representative system. The distinctive property of classical democratic theory lies in the formal constraints it imposes on the relevance of public opinion. That opinion, continuously expressed in random deliberation within political and civil society, ought not to affect state action without being formally acknowledged by the legislature. In this restrictive framework, real discourse has meaning only where it is explicitly acknowledged as a formal procedure within the institutional setting. Rules about mandatory publication and information, regulations enforcing transparency, the participatory rights of members of parliament – all these are ways the legal system formally acknowledges the role of real discourse, thereby incorporating it into the democratic framework. A democracy becomes progressively more deliberative with these procedural safeguards; and real discourse is then a constitutive element of the resulting deliberative democracy.

Discourse theory, however, is not restricted to the small role that real discourse can play within the framework of democracy. When used as the basic rationale for institutionalized democracy, discourse theory explains why new participatory instruments (e.g., Fishkin's deliberative opinion polls) are legitimate even if they were eventually to infringe on formal constraints of classical theories, namely the exclusivity of voting and representation. This 'opening up' of democracy is achieved by identifying *continuous discursive control* rather than the formality of democratic procedures as the relevant source of legitimation.[18] Therefore, discourse theory explains why 'counting heads' is a 'needlessly thin conception of democracy'.[19] It broadens the horizon for new legitimate models of institutionalized democracy without challenging classical models.

4 Conclusion

In summary, we can conclude that deliberation is quite distinct from discourse and that deliberative theory differs greatly from discourse theory. It is discourse theory, not the insular notion of deliberation, that constitutes the comprehensive framework and basic rationale for institutionalized democracy. It gives us, among other things, an explanation why participatory instruments are legitimate even if they were to infringe on formal constraints of democratic procedures. Discourse theory provides the new rationale needed for the deliberative reevaluating of democratic legitimacy: the concept of continuous discursive control.

---

[17] But cf. Dryzek (forthcoming), p. 5.

[18] For the concept of continuous discursive control see Tschentscher, 2000, pp. 220f., 330f.

[19] Dryzek, 2001, pp. 657f.

References

Alexy, R. (1978) *Theorie der juristischen Argumentation: Die Theorie des rationalen Diskurses als Theorie der juristischen Begründung*, Frankfurt a.M. (Suhrkamp).

Alexy, R. (1989/1995) "Probleme der Diskurstheorie", reprinted in *Recht, Vernunft, Diskurs: Studien zur Rechtsphilosophie*, Frankfurt a.M. (Suhrkamp), 109-126.

Bessette, J. M. (1980) "The Majority Principle in Republican Government", in Goldwin, R. A. and W. A. Shambra (eds.) *How Democratic is the Constitution?*, Lanham/London (AEI), 102-116.

Böckenförde, E.-W. (1967) "Die Entstehung des Staates als Vorgang der Säkularisation", in *Säkularisation und Utopie: Festschrift für Ernst Forsthoff*, Stuttgart (Kohlhammer), 75-94.

Cohen, J. (1989) "Deliberation and Democratic Legitimacy", in Hamlin, A. and P. Pettit (eds.) *The Good Polity: Normative Analysis of the State*, New York (Blackwell), 17-34.

Dryzek, J. S. (2001) "Legitimacy and Economy in Deliberative Democracy", *Political Theory* 29, 643-661.

Dryzek J. S. (forthcoming) "Democratic Political Theory", in Gaus, G. F. and C. Kukathas (eds.) *The Handbook of Political Theory*.

Fishkin, J. S. (1991) *Democracy and Deliberation. New Directions for Democratic Reform*, New Haven/London (Yale University Press).

Luhmann, N. (1975) *Legitimation durch Verfahren*, 2nd ed., Darmstadt (Luchterhand).

Madison, J. (1787/1961) "The Federalist No. 10", reprinted in Cooke, J. E. (ed.) *The Federalist*, Middletown (Wesleyan University Press), 57ff.

Sunstein, C. (1985) "Interest Groups in American Public Law", *Stanford Law Review* 38, 29-87.

Tschentscher, A. (2000) *Prozedurale Theorien der Gerechtigkeit. Rationales Entscheiden, Diskursethik und prozedurales Recht*, Baden-Baden (Nomos).

Tylor, T. R. (1990) *Why People Obey the Law*, New Haven (Yale University Press).

Chapter 3

Constitutional Economics in Constitutional Jurisprudence

Axel Tschentscher

Discourse theory is frequently applied as the 'basic theory of the democratic constitutional state'.[1] The impact of constitutional economics on jurisprudence then falls within the expansive theme of analysing the strategic ties of ideal speech communities.[2] A large gap, however, demarcates the border between law and economics – a gap that cannot easily be bridged. The first obstacle arises with the different understanding of 'agreement' and 'consensus' within strategic and moral frameworks of legitimation: decision making and discourse do not overlap (1). A further complication arises from the misunderstanding of discourse as intellectual élitism (2). Finally, the ephemeral connection between law and economics is in fact very one-sided: economics holds legal significance only where economic rationality is normatively acknowledged by law (3).

1. The most fundamental and therefore first question between constitutional economics and discourse theory goes to their difference in legitimizing activity, namely: Is there any similarity at all between the 'agreement' among agents of rational choice and the 'consensus' of real persons in an ideal speech situation? True enough, both concepts are in some way related to the justificatory force of voluntary action by those affected (*volenti non fit iniuria*). They are also both hypothetical procedures when applied as instruments of justification out of the theorist's armory. But what is the relevance of superficial similarities like these? The framework for voluntary action differs notably between the bargaining of self-interested strategists and the arguing of moral agents. Consensus, though sometimes named as the unifying element between contract and discourse theory,[3] is quite distinct in strategic and moral frameworks. This becomes obvious when each of the positions is confronted with the implicit normative claims of the other.

---

[1] 'Basistheorie des demokratischen Verfassungsstaates'; cf. Alexy (1991), p. 417; Alexy (1995), p. 164; Alexy (1996), pp. 343ff.; Müller (1993), pp. 143ff., 146; Tschannen (1995), pp. 388, 391ff.; Tschentscher (2000), pp. 338, 347.

[2] For the perspective of constitutional economics as discussed below cf. Coleman (1984).

[3] Cf. Kaufmann (1989), p. 10f.; Brugger (2000), p. 425.

a) Let us first consider a *Buchanan*-style bargaining situation of social choice where 'Law' is but one public good among others.[4] The ideal of 'ordered anarchy' presents itself within a scenario of maximum threats: 'natural distribution' draws the lawless baseline for strategic cooperation, not even excluding murder or slavery.[5] In real life, contractual agreement frequently perpetuates the disadvantage of social groups and individual participants by treating as 'voluntary' what in fact is an action without alternatives.[6] From the perspective of discourse theory, however, such bargaining with unequal power directly violates the right to equal communicative standing. No agreement under such circumstances could be called 'discursively voluntary' in a sense bestowing legitimacy on the outcome.

b) Taking the reverse perspective we have to consider a *Habermas*-style ideal speech situation of discourse theory where 'Law' is – at least in its communicative connotations – predetermined as a necessary presupposition of discourse theory ('Diskurstheoretische Notwendigkeit von Normen'[7]). The 'ideal speech situation' presents itself within a scenario absolutely free from force or threats: everyone competent to speak and act is allowed to equally participate in non-coercive discourse.[8] From the perspective of social choice theory, however, the difficult conditions of an 'ideal speech situation' entail illegitimate presuppositions: they are twisting the baseline of consent in favor of a liberalistic interpretation of rights. Leaving no place for power, consent under such circumstances fails to mirror the difference in interests among the participants. Discourse becomes as prejudiced as the 'veil of ignorance'.[9]

c) Taking note of the fundamental incompatibility between rational choice and discourse theory, we can conclude that there is no relevant similarity between the 'agreement' among self-interested agents and the 'consensus' in an ideal speech situation. Decision-making and deliberation might both have their place in real world procedures, but they remain distinct, not overlapping concepts.

2. Some constitutional economists regard the counterfactual ideals of discourse theory as a dubious form of intellectual élitism. Were such élitism a consequence of discourse theory, the cost of acknowledging this framework of thought would indeed be high. However, taking discourse theory as some form of modern Platonism fails to understand the distinction between ideal and real discourse. There is, to cut things short, no connection of discourse theory with Platonism at all. The 'ideal' in 'ideal speech situation' bears no similarity to the ideals of Platonism. To

---

[4] For the theory of public choice and (normative) constitutional economics cf. generally Buchanan and Tullock (1962); Brennan and Buchanan (1985); Buchanan (1991); Cooter (2000). For a positive rather than normative application of constitutional economics cf. Voigt (1997) and (1999).

[5] Cf. Buchanan (1975), pp. 60ff., 189.

[6] Caplovitz (1967), pp. XXVff., 81ff.; Ayres and Siegelmann (1995), pp. 307f.; Emmenegger, (1999), pp. 70f.

[7] Tschentscher (2000), pp. 309ff., 311, 317ff.

[8] Cf. Habermas (1990), p. 86; for details see Alexy, (1991), pp. 233ff.

[9] Cf. Rawls (1971), pp. 136ff.

the contrary: discourse theory is firmly rooted in Kantianism, expanding the epistemology of 18th century enlightenment into the communicative reflexivity of contemporary transcendental philosophy.[10] If anything, the resulting framework for public deliberation in real discourse tends to be egalitarian, not intellectually élitist.

3. To show, as I have tried in section 1 above, that approaches of rational choice and discourse ethics do not conceptually overlap within a common notion of 'legitimacy by consent' does not necessarily exclude any relevance of economics to law. However, a number of shortcuts from the realm of economics to the normative world of legal systems are clearly inadmissible.

a) Efficiency and optimality do not straightforwardly fit into the legal framework. Take the optimization criterion according to Kaldor-Hicks or the Pareto criterion as examples.[11] The Kaldor-Hicks criterion would leave the legislator hardly any choice at all if adopted as a constitutional principle.[12] To use the Kaldor-Hicks criterion as a legal norm, therefore, entails quite distinct consequences from using it non-legally as a criterion of economic or political advantage. Even the less intrusive Pareto criterion will hardly ever blend seamlessly into normative systems. If a legislator, for example, were constitutionally required to use every feasible Pareto improvement, the laws could always be challenged on the ground of sub-optimality: a tax code standing scrutiny today might be called unconstitutional tomorrow in a changing economic environment. It is not surprising that constitutions hardly ever mention optimality or efficiency – and if they do, it is in the form of non-binding principles or goals. Regarding efficiency and optimality, the normative order of a legal system deliberately takes a counterfactual standpoint: norms claim validity no matter how costly their implementation might be.[13] Efficiency is usually incorporated *indirectly* by allowing non-state actors to follow their self-interest within the framework of private law guarantees, most prominently by designing contracts according to contract law and in conformity with the standards set by torts law. In public law, deregulation and privatization utilize this effect by expanding the self-interested organization of the private sphere without directly incorporating efficiency into the legal system.

b) Does constitutional economics lend itself more easily to jurisprudence than traditional economics? The starting point for an answer could be the distinctions between realist versus counterfactualist and subjectivist versus objectivist kinds of economic analysis, as suggested by Jules Coleman.[14] Placing constitutional economics of the *Buchanan* school into the realist-subjectivist view on efficiency means that transaction costs are defined by the framework within which the notion of optimality is employed (realist view) and that what is efficient cannot be deter-

---

[10] Cf. Apel (1973), p. 375; Kuhlmann (1992), p. 52, 183; Adorno (1959), p. 56.

[11] Pareto superiority, Pareto optimality, Kaldor-Hicks efficiency; see Coleman (1984), pp. 143ff.

[12] Cf. Tschentscher (2001), p. 188; similarly Möstl (1998), p. 1038.

[13] Cf. Morlok (1998), p. 15.

[14] Coleman (1984), pp. 148ff. (150).

mined independently of actual agreement (subjectivist view). In other words: whatever free participants of cooperation actually agree on in light of the circumstances is by definition efficient.

This view, however, has advantages as well as disadvantages from the legal standpoint. On the one hand, evaluating the efficiency of legal instruments with regard to the actual agreement of real persons within a given legal framework is *more adequate* than counterfactual-objectivist views (of traditional economics and public policy) in capturing the demands of jurisprudence, because it neither ignores the transaction costs imposed by the law, nor assumes an unlimited potential for agreement without regard to the activity of real persons. On the other hand, constitutional economics thus understood is *indeterminate* as a criterion for evaluating the efficiency of legal precepts: no matter what kind of rule is adopted, the resulting action of free utility maximizers is by definition efficient *under this rule.* Hence, if the aim of constitutionalism is to shift focus from particular states of affairs to the institutional frameworks that give them their content and meaning[15] the theory renders 'efficiency' of action meaningless and solely relies on the comparative advantage of different institutional settings.

Coleman presents three criticisms: (a) some transaction costs are unduly subsumed under the institutional setting, (b) the missing argument about why agreement ought to be voluntary, and (c) a paradox unfolds between the subjectivist view of efficiency and the need for an objective criterion to determine the comparative advantage among different institutional settings.[16] The last of these criticisms is of particular concern to jurisprudence. The criterion to compare institutional settings is probably the most pressing question jurisprudence asks of constitutional economics. If the answer comes down to something like 'institutional frameworks are efficient relative to rules of institutional decision making',[17] jurisprudence is sent right back to its own devices because 'rules of institutional decision making' are procedures of legislation and adjudication, even of constitutional amendment, and all of them are *legal rules in themselves.* While realist-objectivist viewers of efficiency might at least claim that one set of court rules is advantageous compared to another, constitutional economics in Coleman's interpretation cannot provide this kind of answer. Whatever the lawmaker adopts within the given legislative procedure is by definition efficient; and on the meta-meta-level: whatever the people adopt as a constitution is by definition efficient. The efficiency calculations of decision making do not entail specific guidelines for the deliberation of lawmakers. In other words – taking up the result of the first section above – decision making and deliberation are not overlapping concepts, they are distinct.

c) What remains of constitutional economics in constitutional jurisprudence? The value of economics in law lies in applying the economic paradigm (self-interested utility maximization, methodological individualism) to legal provi-

---

15 Cf. Coleman (1984), pp. 151ff.

16 Coleman (1984), pp. 152ff.

17 Cf. Coleman (1984), pp. 153ff., who himself does not share this 'realist' view (p. 150).

sions.[18] The legal framework gives incentives and creates additional transaction costs. Therefore, changes of that framework do make a difference for the range of activities rational utility maximizers will freely engage in: legal regulation can inhibit such activity (criminal law) or enable it (law of contracts). Making a difference means that some sets of rules can be of comparative advantage over other sets of rules. In the terms of constitutional and new institutional economics, 'institutional settings' differ. However, the ruling principle to determine comparative advantage of institutions is *not* necessarily that of efficiency or optimality. With many (if not most) institutions such principle or criterion is not even rooted in economic considerations. For example, the indiscriminate use of 'efficient allocation of resources' as a criterion to judge the comparative advantage of institutions does not at all capture all rationales available for legal rules.[19] Sometimes the *effective* – even if exceedingly costly and therefore not efficient – achievement of basic safeguards (human rights, minimum welfare standards) prevails over all other considerations. The rationale is no longer that of self-interested utility maximization, but of universal morality.

Constitutional economics leads to the most basic insight that institutional frameworks, by imposing transaction costs, are responsible for the scope of legal activity that is actually available. This has at least some bearing on law and jurisprudence. Reducing regulation will typically decrease transaction costs and, therefore, seems to be one of the recommendable meta-rules for lawmakers trying to improve the institutional framework by broadening the options for individual activity. Also, submitting issues to the sphere of private rather than public law tends to decrease transaction costs. Both themes have been taken up by lawmakers and jurisprudence theorists under the titles of 'deregulation' and 'privatization'. Furthermore, both themes are good examples for the incorporation of economic rationales as guiding principles in law. Thus, law and jurisprudence are opening small windows for economic analysis.

References

Adorno, T. W. (1959) *Kants 'Kritik der reinen Vernunft'*, reprint 1995, Frankfurt a.M. (Suhrkamp).

Alexy, R. (1991) *Theorie der juristischen Argumentation: Die Theorie des rationalen Diskurses als Theorie der juristischen Begründung*, 2nd ed., Frankfurt a.M (Suhrkamp).

Alexy, R. (1995) "Diskurstheorie und Menschenrechte", in *Recht, Vernunft, Diskurs: Studien zur Rechtsphilosophie*, Frankfurt a.M. (Suhrkamp), 127-164.

[18] Kirchner (1996), p. 71. See also Posner (1992) and Behrens (1981).

[19] Cf. Kirchner (1996), pp. 72ff. regarding the Chicago School of Economic Analysis of Law.

Alexy, R. (1996) "Grundgesetz und Diskurstheorie", in Brugger W. (ed.) *Legitimation des Grundgesetzes aus Sicht von Rechtsphilosophie und Gesellschaftstheorie*, Baden-Baden (Nomos), 343-360.

Apel, K.-O. (1973) "Das Apriori der Kommunikationsgemeinschaft und die Grundlagen der Ethik: Zum Problem einer rationalen Begründung der Ethik im Zeitalter der Wissenschaft", in idem *Transformation der Philosophie, Band 2: Das Apriori der Kommunikationsgemeinschaft*, Frankfurt a.M. (Suhrkamp), 358-435.

Ayres, I. and P. Siegelmann (1995) "Race and Gender Discrimination in Bargaining for a New Car", *The American Economic Review* 85, 304-321.

Behrens, P. (1981) "Aspekte einer ökonomischen Theorie des Rechts", *Rechtstheorie* 12, 472-490.

Brennan, G. H., and J. M. Buchanan (1985) *The Reason of Rules: Constitutional Political Economy*, Cambridge (Cambridge University Press).

Brugger, W. (2000) "Amerikanische Verfassungstheorie", *Der Staat* 39, 425-453.

Buchanan, J. M. (1991) *Constitutional Economics*, Oxford (Blackwell).

Buchanan, J. M. (1975) *The Limits of Liberty: Between Anarchy and Leviathan*, Chicago (University of Chicago Press).

Buchanan, J. M. and G. Tullock (1962) *The Calculus of Consent: Logical Foundations of Constitutional Democracy*, Ann Arbor (University of Michigan Press).

Caplovitz, D. (1967) *The Poor Pay More: Consumer Practices of Low-Income Families*, 2nd ed., New York/London (Free Press).

Coleman, J. L. (1984) "The Foundations of Constitutional Economics", in McKenzie, R. B. (ed.) *Constitutional Economics: Containing the Economic Powers of Government*, Lexington (Lexington Books), 141-55.

Cooter, R. (2000) *The Strategic Constitution*, Princeton (Princeton University Press).

Emmenegger, S. (1999) *Feministische Kritik des Vertragsrechts: Eine Untersuchung zum schweizerischen Schuldvertrags- und Eherecht*, Freiburg i.Ue. (Univ.-Verl.).

Habermas, J. (1990) "Discourse Ethics: Notes on a Program of Philosophical Justification", in *Moral Consciousness and Communicative Action*, translated by Christian Lenhart and Shierry Weber Nicholson, Cambridge, Mass. (MIT Press).

Kaufmann, A. (1989) "Prozedurale Theorien der Gerechtigkeit", vorgetragen in der Gesamtsitzung der Philosophisch-Historischen und der Mathematisch-Naturwissenschaftlichen Klasse am 17. Februar 1989, München.

Kirchner, C. (1996) "Regulierung durch öffentliches Recht und/oder Privatrecht aus der Sicht der ökonomischen Theorie des Rechts", in Hoffmann-Riem, W. and E. Schmidt-Aßmann (ed.) *Öffentliches Recht und Privatrecht als wechselseitige Auffangordnungen*, Baden-Baden (Nomos), 63-84.

Kuhlmann, W. (1992) *Kant und die Transzendentalpragmatik*, Würzburg (Königshausen & Neumann).

Möstl, M. (1998) "Probleme der verfassungsprozessualen Geltendmachung gesetzgeberischer Schutzpflichten", *DÖV*, 1029-1039.

Morlok, M. (1998) "Vom Reiz und Nutzen, von den Schwierigkeiten und Gefahren der Ökonomischen Theorie für das Öffentliche Recht", in Engel, C. and M. Morlok (eds.) *Öffentliches Recht als ein Gegenstand ökonomischer Forschung: Die Begegnung der deutschen Staatsrechtslehre mit der Konstitutionellen Politischen Ökonomie*, Tübingen (Mohr Siebeck), 1-29.

Müller, J. P. (1993) *Demokratische Gerechtigkeit: Eine Studie zur Legitimität rechtlicher und politischer Ordnung*, München (dtv).

Posner, R. A. (1992) *Economic Analysis of Law*, 4th ed., Boston (Little, Brown).

Rawls, J. (1971) *A Theory of Justice*, Cambridge, Mass. (Harvard University Press).

Tschannen, P. (1995) *Stimmrecht und politische Verständigung: Beiträge zu einem erneuerten Verständnis von direkter Demokratie*, Basel (Helbing & Lichtenhahn).

Tschentscher, A. (2000) *Prozedurale Theorien der Gerechtigkeit*, Baden-Baden (Nomos).

Tschentscher, A. (2001) "Indienstnahme der Gerichte für die Effizienz der Verwaltung", in Demel, M. et al. (eds.) *Funktionen und Kontrolle der Gewalten*, Stuttgart (Boorberg),165-198.

Voigt, S. (1997) "Positive Constitutional Economics: A Survey", *Public Choice* 90, 11-53.

Voigt, S. (1999) *Explaining Constitutional Change: A Positive Economics Approach*, Cheltenham (Elgar).

PART II

DELIBERATION AND SOCIAL CHOICE

Chapter 4

A Dilemma for Deliberative Democrats[1]

Philip Pettit

Abstract

The paper begins with the observation that, when decisions have to be reached on the basis of reasons, deliberative democrats face a hard choice on the matter of how individual judgments should be put together. After sketching the ideal of deliberative democracy, a 'discursive dilemma' is introduced, which highlights a serious problem of aggregating individual judgments into collective ones. It is shown that, while other arguments for deliberative democracy fail to give us a lead on how to resolve the dilemma, the republican argument offers strong and persuasive reason for going one particular route. The argument gives us reason to think that, even at the cost of moderating the rule of majority voting, any deliberatively democratic group should be concerned to ensure that the judgments and decisions it collectively endorses are consistent and otherwise rational; it should present itself as a collectivity that relates to others in the manner of a reasoning subject.

The ideal of deliberative democracy prescribes that those engaged in a democratic process should form their voting intentions in the course of debate with others as to what is best for the group overall and should cast their votes on the basis of their final judgment as to what is for the best. But it says little or nothing about the nature of the process itself, in particular on the way in which votes should be put together to yield a collective decision or judgment. This is not an innocuous oversight, for it turns out that deliberative democrats face a hard choice on the matter of how votes should be put together. They have to choose between two options, each of which has an unattractive aspect to it. My aim in this paper is to explain the di-

[1] This is a shortened and substantially modified version of 'Deliberative Democracy and the Discursive Dilemma', *Philosophical Issues* (Supplement to *Nous*), Vol 11, 2001, pp. 268-99. In modifying the paper I benefitted from comments received from my commentators, Frank Michelman and Paul Weithman, when it was delivered at a meeting of the American Philosophical Association in Dec. 2000. The approach taken is further developed, with more emphasis on policy implications, in Pettit, P. (2003): Deliberative Democracy, the Discursive Dilemma, and Republican Theory, in *Philosophy, Politics and Society Vol 7: Debating Deliberative Democracy*, ed. by J. Fishkin and P. Laslett, Cambridge (Cambridge University Press).

lemma involved and to argue for a particular resolution of it, one based on a republican understanding of why deliberative democracy is an ideal.

The paper is in three sections. In the first, I sketch the ideal itself, in the second I introduce the dilemma, and in the third I show that while other arguments for deliberative democracy fail to give us a lead on how to resolve that dilemma, the republican argument offers strong and persuasive reason for going one particular route. The argument gives us reason to think that, even at the cost of moderating the rule of majority voting, any deliberatively democratic group should be concerned to ensure that the judgments and decisions it collectively endorses are consistent and otherwise rational; it should present itself, not just as a collectivity within which reasoning takes place, but also as a collectivity that relates to others – other individuals and other agencies – in the manner of a reasoning subject.

1 The Ideal of Deliberative Democracy

There are many contexts of decision-making where the issue comes up as to whether or not to decide things democratically. The most salient is the context involving the role of the populace in a polity but there are many, more restricted contexts where a parallel issue comes up. The context may involve politicians in a party or parliament or cabinet, for example, the shareholders or directors in a commercial company, the judges in a collegiate court, the workers on a shopfloor, the members on a public board, the public servants in a department of government, or the members in a voluntary club or association.

Deliberative democrats argue that decisions ought to be made democratically in many such contexts – they may differ, of course, about which contexts should be democratized – and, more specifically, that they ought to be made in a deliberatively democratic way. In doing so, they agree on three main points, arguing for the satisfaction of the following constraints on public decision-making (Bohman and Rehg, 1997; Elster, 1998).

- *The inclusive constraint*: all members should be equally entitled to vote on how to resolve certain collective issues, or bundles of issues, with something less than a unanimous vote being sufficient to determine the outcome.
- *The judgmental constraint*: before voting, members should deliberate on the basis of presumptively common concerns about which resolution is to be preferred.
- *The dialogical constraint*: they should conduct this deliberation in open and unforced dialogue with one another, whether in a centralized forum or in various decentralized contexts.

The inclusive constraint means that deliberative democracy is to be contrasted with elitist or authoritarian schemes, even ones in which deliberation and dialogue have an important place. The judgmental constraint requires voters to deliberate or reason about how they should vote, not just vote in an unreflective or spontaneous or reflex manner. In particular, it requires voters to deliberate about how they should vote on the basis of considerations as to what is best for the group as a whole: what is likely to advance those common interests that people would presumptively endorse, if only after some dialogue with others. The kind of voting recommended is sometimes described as judgment-voting rather than preference-voting (Cohen, 1986; Coleman and Ferejohn, 1986; Brennan and Pettit, 1990). The idea is that each voter should make up his or her own mind as to what is for the good of the group in question and should vote on the basis of that judgment, not on the basis of brute preference (Sunstein, 1993b) or bargained compromise (Pettit, 1993, Ch.5; Elster, 1998, pp. 5-8)

The third, dialogical constraint in the ideal of deliberative democracy rules out the sort of plebiscitarian dispensation in which each participant privately forms his or her judgment about common, presumptively avowable interests – rather than doing so in dialogue with others – and then votes on the basis of that judgment. The constraint requires open and unforced dialogue, whether it be centralised or decentralised: whether it occurs in a single assembly of those involved or in smaller groupings, even groupings of two or three. The dialogue must be open in the sense that each can get a hearing and it must be unforced in the sense that no one need fear to speak their mind; it must approximate the conditions for ideal speech that Juergen Habermas (1984; 1989) emphasises.

The three constraints defended by deliberative democrats bear on the need for judgment and dialogue in the formation of voting intention, not on how votes should be put together to form a collective decision. They are focussed, in other words, on the inputs for which we ought to look in democratic decision-making, not on the process of decision-making itself. There is an assumption in place that unanimity should not be required, the grounds presumably being that a requirement of unanimity would reduce any plausible body of people to stalemate on a variety of issues. But that is all. Nothing more is said on how votes should be put together, say among the politicians in a party, the shareholders in a company, or the members of a public board. It turns out however that this raises a problem and that deliberative democrats need to add more detail on how decision-making should be pursued. We turn to that problem in the next section.

2 The Dilemma for Deliberative Democrats

Introducing the Dilemma

Suppose we have a group of three people, each voting on each of three interconnected issues, and with the decision on each issue being determined by majority vote. There can be majority support for each of an inconsistent set of judgments, even though each of the three voters is perfectly consistent in his or her own views. The matrix below makes clear why. In the example represented in the matrix, a majority in a group of three people, A, B and C, support ‘p’; a majority support ‘if p, then q’; and yet nevertheless a majority deny ‘q’.

	First issue: p?	Second: if p, then q?	Third: q?
Voter A	Yes	No	No
Voter B	No	Yes	No
Voter C	Yes	Yes	Yes

As the matrix shows, a majority supports the claim that p, and the claim that if p then q, but still a majority denies that q. Thus if the group view is determined by majority voting on each issue, then the collective set of judgments will be inconsistent and irrational. And yet none of the individuals involved is irrational in the votes they cast. The problem comes of the fact that the majorities on each issue are different. There is only one member in common to the majorities that support 'p' and 'if p, then q' respectively and that is the only person who is rationally required to vote for 'q', and the only person who as a matter of fact does vote that way.

This schematic example illustrates the dilemma that deliberative democrats are bound to face. Not specifying how the decision-making process is to be constrained – focussing, as they do, on the inputs to that process – they do not say how a group in a situation as that illustrated should behave. They have to face the choice, then, between prescribing that the group should always go with the result of majority-voting or some such procedure on each issue that it confronts and prescribing that it should guard, by whatever means available, against collective rationality. The choice constitutes a dilemma – I call it the discursive dilemma (Pettit, 2001a; Pettit, 2001b) – because each option represents a hard alternative to live with. The first would ensure that the group judges in a way that is responsive to the views of individual members but would risk generating collectively irrational positions. The second would ensure that the group generates collectively rational positions but would compromise the responsiveness of the group to the views of individual members.

This dilemma will be familiar to students of law and economics, for a version of it regularly arises in legal decisions; indeed it was first identified in that context as a paradox generated by legal doctrine (Kornhauser and Sager, 1986; Kornhauser, 1992; Kornhauser, 1992; Kornhauser and Sager, 1993. See too Chapman, 1998; Brennan, 2001). Thus consider the case of a three-member court casting votes as to whether someone is liable in tort for something they did that affected another. Legal doctrine requires the judges to make judgments, not just on liability, but also on the related issues of whether there was harm done and whether there was a duty of care. And, more specifically, legal doctrine requires them to let the resolution of those other issues determine the resolution of the liability question: this is a feature of the case, as we shall see, that need not have parallels in other, non-legal cases.

	Was harm done?	Was there a duty of care?	Liable?
Judge A	Yes	No	No
Judge B	No	Yes	No
Judge C	Yes	Yes	Yes

The members of the collegiate court are each individually consistent in the votes. We may assume that not only are they consistent, indeed, they respect legal doctrine by letting their votes on liability be driven – driven in consistency – by their votes on the other issues. But if we look at the majority vote on each issue we see that collectively the court is inconsistent; it supports affirmative judgments on the first two issues – there are two Yes's on each question – and a negative judgment on the third. More specifically, the court collectively breaches legal doctrine, so far as it does not draw the conclusion on liability that its collective positions on the other issues require.

There are two features of the judicial example that are special to it and it is important to see that they need not characterize the sort of case schematically represented in the first matrix, nor all the sorts of cases, therefore, that deliberative democrats will have to deal with. The first feature is that the court typically considers issues like those arising in the tort case simultaneously and members make up their minds on those issues in the course of the same sitting. The second, as already mentioned, is that members of the court are expected not just to be consistent but to let their views on the issues that legal doctrine declares to be primary – in this case their views on whether the defendant caused harm and had a duty of care – drive their view on the issue up for adjudication: in this case, the question of the agent's liability.

The discursive dilemma can arise, however, even in the absence of these features. First, to go back to the schematic example, the group in question may be faced with judgments on 'p', 'if p, then q' and 'q' over a period of time, and vote on each question as it comes up for discussion. The discursive dilemma will continue to be a problem for the group so far as it is bad, not just to be synchronically inconsistent, but also to be diachronically inconsistent: to be inconsistent over time. Diachronic inconsistency would cease to matter only in the unlikely event that there was no aspiration on the group's part to intertemporal continuity.

Second, if the group is to achieve collective consistency, it need not do so by having its judgments on 'p' and 'if p, then q' determine its judgment on 'q', as an analogue of legal doctrine might require in this case. It may achieve consistency just as well – it may achieve consistency and advance all other relevant ideals just as well– by allowing its judgments on the second and third issues to determine its judgment on the first, or its judgments on the first and third issues determine its judgment on the second. In other words, it may achieve consistency by conforming to *modus tollens* as well as *modus ponens*.

In the schematic case given, it may seem easier for the group to go the *modus ponens* way, for individuals A and B can easily reverse their judgments on whether q; this would not require them to change either of their other judgments. But equally A might change the judgment he or she made on the first issue, B the judgment made on the second, or C the judgment made on the first or second. And in any case, the fact that A and B can easily reverse their judgments on the third issue is an artifact of how the example is structured. It would not arise in an example conforming to the following pattern.

	First issue: p?	Second: q?	Third: p and q?
Voter A	Yes	No	No
Voter B	No	Yes	No
Voter C	Yes	Yes	Yes

The discursive dilemma is more general, then, than the doctrinal paradox of legal theory in three ways (Pettit, 2002). It can arise in areas involving interconnected issues of a non-legal kind; it can arise on the basis of diachronic as well as synchronic votes on those issues; and it can present a problem whose resolution is equally well achieved by the reversal of the group judgment on any one of the issues involved.

The discursive dilemma shows that deliberative democrats need to address a question on which the three constraints they defend are silent. Should deliberatively democratic groups – groups that satisfy the constraints given – form their views on interconnected issues in a way that prioritises responsiveness to individuals, and risks collective irrationality? Or should they form their view on such issues in a way that privileges collective rationality and may compromise responsiveness to individuals? Should they put responsiveness first or rationality first?

The Importance of the Dilemma

This question is of the first importance for deliberative democrats, because the answer they give to it will have a major impact on the profile of the position they end up defending. We can see this if we consider briefly the implications of their adopting either a responsiveness-first approach or a rationality-first approach; I assume that they will not attempt to go for a mixed position.

Suppose that they take a responsiveness-first approach, arguing that the important thing in deliberative democratic decision-making is that each individual is included in a judgmental and dialogical way and that the votes of those individuals ought to determine the position of the group on each issue raised. They may hope that should irrationalities arise at the collective level, then this can be taken into account by individuals in a second round of voting and can induce a change of voting that restores consistency. But so far as responsiveness is what matters in the first place, that is all that they can do: hope. For while an individual may be given a practical reason to change his or her view by the fact that this will render the position of the group consistent, it is unclear in many cases – in cases where they simply think that others are mistaken – why this consideration should weigh with them.

Consider the implications of the responsiveness-first approach, then, for what deliberative democrats are going to say about how an organised body like a political party should do its business. Assuming that a political party is to operate in a democratic mould, deliberative democrats who take the approach are going to have to say that the party will be required to live with whatever policies emerge on the basis of inclusive dialogue and judgmental voting. But this is going to make deliberative democracy look like a silly ideal in such a context, as a simple example makes clear.

Take the political party that has to vote in the course of a year leading up to an election, on issues of tax and expenditure. Even if we imagine for simplicity that there are only three voting members, we can see that it is quite possible that majority, individually rational votes on each of three related issues – votes, let us assume, that are taken at different times – will generate a collectively irrational set of decisions.

	Increase taxes?	Increase defence spending?	Increase other spending?
A	No	Yes	No (reduce)
B	No	No (reduce)	Yes
C	Yes	Yes	Yes

A political party that put responsiveness first in such a situation would be incapable of effectively advancing any goals in government, since inconsistent policies will lead in inconsistent directions. And a political party that put responsiveness first in such a way would be a laughing-stock in the electorate; it would just not be a credible contender for government. If deliberative democrats prioritise responsiveness, therefore, they will have to allow that their ideal does not apply in such contexts or that it is has to be governed by higher ideals of effectiveness and credibility.

The lesson illustrated with the political party is going to apply in general with any organised body such as a parliamentary committee, a commission of inquiry, a government agency, a commercial corporation, a trades union, a professional association, a religious group, or whatever. Thus the responsiveness-first approach to the ideal of deliberative democracy would have radical implications for the reach of the ideal. It would suggest that it is at best a partial, secondary ideal for such groups.

The rationality-first approach, by contrast, would certainly allow the ideal of deliberative democracy to apply in such contexts. It would have the effect of adding a further constraint to the three mentioned in the first section, one that articulates the need for collective rationality.

- *The group-rationality constraint*: people should take steps to ensure that where their voting would lead to inconsistent or otherwise irrational policies, this is remedied and group rationality prevails.

What steps could people take to guard against inconsistency or irrationality? It would make good sense for them initially to explore majority voting on each issue and only concern themselves with how to achieve collective rationality in the event of majority voting giving rise to a problem, or threatening to give rise to a problem. And there are a variety of paths that they might take to ensure that when a problem does arise, rationality rules. They might explore second and third rounds of voting as a first recourse. And in the event of that initiative not working, they might have procedures in place that give authority to a certain member or sub-group to decide how to restore rationality, or that give priority to the majority views on certain sorts of issues – say, more general issues or issues resolved earlier – allowing those views to rationally determine the views that the collectivity is to take on other questions (List and Pettit, 2002; List and Pettit (forthcoming)). Or they might have procedures for voting on which of those procedures looks to be the most compelling in the case on hand, and the one therefore to follow.

But as the responsiveness-first approach will have quite significant implications for the reach of the deliberative democratic ideal, so the same is true of the rationality-first approach. It should be clear that many electoral bodies will be incapable of implementing the group-rationality constraint in an intuitively satisfactory way. The small town meeting that gathers monthly to discuss and decide on local issues might be able to do this but not the people in a large-scale electorate, if that electorate uses majority voting in referenda to determine interconnected questions of policy. There might be a procedure in place determining that should the electorate support irrational sets of judgments, then certain sorts of judgment have priority or some privileged individual or group – say, the government – can determine how the irrationality is to be resolved. But such procedures would look like impositions on the deliberations and voting patterns of the population, given the size and lack of organisation of the electorate envisaged; they would have a very different aspect from that which they have in the case of the relatively small-scale, organised group.

The natural line for deliberative democrats to take, if they favor the rationality-first interpretation of their ideal, is to say that large-scale electorates should not be generally given policy-issues to resolve, in view of the likelihood of inconsistencies. Rather the remit of the people should be restricted to the choice of policy-making representatives, together with the associated discussion of the policy programs of candidates and their parties. This line is perfectly consistent with the constraints given, though it is at odds with what many deliberative democrats sometimes seem to envisage.

The considerations in this section show, I hope, that the discursive dilemma is a serious issue for deliberative democrats. I argue in the next section for a resolution that favors the rationality-first interpretation. But before turning to that resolution I should mention that the problem raised by the dilemma is not just an artifact of the assumption that the people in any democratic forum are going to practise majority voting. In work elsewhere, Christian List and I have shown that there is a problem which is independent of that assumption (List and Pettit, 2002; List and Pettit (forthcoming)). Specifically, we have argued for an impossibility theorem – the mathematical proof is due to List – to roughly this effect. Given a rationally connected set of issues, and given individual sets of judgments on those issues that are themselves rationally satisfactory – they are complete, consistent and deductively closed – there is no procedure for aggregating those sets of judgments that will guarantee a rationally satisfactory collective set of judgments and at the same time meet the following constraints: it works for any rational sets of judgment as input and it treats both the issues and the individuals involved as having equal standing.

3 The Resolution of the Dilemma

We come finally to the question of how the dilemma should be resolved. The ideal way to resolve it would be to find that the arguments generally put forward in support of the ideal of deliberative democracy favor one interpretation or the other of the ideal. But it turns out, as I have tried to show elsewhere, that the arguments generally advanced in the literature leave it unclear whether the ideal should be taken in a responsiveness-first or a rationality-first way (Pettit, 2001a). We have to turn elsewhere – to what I call the republican argument for deliberative democracy – in order to find a basis for resolving the dilemma.

The Standard Arguments for Deliberative Democracy

Most of the arguments for deliberative democracy assume that the case for an inclusive democracy is palpable and focus on the benefit to a democratically organised group of having decision governed by deliberation of an inclusive, dialogical kind (Cohen, 1989; Dryzek, 1990; Sunstein, 1993a; Benhabib, 1994; Gutmann and Thompson, 1996). Some of these arguments assert that making democracy deliberative should help to ensure that people's preferences are reflective and informed, as distinct from remaining the brute product of adaptation to circumstance (Sunstein, 1993b); or that it should enable people to do better in reaching beyond the chasms of difference that separate the members of certain groups, even if it does not bring them into consensus (Young, 1990); or that it should stretch people's imagination and empathy as they are forced to take a general point of view (Goodin, 1999). Without alleging any such psychological transformation, other arguments maintain that making democracy deliberative should at least have the effect of screening out self-regarding concerns in favor of more public-spirited considerations, thereby approximating or advancing an ideal of public reasoning among free and equal participants (Habermas, 1984; 1989; Elster, 1986a; Cohen, 1989; Haakonssen, 1991; Elster, 1998). And yet a further range of arguments urge that making democracy deliberative would promote such effects as legitimizing whatever decisions are reached, making them more likely to take account of the relatively powerless, increasing transparency among members of the group, or promoting just outcomes (see Elster, 1998, p. 11, for a summary).

These arguments for deliberative democracy do not compete with one another and I think they make a strong, cumulative case for why it is a good idea to have democratic decision-making done in an inclusive, judgmental and dialogical manner. But they do not give us a line on the dilemma raised. Should deliberative democrats put a premium on maintaining responsiveness to individual voters in the decision-making process they establish? Or should they opt instead for a process that ensures collective rationality? The arguments are silent on that point, for the psychological, sociological and political effects that they cite as benefits which make deliberative democracy attractive would all be available under either version of the ideal.

The arguments mentioned assume the case for democracy, as I already mentioned, and argue that it would be good to make democratic process deliberative. Another line of argument that figures in the literature does the opposite. It assumes that it is necessary on many issues to have deliberation and argues that it would be good to make deliberation democratic. The idea is that many heads are better than one and that if people put their deliberative heads together in a democratic resolution of an issue, then they have an improved chance of getting things right (Estlund, 1993a; Estlund, 1993b; Estlund, 1997). For example, there is a better chance that a jury of twelve, requiring a majority of ten for conviction, will be right about whether someone is guilty beyond reasonable doubt than that a single member will be right on such an issue.

The most famous argument of this kind derives from the Marquis de Condorcet's work in defence of his so-called jury theorem (Black, 1958; Condorcet, 1976; Estlund, 1994). The theorem presupposes that the voters are independent of one another: while they may certainly form their opinions on the basis of dialogue, none of them votes in a way that is blindly deferential to others (Estlund and Waldron, 1989; Estlund, 1994). It shows that if voters each have the same, greater than evens chance of being right on some yes-no issue then, first, their collective resolution of the issue, under majority rule, will have a yet greater chance of being right and, second, it will have a progressively greater chance of being right as the size of the group increases. Indeed the latter element is assured, even if some voters have a less than evens chance of being right; it will hold so long as the average chance of voters being individually right is greater than evens (Owen, Grofman et al., 1989).

Do the arguments in this second category help to resolve the issue as to whether deliberative democrats should prioritise responsiveness to individual voters or the achievement of collective rationality? Wlodek Rabinowicz and I have argued elsewhere that it does not (Pettit, 2001b, appendix). Specifically, we have argued that the Condorcet argument provides no decisive reason for forming a preference between the following two ways of determining a collective judgment on whether 'p and q': first, determine the collective majoritarian judgments on 'p' and on 'q' and then let the collective judgment on 'p and q' be determined by those; and second, let each individual determine his or her judgment on 'p and q' by reference to their individual judgments on 'p' and on 'q' and then let the collective judgment on 'p and q' be determined in the usual majoritarian way.

The Republican Argument for Deliberative Democracy

Republican theory, as I have argued in other work, puts a premium on people's enjoying freedom as non-domination: that is, on people's having a status such that ideally no one else is able to interfere arbitrarily in their lives (Pettit, 1997). If any other person or agency is able to interfere in their lives, then they must be forced to track people's avowed or ready to be avowed interests in the interference they practise; their power of interference must in that sense be non-arbitrary.

That ideal raises the question of how the state can be blocked from enjoying a power of arbitrary interference in the lives of citizens. The state is a necessary institution and it necessarily has a power of interfering with people: it cannot operate without being able to tax, legislate and penalize the governed. So how is its power of interference to be made non-arbitrary? Republican constitutional theory is built around that question and has consistently sought to describe various devices whereby non-arbitrariness may be furthered. These include familiar mechanisms such as democratic election, rule of law, separation of powers, limitation of tenure, rotation of office, and so on.

In this republican tradition of constitutional discussion, one important strand has been the idea that if the state's power of interference is to be rendered non-arbitrary then whatever other devices are in place, people must be able to contest the decisions made by various arms of government. They must have access to the reasons supporting those decisions and they must be able to contest the soundness of those reasons or the degree of support they offer to the decisions made. Moreover they must be in a position, ideally, to expect that such contestations will be heard, will be impartially adjudicated and, if necessary, will be implemented against those in government. The general message is that so far as a government is effectively contestable, to that extent it is less likely to enjoy arbitrary power.

The effective promotion of contestability in the political sphere requires a variety of institutions, especially if it is to guard against unwieldy levels of complaint, and I have tried elsewhere to review some of them (Pettit, 2000). From our point of view, however, only two observations are relevant. The first is that putting in place a regime of participatory or representative democracy is essential in guarding against certain possibilities of non-contestability and domination: the colonial, the authoritarian, and so on. And the second is that any such regime still leaves striking possibilities of non-contestability and domination in place: possibilities associated with the tyranny of the democratic majority, in particular, and the tyranny of what we might describe as the democratic elite (Richardson, 2002): those in the corridors of power – for example, in the bureaucracy, the cabinet, the courts, the prisons, or the police force – who can impose their own will in how they interpret and implement democratic policy.

How are people to be empowered in relation to democratic majorities and democratic elites? How are they to be given a power of contestation against them? Whatever else is necessary, it seems clear that they must be able to ask after the reasons that support the decisions, they must be able to question the relevance of the reasons and they must be in a position to expect a fair hearing. And all of that is going to be possible, of course, only so far as the democratic bodies in question operate in a deliberative mode. There must be a dispensation of deliberation in place in the community as a whole, and in the microcosm of parliament, which establishes a currency of considerations that are admitted on all sides to be relevant to the doings of government. There must be a commitment in the different arms of government to justifying whatever decisions are taken by reference to the considerations that are relevant, by common consent, in their case. And it must be possible for private individuals, or perhaps for designated representatives, to challenge such decisions on the grounds that the reasons quoted are not sound or do not offer the requisite support for the decisions taken. It is only in the event of democracy having this deliberative cast that contestability, and ultimately non-arbitrariness, can be furthered.

This republican argument for deliberative democracy applies also, of course, to forums beyond those of government. Take the workplace community or the community organisation or indeed the family. Even if decisions are taken democratically in such a body, there will be little protection against arbitrariness – short of exit – unless the democracy in question operates in deliberative mode, giving individuals a chance to contest the decisions made. If decisions are made on the basis of interest-group politics, or bargaining from different levels of power, then there will be no grounds on which any contestation can be made. Brute force or naked preference will rule.

Cass Sunstein (1993a) probably has this republican case for deliberative-democratic procedure in mind when he describes deliberative democracy as a 'republic of reasons'. Just as people are in a position to know where they stand in relation to a court judgment, only so far as the judges have to provide statements of their reasons, so more generally people can know where they stand in relation to public decisions only if they know what the grounds adduced in support of those decisions are. They will not be able to take a stand in relation to public decisions, if those decisions are the outcome of interest-group bargaining or of voting on the basis of naked, unargued preference. Such non-deliberatively generated decisions would have the profile of dictats or fiats from on high, where the products of deliberative-democratic procedure would present themselves as reasoned – well-reasoned or badly-reasoned – judgments that people are in a position to examine, assess and if necessary, challenge.

Applying the Republican Argument to the Dilemma

The contestability argument for deliberative democracy ought to have persuasive force, quite apart from its connection with republican theory (see Pettit, 2000). It is of particular interest here because it provides a ground on which to resolve the dilemma raised, offering an argument in favor of the rationality-first approach.

If I am to be able to judge the actions of another individual or agency in relation to alleged reasons – and, ultimately, if I am to be able to contest those actions in the relevant sense – then the individual or agency must prove answerable to those reasons. The individual or agency must be disposed to act as the reasons require or, at the least, to adjust in response to the criticism that the reasons adduced in support of something they did are not appropriate or that what they did was not supported by those reasons. In a word, the individual or agency must prove to be conversable: that is, must prove to be an interlocutor whose words can be taken at face value and, where appropriate, invoked in effective criticism of the things they later do.

A democratic group that fails to put rationality first, no matter how deliberative it is in other respects, cannot ever be held to reasons in this sense, and cannot ever prove conversable. When a group offers reasons for a given judgment or decision it will do so by reference to other commitments that require inconsistency – or perhaps in some weaker analogue of consistency – that it judge or decide as it does in the case in question. But if the group does not enforce consistency on itself at the collective level, then there can be no expectation, for any judgment or decision it makes, that there are other commitments to be cited in this reason-giving role. On the contrary: various commitments – various existing judgments and decisions – may argue for a contradictory judgment or decision.

Consider our original, purely schematic example involving the group of three people that commits itself to the judgment that p and the judgment that if p, then q and then, inconsistently, to the denial that q: the judgment, as we may take it to be, that not q. There is no talking to a group of this kind, no possibility of taking the group into a discursive exchange of reasons. For if it is not structured to find the set of judgments it collectively endorses unacceptable – if it is not prepared to discipline itself to revise such a set of judgments rationally – then there is no hope of ever being able to make a telling objection to it and no hope of ever providing it with a reason for making any particular judgment or decision.

If a group of that kind rules in one's life, then it will represent a completely arbitrary presence. Far from being the sort of power that can be forced to track one's avowable interests in how it behaves – far from being the sort of power that can be ruled by such considerations or reasons – it will be incapable of being subjected to the discipline of any reasons whatsoever. It will be arbitrary, not in the fashion of the self-serving tyrant or the sectionally minded faction, but rather in the even more radical fashion of the completely capricious agent.[2]

Deliberative democracy is said to be appealing, according to the republican argument, because it establishes a republic of reasons within which people know

---

[2] I have tended, in previous writings, to overlook the fact that there are two ways in which a power may be arbitrary, given my characterisation of non-arbitrariness in terms of being forced to track the avowable interests of relevant parties. One mode of arbitrary power will involve tracking other interests – other reasons – instead; the other will involve not tracking any interests at all. Notice, however, that this latter mode of arbitrary power is precisely that: a mode of power that one person or one set of people have over another or others; it is not just the sort of influence that the wind and the rain exercise.

where they stand and are able to contest those imposed decisions that are not, by their lights, well grounded in considerations of common avowable interest. But if deliberative democracy is to have this appeal then clearly it must operate in such a way that the bodies of state in which it is enacted put collective rationality first, and not responsiveness to individual voting. Let responsiveness be what matters more and we can see from the discursive dilemma that that will make the bodies in question into wholly arbitrary powers.

The upshot is significant. It has two implications in particular that are worth noting. Let the discursive dilemma be resolved in the republican fashion, and deliberative democracy requires, first, that those state-empowered bodies that cannot police themselves by the discipline of reason – in particular, the demos as a whole – should not be given charge of policy issues; and second, that those bodies that can police themselves in this way should indeed do so, committing themselves to avoiding inconsistencies and other irrational patterns in the judgments and decisions they make.

The demos or populace as a whole are not really capable of being ruled by collective reason and, this being so, its role in government should generally be restricted to the selection of personnel. Let the populace be given charge of policy, as under a regime that allows of frequent referendums, and it is capable of ruling in the fashion of a capricious tyrant. There may be no consistency in the decisions it supports – and this, even if the individuals involved are wholly rational – and there will be little or no possibility of appealing against such failures of rationality. Power to the people, interpreted in this way, may mean power to a completely arbitrary force.

As against this, it may be said that the populace will be capable of being disciplined by reason, so far as an individual or small assembly has the status of a plenipotentiary that can resolve any issues of inconsistency as is thought best: that is, so far as there is something approximating a Hobbesian representative in place. But this arrangement would not constitute anything seriously deserving of the name of popular rule, since there could be only very little interaction between the representative and the people represented. Short of involving ordinary democratic arrangements, whereby autonomous representatives are checked by the discipline of regular elections, it would hold out a prospect in which the representative becomes effectively a more or less absolute monarch.

But though the first implication of the position taken is that the populace as a whole should not be given charge of policy, that does not argue for a passive role for people in government. The republican argument requires that representatives be disciplined into arguing only on the basis of considerations that are in deliberative currency among the populace, being treated as generally relevant and being accorded this or that level of weight. And the other arguments for the importance of deliberation bolster this case. Thus, quite consistently with the populace not having charge of policy, there are reasons for why republican institutions should try to foster deliberation in public discussions of the policy programs held out by candidates and their parties in the electoral process. The populace may be unable to act as a collectively deliberative body but public-spirited deliberation should still rule, ideally, in the process whereby the merits of different policy programs are established.

The second implication of the position defended here is that those state-empowered bodies that can discipline themselves by reason should do so. The requirement, in effect, is that bodies as disparate as the parliament and the courts, public commissions and government agencies have to constitute themselves as agents that are responsive to reason; agents that can recognise what reason requires, can give an account of the reasons relevant to their decisions, and can bind themselves to act as such reasons require. That deliberative democracy rules in such bodies has to mean, not just that the individuals involved all vote on the basis of dialogue and judgement, but that they commit themselves to a pattern of rationality in virtue of which those bodies take on the semblance of conversable interlocutors.

Is this an unworkable ideal? Not at all. As a matter of current practice, such bodies generally recognise the force of precedent and only adopt measures inconsistent with previously endorsed commitments when they give reason for rejecting the precedent. And all such bodies shrink from putting forward downright inconsistent recommendations; they recognize that this would make a laughing stock of them. The requirement that they should exemplify the rule of reason more systematically – that they should work at ensuring their conversability and their contestability – should not present itself, then, as a utopian demand. It is something well within the reach of the institutions that currently prevail in advanced democracies.

Might the demands of contestability be satisfied to the extent that the individuals in a group, though not the group itself, are conversable and contestable agents? Not really. The group is the entity that continues over time despite changes in its membership, and that fact alone makes it the salient agency that we should want to be contestable and conversable. And not only does the group continue in time across changes in membership. It will often have so many members that no one could hope to secure contestability at the individual level. It will often be, not just the salient agency to make contestable, but the only feasible one available for that role.

To conclude, then. There is a hard choice for deliberative democrats to make, that between a responsiveness-first and a rationality-first interpretation of their ideal. And while most arguments for deliberative democracy give us no reason to go one way or the other in response to that choice, the republican argument is different. It gives us a reason to prefer the rationality-first approach, and makes that approach look quite attractive and persuasive. It shows that for a group to be deliberatively democratic, it has to respect reason not just in the micro, but also in the macro: not just in the deliberations of its members, but also in the overall profile that it displays in its decisions.

References

Benhabib, S. (1994) "Deliberative rationality and models of democratic legitimacy", *Constellations* 1, 26-52.

Black, D. (1958) *The Theory of Committees and Elections*, Cambridge (Cambridge University Press).

Bohman, J. and W. Rehg (eds.) (1997) *Deliberative Democracy: Essays on Reason and Politics*, Cambridge (MIT Press).

Brennan, G. (2001) "Collective Coherence?", *International Review of Law and Economics* 21.

Brennan, G. and P. Pettit (1990) "Unveiling the Vote", *British Journal of Political Science* 20, 311-33.

Chapman, B. (1998) "Law, Incommensurability, and Conceptually Sequenced Argument", *University of Pennsylvania Law Review* 146, 1487-1582.

Cohen, J. (1986) "An Epistemic Conception of Democracy", *Ethics* 97, 26-38.

Cohen, J. (1989) "Deliberation and Democratic Legitimacy", in A. Hamlin and P. Pettit (eds.) *The Good Polity*, Oxford (Blackwell), 17-34.

Coleman, J. and J. Ferejohn (1986) "Democracy and Social Choice", *Ethics* 97, 6-25.

Condorcet, M. de (1976) *Condorcet: Selected Writings*, Indianapolis (Bobbs-Merrill).

Dryzek, J. S. (1990) *Discursive Democracy*, Cambridge (Cambridge University Press).

Elster, J. (1986a) "The Market and the Forum: Three Varieties of Political Theory", in J. Elster and A. Hylland (eds.) *Foundations of Social Choice Theory*, Cambridge (Cambridge University Press), 103-132.

Elster, J. (ed.), (1998) *Deliberative Democracy*, Cambridge (Cambridge University Press).

Estlund, D. (1993a) "Making Truth Safe for Democracy", in D. Copp, J. Hampton and J. E. Roemer (eds.) *The Idea of Democracy*, Cambridge (Cambridge University Press), 71-100.

Estlund, D. (1993b) "Who's Afraid of Deliberative Democracy?", *Texas Law Review* 71, 1437-77.

Estlund, D. (1994) "Opinion Leaders, Independence, and Condorcet's Jury Theorem", *Theory and Decision* 36, 131-62.

Estlund, D. (1997) "Beyond Fairness and Deliberation: The Epistemic Dimension of Democratic Authority", in J. Bohman and W. Rehg (eds.) *Deliberative Democracy: Essays on Reason and Politics*, Cambridge (MIT Press).

Estlund, D. and J. Waldron (1989) "Democratic Theory and the Public Interest: Condorcet and Rousseau Revisited", *American Political Science Review* 83, 1317-1328.

Goodin, R. E. (1999) *Democratic Deliberation Within*, Canberra (Research School of Social Sciences, Australian National University).

Gutmann, A. and D. Thompson (1996) *Democracy and Disagreement*, Cambridge (Harvard University Press).

Haakonssen, K. (1991) "From Natural Law to the Rights of Man: a European Perspective on American Debates", in M. J. Lacey and K. Haakonssen, *A Culture of Rights: The Bill of Rights in Philosophy, Politics and Law, 1791 and 1991*.

Habermas, J. (1984, 1989) *A Theory of Communicative Action*, Vols. 1 and 2, Cambridge (Polity Press).

Kornhauser, L. A. (1992) "Modelling Collegial Courts. I. Path-Dependence", *International Review of Law and Economics* 12, 169-85.

Kornhauser, L. A. (1992) "Modelling Collegial Courts. II. Legal Doctrine", *Journal of Law, Economics and Organization* 8, 441-70.

Kornhauser, L. A. and L. G. Sager (1986) "Unpacking the Court", *Yale Law Journal* 82.

Kornhauser, L. A. and L. G. Sager (1993) "The One and the Many: Adjudication in Collegial Courts", *California Law Review* 81, 1-59.

List, C. and P. Pettit (2002) "Aggregating Sets of Judgments: An Impossibility Result", *Economics and Philosophy* 18, 89-110.

List, C. and P. Pettit (forthcoming) "Aggregating Sets of Judgments: Two Impossibility Results Compared", forthcoming in *Synthese*.

Owen, G., B. Grofman, et al. (1989) "Proving a distribution-free generalization of the Condorcet jury theorem", *Mathematical Social Sciences* 17, 1-16.

Pettit, P. (1993) *The Common Mind: An Essay on Psychology, Society and Politics*, paperback edition 1996, New York (Oxford University Press).

Pettit, P. (1997) *Republicanism: A Theory of Freedom and Government*, Oxford (Oxford University Press).

Pettit, P. (2000) "Democracy, Electoral and Contestatory", *Nomos* 42, 105-44.

Pettit, P. (2001a) "Deliberative Democracy and the Discursive Dilemma", *Philosophical Issues (supp. to Nous)* 11, 268-99.

Pettit, P. (2001b) *A Theory of Freedom: From the Psychology to the Politics of Agency*, Cambridge and New York (Polity and Oxford University Press).

Pettit, P. (2002) "Groups with Minds of their Own", in F. Schmitt (ed.) *Socializing Metaphysics*, New York (Rowan and Littlefield).

Pettit, P. (2003) "Deliberative Democracy, the Discursive Dilemma, and Republican Theory", in J. Fishkin and P. Laslett (eds.) *Philosophy, Politics and Society Vol 7: Debating Deliberative Democracy*, Cambridge (Cambridge University Press).

Richardson, H. (2002) *Democratic Autonomy*, New York (Oxford University Press).

Sunstein, C. R. (1993a) *The Partial Constitution*, Cambridge (Harvard University Press).

Sunstein, C. R. (1993b) "Democracy and Shifting Preferences", in D. Copp, J. Hampton and J. E. Roemer (eds.) *The Idea of Democracy*, Cambridge (Cambridge University Press), 196-230.

Young, I. M. (1990) *Justice and the Politics of Difference*, Princeton (Princeton University Press).

Collective Rationality: A Dilemma for Democrats with a Solution through Deliberation? Comment on Philip Pettit

Natalie Gold

In his paper, Pettit presents a paradox that may arise when a group must vote on an interconnected set of propositions. Even though every individual within the group may be perfectly consistent in her own views, or individually rational, the propositions that the group would accept as the result of a majority vote on each individual proposition are inconsistent, so the group is collectively irrational. Pettit distinguishes between two ways a group may deal with this dilemma: the rationality-first approach, where the institution is committed to some mechanism for prioritising one of the propositions despite the votes of the individuals within it, and the responsiveness-first approach, where, although re-votes may be taken, the institution has no formal means for prioritising propositions when individually rational preferences aggregate to be collectively irrational. Given the argument presented in the paper, you will have to forgive me if I say that, whilst I agree with the conclusion, that we should take a rationality-first approach, I debate the propositions on which that conclusion is based. In my response I will explain why I think that, for all practical purposes, the rationality-first approach is inevitable for democratic institutions, regardless of supporting arguments that deliberative democrats might supply. This implies that the real argument is not whether we should achieve collective rationality but how, so I shall go on to examine whether arguments from deliberation can shed any light on this issue. Finally, I will say something about putting deliberation more directly into this type of decision-making model.

Regardless of contestability and conversability, as Pettit himself points out, the rationality-first approach is effectively enforced on most deliberative institutions. There is an analogy between the institutional and individual agents that may help to make the reason for this clear. An individual has a belief system consisting of multiple propositions which she endorses. Then in decision-making situations her choices are based on these. For an individual, the belief system is primary, in the sense that the beliefs exist prior to the need to make decisions or to act and a person may hold beliefs that she will never act on. In contrast, most institutional deliberation is primarily about deciding what actions to take and the endorsement of propositions happens purely as a stage in this process. Although the action to be taken may depend on the endorsement of certain premises by either the individuals within the group or the group as a whole, inevitably the key question is whether to convict the defendant or which policy to implement. And, unlike the individual case, the decision is probably only taken once, or at least fairly infrequently, so that if there are any inconsistencies in the propositions endorsed, agenda manipulation is more likely to be a problem than the possibility of cycles which is so often discussed in the individual case.

To continue the comparison, whilst an individual may take a responsiveness-first approach and endorse a set of propositions which provide conflicting reasons for action, when the time comes to act these inconsistencies must somehow be resolved. Otherwise the individual faces paralysing indecision with potentially disastrous consequences, as did Buridan's ass. So some reason is found for prioritising certain propositions in the belief system. Of course, an individual could chose to do nothing, but this often amounts to doing something in the sense of promoting a particular outcome. Or another response could be for the individual to chose to randomise between possible actions but, in practice, it is the case that individuals do not like to randomise. Experimental evidence shows that humans are very bad at randomising when asked explicitly to do so[1] but, more importantly, when the issues at stake are important we tend to think that 'I flipped a coin' or 'I threw a dice' is not an acceptable justification for action. We believe that actions should be based on reasons relevant to the case in hand. Unlike an individual agent, an institution does not usually have the luxury of a period where it can endorse conflicting propositions before having to choose an action. The endorsement of propositions happens synchronically with the making of decisions so that, unless we are willing to advocate that our institutions randomise or do nothing when faced with this type of paradox, the rationality-first approach will effectively trump the responsiveness-first approach. This conclusion does not depend for its force on any arguments from deliberation.

The question we are left with then, is which propositions should take priority when inconsistencies arise. Although it might seem that the group itself could decide in each instance, there is reason to think that guidelines should be chosen in advance. If both procedural and substantive reasons are decided at the same time, then there is the possibility of strategic voting by agents on the first question, of which proposition takes precedence, in order to ensure their favored outcome on the second question, of what the policy should be.

As Pettit points out, a deliberative group may be able to achieve consistency by modifying its judgement on any of the three propositions. However, I have nothing to say about this case but instead will focus on the cases where, as in the judicial example, the propositions fall naturally into premises and conclusions. I think that this actually covers more cases than is apparent at first sight. If one grants that people tend to form their judgements about complex propositions from their judgements about simple propositions then a large class of problems, including those involving conjunctions and disjunctions, will have this form, with the simple propositions as the premises and the complex ones as the conclusions. The analogy with the individual case might then suggest that the collective judgements on the

[1] Smith (1999).

premises should drive the collective judgements on the conclusion. That is also the approach that Pettit's republican deliberative democratic conversability and contestability arguments support. I do think that, where the group is such that it is natural to think of the collective as having a single agency, there is a presumption for resolving the dilemma in this premise-driven manner. (So this might cover 'the party thinks...' or 'the government says...' but I am not sure that it includes the judges in the original example.) However, there are other considerations that drive in the opposite direction and I think that there are occasions on which these have force. In order to elaborate on these, I shall draw on work done elsewhere, to which Philip Pettit has been a chief contributor.

As is mentioned in the paper, there is a line of argument which, following the Marquis de Condorcet, advocates democratic procedures because of their increased chance of 'getting it right'. This argument favors a conclusion-driven approach to the paradox, with individual judgements on the conclusion being aggregated to get the collective judgement. The simple intuition is that voting on the premises makes the collective more likely to be correct about the premises and therefore right for the right reasons. But, since the conclusions are a complex combination of the premises, there are other ways of reaching the correct conclusion, though for the wrong reasons. For instance, if the truth is $P \vee Q$, then one could get to the correct conclusion by believing $P \wedge \neg Q$, $Q \wedge \neg P$ or $P \wedge Q$ but only one of these combinations of premises is true. The conclusion-driven approach maximises the collective's chance of reaching the right judgement, albeit for the wrong reasons.[2] The argument by Pettit is that, if a republican deliberative democrat cares about conversability and contestability, then she should care about being right for the right reasons and therefore endorse the premise-driven approach.[3] However, I think that the analogy to the individual case shows why there may sometimes be exceptions to this rule.

When we consider beliefs it is as, if not more, important to endorse a proposition for the right reasons as it is to endorse the correct proposition. But, as I have said earlier, collective decision-making is generally with regard to proposed actions, not abstract belief systems. With actions, it is possible that it is better to do the right thing for the wrong reasons than to increase one's chance of having the right reasons at the expense of one's chance of doing the right thing. In other words, when actions are involved, consequences arguably matter as much as reasons. A concrete example of relevance to deliberative institutions is the criminal trial. In our society we have a preference that the innocent go free. If we take the judicial example in the paper but change it to a murder trial and let P = the defendant killed the victim, Q = the defendant had intent to kill the victim then the verdict of murder depends on the truth of the conjunction $P \wedge Q$. In this case we may prefer to maximise our chances of reaching the correct verdict. It is more important simply to be right than to be right for the right reasons.

Another type of occasion when deliberative institutions may be more concerned about conclusions than premises is when making certain political decisions. In a

---

[2] Pettit and Rabinowicz (2001).

[3] Pettit (2001).

multi-cultural society we need to find a basis acceptable to all on which we can live together. We search for a Rawlsian 'overlapping consensus' on our public institutions even if citizens have differing underlying conceptions of the good. For instance, consider changing the example in that Pettit's paper to the questions of whether we should allow parents to opt out of state schools and educate their children privately. Let P = parents have a right to educate their children privately, Q = we should educate our children within their religious faith. In this case we use a disjunction rule and if $P \vee Q$ is true then we should allow private schooling. Now there might plausibly be three different groups in our society. Libertarians believe $P \wedge \neg Q$, the religious believe $Q \wedge \neg P$ and Liberals believe $\neg P \wedge \neg Q$. If we aggregated premises then we would have a majority for $\neg P$ and a majority for $\neg Q$, so we would not allow people to opt out of the state system. However, if we aggregate conclusions then we would get a majority in favor of $P \vee Q$, so we would allow private schools. In this case we may prefer to aggregate individual judgements on conclusions precisely because we believe that the job of public institutions is not to judge the premises. We are not looking to enforce the 'right' reasons on those we disagree with but to get enough agreement on conclusions about how we structure our society so that its institutions will be acceptable to differing groups within it. Within the political arena, following Rawls, some liberals explicitly do not judge the individual conceptions of the good underlying our shared public intuitions. For them, it is more important to agree on conclusions than to have the right reasons.

Even a deliberative democrat with a presumption in favour of having the right reasons may think that there are occasions when it is more important to either be right about or to agree on the conclusions than to be right about or to agree on reasons. But, anyway, it seems to me that all the preceding arguments could as easily be made by a Rawlsian who believes in public justification without any reference to deliberative democracy. So far, I have said a lot about democracy but very little about deliberation. Finally, let me make some comments about where deliberation might fit into this model. The paradoxes presented are all aggregation problems. In other words they may be faced in any democratic decision-making situation, not just those involving deliberation. Deliberative democrats may have particular reasons to argue that the dilemma should be solved in one way rather than another but the model itself does nothing to capture the deliberation process. Models cannot be expected to capture everything, by their nature they simplify situations in order to clarify key points. One key feature of deliberation, which is often used as an argument in its favour and which is missing from the model, is that deliberation changes peoples' preferences. During deliberation some types of preferences are ruled out and people begin to come to a consensus. These aggregation models assume that voters' opinions are independent of each other. If they have spent time deliberating, then one might hope or expect that this is not the case. Adjusting the model to reflect simple correlation of voter preferences does not affect the mathematical results. However, another way in which deliberation may change preferences is that, rather than correlating opinions on particular issues, it causes voters to structure the argument and the issues at stake in a common manner. It has been formally proved that if deliberation induces sufficient preference structuration then deliberative democrats will avoid such doctrinal paradoxes.[4] Such arguments provide a resolution of the dilemma that is truly unique to deliberative democrats.

References

List, C. (2001) *Mission Impossible? The Problem of Democratic Aggregation in the Face of Arrow's Theorem*, D.Phil Thesis, University of Oxford.

Pettit, P. (2001) "Deliberative Democracy and the Discursive Dilemma", *Philosophical Issues* (supplement 1 of *Nous* 35) 11, 268-95.

Pettit, P. and W. Rabinowicz (2001) "The Jury Theorem and the Discursive Dilemma", Appendix to Pettit 2001, 295-99.

Smith, J. (1999) "How Hard is it to Randomise? Theory and Experimental Results", *Santa Fe Institute working paper* 99-07-048.

[4] List (2001).

Deliberative Constitutional Economics? Comment on Philip Pettit

Christoph Luetge

Philip Pettit has come to the aid of deliberative democrats, helping them clarify their arguments and improve their position. I am no 'genuine' deliberative democrat, so I cannot say for sure whether they will in general accept his republican solution to the discursive dilemma. Instead, I would like to explore the differences and similarities of this solution to the approach of *constitutional economics*. First, I will have a short look at the differences between deliberative democrats and economists in general. I am then going to discuss some advantages of constitutional economics over 'ordinary' neoclassical economics before turning to the similarities of Pettit's approach to constitutional economics. Finally, I will – despite my initial carefulness on this matter – come back to the question of whether the republican solution presented is really acceptable for deliberative democrats. I doubt this. But in any case, I am going to argue that constitutional economists can accept nearly all of this solution.

1 Differences between Deliberative Democrats and Economists

First, what differences are there between deliberation and decision? According to Pettit, the ideal of deliberative democracy can be expressed in terms of three constraints on public decision-making, the inclusive, the judgmental, and the dialogical constraint. The *first* one presents no grave problems for economists. They would accept that everyone is to be equally entitled to vote, and they would also accept that the outcome has to be determined by a non-unanimous vote (though there might be differences in how a criterion of less-than-unanimity should be argued for, but I will leave these issues aside for the moment). The *second* constraint should be quite difficult to accept for most economists, as the idea of judgment-voting implies that the voters in question have common concerns which, for economists at least, should be hard to identify. Pettit stresses that this requires every voter not just to take account of his (narrow?) self-interest, as *homo oeconomicus* would presumably do. One difference between 'deliberation' and 'decision' can be located here.

Another difference can be found in the implications of the *third* constraint. Public formation of preferences in open dialogue is most often not required by economists. Rather – if economics deals with preference formation at all – it does not matter where these preferences come from. Maybe we can paraphrase this as follows: According to deliberative democrats, conflicts should be resolved through debate, not through a process of bargaining. In Habermas' writings, we find the famous quote, that people can be (and often are in fact) motivated not only by self-interest. Instead, the unforced force of the better argument – der 'eigentümlich zwanglose Zwang des besseren Arguments' (cf. Habermas, 1981, Vol. 1, p. 47) – should carry the day. The question which arises in this context is how agreements on the basis of debate can be implemented, how they can be enforced. How is it possible to sufficiently guarantee that the participants in a debate subsequently really *act* according to their prior agreement? This question is addressed in particular by constitutional economics (and by an economic ethics based on it; cf. Homann and Blome-Drees, 1992).

I will now turn to the constitutional approach in economics and discuss what this conception has to say on the two differences between deliberation theory and economics.

2 Constitutional Economics – Can it Answer the Arguments Against Bargaining?

As I said earlier, I want to talk not just about economics, but about *constitutional* economics. By constitutional economics, I mean the research program of James M. Buchanan, which is represented in Germany by Karl Homann and others.[1] This program differs significantly from standard economics. In general, constitutional economists subscribe to five main tenets:

1) Economics is not the science of market processes, but rather the science of costs and benefits. It aims to provide a universal theory of human behavior.
2) Economics deals primarily with interactions, especially with the analysis of dilemma situations (such as the prisoners' dilemma), and not with individual decision-making. Buchanan calls this 'catallactics' (Buchanan, 1979, p. 19).
3) The purpose of economics according to this view is not just a theoretical, but a practical one. The economist should regard it as his main goal to design institutions in order to overcome or maybe to establish dilemma situations.
4) It is only for this purpose – institutional design – that individuals should be modelled as self-interested actors. The model of *homo oeconomicus* thus plays an instrumental role, it is a tool, but not an image of man 'as he really is'. From this perspective, it must be questioned, for example, whether it makes sense to ask if actors – in the 'real' world – act on naked preferences or on reflective judgments. That certainly depends on the modelling, which in turn depends on the problem you want to solve, institutional design or any alternative purpose like reconstructing the situation from the actors'

[1] Cf. Buchanan, 1975; Brennan and Buchanan, 1985; Homann, 1988; Homann and Blome-Drees, 1992; Homann and Suchanek, 2000. For an application to philosophy of science, see Luetge (forthcoming).

perspective (in that case, it might make sense to talk about decisions based on 'naked preference'; Pettit, 2004, p. 102).

5) The normative basis for institutional design is consent. There is no external normative criterion. Rules are efficient if and only if all people in question consent to them. But there is a hierarchy of different levels of consensus. People are not required to consent to every single political measure, but rather to the most general rules of the political process. They agree *unanimously* to decision procedures that require *less than unanimity*.

These points have consequences when applied to the differences between deliberation theory and economics which I mentioned. *First*, the judgmental constraint. A constitutional economist would first contend that there has to be an institution enforcing this constraint, otherwise the constraint would not make any sense. She would then examine whether judgment-voting *should* be promoted, which would be equal to the question of whether all actors involved could *agree* on such an institution. But this agreement would be reconstructed on the assumption that each actor is purely self-interested. So in the end, we (might) have an argument for judgment-voting favored by purely self-interested actors, something that deliberation theory could not get to. And in comparison to standard economic theory, a constitutional economist would not deny that actors can decide on the basis of reflection. She would – as I said, for methodological reasons, – reject the idea that decisions *simply are or can be* made on the basis of naked preferences.

Second, the dialogical constraint. Again, a constitutional economist would focus on an institutional solution. Examples can be found in Pettit's work (cf. Pettit, 2000). There is of course a whole range of institutions promoting discussion and reasoning before finally coming to a decision (some of these are mentioned in Voigt, 2004). Again also, the normative basis must be found in consent.

But most important, we can see that the constitutional approach starts from the problem of the practical *implementation and enforcement* of norms or ideas, not from the problem of their *justification*, whereas deliberative theory, it seems to me, begins with the question of how to justify this or that particular norm. That is exactly what Pettit says, 'it [the ideal of deliberative democracy] says little or nothing about the nature of the process itself'. The original ideal of deliberative democracy relegates the problems of implementation to a secondary level. First, justification of the ideal, then, second, enforcement. Pettit criticizes this in a similar way as constitutional economics would do. I turn to this now.

3 The Republican Solution and Constitutional Economics

The constitutional approach and Pettit's republican solution are very *similar* in that they emphasize the problems of the implementation of ideals and the consequences that these problems have on the ideals themselves. This is paradigm of ethics and political philosophy quite different from the one that deliberative democracy embraces, both in its recent version and in its original form in the discourse ethics of Jürgen Habermas. Today, we have already heard something about the recent version, so let me make my point clearer with regard to Habermas. Habermas has nearly always emphasized the importance of justification of ideals, as, for example, the ideal of unforced dialogue. In earlier writings up to the 1980s, he widely neglected the importance of enforcement of ideals and thereby of institutions.[2] In more recent writings, he has been more flexible on this matter, but has not in principle changed his former position.[3] Quite generally speaking, he now says we need both, i.e., institutionalized implementation *but also* rational justification. This justification is said to have force because citizens in a democracy are (also) motivated rationally and are not only success-oriented. I am not saying he is wrong. But he presents this as a postulate. He starts from the justification of an ideal and not from the problem of how to implement it. That seems to me too weak.

Contrast this with Pettit's main point, the importance of contestability. There is a (maybe rather obvious) analogy to Pettit's emphasis on contestability. Karl Popper – in his social philosophy – has never ceased to stress (nearly in excess) that in a democracy, the people must have the chance to criticize and to peacefully get rid of their government (cf. Popper, 1957). What Popper had in mind on a 'practical' level, is explicitly stated in his 'Open Society': 'Denn ebenso wie Hebel sind Institutionen notwendig, wenn wir etwas erreichen wollen, was unsere Muskelkraft übersteigt', (Popper, 1992, Vol. 1, p. 81). Popper emphasizes the importance of institutions – in the same way as constitutional economics does. For him, this is just another way of the evolutionary method of trial error, of learning from experience.[4]

Popper's arguments seem to me to go hand in hand with Pettit's argument for contestability and also with constitutional economics. All three reject the idea of 'justification first' and instead start from the problems of implementation.

On the other hand, the *differences* between Pettit's approach and constitutional economics seem to me methodological ones. The latter one is *not* opposed to bargaining as the basic process in a democracy, though it assigns bargaining a place different from that of standard economics. Pettit, though, seems to share the arguments of deliberative theorists against the economic approach. Briefly, the following two can be distinguished:[5]

1) A society without a sufficient degree of deliberation is not as *stable* as that envisaged by deliberative democrats.
2) More deliberation reduces the degree of *arbitrariness* of political measures and promotes rationality in politics.

Can constitutional economics address these two arguments against the economic approach to democracy? I think that at least to some degree, it can.

[2] Cf. Habermas, 1981 and 1983.

[3] Habermas, 1992, ch. 1, e.g., emphasizes the importance of legal institutions, but does not abandon the ideal of the 'unforced force of the better argument'.

[4] Cf. Luetge, 2001.

[5] One argument, frequently stated by Rawls and others, does not appear here: The possible subjugation of minorities and, in consequence, the suppression of fundamental human rights.

Arbitrariness and lack of stability are due to the danger of ever-changing majorities, as Pettit says. But is this danger not already – at least to a great degree – reduced by the different-levels approach of constitutional economics? Changing majorities cannot change politics as quickly if there are constitutional safeguards, for example, like those envisaged by Brennan and Buchanan (1980) against arbitrary impositions of taxes. I am not saying that political organizations or bureaucracies should not state the reasons for their acts. But I fail to see how this can work, i.e. provide stability, without institutional implementation. And if we have institutional implementation (and enforcement), then this fits – from a methodological point of view – perfectly within constitutional economics.

4 Deliberative Constitutional Economics?

I must admit that I fail to see major differences between the republican version of deliberative democracy and constitutional economics. Both start from the problems of implementation, both emphasize contestability, both regard institutions as fundamental for working democracies.

Of course, labels do not matter. Why not call the resulting approach *deliberative constitutional economics*, for example? But maybe we overlook something characteristic of many streams of deliberative democracy. Let us go back to the original three constraints. Pettit says that they focus 'on the inputs for which we ought to look in democratic decision-making, not on the process of decision-making itself' (Pettit, 2004, p. 93). And at the end of his paper, he comes to the conclusion – if I may reconstruct it like this – that *some* of this input is indeed important to look at, that the *institutions* which shape the democratic process must prove contestable and conversable (Pettit, 2004, p. 105). But Pettit also says that we can only hope to have contestability and conversability at a *collective* level, not at an *individual* one. And here I doubt that this is what the theory of deliberative democracy originally had in mind. People like Cohen, Habermas, or Sunstein all talk about necessary characteristics of the individuals in a democracy, of certain virtues the citizens are required to have. For Habermas (1981), this is rational motivation of individuals beyond pure success-orientation. For Cohen (1989), these are deliberative capacities. Sunstein (2001) requires common experiences.

I doubt both the necessity and the practical efficacy of these extra qualities and virtues. My argument is a methodological one, as I said before: Better start from implementation and not from justification. Having this in mind, I would like to welcome Philip Pettit as a deliberative constitutional economist.

References

Brennan, G. and J. M. Buchanan (1980) *The Power to Tax*, Cambridge (Cambridge University Press).

Brennan, G. and J. M. Buchanan (1985) *The Reason of Rules: Constitutional Political Economy*, Cambridge (Cambridge University Press).

Buchanan, J. M. (1975) *The Limits of Liberty: Between Anarchy and Leviathan*, Chicago (University of Chicago Press).

Buchanan, J. M. (1979) *What Should Economists Do?*, Indianapolis (Liberty Press).

Cohen, J. (1989) "Deliberation and Democratic Legitimacy", in Hamlin, A., and P. Pettit (eds.) *The Good Polity*, Oxford (Blackwell), 17-34.

Habermas, J. (1981) *Theorie des kommunikativen Handelns*, 2 Vols., Frankfurt/M. (Suhrkamp).

Habermas, J. (1983) *Moralbewusstsein und kommunikatives Handeln*, Frankfurt/M. (Suhrkamp).

Habermas, J. (1992) *Faktizität und Geltung: Beiträge zur Diskurstheorie des Rechts und des demokratischen Rechtsstaats*, Frankfurt/M. (Suhrkamp), in English: *Between Facts and Norms: Contributions to a Discourse Theory of Law and Democracy*, Cambridge, Mass. (MIT Press) 1996.

Homann, K. (1988) *Rationalität und Demokratie*, Tübingen (Mohr).

Homann, K. and F. Blome-Drees (1992) *Wirtschafts- und Unternehmensethik*, Göttingen (Vandenhoeck und Ruprecht).

Homann, K. and A. Suchanek (2000) *Ökonomik: eine Einführung*, Tübingen (Mohr Siebeck).

Luetge, C. (2001) "Popper als Ethiker", *Allgemeine Zeitschrift für Philosophie* 26, 2, 149-162.

Luetge, C. (forthcoming) "Economics in Philosophy of Science: A Dismal Contribution?", forthcoming in *Synthese*.

Pettit, P. (2000) "Democracy, Electoral and Contestatory", *Nomos* 42, 105-44.

Pettit, P. (2004) "A Dilemma for Deliberative Democrats", in this volume.

Popper, K. R. (1957) *The Open Society and its Enemies*, 2 Vols., 3rd ed., London (Routledge and Kegan Paul).

Popper, K. R. (1992) *Die offene Gesellschaft und ihre Feinde*, 2 Vols., 7th ed., Tübingen (Mohr).

Sunstein, C. (2001) *Republic.com*, Princeton (Princeton University Press).

Voigt, S. (2004) "The Consequences of Popular Participation in Constitutional Choice: Towards A Comparative Analysis", in this volume.

Chapter 5

Substantive and Meta-Agreement[1]

Christian List

Abstract

A central problem of democracy is the aggregation of divergent individual inputs into overall collective decisions. Social-choice-theoretic impossibility results famously demonstrate the intractability of a large class of such aggregation problems. This paper develops a taxonomy of two concepts of agreement, agreement at a substantive level and agreement at a meta-level, and discusses the escape-routes these concepts open up from the impossibility problems of social choice. Specifically, two contexts of democratic aggregation are addressed: first, the familiar context of preferences, and second, the largely unexplored context of sets of judgments over multiple interconnected propositions. Drawing on some recent developments in social choice theory and democratic theory, I will defend the view that, when agreement is conceptualised in democratic theory and when it is sought in democratic practice, more emphasis should be placed on agreement at a meta-level than is commonly done. Finally, I will address the more general question to what extent it is acceptable for the stability of institutions for democratic aggregation to be dependent on specific empirical contingencies.

1 Introduction

A great challenge for democracy is the resolution of conflict between divergent individual preferences, views or interests. Sometimes it is held that democracy is about finding 'the will of the people', but if the 'wills' of different individuals bear

[1] This paper is a revised and extended version of an earlier paper that was first published under the title "Two Concepts of Agreement" in *The Good Society* 11(1), 2002, 72-79. The material has been reused with the kind permission of the editor of *The Good Society*. A predecessor of this paper was also presented at the 2000 conference of the New Zealand division of the Australasian Association of Philosophy, held at Victoria University, Wellington, December 2000. The author wishes to thank Stephen Elkin for his encouragement to write this paper, Geoffrey Brennan, John Dryzek, Robert Goodin, David Miller, Philip Pettit and the participants of the conference panels in Wellington and Wittenberg for many useful discussions, and the German National Merit Foundation for financial support. The paper is based on work that was done while the author was a Visiting Scholar at the Center for Basic Research in the Social Sciences at Harvard University and at the Department of Linguistics and Philosophy at the Massachusetts Institute of Technology.

little resemblance to each other, it may be hard to extract anything from the set of individual 'wills' that can plausibly be considered 'the will of the people'.

Condorcet's famous paradox captures some of these problems. If there are three individuals, where one prefers option x to option y to option z, the second prefers option y to option z to option x, and the third prefers option z to option x to option y, then there exist a majority for x against y, a majority for y against z, and a majority for z against x. This means that, if pairwise majority voting is the method for aggregating individual preferences into collective ones, or more grandly, for extracting 'the will of the people', then the resulting collective preferences can be cyclical and thus useless for reaching consistent collective outcomes.

More generally, Arrow's celebrated impossibility theorem (1951/1963) shows that, if the domain of admissible individual preference input is unrestricted (the universal domain condition), there exists no procedure for aggregating individual preferences in this domain into collective ones in accordance with a set of arguably undemanding minimal conditions (the weak Pareto principle, independence of irrelevant alternatives, non-dictatorship and transitivity of social orderings) – conditions capturing the requirement, in a nutshell, that collective preferences be both minimally responsive to individual preferences and consistent.

The difficulties posed by aggregation depend crucially on how divergent the preferences, views or interests of individuals are. In the (rare) limiting case of unanimity the difficulties obviously disappear. If everybody had exactly the same preferences, views or interests, there would be no conflict to resolve. But while unanimity is sufficient for the disappearance of the famous Condorcet and Arrow aggregation problems, it is not necessary. Since Duncan Black's seminal work (1948), it is well known that Condorcet's paradox can be traced back to a 'lack of structure' in the relevant set, also called *profile*, of individual preferences across individuals. Black himself proved that *single-peakedness*, a structure condition to be discussed more formally below, (jointly with the (harmless) technical condition that the number of individuals is odd) is a sufficient (though not necessary) condition for the avoidance of Condorcet paradoxes. A well-known corollary of Black's insight is that Arrow's impossibility result ceases to hold if the domain of admissible individual preference input is restricted to profiles of preferences satisfying single-peakedness.

At one level, Black's result seems only to confirm what we already think we know, namely that, if the disagreement between different preferences, views or interests stays within certain limits – limits that are somehow transcended in situations like the one of the Condorcet paradox –, then familiar methods of democratic decision making, like pairwise majority voting, are available for reaching collective outcomes in reasonably defensible and logically consistent ways. But Black's result teaches us much more than that. It highlights an important distinction between two different concepts of agreement. The two concepts are what we might call *agreement at a substantive level* and *agreement at a meta-level*. It is this distinction that the present paper will explore. The paper discusses two contexts of democratic aggregation: first, the context of preferences, and second, the context of sets of judgments over multiple interconnected propositions. Sections 2 and 3 explore the two concepts of agreement in the first context, section 4 introduces the less familiar context of sets of judgments over multiple interconnected propositions, and sections 5 and 6 explore the two concepts of agreement in this second context. In particular, drawing on some recent developments in social choice theory and democratic theory, I will defend the view that, when agreement is conceptualised in democratic theory and when it is sought in democratic practice, more emphasis should be placed on the concept of agreement at a meta-level than is commonly done. Section 7, finally, takes a step back and addresses the question to what extent it is acceptable for the stability of institutions for democratic aggregation to be dependent on specific empirical contingencies.

2 Agreement at a Substantive Level and Unanimity

Two or more individuals agree *at a substantive level* to the extent that their preferences or views are the same. Perfect *agreement at a substantive level* is the case of identical preferences or views across different people.

In response to the problems of democratic aggregation, it is natural to argue that processes of political deliberation should be encouraged with the aim of somehow reducing the level of conflict between different people's preferences or views and bringing about greater agreement at a substantive level. In his account of the idea of deliberative democracy, Jon Elster summarizes this view quite succinctly: 'The core of the theory [of deliberative democracy] ... is that rather than aggregating or filtering preferences, the political system should be set up with a view to changing them by public debate and confrontation. The input to the social choice mechanism would then not be the raw, quite possibly selfish or irrational, preferences ..., but informed and other-regarding preferences. Or rather, there would not be any need for an aggregation mechanism, since a rational discussion would tend to produce unanimous preferences' (Elster, 1986, p. 112).

If successful, the view outlined by Elster may seem attractive. There are, however, at least two problems with this view. The first, and practical, problem is that the idea that democratic deliberation would produce unanimity may be unrealistic in many circumstances. People may agree on all relevant facts, and arguments, concerning different political options, and yet disagree on their most preferred option. They may agree on what the environmental effects of a new industrial development would be, and yet disagree on whether these effects should be accorded more weight than the expected economic benefits of the new development. In a recent empirical study, Cass Sunstein showed that deliberation, especially if it takes place in clustered homogeneous groups whose members reinforce each other's views, can sometimes even lead to polarization of opinion across different such groups rather than convergence (Sunstein, 2000). Although none of this is to deny the benefits of agreement at a substantive level – *if* it can be reached – it should be clear that democracy needs to have alternative resources for dealing with conflicts of preferences or views in those (plausible and potentially numerous) cases in which deliberation fails to produce unanimity.

The second, and somewhat more theoretical, problem with the view outlined by Elster is that it is unclear whether *convergence towards* agreement at a substantive level (falling short of perfect unanimity) is the most promising strategy for avoiding Condorcet and Arrow aggregation problems. William Gehrlein devised social-choice-theoretic measures of *social homogeneity* capturing basically the question of how closely a given profile of preferences across individuals approximates agreement at a substantive level. Using these measures, he showed that, although there is a positive connection between the level of social homogeneity and the avoidance of Condorcet problems, the connection is much weaker than what one might have hoped to find (Gehrlein, 2000).

3 Agreement at a Meta-Level and Single-Peakedness

Black's insight is to ask not whether two or more individuals have the same preferences over a set of options, but rather whether there exists an ordering of these options from 'left'-most to 'right'-most such that each individual has a most preferred position on that 'left'/'right' dimension and prefers options less and less as these options get more and more distant from his or her most preferred position. If there exists a 'left'/'right' ordering of the options with this property, called a *structuring dimension*, then we say that the given profile of preferences across individuals satisfies *single-peakedness*.

The terms 'left'/'right' are used here in a purely 'geometrical' sense. Any ordering of the options along which individual preferences are systematically aligned in the requisite way could serve as a structuring dimension, whether it orders the options from most urban to most rural, from most secular to most religious, from most architecturally avant-garde to most architecturally conservative, or in any other, however esoteric, way.

Black's concept inspires the following definition. Two or more individuals agree *at a meta-level* to the extent that they agree on a common dimension in terms of which an issue is to be conceptualised. They may reach perfect agreement at a meta-level while at the same time disagreeing substantively on what the most preferred position on that dimension is.

Single-peakedness may thus be an implication of *agreement at a meta-level. If* the individuals agree on a common structuring dimension along which each individual's preferences are systematically aligned in the requisite way, *then* the profile of preference orderings across these individuals satisfies single-peakedness. However, since single-peakedness is only a formal structure condition on a profile of preference orderings across individuals, single-peakedness is logically less demanding than agreement at a meta-level. The latter is sufficient, but not necessary, for the former. A profile of preference orderings across individuals may happen to have the right *formal* structure for satisfying single-peakedness without the individuals *semantically* conceptualising the issue in terms of the same common dimension.

Further, single-peakedness is not merely a consistency condition on individual preferences. Take the preference ordering of a single individual (over a finite set of options). Unless we make reference to a specific structuring dimension, the question of whether this preference ordering is single-peaked is vacuous or, to be precise, must vacuously be answered in the affirmative. For we can simply define this individual's most preferred option to be the 'left'-most option, his or her least preferred option to be the 'right'-most option, positioning intermediate options from 'left' to 'right' in a decreasing order of preference (supposing the preference ordering is strict). With respect to this artificially constructed structuring dimension, the given individual's preference ordering is clearly – but of course uninformatively – single-peaked. The concept of single-peakedness becomes non-vacuous only when applied to the preferences of multiple individuals, for it is in those cases that we can ask whether or not different individuals' preferences are systematically aligned *along the same common structuring dimension.* This is the sense in which single-peakedness truly captures a formal implication of *agreement*, albeit at a meta-level.

Now Black proved the following surprisingly simple, and yet ingenious result. Given a profile of preferences across individuals satisfying single-peakedness, order the individuals (let us assume for simplicity that there is an odd number of them) from 'left'-most to 'right'-most in terms of their most preferred position (their 'peak') on the corresponding structuring dimension. With respect to this 'left'/'right' ordering of the individuals, the *median individual* is simply the one who has as many individuals to the left as he or she has to the right. Then the most preferred option of the median individual will beat, or at least tie with, all other options in pairwise majority voting. A simple corollary of this result is that, *if* the domain of admissible individual preference input consists only of profiles of preference orderings satisfying single-peakedness, *then* pairwise majority voting is a procedure for generating collective preferences in accordance with Arrow's minimal conditions of responsiveness and consistency. Moreover, studies by Niemi (1969) as well as Tullock and Campbell (1970) have shown that consistent social preferences, in accordance with these minimal conditions, are likely to exist if only 75% or even fewer of the individuals have preferences that are systematically aligned along the same common structuring dimension.

Black's result suggests an alternative response to the challenge of democratic aggregation. Rather than seeking convergence towards agreement at a substantive level, which may be hard to achieve, we might seek convergence towards agreement at a meta-level. A recent strand of deliberative democratic thinking advocates precisely this idea (see Miller, 1992; Knight and Johnson, 1994; and Dryzek and List, 2003). The idea is that the key to a deliberative democratic response to Condorcet and Arrow lies not in the idea of deliberation-induced agreement at a substantive level, but rather in the idea of deliberation-induced agreement at a meta-level. As the proponents of this idea emphasize, it is much more realistic, if nonetheless still demanding, to expect processes of political deliberation to produce agreement on what the relevant *questions* are rather than on what the *answers* should be.

Specifically, the idea can be stated as a three-part hypothesis:

(1) that group deliberation leads people to identify a single shared issue-dimension in terms of which the issue at stake is to be conceptualized;

(2) that, for a given issue-dimension, group deliberation leads people to agree on the position of each (policy) option on that dimension; and

(3) that, once an issue-dimension has been identified as relevant, group deliberation leads each individual to determine a most preferred position (his or her 'peak') on that dimension, with decreasing (dimension-specific) preference as options are increasingly distant from that most preferred position.

Neither part of the hypothesis is trivial. And since each part raises difficult social-psychological issues, I am not able to address these questions properly here. To give an intuitive illustration of the issues at stake, suppose in over-simplified terms that (i) the question of what issue-dimension is relevant to a given democratic decision problem is a normative question, (ii) the question of where options are located *on a given issue-dimension* is (often or at least sometimes) a factual question, and (iii) the question of what structure *dimension-specific* preferences of an individual should take is a question of rationality. Under this supposition, the success of part 2 depends on whether group deliberation can bring about agreement on factual matters, for instance by clarifying and supplying information; and the success of part 3 depends on whether group deliberation can induce greater rationality in individuals. While both of these requirements are not undemanding, they are clearly not completely implausible. The success of part 1, on the other hand, depends on whether group deliberation can bring about agreement on normative matters, a much more demanding requirement in many cases. The combination of parts 1, 2 and 3 is, in essence, the hypothesis that group deliberation can bring about agreement at a meta-level, which then surfaces in the form of single-peakedness.

In some cases, an appeal to public reasons and generalizable interests, characteristic of the kind of group deliberation deliberative democrats advocate, may lead to the identification of a single publicly relevant issue-dimension, and in consequence to agreement at a meta-level, the implication of which might be single-peakedness. But in other cases even the invocation of public reasons and generalizable interests may not have this effect, because individuals might still disagree about what is in the public interest, or whether, for instance, ecological integrity or economic growth should be given priority when such interests are in conflict.

Even rational choice theorists of a more traditional orientation are likely to agree that parts 2 and 3 of the hypothesis are relatively undemanding, and that the demanding and difficult part of the hypothesis is part 1. Mueller (1989, pp. 89-90), for example, argues, '[g]iven that we have a single-dimensional issue, single-peakedness does not seem to be that strong an assumption. What is implausible is the assumption that the issue space is one dimensional'.

Obviously, the question of whether the hypothesis that deliberation induces single-peakedness is empirically adequate cannot be answered by pure theorizing. List, McLean, Fishkin and Luskin (2000) have used data from Fishkin and Luskin's deliberative polls (on this method, see Fishkin, 1997) to test the hypothesis empirically. They studied a set of deliberative polls on topics of energy provision in Texas as well as a recent poll on the future of the monarchy in Australia. In these polls, participants were first confidentially interviewed on their opinions, then invited to participate in a weekend of intense group deliberation, and finally confidentially interviewed again, being asked exactly the same questions as in the pre-deliberation interviews. The study showed that the post-deliberation levels of single-peakedness were either strictly greater than the corresponding pre-deliberation levels (in *every* Texan poll in the set) or at least on a par with them (in the Australian poll).

Of course, these findings are not the final word on the introduced hypothesis. There may be situations that are favorable to its success, such as situations in which people on reflection agree that a certain single issue-dimension (for instance, an ecological one) is particularly salient and should guide their conceptualization of the decision problem. But there may also exist situations less favorable to its success, such as situations in which a decision problem is perceived to be so inherently multidimensional, or in which people's value priorities on different issue-dimensions are so fundamentally different, that they neither agree on what the correct answer is, nor even on how to look at the problem.

4 From Preferences to Sets of Judgments

The discussion so far has been centred around the problem of aggregating individual *preferences over a set of options* into corresponding collective ones. Often, however, democratic decision making bodies are faced with the need to aggregate individual *sets of judgments over multiple interconnected propositions* into corresponding collective ones. This need arises when complex policy systems or institutional structures are to be designed or chosen, where the various parts of a policy system or institutional structure constrain each other and consistency is of great importance.

A simple example will serve to illustrate the problem. Suppose the following three policy proposals are simultaneously under discussion:

- P: to introduce a special tax on gasoline (in order to provide an incentive to reduce the amount of 'unnecessary' driving and thereby to reduce the level of pollution);
- Q: to abolish a subsidized commuter railway system;
- R: to give special tax benefits to commuters (in order to compensate for their commuting expenses).

Suppose further that everyone accepts that proposal R should be accepted *if and only if* both proposal P and proposal Q are accepted – formally, $(R \leftrightarrow (P \wedge Q))$ – for the following reason. If the special gasoline tax is introduced (P) and the subsidized commuter railway system abolished (Q), then society will impose an exceptionally great financial burden on commuters, so that commuters should be entitled to some compensation (R). On the other hand, if the special tax on gasoline is not introduced, or if the subsidized commuter railway system remains in service, then nobody needs compensation.

For simplicity, let there be three individuals in the relevant decision making body, with the following sets of judgments on the three proposals (P, Q, R) and on the proposition describing their logical interconnection ($(R \leftrightarrow (P \wedge Q))$).

	individual 1	individual 2	individual 3
P	yes	yes	no
Q	yes	no	yes
R	yes	no	no
$(R \leftrightarrow (P \wedge Q))$	yes	yes	yes

Table 1

Note that each of the three individuals holds a perfectly consistent set of judgments in light of the proposition that R should be accepted if and only if P and Q are both accepted. Now if the individuals choose to determine their collective set of judgments on the basis of majority voting on each proposition, then they will accept both P and Q (each by majorities of 2 out of 3), as well as $(R \leftrightarrow (P \wedge Q))$ (the latter proposition unanimously), but reject R (by a majority of 2 out of 3). But this is an inconsistency, given the unanimous agreement that the acceptance of both P and Q is a necessary and sufficient condition for the acceptance of R.

In short, propositionwise majority voting over a set of logically connected propositions can lead to inconsistent collective sets of judgments, even when all individuals hold perfectly consistent sets of judgments. This problem is a version of what is sometimes called the doctrinal paradox (see, for example, Kornhauser, 1992; Chapman, 1998; Pettit, 2001; and Brennan, 2001).

Generalizing this insight, List and Pettit (2002) have shown that, if the domain of admissible individual sets of judgments is unrestricted (so long as these individual sets of judgments satisfy basic consistency criteria) (the universal domain condition), there exists no procedure for aggregating individual sets of judgments in this domain into collective ones in accordance with a set of minimal conditions similar in spirit to those proposed by Arrow (anonymity, systematicity; and completeness, consistency and deductive closure of collective sets of judgments) – conditions capturing the requirement that collective sets of judgments be both minimally responsive to individual ones and consistent.

Once again, the difficulties posed by this result depend on how divergent the sets of judgments held by different individuals are. I will now show that the two different concepts of agreement we have identified in the context of preferences can also be identified in the context of sets of judgments and that they here, too, point towards two different responses to the problem of aggregation. I will also argue that John Rawls's idea of an *overlapping consensus* (Rawls, 1993) can be seen as a special case of the concept of *agreement at a substantive level* and that it thus differs from the concept of *agreement at a meta-level*.

5 Agreement at a Substantive Level and Overlapping Consensus

Perfect *agreement at a substantive level* in the context of sets of judgments is the case of identical sets of judgments across different people. As before, one might try to solve problems of aggregation in the context of sets of judgments by encouraging processes of deliberation with the aim of bringing about greater agreement at a substantive level. We have noted in the context of preferences that agreement at a substantive level is a rather demanding condition that may be hard to attain in practice. Now, if we are dealing not with preferences over individual options, but with sets of judgments over an entire set of logically connected propositions, agreement at a substantive level may be even harder to attain.

But there is one special case of the concept of agreement at a substantive level that may seem somewhat more realistic, if still demanding. This special case is a version of John Rawls's concept of an *overlapping consensus*. Often the sets of judgments on fundamental moral and political issues held by different individuals are mutually incompatible, in so far as these sets of judgments represent genuinely different comprehensive views of morality, including different supporting reasons even for those judgments the individuals agree on (like 'killing human beings is bad'). However, in a less fundamental and more pragmatic realm of issues, there may actually be much more agreement. Given someone's overall set of moral and political judgments, this overall set will contain some judgments that the individual considers fundamental, maybe even 'axiomatic', and others that he or she considers less fundamental, maybe more pragmatic and applied. Now it is perfectly possible that the different (possibly mutually inconsistent) fundamental judgments held by different individuals may nonetheless have certain *implications* in common at a less fundamental level. This is logically possible because, if there is a relation of logical entailment between someone's fundamental and his or her less fundamental judgments, this relation is usually a one-way relation. The more fundamental judgments may be logically sufficient to determine the less fundamental ones, but not logically necessary. The former ones may logically entail the latter, but not the other way round. The less fundamental and more applied judgments are usually logically *in*sufficient to tell us what the underlying more fundamental judgments are. For instance, consider how many different fundamental reasons might be adduced to support certain welfare provision arrangements. One might believe in certain values of socio-economic justice and equality for liberal reasons or, alternatively, for religious reasons. Or one might believe that the main objective of the state is to keep the streets safe, to prevent crime and to ensure social stability, and that welfare provision arrangements are the only way to achieve this. Or consider how many different fundamental reasons one might have for wanting to implement specific policies for protecting the environment. One might believe in certain rights of future generations; or one might believe that non-human animals have rights that ought to be respected, or that ecosystems have intrinsic value. Or one might believe that environmental disasters would ruin the economy and that the only way to secure a successful economy in the long term would be to implement environmental policies. Many other examples could be given. An overlapping consensus requires the identification of a certain set of policy propositions (usually a proper subset of the set of those propositions that would make up an entire comprehensive view of morality) such that, with respect to these propositions, it is feasible to reach agreement at a substantive level, even if different individuals endorse the same judgments for different underlying reasons.

It is an open question whether, and in what circumstances, processes of political deliberation can bring about an overlapping consensus that is sufficiently broad to give rise to a non-trivial collective set of judgments. In this brief discussion, however, two points should have become clear. First, an overlapping consensus in the sense of agreement at a substantive level over a *restricted* set of propositions is a less demanding condition than agreement at a substantive level over *all* propositions. Second, the concept of an overlapping consensus is different from the concept of agreement at a meta-level. In an overlapping consensus, the individuals agree on certain judgments, without necessarily agreeing on the supporting reasons for these judgments. They agree on certain answers, without necessarily agreeing on what the more fundamental issues or questions are. In a sense, they agree at a substantive level, albeit with respect to a restricted realm of issues, without necessarily agreeing on any meta-theoretical foundations for their substantive agreement.

6 Agreement at a Meta-Level and Unidimensional Alignment

Agreement at a meta-level is defined as agreement on a common dimension in terms of which an issue is to be conceptualized. In the context of preferences, I have argued that the structure condition of single-peakedness may be seen as an implication of *agreement at a meta-level*, in the sense that *if* the individuals agree on a common structuring dimension along which each individual's preferences are systematically aligned in the requisite way, *then* the profile of preference orderings across these individuals satisfies single-peakedness.

While Black's concept of single-peakedness is not straightforwardly applicable to the context of sets of judgments, we will now see that an alternative structure condition can be devised for the latter context (List, 2003), and further that the new structure condition, like single-peakedness, can be seen as an implication of agreement at a meta-level.

In analogy to the context of preferences, the question is not whether two or more individuals hold the same sets of judgments, but this time it is whether there exists a single ordering of the individuals from 'left'-most to 'right'-most such that, for *every* proposition in the relevant domain of issues, the individuals accepting that proposition are either all to the left, or all to the right, of those rejecting it. If there exists a 'left'/'right' ordering of the individuals with this property, once again called a *structuring dimension*, then we say that the given profile of sets of judgments across individuals satisfies *unidimensional aligment*. It is easily seen that the judgments in Table 1 above violate unidimensional alignment. No matter how the individuals are reordered from 'left' to 'right', it is impossible to get the required pattern of acceptance and rejection. By contrast, the judgments of the five individuals in Table 2 below satisfy unidimensional alignment: there exists a single ‘left’/‘right’ ordering of the five individuals (namely: 3, 2, 5, 4, 1) with respect to which, for every proposition, the individuals accepting the proposition are all to the left (they could also be all to the right) of those rejecting it.

	individual 3	individual 2	individual 5	individual 4	individual 1
P	yes	no	no	no	no
Q	yes	yes	yes	no	no
R	yes	no	no	no	no
$(R \leftrightarrow (P \wedge Q))$	yes	yes	yes	yes	no

Table 2

Now, given a profile of sets of judgments across individuals that satisfies unidimensional alignment, order the individuals (again assume for simplicity that there is an odd number of them) on a structuring dimension. Then the set of judgments of the median individual with respect to the structuring dimension will be accepted in propositionwise majority voting (in the case of Table 2, the judgments of individual 5). And provided that the set of judgments of each individual, most importantly the median individual, satisfies the relevant consistency criteria, so will the collective set. A corollary of this result is that, if the domain of admissible profiles of sets of judgments across individuals consists only of those profiles satisfying unidimensional alignment, then propositionwise majority voting is a procedure for generating collective sets of judgments in accordance with the minimal conditions of responsiveness and consistency used in the impossibility theorem by List and Pettit (2002).

The claim that unidimensional alignment is an implication of agreement at a meta-level may seem less straightforward than the analogous claim in the case of single-peakedness, but here is a way of making it plausible. Suppose, firstly, that there is a single common issue-dimension in terms of which all the propositions are conceptualised by the individuals, and suppose that each individual takes a certain position on that dimension. For simplicity, we will call it a ‘left’/‘right’ dimension, but a range of interpretations is possible. And suppose, secondly, that, for each proposition, the extreme positions on the ‘left’/‘right’ dimension correspond to either clear acceptance or clear rejection of this proposition and there exists an ‘acceptance threshold’ on the dimension (possibly different for different propositions) such that all the individuals to the left of the threshold accept the proposition and all the individuals to its right reject it (or vice-versa). If these two conditions are met, then we have a situation of unidimensional alignment. As in the case of single-peakedness, unidimensional alignment requires no agreement at a substantive level: in the case described by Table 2, for example, individual 3 and individual 1 disagree about *every* proposition. Unidimensional alignment requires only the existence of a common ‘left’/‘right’ ordering of the individuals that systematically structures their pattern of acceptance and rejection over the various propositions.

Once again, the claim is only that unidimensional alignment may be an *implication* of agreement at a meta-level, not that unidimensional alignment is by itself sufficient for agreement at a meta-level. A profile of sets of judgments across individuals may happen to have the right *formal* structure for satisfying unidimensional alignment without the individuals *semantically* conceptualizing all propositions in terms of the same common issue-dimension.

Moreover, like single-peakedness, unidimensional alignment is not merely a consistency condition on individual sets of judgments. The singleton profile, consisting only of the set of judgments of a single individual, always trivially – but of course uninformatively – satisfies unidimensional alignment. Like the concept of single-peakedness, the concept of unidimensional alignment becomes non-vacuous only when applied to the sets of judgments of multiple individuals. In this sense unidimensional alignment captures a formal implication of *agreement*, albeit again at a meta-level.

Unlike in the case of single-peakedness, no empirical research has been done on whether group deliberation can induce unidimensional alignment, or indeed on whether there ever exist plausible real-world situations of sufficiently realistic complexity in which a profile of sets of judgments across individuals satisfies unidimensional alignment. But the mere observation that agreement at a substantive level may be hard, if not impossible, to attain in cases of complex and controversial issues and that unidimensional alignment is at least *less* demanding than full agreement at a substantive level should lead us to take the concept of unidimensional alignment seriously.

7 Empirical Contingencies and Institutional Design

A critic might be unconvinced by the claim that agreement at a meta-level and corresponding structure conditions such as single-peakedness or unidimensional alignment open up attractive escape-routes from the paradoxes and impossibility results of aggregation. Specifically, the critic might argue as follows. He or she would concede that, *if* empirical circumstances are such that individual preferences or sets of judgments satisfy the identified structure conditions (or approximate them to a sufficient degree), *then* aggregation procedures like pairwise majority voting or propositionwise majority voting will generate consistent collective outcomes. But, as soon as empirical circumstances are different, the very same aggregation procedures will fail to generate consistent collective outcomes. Social choice theorists can even make precise predictions about when such collective inconsistencies will occur. In other words, what we know about these aggregation procedures is that they work satisfactorily in some empirical circumstances (e.g. for certain profiles of individual preferences or sets of judgments) but not in others. The impossibility theorems tell us, further, that this problem is not just an artefact of pairwise or propositionwise majority voting, but that it is more general. It cannot be resolved by any aggregation procedure, except at the expense of some seemingly attractive minimal conditions. One would not like to design a house just on the basis of the observation that there are some empirical circumstances in which the house would be stable, while there are others in which the house would collapse. Rather, one would seek to design a house on the basis of solid physical calculations confirming its stability. Analogously, the critic argues, it is a risky *ad hoc* response to the problems of democratic aggregation to use aggregation procedures like pairwise or propositionwise majority voting and to rely on the observation that there are empirical circumstances – like situations of agreement at a meta-level – in which these procedures work satisfactorily, while de-emphasizing the existence of other circumstances in which they fail to do so. Like a house, procedures for democratic aggregation should be designed so as to work satisfactorily in *all* relevant circumstances (e.g. for all logically possible profiles of individual preferences or sets of judgments). They should not have to rely on the hope that certain empirical circumstances rather than others obtain. They should be guaranteed to generate consistent collective outcomes, no matter what the empirical circumstances are – so far the critic's objection.

The general question this objection highlights is the following. Should political institutions, such as aggregation procedures, be designed in such a way as to work robustly under all possible empirical circumstances (at least within a relevant domain of circumstances), or is it acceptable for such institutions to rely on specific empirical contingencies that are exogenous to, and not guaranteed by, them?

At first sight, the critic's objection clearly has some force. After all, institutions that rely on specific empirical contingencies may seem prone to erratic behavior, just as the house whose stability can be guaranteed only under specific empirical circumstances may seem a dangerous structure. However, on closer inspection, the objection loses some of its force. Even the most well designed house, designed on the basis of solid physical calculations, will collapse under some circumstances, for example if there is a sufficiently strong earthquake. Strictly speaking, it is therefore not true that a well-designed house will be stable in *all* circumstances. The critic might respond that building standards take that problem into account too. In earthquake zones like California, unlike in Britain, houses are required to meet particular building standards to withstand earthquakes. But, if an exceptionally strong earthquake were to occur, even a house built in accordance with those rigorous standards might collapse.

The observation that can be made from these points is this. Whenever something is to be designed, whether it is a house or an institution, there is a domain of possible circumstances the house or the institution may be confronted with. In some of these circumstances (call them type 1) the house or the institution may have perfect stability, while in others (call them type 2) the house may collapse or the institution may fail to work satisfactorily. Rather than requiring the design of a house or institution for which there are no circumstances of type 2, which may be difficult if not impossible, a reasonable strategy would be the following. First consider the probability distribution over the relevant domain of circumstances, and then ask whether the probability of circumstances of type 2 is sufficiently low (if still nonzero) for the risk of instability under those circumstances to be bearable. For example, even in Britain the probability of the occurrence of a massive earthquake is presumably nonzero. But as this probability is low, it is considered acceptable for houses in Britain not to be built to withstand massive earthquakes. In California, the probability distribution is different, and building standards are adjusted accordingly. Generally, if stability across *all* possible circumstances is difficult to achieve, or impossible, the design of a house or an institution would have to be adjusted to the probability distribution over the relevant domain of circumstances. The idea would be to design a house or an institution in such a way that the probability of corresponding circumstances of type 1 is high and the probability of corresponding circumstances of type 2 is low.

If discursive conditions in a group of individuals are such that (a sufficient degree of) agreement at a meta-level and corresponding structure conditions are extremely probable, while the occurrence of profiles of preferences or sets of judgments leading to collective inconsistencies is extremely improbable, then the use of aggregation procedures like pairwise or propositionwise majority voting seems as defensible as the construction of houses in Britain which do not meet Californian building standards (under arguably undemanding assumptions about the probability distribution over profiles of preferences, it can be shown that the probability of collective inconsistencies decreases towards 0 as the number of individuals increases; see the appendix on the probability of cycles in List and Goodin, 2001). If discursive conditions are different, on the other hand, then the use of such aggregation procedures is much less defensible. The defensibility of an aggregation procedure may thus be sensitive to the relevant probability distribution over the set of all logically possible profiles of preferences or sets of judgments. This probability distribution will itself depend on certain empirical facts about the relevant context and the relevant group of individuals. Moreover, additional institutions, like deliberation settings prior to the use of an aggregation procedure, might be designed with the aim of transforming that probability distribution so as to reduce the probability of circumstances of type 2. The defensibility of the suggested aggregation procedures, then, is no longer an *a priori* matter (as typically viewed by classical social choice theorists), but dependent on certain empirical contingencies, which might differ from context to context.

8 Concluding Remarks

The distinction between agreement at a substantive level and agreement at a meta-level was motivated by Black's response to Condorcet and Arrow. And, as we have seen in the context of preferences, the context of Black's own work, there are both theoretical and empirical results in support of the view that the 'meta-agreement' strategy – the idea that a democracy should seek agreement at a meta-level through processes of political deliberation – is a promising response to the challenge of resolving conflict between divergent individual preferences, given appropriate empirical circumstances.

In the context of sets of judgments over multiple interconnected propositions, on the other hand, our conclusions must remain much more tentative. Again, the two concepts of agreement can be identified, and their logical status, even in terms of avoiding impossibility problems of aggregation, is very similar to that of their more well-known counterparts in the context of preferences. To determine whether a 'meta-agreement' strategy is practically available in this new context, however, remains an open question for democratic theory and a challenge for democratic practice.

In short, many important questions remain open. Most importantly, we will need to tackle the question of whether a certain 'base level of cohesion' – for instance, in the form of (partial) single-peakedness or (partial) unidimensional alignment – is absolutely necessary for any strategy of democratic conflict resolution to be successful, or whether democratic conflict resolution mechanisms can be made so robust as to cope with even the most extreme limiting cases of divergence. The impossibility theorems of social choice would certainly seem to apply in the latter cases.

References

Arrow, K. (1951/1963) *Social Choice and Individual Values*, New York (Wiley).

Black, D. (1948) "On the Rationale of Group Decision-Making", *Journal of Political Economy* 56, 23-34.

Brennan, G. (2001) "Collective Coherence?", *International Review of Law and Economics* 21, 197-211.

Chapman, B. (1998) "More Easily Done than Said: Rules, Reason and Rational Social Choice", *Oxford Journal of Legal Studies* 18, 293-329.

Dryzek, J. and List, C. (2003) "Social Choice Theory and Deliberative Democracy: A Reconciliation", *British Journal of Political Science* 33(1): 1-28.

Elster, J. (1986) "The Market and the Forum", in Elster, J., and Hylland, A. (eds.) *Foundations of Social Choice Theory*, Cambridge (Cambridge University Press).

Fishkin, J. S. (1997) *The Voice of the People: Public Opinion and Democracy*, New Haven/London (Yale University Press).

Gehrlein, W. (2000) "Social Homogeneity and Condorcet Winners: A Weak Connection", paper presented at the annual meeting of the Public Choice Society, Charleston, South Carolina, March 2000.

Kornhauser, L. A. (1992) "Modelling Collegial Courts. I. Path-Dependence", *International Review of Law and Economics* 12, 169-185.

Knight, J. and Johnson J. (1994) "Aggregation and Deliberation: On the Possibility of Democratic Legitimacy", *Political Theory* 22, 277-296.

List, C. (2003) "A Possibility Theorem on Aggregation over Multiple Interconnected Propositions", *Mathematical Social Sciences*, forthcoming.

List, C. and Goodin, R. E. (2001) "Epistemic Democracy: Generalizing the Condorcet Jury Theorem", *Journal of Political Philosophy* 9(3), 277-306.

List, C. and Pettit, P. (2002) "Aggregating Sets of Judgments: An Impossibility Result", *Economics and Philosophy* 18, 89-110.

List, C., McLean, I., Fishkin, J., and Luskin, R. (2000) "Can Deliberation Induce Greater Preference Structuration? Evidence from Deliberative Opinion Polls", paper presented at the conference of the American Political Science Association, September 2000.

Miller, D. (1992) "Deliberative Democracy and Social Choice", *Political Studies* 40 (special issue), 54-67.
Mueller, D. (1989) *Public Choice II*, Cambridge (Cambridge University Press).
Niemi, R. G. (1969) "Majority Decision-Making with Partial Unidimensionality", *American Political Science Review* 63, 488-497.
Pettit, P. (2001) "Deliberative Democracy and the Discursive Dilemma", *Philosophical Issues* 11, 268-299.
Rawls, J. (1993) *Political Liberalism*, New York (Columbia University Press).
Sunstein, C. R. (2000) "The Law of Group Polarization", paper presented at the conference "Deliberating about Deliberative Democracy", University of Texas at Austin, February 2000.
Tullock, G. and Campbell, C. D. (1970) "Computer Simulation of a Small Voting System", *Economics Journal* 80, 97-104.

Economics and the Political Discourse: Comment on Christian List

Rüdiger Waldkirch

To make a comment on an excellent paper is a rather difficult task. Its writer generally faces two different options to make fruitful remarks. The first possibility is to stay within the approach laid out by the paper and to try to discover logical fallacies or aspects that are missing. The second way to proceed is to take a step back and to pose the question of how the problem of social order – which underlies all theorizing in the social sciences – is exposed in the particular approach. Which of its aspects does the approach focus on and which remain unaddressed? In this comment, I have chosen the second option.

The comment comprises three sections. Section I makes some general remarks on the way an economist might see deliberative theory, which serve as a theoretical background of the paper under consideration. Section II addresses the question of what economics may learn from deliberative theory. The intention of List's paper is briefly outlined: A change of approach in the social sciences is needed. In section III the direction of the interrogation is reversed. Now the question is what deliberative theory may learn from economics. It is suggested that the social sciences cannot remain silent on the heuristic quality of mental models concerning the governance of the problem of social order.

I Deliberative Theory and Modern Society

(1) In my opinion deliberative theory has pointed out what many economists have ignored and are neglecting up to this time to a considerable degree. In modern society – a society which is characterized by functional differentiation, individualization, market structures and organizations – a *political discourse* has emerged. Today the entire institutional framework of society, including its constitution, is discussed not only by the politicians within the political system but also by the public at large. Virtually every citizen is confronted by the media with 'reasons of rules', that means with arguments why the institutional framework of society should be as it is now or why certain proposed reforms should be carried through. Together with the incentives provided by other formal and informal institutions these arguments will influence the citizens' actions. To be more precise, the citizens' actions will be governed by their beliefs about the incentive properties and the moral quality of the institutions. Deliberative theorists place this political discourse at the centre of their approach. And in my view it is necessary to do so.

Accordingly, the task of deliberative theory and democracy is defined as enhancing and instructing the public process of deliberation and reasoning in order to set up a better base for political reforms.

(2) Deliberative Theory departs from an approach which focuses on individual interests, preferences or judgments and the ways in which they can be aggregated or transformed into a general will, a collective preference or a common judgment. Often a paradox is formulated as the starting point of theoretical investigation, which points out that under specific conditions aggregation procedures or rules of transformation will generally not lead to a unique, consistent and rational result.

It is this understanding which serves as the theoretical underpinning for the argumentation put forward in List's paper.

II What Economics Can Learn from Deliberative Theory

Substantive and Meta-Agreement is in my opinion a thoughtful and very inspiring contribution, which provides the debate in the social sciences with fruitful insights. As I read it, it proposes a *fundamental change of approach*, which sets deliberative theory on a different – in my opinion: *better* – track in binding it to a 'meta-agreement-strategy'. To put it in List's words: 'The idea is that the key to a deliberative democratic response to Condorcet and Arrow lies not in the idea of deliberation-induced agreement at a substantive level, but rather in the idea of deliberation-induced agreement at a meta level. ... [I]t is much more realistic ... to expect processes of political deliberation to produce agreement on what the relevant *questions* are rather than on what the *answers* should be' (p. 123).

As an economist, I read this 'meta-agreement-strategy' as pointing out the importance of 'basic assumptions', 'Weltanschauungen', 'beliefs' or 'mental models', to which people have recourse in formulating questions concerning the fundamental problem of social order as well as institutional answers to it. To put it straightforwardly, I completely agree with List's assessment that ultimately everyone's interest will be served if social philosophers will instruct the political discourse differently as a result of a change in the approach in the social sciences. In addition to providing information and arguments why a certain institution is the socially desirable answer to a specific political problem, there are another two important tasks that a social theory should accomplish:

(1) Social theory should point out that in an open and free society there is a general need *to create a condition of 'shared mental models'*, common 'beliefs' or 'Weltanschauungen', as the division of labor is likely to go hand in hand with a divergence of the mental models people use in guiding their actions (see among others: North, 1984 and 1993).

(2) Social theory should *assess the fruitfulness*, the adequacy *of widely used 'mental models'* or 'beliefs' which serve as a background of and an input to the

individuals' choices of actions (see among others: Luhmann, 1997; and Waldkirch, 2002).

To summarize it in one sentence: In modern society common knowledge of adequate beliefs is a necessary condition of good societal policy and it is among the primary tasks of social theory to help society in establishing this condition.

III What Can Deliberative Theory Learn from Economics?

There is an argument that a change of approach, a fruitful reformulation of the basic problem of social philosophy – including deliberative theory and economics – is needed. However it seems to me that social scientists have divergent views on the issue of *how* the problem of social order should be redefined. I think that economic theory can make a valuable contribution on this matter, which – in my view – has not received the attention it deserves and should therefore be taken up in future research. As different mental models embody a different *heuristic quality* concerning the governance of the problem of social order, it is important to ask *which kind of mental model* points at crucial aspects of a successful institutional answer to social problems and which kind obscures them. To perform the task of critically analyzing citizens' mental models, social philosophy has to go beyond stating the importance of beliefs and start assessing the fruitfulness of particular mental models for the public discourse. The assessment of the heuristic quality of mental models has been at the core of economic theory right from its start, although this rarely has been made explicit (Waldkirch, 2002). One example of an inadequate mental model and the reasons thereof will be outlined in the remaining lines.

According to the way in which Arrow (1951/1963) exposed the problem of social choice, deliberative theory focuses on the aggregation of individual preferences to a collective one as well as their transformation, their enlightenment through deliberation. Taking this as an idea of what deliberative democracy is about, there are at least two things to be said:

(1) Among others it was the Nobel laureate James Buchanan who stressed that the notion of a social welfare function, a general will or collective preference is misleading the political discourse as it ignores the fundamental fact that social outcomes are the results of interdependent choices of many actors, who retain an inalienable control over some minimal dimensions of their behavior (more recently: Buchanan, 1995). Against this insight the notion of a collective preference draws on the corresponding idea of some powerful social actor, like the state with its monopoly of coercive power, who can impose the chosen institution or policy – also against the will of some other social actors. What is missing here is that to be viable an institution must be incentive compatible, serving the interests of all citizens.

(2) The notion of transforming individual preferences through deliberation is at least inaccurate if not politically dangerous. It was also Buchanan (1991, p. 242) who declared that the principal task of the social philosopher is to facilitate the initial distinction between *interests* and *theories,* between 'what one wants' and 'what one thinks'. Whereas normative theorists should respect the expressed wants of the people, as they are the ultimate source of value, they nevertheless can enlighten them as to adequate beliefs about the institutional framework of the society in order to further their search for mutual gains.

References

Arrow, K. (1951/1963) *Social Choice and Individual Values*, New York (Wiley).

Buchanan, J. M. (1991) *The Economics and the Ethics of Constitutional Order*, Ann Arbor (University of Michigan Press).

Buchanan, J. M. (1995) "Individual Rights, Emergent Social States, and Behavioral Feasibility", *Rationality and Society* 7, 141-150.

List, C. (2004) "Substantive and Meta-Agreement", in this volume.

Luhmann, N. (1997) *Die Gesellschaft der Gesellschaft*, 2 Vol., Frankfurt (Suhrkamp).

North, D. C. (1984) "Transaction Costs, Institutions, and Economic History", *Journal of Institutional and Theoretical Economics* 140, 7-17.

North, D. C. (1993) "Institutions and Credible Commitment", *Journal of Institutional and Theoretical Economics* 149, 11-23.

Waldkirch, R. (2002) *Unternehmen und Gesellschaft. Zur Grundlegung einer Ökonomik von Organisationen*, Wiesbaden (DUV).

The Importance of Information – Remarks on the Constitutional Economics of Deliberative Theory: Comment on Christian List

Detlef Aufderheide

(1) It is the fate of a comment to appear as being either parasitic or pedantic.[1] Faced with these rather unpleasant alternatives, a commentator may even feel free to run the risk of being both – parasitic *and* pedantic. The following few remarks will hopefully reveal that, after all, it was at least not my intention to provoke this conclusion.

(2) Given the common goal of a 'better' or 'stable' democracy, Christian List's contribution shows lucidly that an agreement on the structuring dimensions of a societal problem may well replace an agreement on specific propositions as a conceptual reference, and it may well turn out to be another breakthrough in social choice theory.

The conclusions that Christian List draws are inspiring, and I believe that, given his set of assumptions, the logical conclusions are convincing. What appears to be no less inspiring from a constitutional economist's point of view, however, is the perspective of bringing deliberative theory and constitutional economics closer to each other in terms of a fruitful scientific dialogue. (By now, the reader may have realized my risk of being parasitic.) By shifting the perspective from the level of agreement upon particular policy options to a (meta-)level of agreement on the *structure* of the problem, he paves the way for a 'translation' of the concept he promotes into the language of constitutional economics. What had appeared as a question of divergences in terms of individual preferences before – and what, from the constitutional economist's point of view, would not have been really fruitful – may now be interpreted as a problem of a lack of *knowledge* (or information) of the individuals involved.[2] This means that, to a remarkable extent, both deliberative theory and constitutional economics may be interpreted as different approaches

[1] Following a statement of Gerhard Engel who, in turn, quoted Adorno.

[2] In order to avoid misunderstandings, it should be emphasized here that constitutional economics does not apply standard assumptions of 'mainstream' neoclassical economics. Right from the beginning, it has been on the agenda of constitutional economics to depart from the orthodox neoclassical assumption of so-called full rationality (perfect information) of individuals.

designed to support or even 'produce agreement on what the relevant *questions* are rather than on what the answers should be.' (List, 2004, p. 123; his italics)

(3) The example as presented in the paper is similar but not identical to 'traditional' examples of 'voting paradoxes'. There is, however, reason neither for (logical) suspicion nor for surprise: When looking at the interconnected propositions we find the following (see Table 1 which is taken from Table 1 of List's paper):

	Individual 1	Individual 2	Individual 3
P	yes	yes	no
Q	yes	no	yes
R	yes	no	no
$(R \leftrightarrow (P \wedge Q))$	yes	yes	yes

Table 1

Propositionwise majority voting leads to an inconsistency in this case as a 'No' to proposition R may have different origins which indeed appear in this example: If all voters would vote for R if and only if P *and* Q were accepted as well, i.e., if

$$R \leftrightarrow (P \wedge Q),$$

the *negation* shows the following:

$$\neg R \leftrightarrow \neg (P \wedge Q)$$

$$\text{i.e. } \neg R \leftrightarrow (\neg P \vee \neg Q).$$

This means, List's result is not really surprising insofar as a 'No' to proposition R will appear if and only if there is a 'No' to a combination of P *and* Q, $\neg(P \wedge Q)$: This 'No' to the combination of P *and* Q can, in turn, have no less than three origins. Two of them are: (i) a 'No' to proposition P or (ii) a 'No' to proposition Q. And this is exactly what happens in this example: Individual 2 votes against P (and in favor of Q) but individual 3 votes against Q (and in favor of P). The third possible origin of a 'No' to R is a 'No' to both, P and Q, which indeed appears in Table 2 of List's paper.

(4) I would like to interpret List's approach as an encouragement to include yet another level of agreement which, by the same token, seems to match the concept of meta-agreement very well. It is the agreement on how institutions work or, alternatively, how policy proposals will influence individuals' positions in society. Both approaches, deliberative theory as well as constitutional economics, may well offer each other interesting insights here. From the constitutional economics perspective, we may again take as an example the interconnected propositions that the paper deals with (p. 125). What is the implication of a rebate given to commuters who are confronted with a tax increase on gasoline? First of all, the task of such a tax, from a conceptual point of view, is to confront a consumer with the scarcity of (the quality of) air. This – confronting users of a good with its scarcity – would typically be the task of the price mechanism. The price mechanism usually fulfills

this task to an excellent degree. In this special case, however, it does not work properly as nature, 'the supplier', is unable to place a price tag on this particular scarce good. A tax may (!) be an appropriate substitute. It will, at least, reduce the consumption of gasoline. But a rebate program will reduce the intended effect: Commuters will use a part of that 'fresh money' for more consumption of the good in question. Technically speaking, the negative substitution effect will partly be offset by the income effect of the rebate. In this special case of gas taxes the offsetting income effect will not be dramatic as the income elasticity of gas consumption is rather low,[3] but the income effect should not be neglected, and it may be remarkably larger in other cases. Who would tend to be in favor, who would tend to be against a proposition of this kind? I do not wish to bother the reader with technical details here; the example may only serve as a hint how tedious even the task of achieving an agreement at a meta-level may really turn out to be.

(5) List points out that he does not offer a 'perfect' solution to the problem he addresses but that this should not at all be regarded as a shortcoming of his approach (pp. 130ff.). In support of his arguments I would like to add a more general remark with respect to the (allegedly or factually) imperfect performance of democratic institutions and to the popular lament in the social choice literature that democracy as such does not 'work' as well as some romantic theorists may have expected it to do.

Conflicts of interests – and difficulties to come to terms with them – do not only prevail in democratic societies, but in *any* society. With dictatorships or autocracies, however, the vast majority of individual interests, values or preferences are strictly and systematically *ignored*. Only democracies are organized in such a way that there are options to address each individual's interests, values or preferences properly, in other words: to *respect* them. Or, to put it differently, democracy is admittedly not a sufficient condition, but nevertheless a necessary one for making politicians do what is in the interest of the people. We should keep this in mind when talking about real-world aspects of institutional design.

(6) Following the insights of modern constitutional economic thinking, I would like to go even a step further by asking to what degree the problem of aggregation really is, in its very meaning, a *problem* for democratic societies?[4] I cannot go into details here, but as I may now run the risk of appearing as a pedant, I would like to quote a statement of James Buchanan here: 'My own initial reaction to Arrow's work was, and remains, one of nonsurprise (see Buchanan, 1954). Who would have expected any social process to yield a consistent ordering of results? Only econo-

[3] Cf. Pindyck, 1979.

[4] Besides this, List himself addressed the question of stability in terms of *majority* voting, perhaps implicitly assuming that democracies are stable if majorities are stable. In a constitutional setting one might, nevertheless, be forced to address the question of the unanimity rule as well, in order to prevent individuals from being exploited systematically. See, for example, the approach to majority voting vs. unanimity rule as proposed by Buchanan and Tullock, 1962.

mists who had made the critical methodological error of crossing the bridge from individual to social maximization without having recognized what they were doing would have experienced intellectual-ideological disappointment'.[5]

We have to realize that from the 'inconsistencies' of social orderings we need not conclude that democracy is unstable. Although, for example, repeated heavy policy swings have been observed over a long period of time in the United Kingdom (probably due to the absence of unidimensional alignment), the UK does not appear as an unstable democracy.

When looking at the issue from this point of view, the more pragmatic arguments as outlined in section 7 of List's paper may gain stronger support.

(7) To put it in a nutshell, there is good reason to assume that List's contribution will inseminate further research in this area and that it will thereby give rise to an even more fruitful dialogue between deliberative theory and constitutional economics – provided we keep Buchanan's finding in mind.

References

Buchanan, J. M. (1954) "Social Choice, Democracy, and Free Markets", *Journal of Political Economy* 62, 114-123.

Buchanan, J. M. (1975) "A Contractarian Paradigm for Applying Economic Theory", *American Economic Review* 65, Papers and Proceedings, 225-230.

Buchanan, J. M. and G. Tullock (1962) *The Calculus of Consent*, Ann Arbor (University of Michigan Press).

List, C. (2004) "Substantive and Meta-Agreement", in this volume.

Pindyck, R. S. (1979) *The Structure of World Energy Demand*, Cambridge, MA (MIT Press).

Chapter 6

Democracy and Argument: Tracking Truth in Complex Social Decisions

Luc Bovens and Wlodek Rabinowicz

Abstract

The paper first introduces a complex social decision. A group of individuals has to decide whether a conclusion is true on the basis of two premises. The conclusion is to be accepted if and only if the two premises are judged to be true. Each individual holds views on the two premises and the conclusion. Majority voting on the premises and the conclusion can lead to a paradox, the so-called 'doctrinal paradox' or 'discursive dilemma'. To solve the dilemma, there are two rival procedures. On the 'conclusion-based procedure', the group takes a vote only on the conclusion. On the 'premise-based procedure', the group takes votes on each of the premises, and derives its decision on the conclusion from its decisions on the premises. These procedures may produce divergent outcomes. The paper addresses the relative advantages and disadvantages of the two procedures from an epistemic perspective. Supposing there is an independent truth, it is asked which of the two procedures is better at tracking that truth. Starting from Condorcet's jury theorem, the paper identifies conditions under which the premise-based procedure is the better truth-tracker and conditions under which the conclusion-based procedure is the better truth-tracker.

The Problem

Consider the following example of a complex social decision. Deans of institutions of higher learning in the US yearly make a range of tenure decisions. In many institutions, both the teaching skills and the research skills of the candidates are deemed to be relevant to the decision and the candidates are required to meet some standard on both skills. The dean's decision is informed by a faculty vote in the home department of the candidate. Here is a question about procedure. Either the dean might ask each faculty member to assess the candidate on teaching and research and cast a yes vote for tenure if and only if she deems the candidate to be worthy on both. Tenure will be granted just in case there is sufficient support for the candidate. Let us call this the *conclusion-based procedure* (cbp). Or the dean might ask each faculty member to cast a vote on whether the candidate is worthy on teaching and to cast a vote on whether the candidate is worthy on research. Tenure will be granted just in case there is sufficient support for the candidate both on teaching and on research. Let us call this the *premise-based procedure* (pbp). These procedures are by no means equivalent, as many administrators have noticed in practice. Within legal theory, this has been noticed in connection with jury votes (cf. Kornhauser and Sager, 1986; 1993; Kornhauser, 1992a; 1992b; and Chapman, 1998a; 1998b). There may be a majority of voters supporting each premise, but if the overlap between these majorities is small, then there will be a majority against the conclusion. It is an open question which is the better truth-tracking procedure, i.e. which procedure has a better chance of granting the candidate tenure if and only if he is worthy on both teaching and research. This is a common procedural problem in democratic decision-making. It is confronted by any collective when it has to address a complex issue that can be decomposed into several sub-questions.

Pettit (2001) connects the choice between the two procedures with general political theory, in particular, with the discussion of *deliberative democracy*. (This connection is also made in Brennan, 1999. For a general characterization of deliberative democracy, cf. Elster, 1998.) Deliberative democracy calls for a public process of deliberation and reasoning. An important element of that political ideal comes from the need to impose a *contestability* requirement on democratic regimes. It should be possible for the citizens to contest democratic decisions by questioning their underlying reasons; pbp makes such contestability much easier. This procedure gives the premises of an argument a democratic imprimatur and thus places them in a public arena. Thereby, it allows for the contestation of the conclusion by questioning its premises. On the other hand, cbp keeps the premises out of the public arena, which hinders making the democratic regime accountable for the reasons behind its decisions.

Here, however, the problem we want to examine concerns the relative advantages and disadvantages of the two procedures from the *epistemic* point of view. In some cases one can assume that the question before the committee has a *right answer*, which the committee is trying to reach. How do the two procedures compare as far as truth-tracking is concerned?

It need not always be the case that there exists an independent truth to be reached, which can be tracked by a democratic voting procedure. In some contexts, the right decision is simply the decision that is reached by a legitimate political procedure. Still, it seems that such a purely 'procedural' reading of right and wrong would quite often be inappropriate. For example, in many cases, the voters on the losing side might well consider the majority decision to be wrong, even if they are prepared to abide by it. What they object to is not the legitimacy of the decision-making process but its outcome. And the objections need not be framed in terms of their personal interests; they might well appeal to the goals of the collective. The minority voters might argue that the decision, however legitimate, was an incorrect decision for the collective to take. If such views can be justified, then it is meaningful to evaluate collective decision procedures from the epistemic perspective and compare their capacities as truth-trackers. 'Epistemic' democrats take democracy to be especially valuable from such a truth-oriented perspective. (Cf. Estlund, 1990; 1993; 1997; 1998; and List and Goodin, 2000. The label itself, 'an epistemic theory of democracy', comes from Cohen, 1986.). Rousseau is often seen as a founding father of this approach to democracy. It is central in Rousseau's theory that voters express their views on the 'general will' rather than report their individual preferences. (See Rousseau, 1762, book 4, ch. 2.) In a modified version, this idea is retained by the deliberative democrats, who require the voters to express their opinions as to which decision is best from the point of view of the common goals of the collective. Another French Enlightenment figure, Marquis de Condorcet, is given credit for the theorem that is meant to clarify democracy's epistemic advantage (cf. Condorcet, 1785, pp. 279ff; for an English translation of the relevant passages, see McLean and Urken, 1995). The Condorcet Jury Theorem will be our point of departure in the comparison of the two procedures.

So which of the two procedures is the better truth tracker? As will be shown, the answer to this question is by no means univocal. Starting from Condorcet's Jury Theorem, we will identify the features of the decision situation that determine whether and in what respect pbp or cbp is better at tracking truth. We will show that pbp is clearly superior if we want to reach truth for the *right reasons*, i.e. without making any mistakes on the road to the conclusion. However, if the goal instead is to reach truth for *whatever reasons*, right or wrong, there will be a range of cases in which using cbp turns out to be more reliable. But, for the most part, pbp will retain its superiority. Our results partly confirm and partly disconfirm the conjectures made in Pettit and Rabinowicz, 2001.

The Model

We start with a simple model that is based on the Condorcet Jury Theorem. The theorem itself, in one of its versions, can be stated as follows:

> Suppose we have a group of n voters, with n being odd and greater than 1, who have to assess a proposition A. Suppose that for some p such that $1 > p > .5$, each voter has a chance p of correctly assessing whether A is true or not and that this chance is independent of whether the other voters' assessments are correct or not. Then the probability that the majority vote is a correct assessment of whether A is true or not is greater than p and converges to 1 as the number of voters increases to infinity.

To apply the theorem to the context of voting for tenure we need to make some idealizations that are more or less realistic depending on the situation at hand:
(i) The number of voters is odd;
(ii) Each voter has the same chance p of making a correct assessment of worthiness on teaching and research, respectively;
(iii) The chance of a correct assessment for a given voter does not depend on the corresponding chances for other voters.
Some of these idealizations may be relaxed, but at the price of greater complexity. Concerning assumption (i), it can be shown that for all even numbers $n > 2$, there exists a number $p(n) \in (.5, 1)$, such that the theorem holds for any $p \in (p(n), 1)$. Furthermore, $p(n)$ is a decreasing function of the even numbers n and approaches .5 as n approaches infinity. Concerning assumption (ii), the requirement that a

voter's level of competence is the same for all voters can be relaxed as long as their *average* competence of correctly assessing whether the proposition is true or not is contained in (.5, 1). (Cf. Borland, 1989; Grofman, Owen and Feld, 1983; Owen, Grofman and Feld, 1989). As for assumption (iii), the requirement that voters cast their votes independently also can be relaxed. In particular, the majority still is more trustworthy than a single voter even if the voters to some extent are influenced by common opinion leaders. The Condorcet Jury Theorem still stands as long as the influence of opinion leaders is not too overwhelming (cf. Estlund, 1994). But in what follows we shall ignore these complications.

Essentially, the idea behind the Condorcet Jury Theorem is simple. If the competence of each voter is independent of the competence of the others, then they may be treated as independent witnesses. Clearly, if the independent witnesses are reasonably competent but none of them is infallible and we have to make up our minds one way or the other, then consulting several witnesses rather than one, and going by what most witnesses tell us, is always advisable.

To introduce our methodology, let us construct a function that measures the probability that the majority vote provides a correct assessment of a certain proposition for different values of $p \in (.50,1)$ and for different numbers n of voters (with n being odd). We number the voters from 1 to n. The probability that all and only the first k voters are correct for $k = 1, ..., n$ is:

(1) $p^k(1\text{-}p)^{n\text{-}k}$

There are $\binom{n}{k}$ ways to pick out k individuals out of a group of n voters. Hence, the probability that precisely k out of n voters are correct is:

(2) $\binom{n}{k} p^k(1\text{-}p)^{n\text{-}k}$

For k voters to be a majority among n voters, for an odd n, it must be the case that

(3) k is an integer contained in $[\frac{n+1}{2}, n]$.

Let M be the proposition that a majority among n voters is correct. The probability that M holds (for an odd n) is:

(4) $P(\mathrm{M}) = \sum_{k=(n+1)/2}^{n} \binom{n}{k} p^k (1-p)^{(n-k)}$.

In figure 1 we have plotted this function for p ranging from 0 to 1 and for $n = 3, 11, 101$.

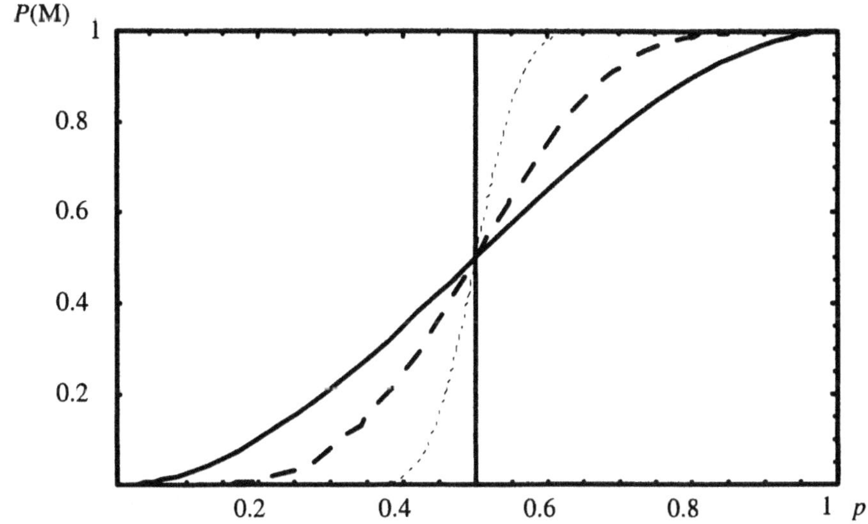

Figure 1: The chance that the majority is correct for different levels p of voter competence and for $n = 3$ (full line), $n = 11$ (dashed line) and $n = 101$ (dotted line) voters

For p above .5, P(M) is always greater than p. And the greater the number of voters, the more confident we may be that the majority gets it right for any particular value of p in the interval (.50, 1).

So far, we have just considered voting on a single proposition A. Let us now turn to the more complex decision that is involved in a tenure vote. Consider the following three propositions:

(P) The candidate is worthy of tenure on teaching.
(Q) The candidate is worthy of tenure on research.
(R) The candidate is worthy of tenure *tout court* (i.e. both P and Q are the case).

Let us first model pbp. Suppose that the dean asks the faculty to vote on P and to vote on Q and will grant tenure if and only if a majority casts a positive vote on P and a majority casts a positive vote on Q. We need to distinguish between four different situations, as regards the actual truth-values of the propositions P and Q:

(S1) P & Q
(S2) not-P & Q
(S3) P & not-Q
(S4) not-P and not-Q.

The candidate is worthy of tenure *tout court* in situation 1, but not in situations 2 to 4.

Institutions tend to have different standards: the chance that some arbitrary candidate makes the mark on teaching or makes the mark on research will be very different from one school to another. Now let us make some additional simplifying assumptions, which again can be relaxed in more complex models: (iv) The ex ante chance that some arbitrary candidate in a particular school is worthy of tenure on teaching considering the standards that are upheld within the school is $P(\mathrm{P}) = q$, where $0 < q < 1$, and there is the same ex ante chance that the candidate is worthy of tenure on research, i.e. $P(\mathrm{Q}) = q$; (v) these chances of P and Q are mutually independent; (vi) For any voter *i*, the chance *p* that *i*'s assessment on teaching (research) is correct is independent of which situation obtains and of whether *i*'s or any of the other voters' assessments on research (teaching) are correct or not.

The chance that pbp will yield a correct assessment of whether the candidate is worthy of tenure is:

$$(5)\ P(\mathrm{M}^{pbp}) = \sum_{i=1}^{4} P(\mathrm{M}^{pbp}|\mathrm{S}i)P(\mathrm{S}i)$$

Given the independence assumption (v), it is easy to determine $P(\mathrm{S}i)$: $P(\mathrm{S1}) = q^2$; $P(\mathrm{S2}) = P(\mathrm{S3}) = q(1\text{-}q)$; $P(\mathrm{S4}) = (1\text{-}q)^2$. To assess $P(\mathrm{M}^{pbp}|\mathrm{S}i)$, we need to assess each situation individually: let us consider situation S2 (in which the candidate is worthy on research but not on teaching) to illustrate the reasoning. In S2, the candidate in question is not worthy of tenure. There are three mutually exclusive ways in which the dean can reach this correct decision: (i) the majority is right in their assessment of the candidate's teaching and is right in their assessment of the candidate's research (note that the two majorities need not coincide); (ii) the majority is right in their assessment of the candidate's teaching, but wrong in their assessment of the candidate's research; (iii) the majority is wrong in their assessment of the candidate's teaching and in their assessment of the candidate's research. Hence,

$$(6)\ P(\mathrm{M}^{pbp}|\mathrm{S2}) = P(\mathrm{M})^2 + P(\mathrm{M})(1\text{-}P(\mathrm{M})) + (1\text{-}P(\mathrm{M}))^2$$

Note that in case (i) the right decision is reached for the right reasons, while in cases (ii) and (iii) the right decision is reached for the wrong reasons.

(5) provides the chance that pbp yields a correct assessment, whether for the right or for the wrong reasons, i.e. *for whatever reason*. But one might also want to know the chance of pbp delivering a correct assessment *for the right reasons* (rr) only. It is easy to see that, in each of the four situations, this chance is $P(\mathrm{M})^2$. Hence,

$$(7)\ P(\mathrm{M}^{pbp\text{-}rr}) = P(\mathrm{M})^2$$

We turn to cbp. For any given situation, the chance that cbp will yield the correct assessment of whether the candidate is worthy of tenure is given by

$$(8)\ P(M^{cbp}|Si) = \sum_{k=(n+1)/2}^{n} \binom{n}{k} P(V \mid Si)^{k} (1 - P(V \mid Si))^{(n-k)}$$

where $P(V|Si)$ is the chance, given Si, that a particular voter casts a vote on tenure *tout court* that is a correct assessment of the candidate in question. Consequently, the unconditional chance that cbp will yield the correct assessment is:

$$(9)\ P(M^{cbp}) = \sum_{i=1}^{4} P(M^{cbp}|Si)P(Si)$$

To illustrate how we go about calculating $P(V|Si)$, we once again focus on situation S2. In S2, to cast a correct vote on tenure *tout court*, the voter has to be either (i) correct on both teaching and research, (ii) correct on teaching, but not on research, or (iii) wrong on both teaching and research:

$$(10)\ P(V|S2) = p^2 + p(1\text{-}p) + (1\text{-}p)^2.$$

Note that in case (i), the voter reaches the right decision for the right reasons, while in cases (ii) and (iii), he comes to the right decision for the wrong reasons.

(9) provides the chance that cbp yields a correct assessment, whether for the right or for the wrong reasons, i.e. *for whatever reason.* But once again, one might want to know the chance of cbp delivering a correct assessment *for the right reasons* (rr) only, i.e. the chance of a majority among the voters making a right assessment of the conclusion for the right reasons. In each of the four situations, the chance that a particular voter casts a correct vote for the right reasons is p^2. Hence,

$$(11)\ P(M^{cbp\text{-}rr}) = \sum_{k=(n+1)/2}^{n} \binom{n}{k} (p^2)^{k} (1 - p^2)^{(n-k)}$$

We can now compare the two procedures for their truth-tracking potential: Which procedure is more likely to provide a correct assessment of the candidate in question?

Sample Results

Concerning the capacity of the two procedures as regards truth-tracking *for the right reasons*, it is easy to see that pbp is superior in that respect. pbp yields a correct assessment of the conclusion based on the right reasons whenever (i) there is a majority that correctly assesses one premise and also (ii) a majority that correctly assesses the other premise. On the other hand, cbp correctly assesses the conclusion for the right reasons if and only if (iii) there is a majority that correctly assesses *both* premises. Obviously, (iii) entails (i) and (ii), but not vice versa. Therefore, whenever cbp makes a right assessment for the right reasons, pbp would make it as well. And there are possible cases, in which pbp would make a right assessment for the right reasons but cbp would fail. Such cases (in which (i) and (ii) hold, but (iii) does not) have non-zero probability as long as the voters' competence with respect to one premise is at least partly independent of their competence with respect to the other premise. And we have assumed that these competences are fully independent of each other.

Still, it is one thing to know that pbp is superior as a truth-tracker for the right reasons and another to find out the extent of this superiority. In Figure 2, we provide the answer to this question by comparing $P(\mathrm{M}^{pbp\text{-}rr})$ with $P(\mathrm{M}^{cbp\text{-}rr})$, for various numbers of voters and for various values of p.

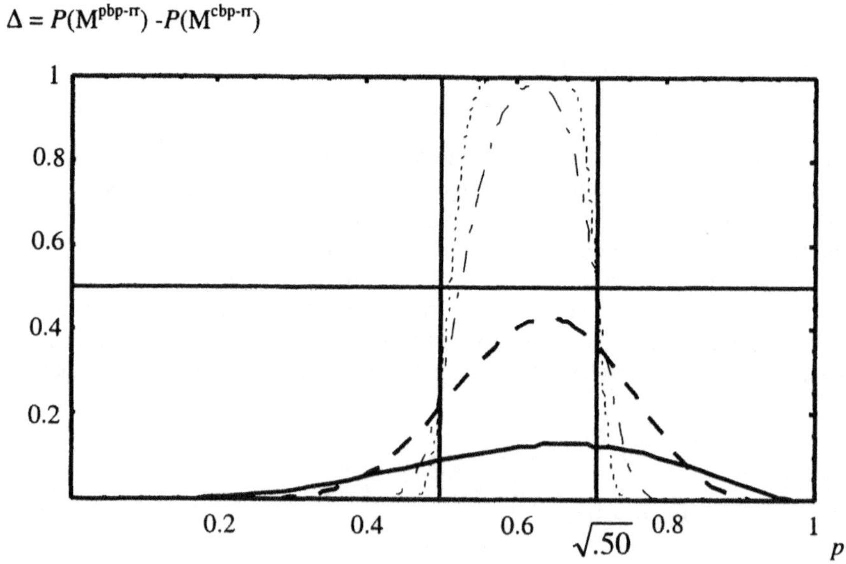

Figure 2: The difference between the chances that the majority vote is correct for the right reasons for the premise-based procedure and for the conclusion-based procedure, for $n = 3$ (full line), $n = 11$ (dashed line), $n = 101$ (dot-dashed line) and $n = 501$ (dotted line)

It turns out that the superiority of pbp is more *pronounced* for larger numbers of voters but the *p-interval* over which that superiority can be observed decreases as the number of voters increases. For n approaching infinity, $\Delta = 0$ for all p in the intervals (0, .5) and ($\sqrt{.50}$, 1), and $\Delta = 1$ for all $p \in (.5, \sqrt{.50})$. For lower n, this curve is rather flat, has a broad base and its maximum is close to $p = \sqrt{.50}$, while as n grows the curve becomes steeper, has a smaller base and its maximum recedes towards $(.50 + \sqrt{.50})/2$.

Suppose, on the other hand, that we are not concerned about the reasons that went into the deliberation: We are interested in the chances that the procedures yield the right results, whether these are arrived at for the right or for the wrong reasons. In Figure 3, we compare the two procedures in their capacity as truth-trackers, for various numbers of voters and for various values of p and q.

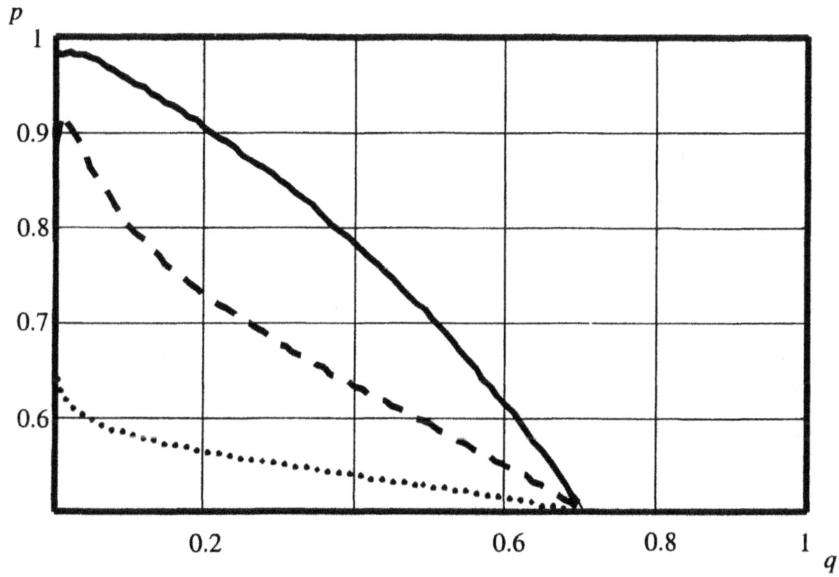

Figure 3: Phase curves for $n = 3$ (full line), 11 (dashed line), 101 (dotted line), for p between .5 and 1, and for q between 0 and 1. Underneath the phase curve, the conclusion-based procedure is a better truth-tracker; above the phase curve, the premise-based procedure is better.

For the most part, pbp is better in tracking truth for whatever reasons. However, the conclusion-based procedure tends to do better as we decrease the size of the committee (low n), the competence of the voters (low p) and the leniency of the context (low q). The reason is simple: (i) cbp does better than pbp when it comes to reaching truth by mistake, i.e. for the *wrong* reasons. Voters are more prone to commit mistakes if there are few of them and if they are less competent; and the room for truth by mistake is larger in less lenient contexts, in which the probability of the conjunction being false is higher. As we know, the truth about a conjunction can be reached by mistake only when the conjunction is false. (ii) As the number of voters increases, pbp does increasingly better than cbp with less competent voters, when it comes to reaching truth for the *right* reasons. But for small numbers of voters, this advantage of the premise-based procedure is smaller and thus it cannot outweigh that procedure's disadvantages as regards reaching truth by mistake.

As an example, consider Figures 4 and 5 below that compare the two procedures for a fixed $q = .5$, for varying values of p and for two different numbers of voters, $n = 3$ and $n = 101$.

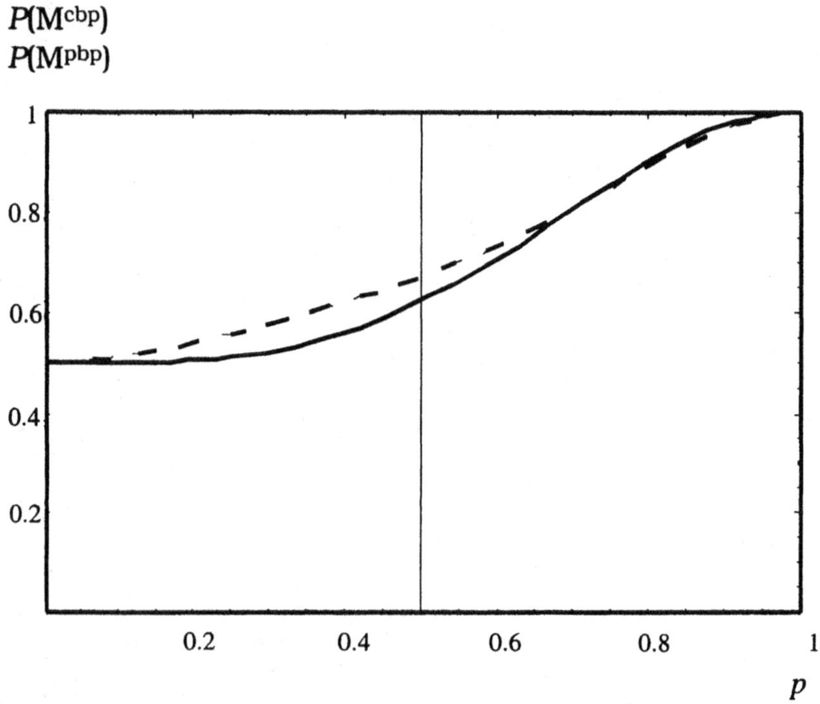

Figure 4: The chance that the majority vote is correct on the conclusion-based procedure for 3 voters (dashed line) and the chance that the majority vote is correct on the premise-based procedure for 3 voters (full line), for q =.5

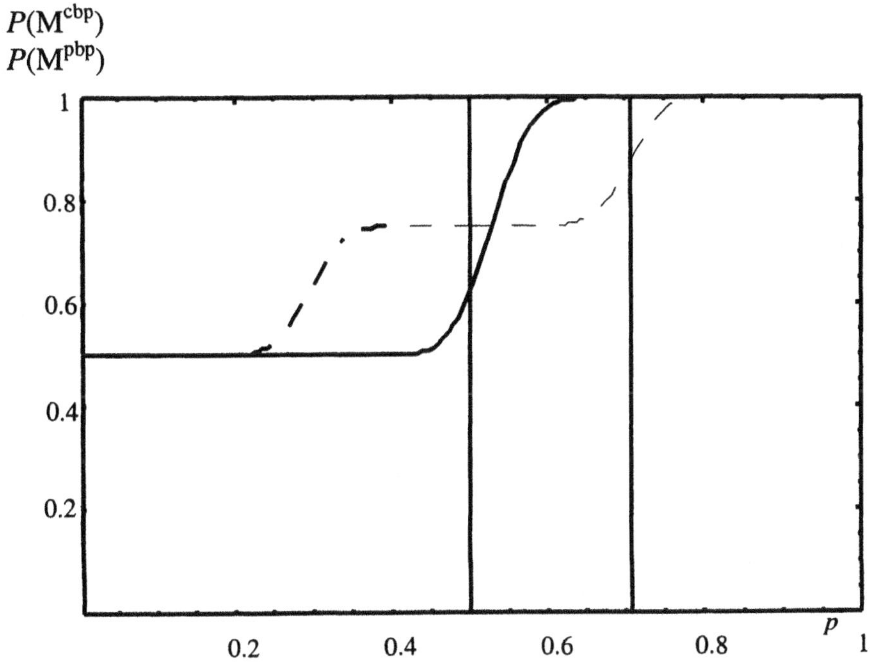

Figure 5: The chance that the majority vote is correct on the conclusion-based procedure for 101 voters (dashed line) and the chance that the majority vote is correct on the premise-based procedure for 101 voters (full line), for q =.5.

We conclude that, in *some* contexts (low p, low q, low n), cbp does better than pbp. This need not be worrying for the adherents of deliberative democracy, for whom a more important concern than true collective belief is collective *knowledge*, i.e. true collective belief supported by right reasons (cf. Pettit, 2001). But other democrats may find this epistemic advantage of cbp attractive. Furthermore, even democrats who put a special premium on collective knowledge should not take lightly the advantages of cbp as a truth-tracker. The classical conception of knowledge as true belief based on right reasons is not uncontested. On the *reliabilist* view, knowledge is true belief arrived at by reliable methods. From the reliabilist perspective, therefore, cbp may sometimes be better than pbp as a generator of collective knowledge. This will be the case in all those contexts in which the former procedure is more reliable in arriving at truth. (We are indebted for this point to Peter Pagin.)

Further Questions

So far we have laid out the basic model and indicated one fairly striking result. The basic model makes a range of assumptions that require careful scrutiny. Here is a range of open questions that need to be addressed:

(i) What can be said about groups of *n* voters for *n* is even?

(ii) Are there convergence results for an infinite number of voters?

(iii) What happens when we increase the number of propositions in the conjunction?

(iv) What happens if we relax our various symmetry and independence assumptions?

(v) cbp keeps the reasoning of the voters locked in the black box while pbp brings them into the open. So does pbp gain in truth-tracking potential when the faculty cannot be trusted to base their decisions on the prescribed criteria, e.g. when they are focusing only on research and ignoring teaching, or when they are adding various private concerns as additional criteria in their decision making?

(vi) But, on the other hand, pbp allows one to vote *strategically*: to vote against a premise one accepts, if one rejects the whole conjunction but suspects that others might accept both conjuncts. Strategic voting is impossible with cbp. How large an epistemic advantage does this give to the latter procedure?

(vii) How is the choice of procedure affected by taking into consideration the respective *utilities* of retaining a tenure-worthy candidate, retaining a non-tenure-worthy candidate, rejecting a tenure-worthy candidate and rejecting a non-tenure-worthy candidate?

(viii) In this paper, we have only considered a very simple type of case, one in which a group takes a stand on a conjunction on the basis of the voters' views concerning the conjuncts. What can be said about complex social decisions in which premises lead to the conclusion via inference rules other than conjunction introduction? Being right in the assessment of the truth value of a proposition is equivalent to being right in the assessment of the truth value of its negation. Since the negation of a conjunction is equivalent to the disjunction of its negated conjuncts, our results concerning conjunction introduction extend to disjunction introduction just as well. We can apply them *mutatis mutandis* to those social decisions in which the conclusion is a disjunction that is being accepted if at least one of the disjuncts gets a majority of votes (pbp) or if the voters who accept at least one of the disjuncts are in majority (cbp). But what about other inference rules, such as modus ponens, disjunctive syllogism, etc.?

(ix) And what about the inference patterns in which the conclusion could be reached by a series of steps rather than in just one move? It is important to note that, in such cases, the premise-based procedure may be applied in different ways. We could either let the voters vote on the propositions from which the main conclusion immediately follows, or instead ask them to vote on the premises that lie farther back in the inference chain. As it turns out, the premise-based procedure may deliver different results depending on the level at which it is applied. In other words, unlike cbp, pbp is *unstable*, as shown by the following example:

Suppose that, in a given group, (i) there are majorities *against* each of the propositions A, B, C, D, but also (ii) majorities *for* A∨B and *for* C∨D. Suppose the group needs to take a stand on the following proposition:

(X) (A∨B) & (C∨D).

If the premise-based procedure is applied at level (i), i.e., if the vote is conducted on each of the propositions A, B, C and D, then the group will reject each of the conjuncts in X and then move on to reject X itself. But if that procedure instead is applied at level (ii), i.e., if the vote is conducted only on A∨B and on C∨D, then the group will accept X. How serious is this instability problem?

These are some of the issues that still await a solution.*

References

Borland, P. J. (1989) "Majority Systems and the Condorcet Jury Theorem", *Statistician* 38, 181-9.

Bovens, L. and W. Rabinowicz (2001) "Democratic Answers to Complex Questions – An Epistemic Perspective", forthcoming in *Synthese*.

Brennan, G. (1999) "Collective Coherence?", manuscript.

Chapman, B. (1998a) "Law, Incommensurability, and Conceptually Sequenced Argument", *University of Pennsylvania Law Review* 146, 1487-1582.

Chapman, B. (1998b) "More Easily Done than Said: Rules, Reason and Rational Social Choice", *Oxford Journal of Legal Studies* 18, 293-329.

Cohen, J. (1986) "An Epistemic Conception of Democracy", *Ethics* 97, 26-38.

* This paper, which is a short version of Bovens and Rabinowicz 2001, has been presented at a conference on Deliberation and Decision (Wittenberg Zentrum für Globale Ethik, September 2001). We wish to thank the participants of that meeting. Special thanks are due to the organizers, Anne van Aaken, Christian List and Christoph Luetge, and to our commentators, Thomas Schmidt and Alois Stutzer. Luc Bovens' research was supported by grants of the National Science Foundation (Science and Technology Studies - SES 00-80580), of the Graduate Committee on the Arts and Humanities of the University of Colorado at Boulder, and of the Alexander von Humboldt Foundation, the Federal Ministry of Education and Research, and the Program for Investment in the Future (ZIP) of the German Government. Wlodek Rabinowicz's research was supported by a grant from the Bank of Sweden Tercentenary Foundation.

Condorcet, J. A. de (1785) *Essai sur l'application de l'analyse à la probabilité des décisions rendues à la pluralité des voix*, Paris (l'Imprimerie Royale); partly translated into English in McLean and Urken (1995).
Elster, J. (1998) *Deliberative Democracy*, Cambridge (Cambridge University Press).
Estlund, D. (1990) "Democracy Without Preference", *Philosophical Review* 49, 397-424.
Estlund, D. (1993) "Making Truth Safe for Democracy", in D. Copp, J. Hampton and J. E. Roemer *(eds.) The Idea of Democracy*, New York (Cambridge University Press), 71-100.
Estlund, D. (1994) "Opinion Leaders, Independence and Condorcet's Jury Theorem", *Theory and Decision* 36, 131-62.
Estlund, D. (1997) "Beyond Fairness and Deliberation: the Epistemic Dimension of Democratic Authority", in Bohman, J. and W. Rehg *(eds.) Deliberative Democracy*, Cambridge (MIT Press), 173-204.
Estlund, D. (1998) "The Insularity of the Reasonable: Why Political Liberalism Must Admit the Truth", *Ethics* 108, 252-75.
Goldman, A. I. (1979) "What is Justified Belief?", in Pappas, G. S. (ed.) *Justification and Knowledge*, Dordrecht (Reidel), 1-23.
Grofman, B., G. Owen and S. L. Feld (1983) "Thirteen Theorems in Search of the Truth", *Theory and Decision* 15, 261-78.
List, C. and R. E. Goodin (2000) "Epistemic Democracy", *Working Papers in Social and Political Theory*, Working Paper 2000 – W9, Australian National University.
Kornhauser, L. A. (1992a) "Modelling Collegial Courts. I. Path-Dependence", *International Review of Law and Economics* 12, 169-85.
Kornhauser, L. A. (1992b) "Modelling Collegial Courts. II. Legal Doctrine", *Journal of Law, Economics and Organization* 8, 441-70.
Kornhauser, L. A. and L. G. Sager (1986) "Unpacking the Court", *Yale Law Journal* 82.
Kornhauser, L. A. and L. G. Sager (1993) "The One and the Many: Adjudication in Collegial Courts", *California Law Review* 81, 1-59.
McLean, I. and A. B. Urken (translators and editors) (1995) *Classics of Social Choice*, Ann Arbor (University of Michigan Press).
Owen, G., B. Grofman and S.L. Feld (1989) "Proving a Distribution-Free Generalization of the Condorcet Jury Theorem", *Mathematical Social Sciences* 17, 1-16.
Pearl, J. (1988) *Probabilistic Reasoning in Intelligent Systems: Networks of Plausible Inference*, San Francisco, (2nd ed. Morgan Kaufmann).
Pettit, P. (2001) "Deliberative Democracy and the Discursive Dilemma", *Philosophical Issues* (supplement 1 of *Nous* 35) 11, 268-95.
Pettit, P. and W. Rabinowicz (2001) "The Jury Theorem and the Discursive Dilemma," *Philosophical Issues* 11 (supplement 1 of *Nous* 35); appendix to Pettit 2001, 295-99.

Rousseau, J.-J. (1762), *Du Contrat Social ou Principes de Droit Publique*, translated into English by G.D.H. Cole, see http://www.constitution.org/jjr/socon.htm.

Deliberative Democracy and Collective Truth-Tracking: Comment on Luc Bovens and Wlodek Rabinowicz

Thomas Schmidt*

Suppose a committee of three members (A, B, C) has to judge whether a certain conclusion R is true or not. It is agreed that R follows from two premises, P and Q, and each committee member accepts R if, and only if, he accepts both P and Q. After having discussed the matter for a while, the members individually assess the truth value of P, Q and R. When deciding whether to accept or to reject the conclusion, the committee can employ one of the following two procedures: either the members vote on the premises individually and collectively accept the conclusion if, and only if, each of the premises is accepted by a majority. Or else they cast a vote on the conclusion straight away. I follow Bovens and Rabinowicz (2004) in labelling the first option *premise-based procedure* (pbp), and the second *conclusion-based procedure* (cbp).

The pbp and the cbp do not always lead to the same group verdict on the conclusion. Here is an example situation:[1]

	P	Q	R
A	Yes	No	No
B	No	Yes	No
C	Yes	Yes	Yes

Adopting the cbp requires the committee to reject the conclusion. Each of the premises, however, is accepted by a majority, which is why the pbp leads to accepting the conclusion. Two features of this example are worth noting. Firstly, a problem arises since the premises are accepted by majorities which are not identical, although they overlap (in voter C). If all individuals who accept one of the premises also accept the other, the cbp and the pbp would lead to identical results. Secondly, all individuals are consistent in only accepting the conclusion in case they accept both premises.

Pettit labels the problem revealed by examples of this kind the 'discursive dilemma'.[2] The situation is a dilemma since there does not seem to be an easy way of

[1] See Pettit, 2001, pp. 272-273, and Pettit, 2004, pp. 93ff.

[2] The discursive dilemma is a close relative of the 'doctrinal paradox' discussed in jurisprudence (for references, see Pettit, 2001, p. 272).

deciding which of the two procedures to adopt. Following the pbp leads, in the above example, to a decision rejected by the majority. Adopting the cbp, on the other hand, involves deciding against majority votes on the premises. Pettit argues that the problem is not at all artificial but rather highly relevant to the theory of deliberative democracy.

One idea supported by deliberative democrats is that group verdicts and decisions ought to be *contestable.* Suppose the committee in the example above decides to accept the conclusion by following the pbp. There seems to be a fairly clear sense in which the committee can be said to have a reason for its decision: a majority accepts P, a majority accepts Q, and therefore the committee accepts P and Q, which is why it accepts R. The committee's stance with regard to the relevant premises is clear and contestable. Note that this is not the case when the cbp is followed. Hence, the contestability requirement favors the pbp.[3]

Here is another relevant question for assessing the two procedures: how do they compare with regard to their truth-tracking potential? Following the idea of Condorcet's jury theorem, this question is addressed by Rabinowicz and Pettit in an appendix to Pettit 2001, and it is studied further and in greater generality in Bovens and Rabinowicz 2004.[4]

Bovens and Rabinowicz investigate a model in which a group of an odd number of n voters faces a situation of the type introduced at the outset. The ex ante probability of P being true is q, and so is the ex ante probability of Q being true. Each voter is assumed to be right about P with the probability p, and he has the same chance of correctly assessing the truth value of Q. All probabilities involved are independent.

Suppose that the committee has correctly assessed the conclusion. If it has arrived at the conclusion following the *pbp*, it is said to have done so *for the right reasons* if, and only if, a majority is right on premise P and a majority is right on premise Q. To give an example: suppose that in the situation introduced above, as a matter of fact P, Q and R are true; then the pbp leads to the right decision for the right reason. If the committee has arrived at the conclusion using the *cbp*, Bovens and Rabinowicz say that it has done so *for the right reasons* if, and only if, a majority correctly assesses *both* premises. For example, let it be the case that P, not-Q, and not-R; voters A and B cast a 'no' on P, a 'yes' on Q and a 'no' on R; as above, let there be only one further voter; then, the cbp leads to the truth for the wrong reason since both A and B, i.e. a majority, wrongly assess P and Q, despite their being right on the conclusion.[5]

---

[3] A detailed argument in favor of the pbp along the lines just sketched is provided in Pettit, 2001, pp. 283-287.

[4] For a longer presentation, see Bovens and Rabinowicz, 2001.

[5] In passing, here is a quick remark on Bovens' and Rabinowicz's notion of arriving at the truth for the right reasons under the cbp. One would expect that if the cbp leads to the truth but not for the right reasons, it has done so for the wrong reasons. This, however, is generally not the case. If both R and P are false, and if Q is true, and if the belief structure is as described above, then the cbp leads to the right conclusion, and it does not do so for the right reasons. However, this does not imply that the cbp leads to the right conclusion for the

In a nutshell, Bovens' and Rabinowicz's results are as follows. As far as *truth-tracking for the right reasons* is at issue, the pbp always does better than the cbp. This is fairly obvious, since in each case in which the cbp reaches the truth for the right reasons, so too does the pbp, and there are cases in which the pbp reaches the truth for the right reasons in which the cbp does not reach the truth at all (for an example of the latter type of case, consider the belief structure of Pettit's example, with P, Q, and R being true). As regards *truth-tracking for whatever reason*, in most cases the pbp also does better than the cbp. There are, however, contexts in which the probability of arriving at a true judgment is higher when the cbp is applied (low n, low p, low q).

For the overall question of whether the pbp or the cbp should be adopted, these results appear to be in line with Pettit's argument for the pbp. Deliberative democracy is concerned, among other things, with collective knowledge, and the classical concept of knowledge has it that knowledge is (at least) true belief based on the right reasons. This is why Bovens' and Rabinowicz's result does not seem to create problems for those wishing to support pbp along the lines described above.[6]

In what follows, I shall argue that this is not the case and that there is more to Bovens' and Rabinowicz's result from the point of view of deliberative democracy. Consider the following example:[7]

> A general is in charge of deciding when to issue a flight alarm to a city during a time of war. Since a false alarm has considerable negative effects on the population (casualties due to chaos etc.), he has orders to issue an alarm only when he believes the probability of an enemy aircraft approaching to be 0.6 or higher. He bases his judgment on the independent observations of three soldiers. Since the planes typically fly rather high, it is difficult to identify them correctly. An aircraft is an enemy aircraft (R) if, and only if, it has a certain shape (P) and makes a specific sort of noise (Q). Suppose that the general has good evidence for believing that each of the soldiers correctly assesses both P and Q with a probability of 0.4 (this fact has been confirmed by individual tests in a simulator). Assume further that the probability for an individual plane being P is 0.5, as is the probability for it being Q. Let all probabilities be independent. –

---

wrong reasons. Rather, there is *no* reason of the kind Bovens and Rabinowicz seem to have in mind and of which it would make sense to ask whether it is right or wrong.

[6] See Pettit, 2001, p. 292, and Bovens and Rabinowicz, 2004, p. 153. However, Bovens and Rabinowicz argue that their results would be awkward for deliberative democrats who adhere to a *reliabilist* interpretation of knowledge.

[7] My story is a modification of an example introduced by Clarke, 1972, p. 759. Clarke's example and related ones play a prominent role in the discussion of reliabilism in epistemology.

> The general has reason to believe all of this. In deciding on when to issue a warning, should he follow the pbp or the cbp?[8]

Bovens' and Rabinowicz's calculations say that in a situation of this kind, only the cbp leads to a correct assessment of R with the required probability of at least 0.6 (see Bovens and Rabinowicz, 2004, p. 152, Figure 4). This is why the general, and, indeed, everybody informed about the structure of the situation and about Bovens' and Rabinowicz's result, has reason to follow the cbp in the case described.

This example demonstrates that there are situations in which there are good reasons to believe that the cbp is a better truth-tracker than the pbp. In these situations, it can be advisable to follow the cbp *for this reason*. Provided that there are good reasons for believing that the cbp, in the respective context, is a more reliable method for reaching the truth than the pbp is, these reasons speak in favor of accepting the cbp's verdict. Analogously, one can think of situations in which one has reason to believe that the pbp is the better truth-tracker, in which case there is, *ipso facto*, reason to accept the pbp's verdict.

With regard to the possibility of comparing the pbp's and the cbp's truth-tracking ability in specific contexts, two points should be noted. Firstly, if a group has reason to believe the pbp to be the better truth-tracker in a given situation and if the group, *for this reason*, accepts the pbp's verdict, then the reasons stemming from majority assessments of the premises lose their importance. When a group has good reasons for believing that the pbp is the better truth-tracker in a specific situation and when pbp says that the conclusion ought to be accepted, the group does not have to take a stand on whether P and Q are correctly assessed by majorities or not.

Secondly, looking at possible conflicts between the pbp and the cbp from the perspective of the reliability of the procedure involves a specific stance towards the initial beliefs of the individuals. These beliefs are treated somewhat analogously to outcomes of experiments: they are uttered and then fed into the collectively accepted procedure. Out comes the collective verdict which all members of the group have reason to accept. The individuals' initial beliefs, hence, do not count as premises for arguments but rather as data for a mechanism.

Both these remarks point towards a certain oddity of the proposal under discussion. For one thing, when a group accepts a conclusion in following a procedure on grounds of reasons favoring its reliability, the group's verdict is not contestable in the sense introduced above. Whether the group, as a group, accepts the premises or not does not matter. However, the group's verdict can be contested in another sense: people can discuss whether there really have been good reasons for adopting the procedure employed by the group. What is more, all group members *individually* can accept both the group's verdict and the group's reason for it.

---

[8] The example might be objected to by pointing out that not the group but rather the general makes the decisions. The general, however, has just been introduced for expository purposes and might well be omitted from the story (the same applies to the dean in Bovens' and Rabinowicz's example, see Bovens and Rabinowicz, 2004, pp. 143f.)

To sum up: there are situations in which a group has reasons to follow a procedure in virtue of its truth-tracking potential in situations of the kind the group typically faces. In these situations, the group's reasons for its verdict are quite different in kind from the sort of reasons Pettit and Bovens and Rabinowicz address in their arguments. Consequently, the notion of contestability has to be modified in order to cover cases of the kind discussed above.

An open question should be noted. In most situations reasons favoring one procedure over the other as regards truth-tracking potential are *epistemically* not available. We normally do not have epistemic access to the relevant probabilities. However, is the non-availability of reasons of the type just mentioned always an epistemic problem? The example of *moral issues* seems to suggest that this is not the case. It sounds odd to compare procedures such as the pbp and the cbp with regard to their truth-tracking potential on moral matters.

Odd though this may sound, this observation does not show much. However, the question of how this oddity can be explained is important. The seeming oddity points towards an asymmetry between descriptive and normative issues, which asymmetry is likely to have consequences for how voting procedures are to be appropriately interpreted.

There is ample reason to believe that the epistemic stance towards procedures of the kind described in this paper can be justified when it comes to descriptive issues. If, however, one wants to extend the epistemic interpretation of voting to moral (and other normative) issues, a naive realist outlook, which might be sufficient as a foundation for that interpretation in the descriptive case, is not straightforwardly available any more. One seems, rather, to require a sophisticated conception of moral realism. However, many find even such a sophisticated realist view of morality unattractive, and, consequently, the possibility of such a position is a matter of debate.

References

Bovens, L. and W. Rabinowicz (2001) "Democratic Answers to Complex Questions – An Epistemic Perspective", forthcoming in *Synthese*.

Bovens, L. and W. Rabinowicz (2004) "Democracy and Argument: Tracking Truth in Complex Social Decisions", in this volume.

Clarke, T. (1972) "The Legacy of Skepticism", *Journal of Philosophy* 69, 754-769.

Pettit, P. (2001) "Deliberative Democracy and the Discursive Dilemma", *Philosophical Issues* 11 (supplement 1 of *Noûs* 35), 268-295.

Pettit, P. (2004) "A Dilemma for Deliberative Democrats", in this volume.

Pettit, P. and W. Rabinowicz (2001) "The Jury Theorem and the Discursive Dilemma", *Philosophical Issues* 11 (supplement 1 of *Noûs* 35), 295-299 (appendix to Pettit 2001).

---

* For helpful discussions I am indebted to Holger Baumann and Wlodek Rabinowicz.

Where Can the Insights from the Condorcet Jury Theorem Be Applied? Comment on Luc Bovens and Wlodek Rabinowicz

Alois Stutzer

Marquis de Condorcet wanted to contribute to the discussion on the new constitutions in France and America after their respective revolutions. Thus, he had complex social decisions in mind when he did his analysis. It is understandable that his work is not always without contradictions as is mentioned by experts of Condorcet's work such as McLean and Hewitt (Condorcet, 1996). Maybe it is due to the difficulty in getting policy recommendations from tractable models of decision-making; models that are by necessity based on simplifying assumptions. It is precisely this area of conflict that led to my commentary on the paper entitled 'The Condorcet Jury Theorem and Complex Social Decisions'.

The authors Bovens and Rabinowicz want to contribute to the understanding of decision-making in two settings. On the one hand, they mention decision-making among small bodies of people, like a jury or a faculty, and on the other hand, they refer to democratic decision-making in society as a whole. Their formal analysis refers to the first setting and is based on an extension of the Condorcet Jury Theorem (CJT). In order to gain new insights, they investigate the capacity of two different procedures to track the truth. In brief, a *conclusion-based procedure* asks each member of a body to vote on a candidate, taking two particular criteria into consideration. If, according to their information, the candidate fulfils both criteria, they should vote for that candidate. The second mechanism is called a *premise-based procedure*. With this procedure, the members are asked to vote twice on each candidate. For each separate criterion, they are asked to assess the candidate and form their opinion in a vote. The results of the analysis are clearly presented and fit in well with previous literature on the CJT. However, the transfer of the results to democratic decision-making – although intended – is less obvious and not explicitly provided by the authors. Leaving the transfer open provides room for speculation. A related pair of procedures could be party voting in purely representative democracies and issue voting in direct democracy. A combination of representative and direct democratic elements in political decision-making would allow the unravelling of issues similar to the premise-based procedure. Given this as a starting point, the question is whether the transfer of the results for the small body to the democratic process is fruitful or, in other words, whether the insights contribute to recommendations for institutional design at the level of democratic decision-making.

I will address the question from the point of view of five basic assumptions underlying the CJT.

Truth. The CJT is about mechanisms that are to be applied in the quest for truth. The quest for truth is the basic task of any jury: did a certain person commit a crime or not? However, in most cases of democratic-decision making, it is not a question of truth but of overcoming social dilemmas, as for example in the case of social policy. This fundamental difference in focus restricts any simple transfer of the results of models based on the CJT.

Individual interests. The CJT is based on a strong assumption of common interest. A society is assumed to be composed of individuals with identical preferences with regard to the issue in question. However, this limits the range of decisions to decisions that allow for Pareto improvements. These are very rare in political decision making, and have mostly distributional consequences, which people might well dislike.

Voting behaviour. In the simple versions of the CJT, it is assumed that voters are sincere and vote to the best of their knowledge. This assumption has been criticised before (Austen-Smith and Banks, 1996) and it has also been shown that the theorem holds under less restrictive assumptions (McLennan, 1998; Wit, 1998). For an application to the democratic process, however, we have to consider an enriched model of voting behaviour, with instrumental as well as expressive aspects (e.g. Brennan and Lomasky, 1993).

Voters' competence. Each voter's competence is assumed as given and independent of other voters in the CJT. This is a very restrictive assumption; for example, it excludes opinion leaders. For decision-making in a body of people, this assumption has been mitigated and it has been shown that in situations with dependency between judgements, negative inter-voter correlation improves the likelihood of a correct decision (Berg, 1993). If the democratic process is taken into consideration, integration is more difficult. It is not only important that voters' competence be studied from an inter-dependent point of view, but also from an endogenous point of view. Voters' incentives to collect information and to share information are most relevant. This has been systematically studied in the direct democratic process of decision-making (Bohnet and Frey, 1994; Frey, 1994).

Voters' utility. In the CJT, utility is gained from the outcome of the process. However, there is ample reason to think that people not only consider outcomes, but also the process of decision-making itself (Frey and Stutzer, 2002; Stutzer and Frey, 2003). People have preferences about the conditions which lead to certain outcomes. This *procedural utility* is quite a different source of an individual's well-being than instrumental outputs, such as in a traditional utility function. An extended view that considers procedural utility is of particular interest if democratic decision-making is studied rather than decision-making in a small body.

The discussion suggests that the insights from the study of the CJT (and its extensions) are more applicable to decision-making in small bodies, like a jury, than to democratic decision-making in society. Thus, the concise analysis has its price: it neglects important aspects, like people's motives at the poll, voters' collection of information and voters' utility from the process itself.

References

Austen-Smith, D. and J. S. Banks (1996) "Information Aggregation, Rationality, and the Condorcet Jury Theorem", *American Political Science Review* 90(1), 34-45.

Berg, S. (1993) "Condorcet's Jury Theorem, Dependency among Jurors", *Social Choice and Welfare* 10(1), 87-95.

Bohnet, I. and B. S. Frey (1994) "Direct-Democratic Rules: The Role of Discussion", *Kyklos* 47 (3), 341-354.

Brennan, G. and L. Lomasky (1993) *Democracy and Decision: The Pure Theory of Electoral Preference*, Cambridge (Cambridge University Press).

Condorcet, M. J. A. N. de Caritat (1996) *Condorcet: Foundations of Social Choice and Political Theory*, translated and edited by Iain McLean and Fiona Hewitt (eds), Aldershot (Elgar).

Frey, B. S. (1994) "Direct Democracy: Politico-Economic Lessons from Swiss Experience", *American Economic Review* 84 (2), 338-348.

Frey, B. S. and A. Stutzer (2002) *Happiness and Economics: How the Economy and Institutions Affect Human Well-Being*, Princeton (Princeton University Press).

McLennan, A. (1998) "Consequences of the Condorcet Jury Theorem for Beneficial Information Aggregation by Rational Agents", *American Political Science Review* 92 (2), 413-27.

Stutzer, A. and B. S. Frey (2003) "Institutions Matter for Procedural Utility: An Econometric Study of the Impact of Political Participation Possibilities", in R. Mudambi, P. Navarra and G. Sobbrio (eds) *Economic Welfare, International Business and Global Institutional Change*, Aldershot (Elgar).

Wit, J. (1998) "Rational Choice and the Condorcet Jury Theorem", *Games and Economic Behavior* 22 (2), 364-76.

PART III

DELIBERATION AND SOCIAL ORDER

Chapter 7

What is Meant by Consent?

Andreas Suchanek

I Introduction

Consent is an elusive concept. Everybody knows its meaning, and still it is quite difficult to explain how the concept works. The main problem seems to lie in the tension between the importance of the idea of unanimous agreement on collective decisions or on social norms and the fact that real consent never seems to be observed in society. Bridging this gap is, in a sense, a key task of social philosophy.

In this paper I will discuss two approaches to a theory of consent, a justificatory one and an economic one along the lines of Constitutional Economics. The basic idea for the evaluation of these theories is that consent, as a normative concept, must be self-enforcing (in a specified sense). According to this criterion, I will demonstrate that the economic approach meets this test better than the justificatory one and how it does so.

II The Basic Problem of a Theory of Consent

As a starting point it is useful to define the problem which the concept of consent is designed to solve. This problem is well known as "the problem of social order" and can be stated as follows: the citizens of the (global) society themselves have to define, implement, and maintain the rules of their "venture of social cooperation for mutual advantage" (Rawls, 1971). Based on the fact that there exists no external authority who would help to overcome this problem, consent becomes the basis for legitimization of collective rules, norms, and decisions. The idea is that those who are affected by a collective decision or who are required to adhere to a legal, social, or moral norm should be able to accept it out of their own free will. In this respect, consent is the ultimate basis for legitimization of collective decisions as well as for legal, social, and moral norms – in the words of James Buchanan, "individuals are the ultimate source of value" (1987, p. 586).

From this perspective, consent is a concept of a normative theory which tries to develop an appropriate semantics for a rational discourse on the rules for ensuring the social order. As such, consent theory has the function to encourage unanimous agreement – whatever that actually means – on social norms and collective decisions in a similar way that justice as a theoretical concept is designed to promote the realization of justice. Consequently, the concept of consent has to be *self-*

enforcing[1] in the sense that its application should help to find consent in society; i.e. the theory of consent should improve the prerequisites of the "venture of social cooperation for mutual advantage".

A presupposition underlying this perspective is the idea that the citizens, inasmuch as they are (however indirectly) the addressees of the consent theory, must be understood as autonomous persons. Obviously one can object to this premise on the basis that human beings, as we know them, do not meet this feature of reasonableness. An answer to this objection is that apparently there is no better premise for a normative theory of the social order which would be more appropriate to promote the quality of public discourse about the rules of the game.[2]
Nonetheless, this objection raises an important question, i.e. how to deal with the diverse aspects of human life such as conflicts of interest, limited knowledge, pluralism of "Weltanschauungen" and, last but not least, the complexity of social reality. These intriguing aspects of the problem of social order have to be considered within the framework of consent theory if it intends to successfully meet the criterion of being self-enforcing.

As I will try to show, the main task of consent theory does not consist in giving compelling reasons for obligations of what should be done; these reasons are rarely self-enforcing. Instead it should be understood as a heuristics for generating information about those empirical conditions that are prerequisites for a better realization of social cooperation.

III Critique of Justificatory Theories of Consent

The first approach to be discussed will be called Justificationism. The basic idea of this approach is to understand consent as a norm which every reasonable individual has to agree to because of its properties.

In discourse ethics, for example, it is argued that the fundamental structure of language implies that everyone who is able to communicate is to be recognized as a moral person. Further, it is held that this fact implies the renunciation of acting in a way that might harm other persons if they do not agree to the reasons for this behavior. Consequently, the norm of consent implies that every reasonable person should act only according to those interests which can claim to be universally valid; thus every person B who is concerned with the action of a person A should,

---

[1] It may seem that this notion of self-enforcement is different from the one that is used in economics with reference to contracts: a contract is self-enforcing when the contracting parties have incentives to abide by its terms. Consent theory, however, can be seen as the theory which works out the terms of the *social contract*. That contract must, obviously, be self-enforcing since there is no third party which could enforce it. Seen from this perspective, one can argue that arguments act, as it were, as incentives by taking the form of information, where it is in the (enlightened) interest of an individual to accept that information and, should the occasion arise, to behave accordingly.

[2] In this context see the discussion of the first aspect of the meaning of consent in section IV below.

in principle, be in a position to assent to it. This line of argument can also be called a Kantian approach in that it requires everyone to give priority to the duty to act according to those norms (or to accept those collective decisions) which can be seen as having universal validity.

A typical characteristic of this sort of Kantian consideration is the idea that the addressees of the theory must – as reasonable persons – accept certain norms that are deduced from a normative theory on the basis of deliberative reasoning. It is a further characteristic of this approach that the claim for validity is neither based on empirical facts nor presented as an argument of prudence, but that it rests solely on ethical deliberations, i.e. practical or communicative reason.

This line of reasoning can be traced back to Kant. According to Kant, the fundamental basis of free will and moral behavior is reason alone. It is a central feature of the freedom of a person that she does not follow her wants and inclinations ("Neigungen") but acts according to the voice of reason. It is only in isolating deliberative reasoning as the foundation for moral behavior from contingent empirical conditions that moral norms allow for strict universal validity (Kant, 1968a).

The ultimate reason for this line of argument is, in my opinion, the attempt to solve the problem of stability of those rules which are to guarantee the social order. Due to a strict priority of moral commands over contingent wants and, more generally, over contingent empirical conditions, Kant intends to avoid the problem of allowing exceptions to obeying norms. According to him it is a compelling demand of reason to adhere to universal laws independent of one's own interests to secure the stability of social order; otherwise the manifold contingencies of reality would result in a loss of the reliability of norms.[3]

Unfortunately this approach leads to shortcomings and fallacies which can be called "normativistic fallacies" (cf. Suchanek, 2001). It is exactly this dualism between moral demands, or moral norms, and empirical conditions that prevents this kind of consent theory from contributing to the improvement of the conditions of social cooperation. The reason for this assertion is the fact that the compliance of an individual with a collective decision or norm depends strictly on empirical circumstances too. Consequently, a consent theory which does not take those empirical conditions into consideration will, as a rule, not be able to derive the above mentioned kind of self-enforcing arguments. This relationship will be explained in two steps.

The first step consists in a differentiation between moral ideals on the one hand and practical norms that guide individual behavior or collective decisions on the other:

---

[3] Cf. for example Kant's introduction to his "Metaphysik der Sitten" (Metaphysics of Morals).

(1) moral ideals
(2) empirical conditions

---

(3) practical norms

The level at which the question of individual consent gains social importance is (3) because this level is relevant for individual behavior, e.g. the adherence to norms or the acceptance of collective decisions. Now (3), i.e. individual consent, depends invariably on two kinds of premises, i.e. on (1) the moral ideals and values of the individual and (2) the empirical conditions of the particular situation. Consequently actual consent as well as behavior will, as a rule, be influenced by the structure of the particular situation; hence if a theory intends to say something about (3) (i.e. about the practical norms which the individuals are urged to assent to), the empirical conditions (2) have to be considered in a systematic manner. If this does not happen, that is, if practical norms are derived from (1) without appropriate consideration of (2), one can speak of a "normativistic fallacy".

This relation can further be elaborated by means of the well known prisoners' dilemma.[4]

		B	
		c	*d*
A	*c*	*I* 3, 3	*II* 1, 4
	d	*III* 4, 1	*IV* 2, 2

In a situation like this, moral behavior, i.e. cooperation,[5] risks exploitation: if *A* cooperates, she risks ending up in cell *II* and, hence, with her worst outcome. In reality this is not a compelling consequence but there are typical features of particular situations which will lead to this result. This consequence is socially undesirable in at least two respects: firstly, the morally acting individual has to face – sometimes severe – consequences of her behavior, often without realizing the end

---

[4] I will take this scheme as the paradigmatic representation of the problem of social order and therefore of the problem of an adequate concept of consent.

[5] I do not want to assert that cooperation in the prisoners' dilemma is always equivalent to moral behavior. Obviously there are several instances like cartels or corruption in general where cooperation between two individuals can harm third parties and can therefore hardly claim to be morally desirable. Nonetheless I will equate cooperation in the prisoners' dilemma with moral behavior for the rest of the paper to avoid unnecessary complexity in my argument.

she sought. Secondly, this result might lead to an erosion of the readiness to act morally which is obviously undesirable from the viewpoint of society.

My fundamental critique of Justificatory approaches is that they do not take this "reciprocal nature of the problem"[6] *systematically* into account and therefore lead to "normativistic fallacies". In a situation of the type of the prisoners' dilemma – as the paradigmatic formal description of the problem of social order – there exist two systematic problems which are interrelated but different. The first is usually treated in justificatory approaches: *A* has to choose between the strategies *c* and *d* and the problem of this choice can be modelled as a conflict between self-interest and morality; Kantian approaches of ethics characteristically argue that only strategy *c* is universally valid and must therefore to be chosen.

I do not want to question that this line of argument will sometimes have its place and may even generate interesting arguments, but not necessarily. More often it will miss the point in that it does not take into account a second problem: if *A* is to be persuaded to cooperate then she has to be assured that *B* will also cooperate and will not defect. The negligence of this aspect leads to typical consequences of normativistic fallacies that are mentioned above.

This "reciprocal nature of the problem" is, in my opinion, one of the central aspects of the problem of social order – and consequently of consent theory. The claim that *A* should cooperate, i.e. agree to a norm or a collective decision, demands the offer of sound arguments that *A* can expect not to be exploited by *B*. This kind of argument, however, cannot be supported by ethical reasoning alone for it is an *empirical* question of the (presumed) behavior of *B* and the incentives he is confronted with. This might include the incentive to act morally, that is, not to exploit *A* but such presumptions are contingent and thus have to be based on empirical facts.

The relevance of this problem becomes apparent when we consider a central feature of modern societies, that is, the productivity of competition. The point to stress here is that competition is a sort of conflict that is sometimes, but not always, socially desirable. Again it is a question of empirical conditions which have to be taken into consideration when one reflects upon questions of how social problems could be overcome.

A consequence of these considerations is that a Justificatory approach will not meet the aforementioned condition of self-enforcing arguments[7] because it does not lead *in a systematic way* to considerations of how to take empirical constraints into account. One cannot expect that individuals will agree to norms independently from the conditions of the particular situation in which they find themselves. Similarly, it is to be expected that individuals will agree to institutional arrangements

---

[6] In his famous article "The Problem of Social Cost", Coase criticized Pigou and Welfare Economics in that they did not see "the reciprocal nature of the problem" of external effects. If *A* exerts a negative external effect on *B* by doing *x* then *B* has in principle an incentive to react, e.g. trying to prevent *A* from doing *x*. By not taking account of these possible reactions – and the reasons why they possibly do not occur – Welfare Theory misses fundamental aspects of the problem.

[7] See footnote 1.

only if they can understand the way these institutions coordinate the actions of the individuals and hence foster the cooperation for mutual advantage. Since Justificatory approaches are, from a methodological viewpoint, "incommunicado" in relation to empirical conditions, they systematically miss important features of the problem.

IV Consent (Theory) as a Heuristics

How can consent (theory) contribute to the process of social cooperation for mutual advantage? I propose using the economic method as a tool for analyzing social interactions and their problems.[8] To elaborate, I begin with a distinction of three different but related specifications of consent:

(a) consent as a (normative) regulative idea,
(b) the idea of an implicit consent as a methodological heuristics for positive analysis of social structures, and
(c) the idea of a hypothetical consent as a heuristics for institutional reform.

(a) Consent as a (Normative) Regulative Idea

It is one of the fundamental insights of Kantian philosophy to regard every human being as a person who has dignity. Kant has conceptualized this idea as follows: a person must not be offset in political calculations against her will. In the language of consent theory, every person has a fundamental right of veto against collective decisions.

I will not try to give a philosophical argument for this premise. Suffice it to say that history has proven the enormous effectiveness of this regulative idea: modern societies – representative democracies with market economies – and their institutions are based on this premise and there does not seem to exist a superior alternative in our times in relation to such a normative starting point.

Justificationist approaches have a point here in elaborating upon this regulative idea. Unfortunately this elaboration remains mostly fruitless as long as it is not connected systematically to a method for working out how this normative ideal can be made practical. Thinking of a decision, an action, or a norm as being universal, i.e. acceptable for all those concerned, is obviously not equivalent to the fact that everyone who is actually concerned will in fact agree and act accordingly.

Therefore, it is important to note that the regulative idea of consent must not be confused with an operational concept. Consequently the question arises as to how to analyze what people do in fact agree to, i.e. take as a basis for their actions. At this point the second interpretation of consent comes into play.

---

[8] For a corresponding approach to economics see Homann and Suchanek, 2000.

(b) The Idea of Implicit Consent as a Heuristics for Positive Analysis

The central assumption of this idea is that implicit consent can be stated as follows: within the status quo, everyone acts in his own interests, i.e. each individual chooses exactly the course of action he prefers, given the constraints of action including his pool of resources, his abilities, his knowledge.

Ostensibly, this assumption seems to support the view that economists are cynical, along the lines "if a poor person does not buy a car, then this suggests that he does not want one". Actually, it is a tough question to what extent individual assent can be interpreted as voluntary.[9]

Nonetheless, to find out which social norms, rules, and decisions can actually be expected to be agreed upon, it is crucial to analyze the preferences of the people *in reality*, that is, to learn something about their preferences as the basis for their actual behavior. This task demands the consideration of the conditions of scarcity, of existing conflicts of interest, and of institutional structures. When investigating the actual possibilities of acquiring consent, it is less important to know what people desire provided they have not had to pay for it. However, it is important to learn how they actually behave under the conditions of the status quo. For this purpose, the economic method offers a substantial body of theoretical models and concepts. With the aid of these models typical constellations of social situations, reactions of individuals, and the resulting social states may be analyzed.

This assumption compels one to seek out why people act the way they do. In order to learn something about social situations and about the different ways of behavior in a variety of circumstances, one has to assume that they react systematically to the conditions, especially the incentives of particular situations. By using this method, one gains information about typical structures of social situations and of the conditions of successful social cooperation as well as those kinds of problems that prevent the realization of gains through cooperation.

To put it differently, if the social philosopher assumes that it would be better for people to behave in a way that differs from their actual behavior, the question arises: why do they not do it? What are the reasons why, in a particular situation, an observer should know better what to do than the individuals themselves? F. A. v. Hayek rightly called the general presumption of such a superior knowledge a "pretence of knowledge" (Hayek, 1975).

In summary, it is possible to say that this meaning of consent is a heuristics for the analysis of the status quo or, in other words, for a 'diagnosis' of the problems the citizens face in their "venture of social cooperation for mutual advantage". As such, it establishes the basis for the recommendations, the 'therapy', which the consent theorist gives in terms of a proposal for which hypothetical agreement is sought. But is there still a place for normative assertions and recommendations? The answer is, in principle, yes.

---

[9] See, for instance, Vanberg, 1994, pp. 208ff.

(c) The Idea of Hypothetical Consent as a Heuristics for Institutional Reform

Social philosophers are specialists and as specialists they may have (fallible) knowledge others do not have in the same way. Therefore, it may happen that social philosophers will, perhaps rightly, see some possibilities for gains from cooperation that the participants have not yet realized. It is a matter of judgment, and finally of reality, whether this assumption is justified or not.

To explain the difference between b) and c) above, it might prove helpful to make use of the prisoners' dilemma once more.

		B	
		c	*d*
A	*c*	*I* 3, 3	*II* 1, 4
	d	*III* 4, 1	*IV* 2, 2

The cells *IV* and *I* can represent, respectively, the concepts of implicit and hypothetical consent. In the status quo (cell *IV*) every individual acts according to his own interests and in this sense a (sort of) implicit consent arises. In this interpretation (implicit) consent means exactly this – *every person acts in accordance with his own interests given the alternatives as he perceives them.*[10]

This interpretation of individual consent reflects a fundamental feature of modern society, that is Individualism: individuals differ in their *Weltanschauungen,* their knowledge, their interests and values. In an open and free society, these differences will necessarily continue to exist.[11] Consequently, it is important to have a notion of consent that is applicable in light of these differences and the concomitant problems of cooperation; or to put it differently: to gain a better understanding of the structures of society, it is an expedient method to assume that the status quo is reasonable (Hegel, 1993) notwithstanding the substantial evidence against such an assumption.

It is important to note that this sort of analysis is not to be taken as the final result but rather as an essential step on the way to improved conditions of social cooperation. As I said before, acquiring this knowledge is a requirement for con-

---

[10] It is noteworthy that this interpretation of consent is strictly related to the decisions or the behavior of individuals, not to their abstract preferences as such.

[11] In this respect, the usual assumption of common knowledge in the prisoners' dilemma is misleading. Although it puts the problem of social order in a nutshell, in a crucial respect, the conflict between self-interest and the common good (another fundamental aspect of the problem) is missed out. What is overlooked is the problem of common ground for a rational public discourse which considers the enormous complexity of the institutional structures of society. In a certain sense, consent theory has the task of providing focal points for this problem of coordination in the form of theoretically profound concepts that can also be used in everyday language.

sent theory if it is to overcome the obstacles of social cooperation. In this place the idea of a hypothetical consent comes into play. Informed by the positive analysis of crucial features of social situations, conditions of information and incentives, and institutional arrangements, the social philosopher is in a position to contribute to public discussions about social problems, that is, about the problems that prevent the realization of further gains from cooperation and, possibly, about institutional means to overcome these obstacles.

This interplay of implicit and hypothetical consent, seen from the viewpoint of constitutional economics, can also be described as compliance with the incentive-compatibility-constraint. A person will only grant her agreement if it is in her own interest, that is, if it is compatible with the incentives of her situation. This idea will be illustrated in the following section.

V Illustrative Considerations

There are several ways to illustrate the foregoing statements about consent (theory) as a heuristics. Take as an example voluntary agreements as an instrument of environmental policy: firms increasingly accept committing themselves in the form of a voluntary agreement, e.g. not to use some components of production that harm the environment. This voluntary agreement is usually a substitute for governmental regulation and as such it can – sometimes – be seen as a socially desirable form of cooperation between the industry and the government. On the basis of the notion of implicit consent, i.e. with the help of economic theory, you can learn something about the structure of the situation and thus analyze whether this form of cooperation is really desirable in the particular situation or not. As a result, a particular voluntary agreement may be shown to be the best alternative compared with other forms of regulation and hence can be assented to by all parties.[12]

I do not want to venture further into this kind of illustration. Instead, I will briefly expound some general considerations about democratic institutions as a form of securing consent at a practical level.

The first step is to recognize that strict consent, in the sense of a veto right for everyone, is obviously Pareto-inferior, since nearly every collective decision could be blocked.[13] Consequently it can, in principle, be acceptable for everyone to have procedures for collective decisions without individual veto rights, e.g. the majority rule (Buchanan and Tullock, 1962).

Similarly, a situation without rules, i.e., without any constraints of individual freedom, is disadvantageous for all. Consequently, it is in the common interest to accept forms of collective decisions as well as rules which serve to promote gains from cooperation although they will burden individuals in particular situations.

---

[12] Obviously the analysis can also come to the result that a voluntary agreement is not a suitable solution for the problem at hand.

[13] This assertion is to be understood in relation to modern society. Undoubtedly, some tribes or groups are successful in using consent in this sense.

It is important to note that, from the perspective of consent theory, a judgment about the relative advantages or disadvantages of an institutional arrangement, a voting procedure or a norm, is *not* a question of aggregating different costs the individuals have to bear. The right question to ask is *under which conditions* individuals will surrender their veto right and accept divergences from strict consent as well as obey certain norms of behavior.

Both aspects can be reduced to the question of under which conditions individuals will accept either certain rules of behavior or procedures for reaching collective decisions. Certainly there is much to say on this topic, but I will only mention one aspect of this complex question, that is, the importance of clarifying the mode of functioning of a particular rule, for this knowledge is the basis of arguments that serve to convince autonomous persons to assent to this rule. This analysis focuses on three different but related aspects, (1) its function, (2) its credibility, and (3) its incentive-compatibility.

(1) The first elementary aspect concerns the question of whether a particular rule is, in the technical sense, suitable. Although rules and institutions are often complicated, it is important to present an interpretation of these rules that is understandable on the basis of common sense. It is a crucial problem of modern society that, in view of its complexity, regulations are hard to explain to the public.[14] This helps to give the heuristic quality of consent theory its significance.

(2) A rule may in principle be suitable for a particular problem but may turn out to be inadequate in that its enforcement is not credible. A rational individual will accept a rule only on the basis that other individuals will also adhere to it. As discussed before, this is not a question of (purely) normative considerations although these may indeed matter. First and foremost, it depends on the incentives the other people face in a particular situation. A rule can be said to be credible when incentives exist for each concerned individual to respect this rule. This idea is in principle well known; nonetheless it is not trivial to see the connection with the consent theme: to get the agreement of an individual to a rule of behavior or a (procedure of a) collective decision, it is necessary to demonstrate that others are exposed to incentives that will not lead them to exploit this agreement.

(3) Usually it is insufficient to demonstrate that a norm or an institution is advantageous per se. Since consenting to an institution places some cost on an individual, it also has to be shown that it is in her particular interest. This is the reason why people often say that consent is actually not observed; accepting these costs seems to be unacceptable for a rational and self-interested individual.[15]

---

[14] A typical example is the instrument of environmental licences which are sometimes rejected with reasons which demonstrate that the critics did not understand the function of this instrument.

[15] This is obviously the well-known free-rider-argument. Although it often applies, it is important to consider *all* incentives in a particular situation. Economists sometimes tend to judge situations in isolation from a broader context and consequently underestimate the

Again, the incentive-compatibility-criterion is crucial for clarifying under which circumstances an individual will assent to a norm and actually act accordingly. Here it is important to note that the criterion for (implicit) consent is not necessarily the advanced opinion of an individual. Instead it is useful to look at the *behavior* of people to learn something about their preferences.

To illustrate, take the German law of codetermination ("Mitbestimmungsgesetz") of 1972. After the commencement of the Act employer organizations sued against it. Finally, the Federal Constitutional Court rejected their claim and the law became effective. It is a question of interpretation to say whether the employers consented to this Act or not. In a sense it is safe to assume that they did not want it. On the other hand, it is obvious that they did not revolt against the law; for them it was actually a better alternative to accept it notwithstanding the fact that they would rather live without it. Thus it is justified to claim that they have assented to the law in a similar way to the one in which an employee accepts an unpleasant order from his employer.

It is of utmost importance to realize that it is only this last interpretation of consent which has the capacity to assist in improving the terms of social cooperation because it allows us to consider the reality of conflicting interests and, more generally speaking, of the manifold empirical constraints of behavior. Only in considering the structures of social life, consent theory will be able to come to a practical level and hence generate arguments that contribute to the endeavour of social cooperation.

VI Final Remarks

From the perspective of an economist, the consent of an individual can, as a rule, be seen as a kind of investment. Buchanan has shown that rules can be interpreted as capital goods (Buchanan, 1975, ch. 7) since they are prerequisites for successful social cooperation. Now, the value of rules as capital goods depends on the behavior of the individuals. Their adherence to a particular rule will, ceteris paribus, strengthen its validity and hence decrease the cost of its enforcement. By contrast, violating it will, ceteris paribus, impair its validity and hence increase its enforcement costs. Securing consent in relation to the adherence to this form of social asset is one of the most fundamental requirements for the functioning of society. For that reason, consent theory can be seen as the science of the prerequisites for investments in the social cooperation for mutual advantage.

---

forces that lead to social cooperation. To put it differently: This argument is useful as a methodological assumption for asking in a systematic manner why people sometimes cooperate and sometimes not; it is inadequate as a general conjecture about human behavior.

References

Buchanan, J. M. (1975) *The Limits of Liberty: Between Anarchy and Leviathan*, Chicago (University of Chicago Press).

Buchanan, J. M. (1987) "Constitutional Economics", in: Eatwell, J., M. Milgate, and P. Newman (eds.): *The New Palgrave: A Dictionary of Economics*, 585-588.

Buchanan, J. M. and G. Tullock (1962) *The Calculus of Consent*, Ann Arbor (University of Michigan Press).

Coase, R. H. (1960/1988) "The Problem of Social Cost", in: *The Firm, the Market, and the Law*, Chicago, London (University of Chicago Press), 95-156.

Hayek, F. A. v. (1975) "The Pretence of Knowledge", in: *Swedish Journal of Economics* 77, 433-42.

Hegel, G. W. F. (1993) *Grundlinien der Philosophie des Rechts*, Gesammelte Werke Bd. 7, Frankfurt am Main (Suhrkamp).

Homann, K. and A. Suchanek (2000) *Ökonomik: Eine Einführung*, Tübingen (Mohr Siebeck).

Kant, I. (1968a) *Grundlegung zur Metaphysik der Sitten*, Gesammelte Schriften (Akademie-Ausgabe) Bd. 4, Berlin (de Gruyter), 385-463.

Kant, I. (1968b) *Metaphysik der Sitten*, Gesammelte Schriften (Akademie-Ausgabe) Bd. 6, Berlin (de Gruyter), 203-494.

Rawls, J. (1971) *A Theory of Justice*, Cambridge, Mass. (Harvard University Press).

Suchanek, A. (2001) *Ökonomische Ethik*, Tübingen (Mohr Siebeck).

Vanberg, V. (1994) *Rules and Choice in Economics*, London, New York (Routledge).

On the Normative Notion of Consent: Comment on Andreas Suchanek

Martin Rechenauer

In his paper, Andreas Suchanek has outlined several uses of the normative notion of consent. His main contention, as I understand him, is that there are basically two notions of consent, a justificatory one and an economic one. The first resembles in various respects the well-known conception of consensus put forward especially by German philosophers of discourse theory like Habermas and Apel. The second is inspired by ideas from institutional economics. Suchanek holds that the economic notion is better suited for several purposes because of its self-enforcing character. This does not mean, though, that the justificatory notion is unimportant or wrong-headed; it just has to be complemented by an economically sustained conception of rationality.

I will comment on Suchanek's paper mainly from the point of view of a philosopher, who is interested in the notion of consent as a justificatory device in normative contexts. This does not necessarily mean concentrating only on the first notion of consent, for I think that rationality considerations have to be included in the justification of rules and institutions as well, thereby paying tribute to ideas about incentive structure. It seems to me that I come to somewhat similar conclusions as those in Suchanek's paper. The degree of similarity is to be judged by others, however.

Philosophers are naturally interested in the notion of consent as an element of justification. Some notion of agreement or consent plays a role in theories like those of Rawls, Gauthier and other contractarians or contractualists as well as among the German discourse theorists (see Rawls, 1971; Gauthier, 1986; Apel, 1973; Habermas, 1983). The main idea is that there is some important connection between the justification of a certain rule of the moral or political code or an institutional structure on the one hand, and consent among the concerned ones about the value of this rule or institution, on the other. Suchanek rightly points out that this connection expresses a basic stance of individualism in that it is the individual preferences and attitudes that are the ultimate base of justification. Here, I think, we are all in broad agreement.

Now the first fundamental distinction is that between actual and hypothetical consent. Most philosophical theories whose aim is the justification of moral rules or institutional structures etc. appeal to hypothetical consent, and this for good reasons. For the trouble with actual consent is: we do not normally observe it in normative matters. Moreover, if there happened to be some actual consent over some rule, proposition, institution etc., there would always be the possibility that this consent was based on lack of information or some other bias on behalf of the consenting people. Furthermore, to base justification on actual consent would mean to give everyone a veto right. In most actual situations this is implausible. Thus in the context of philosophical theories about the justification of something, actual consent is not a well-suited normative notion. I take this point to be rather obvious.

The usual way of approaching justification problems in normative contexts seems to rest on the idea of hypothetical consent, then. If all concerned people were to assent to a certain rule, or if they were to consent to a certain institutional structure under some specified conditions, then this structure or rule would be justified. Now of course everything depends on how we specify these further conditions and how we spell out who the relevant people are. Usually a key idea is this: if people were fully informed, perfectly rational and unbiased, then they would consent to the structure to be justified.

At this point the justification process can get complicated. Normally we observe a tension between having full relevant information and the removal of informational factors that might contribute to biased decisions or judgments. And usually philosophers decide to include ideas of how to avoid bias as a kind of restriction on available information.

In different theories these restrictions take different forms. Rawls, for one, places his agents behind a thick veil of ignorance, to the effect that nobody knows which person she is. The intention behind this move is to ensure that everybody will indeed decide in an unbiased manner. German discourse theorists envisage a situation in which people might discuss the issues in an open-ended way and will be prepared to let the better argument win. In all these models the central idea behind the justificatory procedure seems to be something like this: an institutional framework or a moral rule will be justified if everybody *would* consent to it.

Now this last statement can be given two different readings: it could be taken to say that *it is the fact that people would consent to X* under specific circumstances that justifies X. Or it could mean that *the consent under the hypothetical circumstances is an indication for the proper justification of X*, which nevertheless is grounded in something other than the mere fact of everybody consenting to X. In the first case consent is the basic normative notion, in the second case consent is a side effect of the application of other normative considerations.

As far as I understand them, the consensus theories of Habermas and Apel tend to conform to the first reading. If so, I would concur with Suchanek's implicit criticism of these approaches, but for somewhat different reasons.

Let me put the main point thus: we all agree that actual consent is often not enough. Hypothetical consent is an altogether different notion. It arises in hypothetical contexts which are designed in such a manner as to elicit (hypothetical) consent. Now take the classical contractualist justifications of moral principles, as they have been proposed in various forms. (It does not matter which one is considered.) Every version proceeds (roughly) by constructing a kind of original position, which is framed by taking away some available information. The reason for this is that the availability of some kinds of information would encourage rational individuals to make decisions on rules and institutions which would give them an unfair advantage. So there are reasons for screening off some information on personal characteristics because nobody should decide in favor of persons like herself.

These reasons come from considerations of equality, of equal standing of every individual with respect to each other.

Of course principles like the assumption of general equality of all individuals in certain respects might be objects of consent, too. But the reason for their being central moral tenets is not the fact that they will be based on consent. They are grounded in certain moral and rational ideals like the equal standing of everybody, protection of those worse off, risk aversion, maximizing etc. Think of the whole list of principles (ethical ones as well as rational ones) which have been defended by original position arguments and reflective equilibrium considerations. The individualist assumptions give us reasons to frame the original position in the way we do. We all have needs, want certain opportunities etc. These are the bases for claims which should be respected as far as possible. The limits are set by others which have similar claims. In the end we should reach agreement on this; but this agreement follows the acknowledgement of other reasons.

Note the role consent takes in this: it is not the primary source of the normativity of certain principles and rules. Instead, it is to be conceived more as an epistemic indication for getting the principles right. If we arrive at a set of rules or principles in a hypothetical justification situation which gains universal consent then it seems that the structure is the right one, or at least a defensible one. Any rule which cannot get this universal consent is not acceptable. But this in itself does not make consent the basic notion for justification.

To put it another way: something will be the primitive normative concept. What I want to point out is that this is not consent. Following Scanlon (1998), I would put the notion of *reason* at the beginning. This also allows to bring in other factors beside the high realm of moral reasons, which might help to alleviate Suchanek's concern over normativistic fallacies. The better reasons are of course those which will get the agreement of all. But it is a hypothetical agreement in circumstances which are devised to bring certain reasons to full force while silencing others. To determine which ones should be heard, and which ones not, is the task of moral or practical reasoning, the weighing of reasons. And in the hypothetical situation, consent is an indication for having found acceptable and justifiable structures.

I believe that this sketch amounts to a sort of parallel argument to that of Suchanek's paper. Consent has a kind of heuristic function. When it arises, it is an indication of having a justifiable rule or institution before us. And the more strongly consent persists in hypothetical refinements of the original decision situation, the stronger the indication of having a justifiable rule or institution.

There is one important difference, though. Suchanek's remarks on the heuristic function of consent addresses economic applications in real-life cases, while my considerations address the original position reasoning of contractualist philosophy. Nevertheless, I think that there are important parallels. The original position arguments must rely on the rationality of the participants. This means (among other things) that the rules or institutions must not make requirements which are not defensible against rational agents, i.e. they must be in a sense self-enforcing.

There is still a worry. We might grant that we will reach some agreement on rules and institutions in a hypothetical justification procedure, but why should one accept the restrictions on information? We are told that the individuals do not know their identities in order to be screened off from information which might motivate them to make biased decisions. But who is to say that we should accept these restrictions? They are normative in character, so they must be based on further arguments, and are these not based on consent?

This consideration points towards a problem in broadly contractualist arguments, but note first that it is of no help for a consent theorist who wants to make consent the central normative notion. For he is confronted with the same sort of question: why should we take consent as basic? Philosophers like Habermas and Apel would point out that participating in a discourse would in itself necessarily mean to acknowledge every other participant as a person with certain rights. This raises the question on which reasons one should do so. To say that this is an implication of the very notion of consent, does not really answer the question. Habermas once said that it is built into the notion of communicative action that one will regard everyone as an equal participant with equal rights. But this is a sort of technical move, completely parallel to that made by contractualists. And therefore the considerations above on the role of consent apply.

Secondly, there are arguments to answer the aforementioned sceptic. If someone were to impose on me rules which are obviously biased towards his own advantage and my disadvantage, I would reasonably object – and vice versa. This consideration gives us reason to remove all partial reasons from the process of weighing reasons in the hypothetical justification situation. (I am borrowing here ideas from Scanlon, 1998.)

To summarize: the notion of consent is not of primary normative significance in processes of hypothetical justification. It is more like an epistemic criterion for having found the right (or at least an acceptable) justificatory basis for normative claims.

Now let me comment on a point in Suchanek's paper which might give rise to some puzzlement given what I have said. Up to now, I discussed the notion of consent in its justificatory use: a norm or institution would be justified if it would get consent from everyone. But Suchanek speaks of consent as being itself a norm which 'every reasonable individual has to agree because of its properties'. This is obviously something different. Consent, it seems to me, is seen here as a kind of meta-norm which then is used for further normative purposes. And Suchanek seems to think that this kind of meta-norm is of very little use in giving us reasonable justifications of norms.

I do not think that this is the central problem with the notion of consent. To be sure, some Kantian theories and theories from discourse ethics come very close to the conception Suchanek criticizes in his paper. But these theories are extreme in their almost complete neglect of empirical circumstances. Most of the theories I would like to classify as broadly contractualist do not fall under the criticism. This is due to the fact the notion of consent does not bear great justificatory weight in them, as I have tried to explain before.

So I do not see any substantial disagreement here; I just want to stress that different ideas are presented. Perhaps we can agree on this: that rational people should be able to reach agreement on certain rules or institutions is a kind of epistemic indication for having the right principles justified. This does not make it necessary that everybody actually agrees.

Concerning the three types of consent distinguished by Suchanek, let me just make some short remarks. The first type corresponds to what I called the meta-concept of consent. I agree with Suchanek on its limitations. The most interesting concept seems to be the notion (c), which bears some similarities to the role of consent I suggested for contractualist theories of justification. Concerning the notion (b) of implicit consent, I am somewhat sceptical if one talks of consent at all in the context of a pure economic analysis of social behavior. This notion of consent seems to play a large part of the role that the notion of equilibrium is usually assumed to play. So we should stick to that useful and well-established concept. It seems somewhat unnatural to say of individuals acting on their preferences that they consent to this. Maybe they would all agree on the institution of a market, if asked about this, but that is another story.

Let me close with some remarks on the use of game-theoretic models in the analysis of problems of morality and social order. There is no doubt that the prisoner's dilemma (PD) describes a very important structural feature of some human interactions. And I do not want to object at all to the use of it in Suchanek's paper. But I see a tendency to overgeneralize the lessons from the PD. In reading the vast literature of the last years one can get the impression that the PD models *the* paradigmatic social situation. This surely is an overstatement. One of the central features of our predicament is the simultaneous existence of conflict and the need to coordinate. Not every situation which can be characterized in these terms offers one or several parties the opportunity to exploit others. Thus the game structure of 'Battle of the Sexes' (or 'Bach or Stravinsky', as Osborne and Rubinstein 1994 call it more neutrally – the acronym BoS always serving as a neutral label) captures this aspect of social structure sometimes better than the PD. As for the modelling of the problem of social order, both structures seem equally important. So if we use these models for analysis (which in my opinion is a good idea), we better keep our eyes on both (and some others beside them).

There is one feature of the BoS structure which I want to highlight with respect to the general topic of deliberation and decision. The game has in its usual two-person non-cooperative interpretation three equilibria, the one in mixed strategies being inefficient. If the players have the possibility to communicate, they can use a coordinate strategy which is an instance of a correlated equilibrium: just let a fair lottery decide which of the efficient equilibria should be implemented (see Aumann 1987 for the notion of correlated equilibrium). Of course, the correlation presupposes the possibility of coordination and communication, and it therefore opens a possibility for joint deliberation on which strategy to implement. This is not always possible, but if it is, all concerned parties have an incentive to coordinate their strategies. So the structure of BoS might actually help seeing the importance of joint deliberation in order to find the best solution to a problem of social cooperation.

References

Apel, K.-O. (1973) *Transformation der Philosophie*, 2 Vols., Frankfurt (Suhrkamp).

Aumann, R. (1987) "Correlated Equilibrium as an Expression of Bayesian Rationality", *Econometrica* 55, 1-18.

Gauthier, D. (1986) *Morals by Agreement*, Oxford (Oxford UP).

Habermas J. (1983) *Moralbewußtsein und Kommunikatives Handeln*, Frankfurt (Suhrkamp).

Osborne, M. and A. Rubinstein (1994) *A Course in Game Theory*, Cambridge (MIT Press).

Rawls J. (1971) *A Theory of Justice*, Cambridge (Harvard UP).

Scanlon T. (1998) *What We Owe to Each Other*, Cambridge (Harvard UP).

The Morality and Heuristics of Consent: Comment on Andreas Suchanck

Jurgen De Wispelaere

Introduction

In his fairly short but stimulating paper Andreas Suchanek investigates one of the persistent bottlenecks of modern political theory.[1] What, if anything, is the role of individual consent in the constitution of a society? Since the writings of Hobbes, Locke and Rousseau, political theorists have seriously contemplated the idea that the consent of individuals has a crucial role to play in the related problems of justifying the state and legitimizing state action (Simmons, 2001, ch. 7). The bulk of philosophical effort in the writings of Hobbes or Locke, as well as contemporary thinkers such as Rawls, Scanlon, Gauthier or Buchanan, has gone towards explicating the conditions under which consent can be said to *normatively legitimate* a decision or set of rules – especially where these significantly affect the members of a particular political unit.[2]

Suchanek's contribution advances a radical critique to the enterprise of political justification, maintaining that consent theory should not be concerned with the search for 'compelling reasons for obligations of what should be done' but rather with 'those empirical conditions that are prerequisites for a better realization of social cooperation' (p. 170). He argues that consent theories cannot play a justificatory role because they commit what he calls the *normativistic fallacy*: consent theories generally advance moral demands that are completely devoid of relevant empirical considerations, fail to be self-enforcing,[3] and consequently render them-

[1] Suchanek, 2004: page references throughout the text refer to this paper. This commentary was originally written for a conference on *Deliberation and Decision: Discourse Ethics meets Constitutional Economics*, Wittenberg. I would like to thank the organizers for their kind invitation and subsequent support, and Els Compernolle, Hans Kribbe, Cillian McBride and Lindsay Stirton for comments.

[2] Suchanek rightly suggests that 'consent becomes the basis for legitimization of collective rules, norms, and decisions' because 'those who are affected by a collective decision or who are required to a legal, social, or moral norm should be able to accept it out of their own free will' (p. 169). I have serious reservations with the inclusion of 'norms' in the above quotation since norms cannot be consciously proposed and consented to in the same way that rules or decisions can be.

[3] Suchanek suggests that the concept of consent has to be self-enforcing in the following way: 'its application should help to find consent in society, i.e. the theory of consent should improve the prerequisites of the "venture of social cooperation for mutual advantage"' (p. 170). It remains unclear to me whether Suchanek advances the strong claim that consent

selves impractical and effectively futile. Suchanek proposes that, instead, we regard consent theory chiefly as a heuristic device that provides us with essential insight in the conditions under which individuals consent to a rule as well as the conditions necessary for changing a rule. On this view, taking a heuristic turn would allow us to vindicate the central role of consent in social theory without committing ourselves to an inherently fallacious position.

In this commentary I want to challenge Suchanek's views on two counts. First, I argue that his critique of the justificatory role of consent theory is invalid and largely fails to achieve its stated goal of discrediting Justificationism.[4] I think Suchanek may have a point against those consent theorists that fail to respect the division of labor between ethical reasoning and institutional design (though the merit of the argument obviously needs to be considered on a case-by-case basis). But I simply do not think his critique extends well to justificatory consent theories *in general*. I argue that he misrepresents both the main insights and purpose of justificatory consent theory; furthermore I suggest that this is in part due to a failure to acknowledge a number of key distinctions within the political theory of consent. Second, I point out some difficulties with the alternative approach of reconstructing consent as a heuristic device. It seems to me that the heuristics of implicit and hypothetical consent – the two cases Suchanek discusses – is a bit of a red herring. In my view neither contributes much to social theory that is not already present in standard rational choice theory and game theory, which of course begs the question what can be gained from introducing yet another conceptual scheme. However, I do think there is some mileage to the heuristic approach in relation to *express consent* – which Suchanek somewhat surprisingly ignores – and in the final section I briefly outline what role the 'heuristics of express consent' can play in contemporary democratic theory.

The Morality of Consent

Suchanek's critique relies heavily on the argument that justificatory consent theories commit what he calls the *normativistic fallacy*. The central idea is a familiar one and indeed embodies an old chestnut in political theory: to be of practical importance rules need not only satisfy a set of desirable properties but also operate within certain feasibility constraints.[5] Because justificatory consent theory implies a dualism between moral demands and empirical conditions, preventing 'consent theory from contributing to the improvement of the conditions of social cooperation', *mere* consent cannot fully justify a particular set of rules or decisions

---

should *produce* the relevant background conditions for mutually advantageous social cooperation, or whether he instead endorses the weaker claim that they should be merely *compatible with* them.

[4] 'Justificationism' is Suchanek's term for approaches that attempt to legitimate political arrangements by appeal to the normative force of consent.

[5] Compare Griffin (1996) for an interesting philosophical critique of the 'ought implies can' doctrine which underlies the distinction between 'desirability' and 'feasibility'.

(p. 171). I want to challenge this radical conclusion by pointing out three key distinctions that Suchanek fails to take into account in his analysis.

First, consider the problem of social order which, Suchanek maintains, constitutes the basic problem of consent theory. The problem of social order arises when collective action gives rise to coordination problems and social antagonism. Social order has both a production and a distribution component that need to be resolved together to avoid persistent social conflict (Knight, 1992). Avoiding social conflict is considered a social good that allows us to efficiently organize social cooperation and, in principle, to distribute the gains from social cooperation such that all have a rationale to cooperate. This is where the 'mutual advantage clause' in Suchanek's conception of social order carries the bulk of the argument.

One crucial aspect of the problem of social order concerns what James Buchanan has termed the *natural distribution*. On this view the starting point for resolving social conflict must be the existing distribution of power and opportunities and their associated costs and benefits.[6] In recent years many political theorists have argued that this starting point cannot constitute a just or *moral* order. For a social order also to constitute a moral order we need to ensure some sort of fair baseline underlying subsequent Pareto-superior moves. Rawls, for instance, famously proposed that the natural distribution of talents and the social distribution of opportunities is morally arbitrary and therefore cannot be allowed to play a role in the constitution of a just cooperative venture.[7] Brian Barry (1989; 1995) has taken Rawls' arguments a step further and has even challenged Rawls' idea of justice as reciprocity for giving in too much to the bargaining position of those who hold a disproportionate share of natural or social talents. Naturally, the problem of moral order overlaps with the problem of social order. Social order is often a precondition for achieving a socially optimal moral order; norms of fairness in turn often contribute significantly to a stable social order.[8] But both goals in fact *may* – and often *do* – conflict, at which point the constitution of a moral order poses more stringent demands than the constitution of a social order.

Contrary to what Suchanek seems to suggest, then, I believe justificatory consent theories are best appreciated as attempts at regulating the moral order, not simply as an approach to resolving social conflict. Of course, traditionally avoid-

[6] James Buchanan (1975, pp. 54-58) defines the natural distribution in terms of the combined outcome – an independently adjusted equilibrium – resulting from each person's preference and production functions under conditions of a genuinely anarchic order. The same background condition roughly underlies David Gauthier's social contract theory (Gauthier, 1986).

[7] 'The natural distribution is neither just or unjust; nor is it unjust that persons are born into society at some particular position. These are simple natural facts. What is just or unjust is the way that institutions deal with those facts' (Rawls, 1991, p. 87). Rawls suggests we regard distribution of native endowments, but *not* the endowments themselves, as a common asset (Rawls, 2001, pp. 74-77). For discussion see Thomas Pogge (1989, pp. 73-81).

[8] Experimental studies have shown that norms of fairness significantly contribute to stable outcomes in a variety of social domains. The importance of fairness is most evidently illustrated by the Ultimatum Game, in which individuals are regularly willing to incur costs to counteract being treated unfairly. See Thaler (1992, ch. 3).

ance of social conflict has been an important motive for setting up a strong state. This was most clearly the rationale behind Hobbes' social contract theory (Hobbes 1991), and its motivational force remains very much unchallenged to date.[9] But other social contract and consent theorists have broadened their moral scope to include other types of reasons, taking into account more stringent normative limitations.[10]

The key concern in the philosophical debate surrounding the role of consent in the constitution of society has been to examine the extent to which contingent conditions can be said to validate the legitimizing force of individual consent. Locke's proposed move from express to implicit consent, for instance, has rightly been subjected to fierce criticism on the grounds that it renders individual consent hostage to individual circumstances. Here is David Hume's characteristically lucid view:

> Can we seriously say, that a poor peasant or artisan has a free choice to leave his country, when he knows no foreign language or manners, and lives from day to day, by the small wages he acquires? We may as well assert, that a man, by remaining in a vessel, freely consents to the dominion of the master; though he was carried on aboard while asleep, and must leap into the ocean, and perish, the moment he leaves her (Hume, 1987, p. 475).

Rousseau (1973), and in particular Immanuel Kant (1993), went a significant step farther by suggesting that moral agreement arises from an independent source – human reason – thus rendering consent a hypothetical notion.[11] Consent theories range from the strong (Hobbesian) interpretation of consent, which maintains that an individual's consent is the sole source of moral and political obligation, to the weak (Kantian) notion that consent may contribute some additional legitimacy to a particular decision provided it accords with the dictates of Reason. But despite their differences and disagreements, the adherents of these consent theories all seem to share a common goal: to *justify* or *legitimate* the establishment of rules or decisions that affect personal action. To ignore this is to misrepresent the nature and purpose of consent theory in both its traditional and contemporary form.

Part of the problem lies in Suchanek's failure to appreciate that the *acceptance* of rules or decisions is distinct from the *compliance* with such a set. To comply with a decision is to exhibit the sort of behavior that is merely compatible with it.

---

[9] In a recent article, Adam Przeworski argues along similar lines that the primary function of a democratic state is to regulate the non-violent transition of rulers (Przeworski, 1999).

[10] Most famously, John Locke (1960) thought that an individual's action, and by implication also her consent, must abide by the Laws of Nature, laid out by God and even operative in the State of Nature. The distinction between the Hobbesian and Lockean conception of the State of Nature is essential to understanding the *political* versus *moral* nature of their respective theories of consent (Simmons, 1993).

[11] Some scholars may object to my depiction of Rousseau's consent as a hypothetical device. But once taking into account his celebration of the General Will and its implications for individual freedom and consent, I fail to see how we can grant it anything but a hypothetical status.

To accept a decision implies that one further entertains a voluntary commitment to endorse and perhaps even promote it. Consider Brad Hooker's analysis:

> Acceptance of rules also involves the disposition to encourage others to comply with them, dispositions to form favourable attitudes towards others who comply with them, dispositions to feel guilt or shame when one breaks them and to condemn and resent others' breaking them, *all of which dispositions and attitudes being supported by a belief that they are justified* (Hooker, 2000, p. 76, italics added).

The problem of social order is very much a problem of ensuring that a sufficient number of individuals *comply* with a particular decision to avoid social conflict. But does this necessarily demand that they *accept* the decision in any morally relevant sense? I think not.

As Suchanek points out, social and political rules often alter individuals' behaviour; by effectively ruling out certain behavioural options or by significantly altering the opportunity costs associated with a particular action. This means that there are means of ensuring compliance with a decision that are independent of full acceptance of it. This is not to say that acceptance of a decision might not have a positive impact on the compliance with a particular rule: in many cases people accepting a rule does constitute the most efficient route to ensuring compliance. But scholars also have pointed out instances where people seem to accept a particular rule or decision as appropriate, yet fail to comply with it – whether because of inherent weakness-of-will or a free-rider problem rooted in the structure within which individuals operate (Elster, 1985). The solution to ensuring compliance in cases of weakness-of-will, or to otherwise deter free riding, is generally to install a mechanism for detecting and sanctioning such undesirable behaviour. It is important to realize that, even if one expects widespread acceptance of a particular decision or rule, this often does not lessen the need for such a detection and sanctioning device. In addition, it is in fact often in a person's rational interest to endorse such a device even if this also prevents her from shirking on a particular rule.

I think the distinction between acceptance and compliance is important to fully appreciate how justificatory consent theories operate. Justificationism is mainly concerned with the reasons we advance to *accept* certain rules or decisions. A strong Hobbesian interpretation would argue that individual consent is the only moral ground for instituting a particular rule, whereas weaker interpretations tend to put bounds on the weight we grant consent compared to other moral reasons. But the crucial point is that there is little reason why a justificatory consent theory, except maybe in its most stringent form, cannot be made compatible with different regulatory procedures or mechanisms that take empirical conditions into account.

This brings us to my final point. I believe Suchanek ignores a crucial distinction between *principles of consent* and *consent mechanisms*. Principles of consent are normative statements or moral guidelines that express the moral reasons underlying the justification of rules or decisions. They are often expressed in universal and general terms, and essentially reflect the moral status individuals embody and the normative relationship between moral persons with potentially competing interests. Principles of consent often endorse an ideal of equality: famous examples include the Kantian maxim that no person should be treated as a mere means to an end or the Dworkinian idea that one should treat all persons with equal concern and respect (Kant, 1993; also O'Neill, 1989, ch. 7; Dworkin, 1977, pp. 180-183; 272-278). It is by virtue of these ideals that principles of consent claim to be universally valid.

It is true that universal validity comes at a price: universalism is only possible by restricting the analysis to a certain level of formality. Hegel (1967) famously criticized Kant for refraining to move beyond 'abstract right'. Suchanek seems to take Hegel's lead, challenging Justificationism for 'isolating deliberative reasoning as the foundation for moral behavior from contingent empirical conditions' (p. 171). But this claim is false. Consent theory does *not* isolate deliberative reasoning from empirical contingencies; that the contrary is true can be easily ascertained by looking at some of the recent literature on deliberative democracy (Nino, 1996; Dryzek, 2001). Justificationism does not demand that all rules or decisions are universally valid in the sense that they can be agreed upon by all persons.[12] What consent theory demands is that the moral grounds that determine whether a particular rule is morally acceptable are universally valid in the sense of according with the moral status of persons and the moral relationship between them.[13]

In order to combine universally valid moral reasons with stable and practical rules, society needs procedures or mechanisms to mediate between competing interests. Contemporary political practice gives us plenty of examples of how to institutionalise different consent mechanisms: modern polities regularly employ various forms of representation, co-determination, voting and deliberation at different levels of decision-making to arrive at a legitimate set of rules. What is important from a justificatory point of view is that these mechanisms are supported by universally valid moral reasons. Of course, from an institutional design point of view they must simultaneously satisfy properties such as incentive-compatibility. But it is the *mechanisms* and not the underlying *values* or *principles* that need to be made compatible with existing circumstances. Suchanek's failure to distinguish between principles and mechanisms, in my view, betrays a misunderstanding of the appropriate division of labor between ethical reasoning and institutional design.[14]

---

[12] I think Suchanek is also seriously mistaken by insisting that 'consent theory has the function to encourage unanimous agreement' (p. 169).

[13] I think Suchanek is wrong in assuming that because 'the norm of consent implies that every reasonable person should act only according to those interests which can claim to be universally valid', this means every person must actually assent to it (p. 171). This seems a clear misunderstanding of the rationale behind Kantian universalism. Roger Scruton, for instance, has shown that Kant in fact holds the contrasting view that a law must be framed such that it is merely *possible* for all the people to give their consent, even if they at present would be inclined to refuse to do so (Scruton, 1992, pp. 213ff; compare Korsgaard, 1995, ch. 2).

[14] It remains a matter of some controversy what exactly constitutes the proper division of labour between political philosophers and institutional designers or policy analysts. For an interesting account see the Postscript in Shue (1996).

The Heuristics of Consent

In the previous discussion I wanted to point out that the problem of social order is distinctive from the problem of the moral order, that complying with a rule and accepting a rule are two different things, and that mechanisms and principles remain substantially different in nature even when both form an essential component of a general consent theory. I believe Suchanek invalidly collapses these distinctions together and that this has serious implications for his case against Justificationism: while his arguments are genuinely informative along many dimensions, they fail to invalidate Justificationism in general.

In the second part of his essay Suchanek proposes that we adopt a constitutional political economy approach and investigate the extent to which consent theory may serve as a heuristic for resolving the problem of social order. The idea underlying the heuristics of consent is that we can obtain crucial information by analysing the circumstances under which individuals consent to a given rule. However, I believe his restrictive use of consent as compliance also poses serious problems for the heuristics of consent. In this section I elaborate briefly on this point.

Suchanek develops his alternative approach along two lines. First, he argues that a heuristic approach to implicit consent allows us to 'learn something about [people's] preferences as the basis for their actual behavior' (p. 175) This is then meant to serve as a diagnosis of the constraints individuals face when agreeing to a rule, which under Suchanek's restricted view boils down to deciding whether or not to comply with a particular rule. Second, Suchanek also maintains that an analysis of the structure of the situation within which individuals operate is a necessary condition for improving conditions of cooperation. This is captured by the notion of hypothetical consent.

Unfortunately, I fail to see how an analysis of revealed preferences (implicit consent) or the background structure of individuals' rational choices (hypothetical consent) tells us anything more about the nature of *consent*. By restricting the notion of consent to compliance with a set of rules or decisions, Suchanek renders his theory vulnerable to the objection that the heuristics of consent in either its implicit or hypothetical form contributes little to social theory that is not already covered by mainstream rational choice and game theory. If the heuristics of consent generates equivalent insights to contemporary rational choice theory, what explanatory value has Suchanek's proposal to offer? For the heuristics of consent to have theoretical bite it must be the case that the act of consenting itself generates valuable information; information which, in turn, supports a stable system of mutually advantageous social cooperation. I believe *express consent* might satisfy this requirement. Let me demonstrate the argument by drawing a rough parallel between rules and consent.

Social theorists generally accept that, from the perspective of the individual, rules play two important roles. First, a rule provides important information about the sort of behavior that is expected from an individual. Second, because of its association with a sanctioning device, rules also provide important information about the overall likelihood that certain behavior will occur. This is often regarded as an extremely valuable property of rules, not only for institutional design at the societal level but also for individuals themselves.[15] It seems there are two ways in which we can secure a baseline of expected desirable behaviour. The first is by attaching sufficiently effective monitoring and sanctioning devices that make it costly for individuals to exhibit unwanted behaviour. The problem with this solution, familiar to economists and policy-makers, is that monitoring and sanctioning may be extremely costly in their own right – up to the point that it may be more efficient to allow a certain level of misconduct instead of introducing overall heavy monitoring and rule-enforcement (Milgrom and Roberts, 1992).

But there exists a second solution that builds on two assumptions. First, individuals who fully accept a given rule on balance are more likely to comply with it than individuals who do not accept it. Second, under certain conditions the overall level of acceptance of a rule gives a good indication of the expected level of compliance with that rule. This in turn generates valuable information about the practicality of instituting a particular rule. The information entailed by the *signalling* of general acceptance with a rule, then, does not only provide institutional designers with an indication of the level of sanctioning that is required to ensure that non-accepting individuals comply with a rule. It also forms a central piece of information for individuals who often decide to accept a certain rule based on information on how likely it is that other people accept it.[16]

Clearly, the 'heuristics of express consent' has important implications for the design of consent mechanisms. To begin with, it is clear that the relevant information must be *attainable to all relevant parties* – individuals as well as decision-makers. Some scholars have gone so far as to demand that votes should be made publicly accountable (Brennan and Pettit, 1990). At the very least it means adequate dissemination of information throughout all layers of the polity is essential. In addition, the background conditions under which individuals express their consent must be designed such that their acceptance of a rule has the highest *expressive value* – that is, it can be regarded by all relevant parties as expressing a free and genuine choice (Brennan and Lomasky, 1993; Schuessler, 2000).[17] If I have a reason to believe that your consent does not in fact properly reflect your acceptance of a decision, its signalling value is of little use. It goes without saying that combining these two features imposes serious demands on the types of procedures and mechanisms decision-makers can employ. Given the complexity of the matter it seems plausible that we need to think in terms of a set of mechanisms to jointly ensure as best as possible that people can freely express their consent with rules and decisions.[18] Needless to say it goes beyond the scope of this commentary to

[15] Jeremy Bentham, for instance, suggested that the expectation of behaviour is an important source of utility for the individual, thus providing a utilitarian justification for instituting a system of law. For an extensive analysis of this argument, see Kelly (1990a; 1990b).

[16] This is the 'reciprocal nature' of consent which Suchanek rightly draws our attention to on pp. 6-7. Many decisions take the form of an Assurance Game (Taylor, 1987).

[17] The present use of 'expressive value' is instrumental and accords more with Schuessler's than Brennan and Lomasky's approach to democratic politics.

[18] In practice a functional democracy is likely to contain a voting system in addition to other forms of representation, participation and deliberation. Political philosophers often fail to

further specify the heuristics of express consent. I would like to stress, however, that the present argument appears to genuinely validate a heuristic in addition to, and fully integrated with, a justificatory approach to the meaning of consent.

Conclusion

In this commentary I challenged Suchanek's essay on two grounds. First, I argued that his critique of the justificatory role of consent theory largely misses its target. Once we acknowledge the central role of distinctions such as moral vs. social order, acceptance of vs. compliance with rules, and principles vs. mechanisms, it seems Suchanek's concerns are at best orthogonal to the issues that justificatory consent theories traditionally address. I concluded that Suchanek might have a ground for complaints against those justificatory consent theorists who venture into practical issues without considering empirical constraints. But I have also argued that this in no way invalidates justificatory consent theory *in general*.

In addition, I listed some sceptical thought about the heuristic approach championed by Suchanek. The heuristics of implicit and hypothetical consent seem to me to simply repeat insights already obtained from rational choice theory and game theory. I have suggested, however, that one might vindicate the heuristic approach by focussing on express consent. Express consent serves an important signalling function under conditions of imperfect information and moral pluralism, and contemporary democratic theory would do well to integrate this function in its analysis of consent.

---

appreciate the contingencies associated with the choice of mechanisms, and normatively analyse one single mechanism. This probably constitutes one of the best examples of failing to appreciate the division of labour between political philosophers and institutional designers.

References

Barry, B. (1989) *Theories of Justice*, Hemel Hempstead (Harvester-Wheatsheaf).

Barry, B. (1995) *Justice as Impartiality*, Oxford (Clarendon Press).

Brennan, G. and L. Lomasky (1993) *Democracy and Decision: The Pure Theory of Electoral Preference*, Cambridge (Cambridge University Press).

Brennan, G. and P. Pettit (1990) "Unveiling the Vote", *British Journal of Political Science* 20, 311-333.

Buchanan, J. (1975) *The Limits of Liberty*, Chicago (University of Chicago Press).

Dryzek, J. (2001) *Deliberative Democracy and Beyond*, Oxford (Clarendon Press).

Dworkin, R. (1977) *Taking Rights Seriously*, London (Duckworth).

Elster, J. (1985) "Weakness of Will and the Free-Rider Problem", *Economics and Philosophy* 1, 231-265.

Gauthier, D. (1986) *Morals by Agreement*, Oxford (Clarendon Press).

Griffin, J. (1996) *Value Judgement: Improving Our Ethical Beliefs*, Oxford (Clarendon Press).

Hegel, G.W.F. (1967) *Philosophy of Right*, Knox, T.M. (ed.), Oxford (Oxford University Press).

Hobbes, T. (1991) *Leviathan*, Tuck, R. (ed.), Cambridge (Cambridge University Press).

Hooker, B. (2000) *Ideal Code, Real World: A Rule-Consequentialist Theory of Morality*, New York (Oxford University Press).

Hume, D. (1987) "Of the Original Contract", in *Essays. Moral, Political and Literary*, rev. ed. by Eugene Miller, Indianapolis (Liberty Classics).

Kant, I. (1993) *Grounding of the Metaphysic of Morals.* 3rd ed., trans. James Ellington, Indianapolis (Hackett Publishers).

Kelly, P. (1990a) "Utilitarian Strategies in Bentham and Mill", *Utilitas* 2 (2), 245-266.

Kelly, P. (1990b) *Utilitarianism and Distributive Justice: Jeremy Bentham and the Civil Law*, Oxford (Clarendon Press).

Knight, J. (1992) *Institutions and Social Conflict*, Cambridge (Cambridge University Press).

Korsgaard, C. (1995) *Creating the Kingdom of Ends*, New York (Cambridge University Press).

Locke, J. (1960) "Second Treatise of Government", in Peter Laslett (ed.) *Two Treatises of Government*, Cambridge (Cambridge University Press).

Milgrom, P. and J. Roberts (1992) *Economics, Organization & Management*, Englewood Cliffs (Prentice-Hall).

Nino, C. S. (1996) *The Constitution of Deliberative Democracy*, New Haven (Yale University Press).

O'Neill, O. (1989) *Constructions of Reason*, Cambridge (Cambridge University Press).

Pogge, T. (1989) *Realizing Rawls*, Ithaca (Cornell University Press).

Przeworski, A. (1999) "Minimalist Conception of Democracy: A Defence", in Shapiro, I. and C. Hacker-Cordon (eds.) *Democracy's Value*, Cambridge (Cambridge University Press).
Rawls, J. (1991) *A Theory of Justice* (rev. ed.), Oxford (Oxford University Press).
Rawls, J. (2001) *Justice as Fairness: A Restatement*, Erin Kelly (ed.) Cambridge, (Harvard University Press).
Rousseau, J. J. (1973) "The Social Contract", in Cole, G.D.H. (ed.) *The Social Contract and Discourses*, London (Dent).
Schuessler, A. (2000) *A Logic of Expressive Choice*, Princeton (Princeton University Press).
Scruton, R. (1992) "Contract, Consent and Exploitation: Kantian Themes", in Williams, H. (ed.) *Essays on Kant's Political Philosophy*, Cardiff (University of Wales Press).
Shue, H. (1996) *Basic Rights: Subsistence, Affluence and U.S. Foreign Policy* (2nd ed.) Princeton (Princeton University Press).
Simmons, A. J. (1993) *On the Edge of Anarchy: Locke, Consent, and the Limits of Society*, Princeton (Princeton University Press).
Simmons, A. J. (2001) *Justification and Legitimacy: Essays on Rights and Obligations*, Cambridge (Cambridge University Press).
Suchanek, A. (2004) "What is Meant by Consent?", in this volume.
Taylor, M. (1987) *The Possibility of Cooperation*, Cambridge (Cambridge University Press).
Thaler, R. (1992) *The Winner's Curse: Paradoxes and Anomalies of Economic Life*, Princeton (Princeton University Press).

Chapter 8

The Consequences of Popular Participation in Constitutional Choice – Towards a Comparative Analysis

Stefan Voigt*

Abstract

Discourse ethics and constitutional economics are usually perceived as normative ventures. Notwithstanding substantial differences, representatives of both programs can agree on the claim that 'discourse matters', or rather that 'discourse should matter'. Representatives of the young research program of positive constitutional economics are, in turn, interested in testable hypotheses concerning choice and development of constitutional rules. In this paper, the conjecture that 'discourse matters for the choice and development of constitutional rules' is taken as the starting point. After dealing with the issue of how one can make the notion of 'discourse' empirically tractable, possible transmission mechanisms between (a) 'discourse' and the content of the constitution, and (b) 'discourse' and the success of a constitution are generated. It is shown that the hypotheses are, in principle, testable.

... and were one to choose a period of time, when the people's consent was the least regarded in public transactions, it would be precisely on the establishment of a new government. In a settled constitution, their inclinations are often consulted; but during the fury of revolutions, conquests, and public convulsions, military force or political craft usually decides the controversy.

(David Hume, 1777/1985, p. 474).

1 Introduction

When South Africa's constituent assembly discussed the possible contents of a new Constitution in 1996/97, South Africa's citizens were encouraged to participate actively in the process by making proposals. This is by no means the only case in which active participation of citizens was solicited: another example for encouraged citizen input is Poland's post-socialist Constitution (Czeszejko-Sochacki and Machacek, 1992). In these two cases, a new regime went along with a new constitution. But active participation has also been encouraged when the aim was constitutional reform within a stable regime: when the old Soviet Constitution of 1936 was reformed in 1978, more than half a million proposals from citizens were counted.

Drawing exclusively on these three examples, the effects of broad popular participation in constitutional choice seem mixed at best. But three examples taken at random do not make for convincing empirical evidence. In this paper, we will try to deal a bit more systematically with two aspects of popular participation in constitutional choice: the first is concerned with the consequences of popular participation: does it have a discernible effect on the contents of the constitution, does it influence its legitimacy, will constitutions be more successful when broad participation in its genesis has taken place? The second aspect is concerned with the preconditions for popular participation: can we identify conditions under which it is more likely that popular input will be solicited?

Discourse Ethics and Constitutional Economics are conventionally perceived as normative ventures. My interest is, however, rather with testable hypotheses, i.e. with positive theory. I will therefore distinguish between the more traditional Normative Constitutional Economics and Positive Constitutional Economics (Voigt, 1997). My interest in this paper is in identifying the (implicit) hypotheses that the representatives of the two normative approaches might have, in spelling them out explicitly, and making them amenable to empirical tests. Both Discourse Ethics and Normative Constitutional Economics can be understood as procedural theories. I therefore assume that representatives of both approaches could agree on the simple conjecture that 'procedure matters'. In this paper, the central question is to what degree the procedures used for choosing constitutional rules matter for their subsequent success. As representatives of both approaches emphasize the importance of voluntary consent of all those possibly concerned, the participation of all those possibly concerned will supposedly have some effects.

The rest of the paper is organized as follows: the next section serves to identify some of the central notions of Discourse Ethics as well as of Normative Constitutional Economics. In the third section, the terms 'participation' and 'deliberation' are delineated and possible criteria for comparing contents and success of constitutions are presented. Section four contains a number of hypotheses. Section five concludes.

2 From Discourse Ethics to Constitutional Economics

Discourse Ethics as developed by Karl-Otto Apel and Jürgen Habermas and Normative Constitutional Economics as developed by James Buchanan and his various co-authors share a number of commonalities. At the same time, there are important differences in aim, approach, and assumptions between the two programs. Some of the commonalities and the differences will be highlighted in the first subsection. Special emphasis will be on the relationship of aim, approach, and assumptions of both these programs in comparison with the more standard economic approach of which the representatives of both programs are highly critical. In the second subsection, one attempt to apply some concepts that have been proposed and developed by Habermas to the study of empirical phenomena will be summarized and critically evaluated. It is Jon Elster's (1991; 1995) attempt to analyze the proceedings of two constituent assemblies – namely the U.S. American one of 1787 and the French one beginning two years later – within an analytical framework based on central notions of Discourse Ethics.

2.1 Commonalities/Differences between Discourse Ethics and Constitutional Economics

The two programs share a common starting point: drawing on metaphysics or religion can no longer legitimize the rules which are to structure individual interaction. Representatives of both programs develop a procedural approach which is to help in identifying legitimate rules. Buchanan is interested in identifying rules that everybody could agree to and that therefore promise to be Pareto-improvements. Habermas is more pretentious: he is not only interested in the legitimacy of positively made law, but is interested in identifying the conditions under which a universally acceptable ethics could be brought about. Under ideal conditions, consensus is – sufficient for Habermas to pronounce truth judgments.

Habermas is not interested in unanimity as such. A unanimously agreed compromise could also be the result of promises or threats that are connected with the resource endowment of those compromising and not – at least not solely – the quality of their arguments. He distinguishes between pragmatic, ethic, and moral discourses (1992, pp. 198ff.) but knows that there will be situations in which bargaining instead of discourse will carry the day. For Buchanan, on the other hand, unanimity – as long as it was not achieved by using force – is sufficient to legitimize rules. If nobody vetoes a proposal for a new rule, this is interpreted as sufficient reason to assume that nobody expects to be worse off with the newly proposed rule. Unanimity is thus sufficient to conclude that a rule which has passed that test ought to be implemented. In comparing Discourse Ethics with Normative Constitutional Economics, Vanberg and Buchanan (1991) have put on a par the notion of contract with 'agreement as compromise' and the notion of discourse with 'agreement as truth-judgment'. But they do introduce a distinction reminiscent of the Habermasian distinction between discourse and bargaining, namely the one between 'interests' and 'theories'. In disagreements concerning interests, it is the evaluative component which is more important; in those concerning theories, it is the cognitive component.[1]

[1] Elster (1998, pp. 100f.) assumes that members of constitutional assemblies will have fundamental preferences, beliefs about ends-means relations, and policy preferences which follow from the first two. In the language of Vanberg and Buchanan, fundamental preferences are equivalent with interests, and beliefs with theories of the actors. He notes that there might be cases in which both fundamental preferences and beliefs deviate among delegates which could result in their canceling each other out. He believes this to be quite a common phenomenon. Consent may thus be the consequence of non-compatible theories. Had the participants aligned their theories first would they not have reached agreement.

Getting to yea or: how to reach consensus Representatives of neither program are very keen on empirical consent. Whereas representatives of Discourse Ethics go through pains in specifying an ideal speech situation, representatives of Normative Constitutional Economics introduce a veil of ignorance (Rawls, 1971) or uncertainty (Buchanan and Tullock, 1962). Behind that veil, discourse participants do not have at their disposal knowledge concerning their individual interests, which leads them to opt in favor of 'fair' or 'impartial' rules. Vanberg and Buchanan (1989) have argued that it would be desirable to have a situation in which there is a very thick veil concerning the interest dimension, yet a very thin one concerning the theory dimension. Representatives of Discourse Ethics go on and compare the ideal speech situation with realized or realizable speech situations whereas some normative constitutional economists claim that it would be in the interests of the relevant actors to artificially make the veil thicker (see Tschentscher, 2000 for the different speech situations as well as for the different notions of consent between the two programs and Voigt, 1994 for a critique of the use of the veil in Normative Constitutional Economics).

Getting rid of homo oeconomicus *or: criticizing the behavioral model of mainstream economics* Another commonality is the critique concerning the assumptions of standard economics. Naturally, this critique is spelled out in much more detail by Buchanan. Habermas points out that rational choice theory is still concerned with solving the Hobbesian problem of order (1992, p. 408). It has often been pointed out that on the basis of the standard *homo oeconomicus* assumptions, the emergence of stable order cannot be explained convincingly. This is a critique that Buchanan cannot claim to have solved: his version of the social contract is susceptible to the critique that has been brought up against these theories ever since Hume (Voigt, 1999).

Buchanan's problems with economics deal with welfare economics: he evaluates the notion of an omniscient observer as 'wholly unacceptable' (1959, p. 126). According to Buchanan, utility is a subjective concept, which does not allow for intersubjective comparison. Since an economist reflecting on efficiency will only express her assessments concerning the preferences of others and not their true preferences, Buchanan deems it appropriate to talk of 'presumptive efficiency' (ibid.), or of hypotheses of an economist on what could be efficient. To find out whether it really is efficient, one would need to test whether unanimity for the policy proposed can be achieved. In his early writings, Buchanan thus clearly parted from the approach according to which it is sufficient that a solitary scientist claims to have identified better rules in his ivory tower. Buchanan then added the necessity to put the hypotheses generated to an empirical test, i.e. to really ask empirically existing people.

Habermas would supposedly share some of this critique: his switch from practical to communicative reason has a similar purpose. In his case, it is not the assumption of perfect knowledge concerning the preferences of millions of others that forms his practice target but the assumption that by drawing on practical reason, one would be able to identify universally acceptable law or ethics. Whether

Habermas – and Buchanan – leave the Kantian monologue convincingly behind will be discussed below.

Concerning rational choice theory, Habermas criticizes two assumptions (stable preferences, utility-maximizing behavior) as 'unrealistic' (1992, p. 408). Although Buchanan is an economist, he has also frequently parted from the assumption of stable preferences (e.g. in 1954; 1959; 1994).[2] Economists usually assume preferences to be stable not because they believed that this assumption was 'realistic' in the sense of a reasonably good description of reality but out of methodological concerns. Economists work with models that abstract from many traits found in reality. Complexity reduction is a precondition for constructing models that can be used to generate predictions. Economists thus evaluate models according to the quality of the output achieved with them, i.e. the quality of the predictions, and not by the realistic 'fit' of the input, i.e. the assumptions.

Do not try to argue with homo oeconomicus*? Or: why the assumption of stable preferences is not necessarily an impediment to a fruitful dialogue* Habermas emphasizes that individually declared preferences are not necessarily those preferences that individuals would pronounce were they better informed after deliberating the pros and cons (1992, p. 408). This is apparently meant as 'proof' that the stable preferences assumptions of rational choice theory would be 'unrealistic' or inadequate. *Prima facie*, deliberation and discourse seem to be incompatible with a *homo oeconomicus* who has stable preferences. Deliberation and discourse imply that individually *declared* preferences can change, otherwise deliberation would be pointless.

As pointed out earlier the 'realistic fit' of assumptions is not a good criterion for evaluating the assumptions used in economics. Even if that argument is not accepted for whatever reasons, Habermas' observation is not sufficient for proving that the preferences of real individuals are not factually stable. It might be helpful to distinguish two aspects of this observation: (1) participants in a discourse can have incomplete information concerning the existence or availability of options, or (2) they can have incomplete information concerning the different consequences of alternative options. They might, e.g. continuously buy C-Cola because they have never heard of D-Cola. Communicating with others, they might learn of the exis-

2 Note that 'the early Buchanan' argued very similarly (1959, p. 136): According to Buchanan, the meaning of discussion is 'precisely that of changing "tastes" among social alternatives'. An interesting example in which Buchanan combines the assumption of instable preferences with an unsurpassed paternalism is this (1986, pp. 89f.): 'Auf einer zweiten oder "konstitutionellen" Ebene des Diskurses müssen aber vorhandene Sets von Präferenzen nicht als gegeben akzeptiert werden, und eines der Ziele eines solchen Diskurses ist ja in der Tat eine wirksame Kritik solcher Präferenzen, die auf eine Verbesserung durch angemessenen institutionellen Wandel abzielt. Präferenzen für Kitsch sind auf dieser Ebene nicht so gut wie Präferenzen für Dichtung, und eine der Hauptaufgaben des Sozialphilosophen und Wissenschaftlers ist die Gestaltung einer konstitutionell-institutionellen Struktur, welche die Hervorbringung "besserer" Präferenzen (z.B. Dichtung) fördert'.

tence of D-Cola and realize that its consumption contributes more to their individual utility than C-Cola. The subsequent change in behavior is not due to a change of preferences that was brought about by this 'discourse' but to the more complete information.

The second aspect is very similar to the first: before entering into a discourse, an individual might have opted in favor of liberalizing opening hours of stores. After discussing the pros and cons with others, he might have learned of a number of cause-effect-relationships, possibly consisting of externalities and more indirect – and less obvious – consequences that these others expect to be relevant. After a discourse, he might indeed declare a preference different from the one declared before entering into a discourse.[3] But again, it does not seem to make sense to interpret this as a case of unstable preferences but simply as one of incomplete information. We can draw an important insight from this discussion: the assumption of stable preferences does not preclude the possibility that after a discourse people prefer options different from those they had declared to prefer before entering into the discourse.[4] It is, however, important to highlight the incompatibility of another standard assumption of economics with the discourse notion, namely the concept of 'perfect' or 'complete' rationality. A completely rational individual has been described as endowed with the capacity to foresee everything that could possibly happen and be capable of weighing all possible outcomes against each other and to optimally decide between them, all in an instant and costlessly (Kreps, 1990, p. 745).

Incomplete information is a logical precondition for the possibility of a useful dialogue.[5] Discourse might have yet another function difficult to incorporate into standard models based on standard assumptions of rationality: together with the assumption of incomplete information as just introduced we have implicitly introduced the assumption that the entire available knowledge is not concentrated in one representative head (i.e. is available for everybody) but is scattered. To draw on a Hayekian idea: there is not only a division of labor but also a division of knowledge. The next modification would be no longer to assume that all knowledge is given but that communication can lead to the generation of new ideas and new hypotheses. An implicit assumption of the discourse notion seems to be that chances to generate new ideas or hypotheses are higher while discussing than while sitting solitarily in one's armchair.[6]

---

3 For decades, the political magazine 'Pro & Contra' on German television was built exactly on that idea: let the audience vote *ex ante*, then have an intense discussion, and let the audience vote again *ex post*.

4 It seems that the analytical distinction between interests and theories is not of great help here: cognition is a precondition for evaluation, the distinction is thus difficult to carry through.

5 This does, however, not mean that more information will necessarily lead to better decisions. This would only be true for complete information.

6 Economists might accept this argument but would immediately think about the optimal number of participants in a discourse: surely, there would be a tradeoff between more hy-

But introducing bounded rationality in order to create space for deliberation seems to be *ad hoc*. Although it seems to be quite plausible to work with the assumption of bounded rationality, this concept needs to be specified before one can use it in formal models. It has been noted (Kreps, 1998) that this is often done in an *ad hoc*-manner.

Can it be rational to remain mute? Or: why rational ignorance might make people abstain from participating in deliberation For economists, it is not sufficient to point towards the fact that with regard to constitutional choice, actors have incomplete information about the different consequences of alternative rules. Representatives of discourse theory seem to assume at least implicitly that those affected have incentives to participate in a discourse in order to increase the commonly consensual knowledge. Economists would ask what incentives individuals could have to spend resources on such an activity. In questions of constitutional choice, all members of a society are 'affected'. Supposedly, however, the individual impact on those rules chosen will be marginal at best. Thus, participation in a discourse on constitutional rules seems irrational. This is called rational ignorance in economics.

Bruno Frey (1979, p. 317; see also McCormick and Tollison, 1981, pp. 127f.) tries to make broad participation in constitutional choice plausible: '... it is relatively easy to bring latent groups to participation in the working out of a constitutional contract with its once-and-for-all character even where they cannot be induced to participate continuously'. The argument is based on the assumptions (1) that constitutions comprise a multitude of rules which will have substantial consequences for every actor and (2) that constitutions are made to last, which makes their allocative and distributive effects even more severe. Once the basic constitutional decisions have been made and constitutional change only occurs at the margin, the potential external costs that can be put onto individuals are relatively small so that participation will only be rational for organized interest groups with special stakes. These arguments imply that the rational interest of individuals leads to a public discourse in constitutional matters. Given that constitutions will be implemented and will last, effects on the individual will indeed be substantial. This does, however, not change anything with regard to the marginal influence an individual can rationally expect to have on the constitution. Standard theory will thus repeat that remaining mute is rational.

Do we have a deal? Or: how to ascertain consensus One problem that Discourse Ethics and Normative Constitutional Economics share is the issue of how to ascertain consensus. Remember that Habermas criticizes the Kantian notion of *prak-*

---

potheses generated due to more participants on the one hand and less chances of consent on the other.

Van Aaken (2001) criticizes representatives of Discourse Ethics for not sufficiently taking opportunity costs and scarcity in general into account.

tische Vernunft as leading to monologues. In order to be of additional value, a *real* discourse has to take place. The relevance of consensus under non-ideal circumstances remains, however, unclear.[7] In 1959, Buchanan was still pleading to test whether consent could be factually attained (1959, p. 127). In the meantime, he has retreated to a hypothetical consent which opens the door for broad discretion by all those external observers who ask themselves whether a particular rule could have generated general agreement (see Voigt 1996, 169f. for a more detailed critique).

The main argument of *Facts and Norms* is that the rule of law cannot be sustained without radical democracy (1992, p. 13). Regrettably, Habermas says very little about origin and rise of the rule of law. For most of his analysis, the constitution seems to be exogenously given. In the chapter on deliberative politics he explains, e.g., that the success of deliberative politics depends on the institutionalization of respective procedures (ibid., p. 361). This may well be true but as someone interested to know how procedures originate and evolve, I would have liked to learn how they come about or – for the more normatively inclined – how they could be brought about.[8]

To sum up: Discourse Ethics and Normative Constitutional Economics share an emphasis on procedures. For normative constitutional economists, agreement will be sufficient to legitimize rules whereas representatives of discourse ethics are interested in truth-judgments. Due to their emphasis on procedures both programs have difficulties with standard welfare economics with its emphasis on concrete results. For discourse to be possibly relevant, one however does not have to give up the assumption of stable preferences but has to focus on incomplete information and bounded rationality. Under such circumstances, the readiness of actors to invest in information concerning the working properties of alternative constitutional rules cannot simply be assumed but needs to be explained. Both approaches have problems in transferring their procedural proposals into the real world. It is thus no mean feat for somebody interested in positive analysis to draw from these theories.

---

7 Habermas (1992, p. 392) writes: 'Die kontrafaktischen Voraussetzungen, von denen Argumentationsteilnehmer ausgehen müssen, eröffnen zwar eine Perspektive, aus der sie die im Handeln und Erleben unentrinnbare Provinzialität ihrer raumzeitlichen Kontexte und die vor Ort eingespielten Praktiken der Rechtfertigung übersteigen, also dem Sinn *transzendierender* Geltungsansprüche gerecht werden können. Aber mit den transzendierenden Geltungsansprüchen versetzen sie sich nicht selbst ins transzendente Jenseits eines idealen Reiches intelligibler Wesen. Anders als beim Entwurf von Idealen, in deren Licht wir *Abweichungen* identifizieren können, kommt "ein Entsprechungsverhältnis oder ein Vergleich zwischen Idee und Realität bei den idealisierenden Unterstellungen, die wir immer schon vornehmen müssen, wenn wir uns überhaupt miteinander verständigen wollen, gar nicht ins Spiel"' (Habermas quotes Hauke Brunkhorst here).

8 In the chapter on the principles of the rule of law, he concedes that there might be situations in which there will be no place for moral or ethic-political discourses but only for bargaining. But even in such situations, there is a place for the principle of discourse, namely in the procedures that regulate the bargaining processes according to fairness-aspects (ibid., pp. 204f.). Again, one would have liked to know how they came about. I suspect that Habermas' reasoning is subject to an infinite regress here.

In *Facts and Norms*, Habermas (1992, pp. 195f.) endorses Kriele's judgment 'daß die Logik des Diskurses mit den rechtsstaatlich institutionalisierten Verfahren nicht auf kurzschlüssige Weise zusammengeführt werden darf. Eine unvermittelte Anwendung der Diskursethik oder eines ungeklärten Diskursbegriffs auf den demokratischen Prozeß führt zu Ungereimtheiten; diese bieten dann Skeptikern Vorwände, um den Entwurf einer Diskurstheorie des Rechts und der Politik schon im Ansatz zu diskreditieren'. I cannot help but read this as a strategy of immunization: if you try to apply Habermas' reflections on the real world, he might reply that you did it in a short circuit manner.[9] Against the immunizing-strategy, two aspects are encouraging: (1) There is somebody else who has tried to apply Habermasian notions to the analysis of constitutional choice, namely Jon Elster and (2) Habermas even describes his approach approvingly (ibid., p. 413). This is why Jon Elster's approach will be described and its shortcomings critically evaluated in the next subsection.

2.2 Making Discourse Ethics Susceptible of Positive Constitutional Economics

As already spelled out above, Habermas distinguishes between various modes of discourse (pragmatic, ethic-political, moral) on the one hand and bargaining on the other. In his analysis of the proceedings of two constitutional assemblies – namely the U.S. American one of 1787 and the French one subsequent to the revolution – Elster distinguishes between two kinds of speech acts: arguing and bargaining. In arguing, it is the better argument that counts whereas in bargaining, the credibility of the pronounced promises and threats are decisive. In discourse processes, strategic misrepresentation of one's own preferences does not make any sense, whereas they are the name of the game in bargaining. In rational discourses, due to the introduction of a veil of ignorance, the concrete traits of the participants are irrelevant whereas the flesh and bone does enter into bargaining.

But Elster does not stop here: he observes that in the two constituent assemblies, there were many instances in which representatives attempted to use arguments strategically, i.e. situations in which they tried to disguise self-interested behavior in terms of the public good. The central question then becomes: '*why argue at all?*'. One could, after all, bargain right away or even vote without any prior discussion at all.

Elster (1991) presents three possible answers.

1. If others believe that one really is arguing from principle, they may be ready to give in more easily. This will, however, only work if others are convinced that among the given population, there are some people who really act on principle. If nobody does, pretending to act on principle does not make any sense. To use Weber's (1922/1985) terminology, the argument presupposes that there are some people who act according to *Wertrationalität*, and not solely to *Zweckrationalität*. Such behavioral assumptions are, however, incompatible with homo

[9] I wonder why the concept of discourse is still 'unclear' or 'obscure' after so many years of deliberation about it.

oeconomicus as generally conceived. The argument further presupposes that actors are incapable of sorting perfectly between types who really act on principle and those who only pretend to.
2. Macey (1986, p. 251) has suggested that public-regarding language is often used as 'subterfuge' for deals that are special interest deals. This subterfuge would make it more costly for the public and concerned rival groups to discover the true effects of such legislation. For this argument to go through, we must again assume positive information costs and/or bounded rationality.
3. People who are uncertain as to who has the better argument might actually be persuaded by a strategic use of argument. Elster supposes that there are some people who are neutral with regard to a given proposal, i.e. their individual interests are not at stake. This could work even if the third party knows that the others are moved entirely by self-interest.

Elster then asks under what conditions a norm against pronouncing purely self-interested claims can be expected to be strong and hypothesizes that it will be stronger in constituent assemblies than in ordinary legislatures. Secondly, the norm will have more impact in public settings than in cases in which discussions take place behind closed doors. He expects this to be the case because a broad public will not accept its representatives resorting to outright power games. In order to assess the consequences of strategic uses of argument, Elster goes on to compare the consequences of bargaining on efficiency and equity with those of strategic uses of arguing:

1. With regard to bargaining, the parties have incentives to misrepresent their preferences, which might lead to outcomes inferior to those that would attain had they reported their true preferences. There is no analogue to this in the strategic use of argument.
2. If credible promises are impossible, outcomes that might be attainable if that were the case may be unreachable in bargaining; this could be less severe in the strategic use of argument because 'the very same motives that make speakers adopt the arguing rather than the bargaining attitude in the first place will also induce them to keep their promises' (ibid., pp. 249f.).
3. If commitment is possible, the bargaining mode might lead the parties to commit to incompatible solutions, which might lead to an impasse. This would also apply to strategic uses of bargaining.

Elster (ibid., p. 250) concludes: 'It follows, I think, that neither bargaining nor strategic use of impartial reasoning is unambiguously more efficient than the other. By contrast, I believe we can assert that argument – even when purely strategic and based on self-interest – tends to yield more equitable outcomes than bargaining'. He calls this effect the 'civilizing force of hypocrisy' (1991, pp. 83ff.). The discussion is summed up (1995, p. 250) with the claim that 'according to this criterion private settings are always better than public settings, for a given mode of communication; and that arguing is always better than bargaining, for a given setting'.

This result can be represented in a simple 2x2-matrix:

	Arguing	Bargaining
Secret	1 →	2(3)
Open	3(2) ←	4

If the two dimensions were independent of each other, one would choose a secret setting in which the participants would argue. Elster, however, believes them to be interdependent: secrecy would induce bargaining, whereas openness would increase the chances of the participants to be arguing (as indicated by the arrows). The rank ordering shows that the best (1) and the worst combination (4) can be clearly named but that there is uncertainty concerning the 'middle options'. Now if that is true and the two dimensions are indeed not independent of each other, then there is not much of a recommendation that can be drawn from this exercise: whether participants can be induced to argue or whether deliberation takes place in public or not does not seem to make much of a difference. In a later paper (Elster 1998, p. 117), Elster proposes a combination of openness and secrecy taking the conflicting elements explicitly into account: elements of secrecy (committees) should be combined with elements of openness (plenary discussions held publicly).

After having described Elster's approach, we now turn to (i) highlight some possible implications, (ii) then to criticize the approach, and finally (iii) identify the questions that follow from it. The last topic serves as a prelude to our own research agenda.

Implications For a given mode of communication, Elster would always prefer secrecy to openness on the grounds that openness in constitutional debates leads participants to pronounce claims that they have difficulty resorting from later on. It is astonishing that someone who derives his argument with notions taken from Discourse Ethics pronounces such a claim. He argues explicitly against the possibility of a broad public to follow the deliberations on the constitution. This presupposes that he also argues against a broad active participation of the public or parts thereof. He is thus in favor of representation as well as of intransparency.

Suppose his hypothesis that arguing is to be preferred over bargaining on grounds of efficiency and equity is correct. Then, institutional structures that encourage arguing should be established. This is exactly the method Elster uses to explain the differences in the use of argument and bargaining between the two constituent assemblies.[10] One of the more concrete hypotheses (1995, p. 249) reads: 'The norm against self-interested claims can be expected to be stronger in constituent assemblies than in ordinary legislatures'. Now if that is true and strategic use of

---

10 1995, p. 244: 'My strategy in this chapter will be to treat these differences between the two assemblies as endogenous to the institutional context'.

argument will lead to more equitable outcomes, then this would be an argument in favor of having constituent assemblies.

In a later paper, Elster (1998) explicitly draws some normative conclusions. They are: (1) specially convened constitutional assemblies ought to write constitutions. (2) Other actors whose behavior is to be regulated by the constitution such as the executive, the judiciary, and the military should not be part of the constitution-making process. (3) There ought to be a mix between secrecy and openness. (4) Elections to the constitutional assembly ought to be based on proportional representation. (5) The constitutional assembly should be convened outside the capital and other major cities. (6) The constitution should be ratified by referendum. (7) The constitution should only enter into force after x years (Elster proposes 20) after having been completed.

Critique Elster's approach is based on the presumption that it is possible to distinguish unequivocally between the three modes of communication. This might, however, not be as easy as Elster implicitly seems to assume: if participants can be made to believe that one is really arguing out of concern for the public good and not only out of pretending to do so, why should an observer not be subject to the same sorting problems?

Elster uses an unspecified combination of efficiency and equity to rank arguing and bargaining. It is curious that the strategic use of arguing is not ranked as a separate communication mode of its own. Different from what Elster assumes, the name of the game in the strategic use of arguing is the misrepresentation of one's preferences. But the more general critique is this: for normative constitutional economists, efficiency and equity are consequences of the rules chosen unanimously on the constitutional level. A result-oriented efficiency-criterion is substituted for a rule-oriented one. Following Wicksell (1896), rules are assumed to be efficient if they have been agreed to unanimously. Re-introducing the standard efficiency criterion in order to evaluate the alternative efficiency criterion that was only introduced because the feasibility of the standard criterion was questioned thus seems to make little sense.

Elster never specifies his notion of equity. But he assumes that the (strategic) use of argument will lead to more equitable outcomes than bargaining. This is evaluated positively and called the civilizing force of hypocrisy. Suppose a constituent assembly decided to use unanimity as the voting rule for passing the final constitutional draft. I fail to see why results should be more equitable with the strategic use of arguing than with bargaining. Strategic use of argument is nothing but bargaining in disguise. If one is not only interested in the document produced by a constituent assembly but in its chances to be structuring collective choices later on (thus the general function of a constitution), ignoring the bargaining power of the relevant interests will reduce the chances of the document ever becoming relevant in any meaningful sense. In order to be implemented, a constitution needs to be self-enforceable, i.e. no relevant actor must have incentives not to act according to the rules laid down in the document. If – while formulating the document – the bargaining power of the relevant actors, i.e. their ability and willingness to inflict costs on others, is not sufficiently taken into account, this will reduce chances that the constitution will be self-enforceable.

The mix between secrecy and publicness seems to be a safe middleway between two extremes. Yet, Elster has not shown with any rigor that this middleway can be expected to lead to better outcomes, indeed he did not even make a plausible verbal argument in its favor. It thus remains to be shown.

Questions We have criticized Elster's approach for not generating solid hypotheses. One question then almost suggests itself: why draw on it at all? Simply stated: because he explicitly raises a host of very interesting questions that he then does not deal with or does not answer. The nice thing about his approach is thus exactly its incompleteness. Let me explain.

Elster compares two historic constituent assemblies and comes up with the result that in both arguing and bargaining played a certain role. Although he presents the hypothesis that arguing and bargaining are induced by respective institutional structures and can thus be endogenized, it does not lead to any solid results since it is unclear how bargaining conducted behind closed doors compares to arguing publicly. That 'there was' arguing and bargaining in both assemblies is not an interesting result as such. But three questions almost seem to suggest themselves: (1) are there any systematic consequences concerning the *content* of the constitutional document that can be explained with the differential use of arguing and bargaining? (2) are there any systematic consequences concerning the *success* of the constitutional document that can be explained with the differential use of arguing and bargaining? (3) under which conditions can we expect a constituent assembly to be formed?[11]

Although Elster does explicitly not deal with the second question (1991, p. 15: 'Specifically, I shall not try to explain why the American constitution succeeded whereas the French did not'), he offers criteria for the success of constitutions that will be taken up later. Moreover, he suggests a host of interesting questions how the procedures being used for drafting a constitution could influence its content, e.g., (i) what are the consequences of time limits for constitutional conventions, (ii) how do constitutional conventions that simultaneously serve as legislatures allocate their time between the two functions?, (iii) what are the effects of conducting the discussions behind closed doors?, (iv) what are the effects of regularly informing the public about the progress of the constitutional negotiations? and (v) how can certain super-majorities and election rules determine the outcome of conventions?

Economists would start to derive hypotheses by drawing on some behavioral model. As a second step, they would then try to test these hypotheses explicitly. Qualitative data as those provided by Elster with regard to his two constituent assemblies will not convince many economists. They would prefer quantitative in-

---

[11] There are other interesting questions: is it possible to assess the relevance of the civilizing force of hypocrisy empirically? Are there any discernible differences between societies concerning the strength of the underlying norm? Is the underlying norm issue-specific, i.e. does the force depend on the issue dealt with? Etc.

stead of qualitative analyses. By critically reviewing Elster, we have thus identified our own research agenda with regard to constitutional choice: we are interested in the consequences of constitutional deliberation on the content of the constitution as well as on its success. In order to test our hypotheses, we would prefer quantitative instead of qualitative evidence. Ideally, we would also aim at identifying the conditions that lead to implement various options of having a constitution drafted.

3 How to Measure Deliberation, Content, and Success

The basic conjecture that we would like to test is whether deliberation or, more broadly, participation matters. It could matter for the content of a constitution as well as for its success. To make the conjecture plausible, three elements are necessary. We first need an indicator for deliberation or participation. We secondly need an indicator for the content as well as for the success of a constitution. The third ingredient, hypotheses on transmission mechanisms from participation to content and success will be the topic of section 4.

3.1 Deliberation and Participation Indicators

Attempting to measure the deviation of some empirical deliberation process with some ideal speech situation seems to be an impossible task: one would need some metric to be able to measure the deviation. An ideal speech situation comprises many dimensions and a one-dimensional measure would thus presuppose solving tradeoff and weighting problems, which would have to be based on some criteria. This approach thus appears to be infeasible. But we are interested in factual, real or empirical discourses and therefore need some way to compare them.

Participation can be conceived of as the possibility of a number of members of a society (at the margin all of them) to have the right to speak and to see their pronouncements enter into decision-making. Deliberation presupposes discussion. Discussion presupposes the participation of at least two discussants. In that sense, participation is a precondition for deliberation. It is a necessary, but not a sufficient condition for deliberation.

We now turn towards naming possible components of deliberation with regard to constitutional choice that are, at least in principle, measurable and thus comparable. The relevance of deliberation in a given society can be ascertained by asking whether the constitution was brought about by a body exclusively created for that purpose. Parliaments that also serve as constitutional assemblies have to allocate their time between discussing the possible contents of a constitution and their normal duties as legislators. The existence of a constitutional assembly whose only job it is to come up with a new constitution can thus be interpreted as enabling a higher degree of deliberation.[12] If parliament forms a committee with the exclusive task of

[12] Mueller (1996, ch. 21) makes the following observations with regard to this topic: When legislators draft and/or enact a constitution, they (1) will allocate a disproportionately high

drafting a constitution, this will not count as a constitutional assembly in our sense because the members of the committee are still parliamentarians and play repeated games involving party loyalty and the like. If deliberation matters, then constitutions drafted by constitutional assemblies in our sense should be different from those drafted by other bodies. This should show in their contents as well as in their success.

But not all constitutional assemblies are alike. We propose a number of criteria that enable us to compare them with regard to deliberation. These criteria measure neither deliberation nor participation directly but some *institutional prerequisites* favorable to deliberation: (i) According to what procedures are the delegates chosen or are they named by representatives of the former regime now to be replaced? Are they elected by universal suffrage? Are they elected as individuals or as representatives of a political party? What is the election rule used? How many electoral districts are used? Election of individuals could advance the possibility that constitutional experts be elected to the constitutional assembly. Their presence would supposedly be correlated with the quality of deliberation to be expected.[13]

It is well known that there are two views of representation (Breton and Galeotti, 1985; see also Mueller, 1989, chapter 12): representatives of the first view concentrate on decisions being made and carried out while representatives of the second view stress the desirability to have as many currents of political thinking represented. Representatives of the first view would opt for plurality rule, which induces two party-systems whereas representatives of the second view would opt in favor of proportional representation, which induces multi-party systems (Duverger's Law). Usually, the voting rule is part of the constitution and the number of parties is determined on the post-constitutional level of choice. But these considerations can also be applied to an anterior level, namely the 'constitution of the constitutional assembly', i.e. to the procedures that are used in order to elect the delegates. If proportional representation is used, this is thus interpreted to be more in favor of deliberation than plurality rule.

(ii) Deliberation in the real world takes time. If participants are to listen to each other, no more than one participant can speak at a time. On the other hand 'If it did

---

percentage of time on deciding short-term issues, thus neglect constitutional issues that are more relevant in the long run. (2) As members of parliament who want to be re-elected, representatives of the constitutional assembly will be less ready to sacrifice the interests of their constituents in favor of the good of the whole nation. (3) Representatives might play an outright power game and support only those proposals that are in the interests of their parties or even only in their personal interests.

[13] Elster (1998, p. 109) presumes that '(t)hose who know a great deal about a subject also tend to have an interest in it or to be moved by strong passions'. If that presumption was correct, the normative implication could be to try to keep experts out of deliberations. Note that his presumption runs counter to what unites representatives of Discourse Ethics and Normative Constitutional Economics, namely that presence and use of theoretical knowledge will further the common good, however defined.

not matter when people agreed, it would not matter whether or not they agreed at all' (Cross, 1965, p. 196). There is thus a premium on time. The more generous the time limit given to a constitutional assembly, the more weight is supposedly given to deliberation. Often, new constitutions are written in times of crises and the premium can be very high. This shows that deliberation might come at substantial costs.[14]

(iii) The voting rule used within the constitutional assembly can also be used as a proxy for the importance of deliberation. The deliberative ideal of consensus is easily translatable into the unanimity rule. The less inclusive the necessary majority, the less importance is attributed to deliberation.

Let us now turn to the more inclusive concept of participation. A first aspect of participation could be the size of the constituent assembly: the larger it is, the broader is formal participation.[15] If we assume that for reasons of practicality, most constituent assemblies cannot be made up of all members of society but of representatives, we can ask whether there are formalized ways to participate in the deliberations on the constitution for those who are not delegates. (i) There might be a provision that gives certain groups a right to make proposals concerning the constitution. (ii) There might also be a provision that gives individuals this right.[16] [17] (iii) The criterion discussed at length by Elster (1991) is the openness of the constituent assembly: is the public regularly informed on the progress of the proceedings? We argue that this is a (formal) precondition for more informal ways of participation such as demonstrations to be discussed in an instant. (iv) A constitution can be ratified with more or less participation: if a general referendum needs to be held in order to ratify the constitution, the populace at large participates in the process of constitution-making. (v) Broad media coverage concerning the activities of the constituent assembly is a more informal – and also a more indirect way – of participation. It is based on the – formal – precondition of an independent press.[18] Again,

---

[14] Elster (1991, p. 22) observes: 'In a crisis, time is at a premium. The urgent need to reach agreement has the effect of equalizing bargaining power'. The necessity to be fast is thus a mixed bag: on the one hand, it reduces the chances of deliberation, on the other hand, it equalizes bargaining power and might therefore lead to more equitable outcomes.

[15] Elster (1998, p. 107) argues that bargaining can only occur within small-number settings and that 'in large, fragmented assemblies interaction must take the form of arguing'. Fragmentation in large assemblies can, however, be reduced by the existence of a small number of political parties.

[16] There is a huge difference between these two possibilities: Olson (1965) has shown that specific conditions must be met if a latent interest group is to turn into a manifest one. Allowing only recognized interest groups to participate thus excludes positions held by people who are potential members of latent interest groups.

[17] But note that low entry barriers will be connected with high recognition barriers in these cases.

[18] This will often be difficult to ascertain empirically since logically the freedom of the press cannot be secured in the constitution which is only in the making. If former regimes were more oppressive, their dealing with the press will often not adequately reflect its status during the process of writing a constitution.

this can be measured. (vi) Demonstrations are another possible component of a 'participation'-index concerning constitutional choice. Again, their legal occurrence depends on formal preconditions such as the right to demonstrate which can be ascertained.

Summing up, it seems important to distinguish between the *demand* for participation, the *possibility* to participate, and the *actual* level of *participation* that was observed.

3.2 Content Indicators

Remember that the basic hypothesis to be tested reads: Deliberation matters. We aim at making this general conjecture more concrete with regard to two aspects: (1) Does it matter for the content of the constitution and (2) Does it matter for its success? We now turn to present some indicators for ascertaining the content of a constitution.

Concerning the content, there are a host of possible criteria which basically suggest themselves and which will therefore be just named but not spelled out in any detail: (i) does the constitution preview a democratic system? (ii) what weight is given to basic human rights? (iii) does it preview a parliamentary or a presidential system? (iv) are elections based on the plurality rule or on proportional representation? (v) does the constitution preview a unitary state or a federation? (vi) a unicameral or a bicameral system? (vii) is it completely based on representation or does it preview direct democratic elements? (viii) what is the degree of delegation of competences to agencies not elected by popular vote?

3.3 Success Indicators

It was already mentioned that Elster (1991) does not try to explain why some constitutions succeed and others do not. Although he does not, he still proposes three criteria that a successful constitution should fulfill: (1) the constitution matters. By that, Elster (ibid., p. 15) means that (i) it 'must have precise, enforceable implications for behavior' which must be (ii) factually enforced, and (iii) the enforcement must be caused by the existence of the constitutional rules. (2) the constitution works in that collective decisions are taken and carried out in an orderly way. (3) the constitution lasts. He then goes on to propose that for purposes of positive analysis (our interest here) one better drop the second criterion because it would be value-laden.

To ascertain whether a constitution matters is not simple. One would have to show that without the currently valid constitution, i.e. with a different one, other equilibria than those that have been realized under the given constitution would have been realized. In other words, we are dealing with an 'as if'-comparison that must remain hypothetical for logical reasons. But there might be reasonably good proxies that could help us in ascertaining whether a constitution matters. We simply assume that it does if the stipulations contained in the constitution are abided by the relevant players, in other words if the *de jure* constitution is more or less equivalent with the *de facto* constitution. There are a number of organizations that regularly publish indicators that can be interpreted as dealing with these questions. The authors of the International Country Risk Guide have, e.g., regularly published an indicator on the rule of law as factually implemented in a country (for use in econometric analyses, see Knack and Keefer, 1995).

Elster's third criterion is easily operationalized: how long a constitution has lasted is readily measurable. As long as constitutional change is brought about within the rules laid down in the constitution, at least one of its central traits – the modification rule – lasts. It only ceases to last if the constitution is changed in an unconstitutional way. It is true that this might lead to awkward 'counts': some of the constitutional changes brought about in Central and Eastern Europe over the last ten years were done within the frame of the socialist constitutions. Thus no need to start counting anew.

We want to propose four additional criteria for the success of a constitution. Above, the precarious role attributed to efficiency and equity has been critically discussed. Nevertheless, we assume that most people would prefer to live in a country with high average income to one with low average income. Among those with high average income, people *might* prefer countries with a more equal distribution of incomes. If constitutions matter, then they will be one determinant of income levels and their distribution. Two additional criteria could thus be: (4) income levels and (or) growth of income levels, and (5) distribution of income and wealth. (6) Recently, economists have returned to realizing that income is not all that matters (most prominently, Frey and Stutzer, 2002). They have proposed to ask for the determinants of a more inclusive variable, namely happiness. If people are happy, this could be due to the way interactions are structured in their society. Average happiness could thus be used as a proxy for the success of their country's constitution. A related success indicator is the (7) legitimacy that the citizens of a country attribute to its constitution. This will be spelled out in greater detail later.

4 Some Hypotheses on Possible Transmission Mechanisms

4.1 Introductory Remarks

In the last section, a couple of indicators for assessing deliberation and participation were proposed. Among them, constitutional assemblies and referenda on the constitution figured prominently. In order to assess the possible consequences of participation, we begin by developing hypotheses in which we take the existence of a constitutional assembly as exogenously determined. Only later on will the choice of this institutional device be endogenized.

Among the exogenously given participation possibilities, we will further distinguish between effects on constitutional choice (4.2.1) and effects on post-constitutional choice (4.2.2). This is very similar to the distinction between the effects of popular participation in constitution-making on the content of the constitution on the one hand and on its success on the other.

4.2 Exogenously Given Participation Possibilities

4.2.1 Effects on the Content of the Constitution

Hypothesis #1: The structure of the constitution will mirror the structure of the constitutional assembly.

This hypothesis is advanced by Elster (1996) with regard to constitutional conventions that simultaneously serve as legislatures. In particular, it is argued that they will give heavy weight to the legislature in comparison to the executive and judiciary. They will further assign an important role to the legislature in the amending process at the expense of extra-parliamentary ratification possibilities, such as referenda. Third, they will mirror the current structure of parliament, i.e. unicameral (bicameral) conventions will create unicameral (bicameral) systems.

We are here particularly interested in constitutional assemblies that serve exclusively as such. Here are some hypotheses concerning differential effects of alternative institutional settings:

(1a): If at least some of the delegates are nominated by representatives of the old regime, then it seems unlikely that universal suffrage to parliament will be the outcome of constitutional deliberation. Conversely, if the delegates are elected on the basis of universal suffrage, then universal suffrage will be the election rule to parliament.

(1b): If the delegates are elected on the basis of proportional representation, then it seems likely that the election rule to parliament will likewise be proportional representation. Conversely, if they are elected on the basis of majority rule, this will also be the election rule to parliament.

(1c): If the entire country is a single district, then it seems likely that a relatively centralized system will result. Conversely, if there are many districts, the system will be more tilted towards federalism.

(1d): If popular referendum is necessary to ratify the constitution, it seems likely that the possibility of popular referenda for issues other than constitutional ones will find their way into the constitution.

(1e): If delegates are elected as individuals who are experts in constitutional issues, it is less likely that they will attribute a dominant role to the legislature *vis-à-vis* the other two branches. If many of the experts are constitutional lawyers, one could even expect the constitution to be tilted towards judicial independence.

This list is, of course, not exhaustive.

Hypothesis #2: The existence of a constitutional assembly with members who will not seek political office later on tends to lead to a document emphasizing the public good.

This is a straightforward application of economic reasoning. If the drafters of the constitution expect to hold political office later on, they will try to influence the document in such a way that serves their own interest or the interest of their party (see footnote 13). If they do not expect to hold political office later on, they have more incentives to try to establish a document that serves the public good. This consideration seems to be at the base of the recommendation to have a constitutional assembly with the sole purpose of drafting a constitution. Yet, there might be some counterarguments similarly based on economic reasoning. If the delegates will not stay in politics, what incentives do they have to acquire knowledge concerning the working properties of alternative constitutional rules? If the delegates have an extra-political reputation to defend – say as social scientists convinced of their own hypotheses – why should they be ready to accept compromises? If the delegates represent specific interests, they might well represent them even if they do not expect to hold political office later. If the delegates do, however, not represent specific interests why should they bother to take the bargaining power of the relevant interest groups explicitly into account? If they do not, the chances that the formal constitution will ever be factually enforced seem to be slim indeed (see also hypotheses 7 and 8 below). In other words, there are some convincing arguments in favor of having a sitting legislature draft the constitution.

Hypothesis #3: Use of referenda in order to ratify a draft constitution will lead to a document that takes the preferences of the citizens at large explicitly into account.
One assumption underlying this hypothesis is that one can draw a meaningful line in separating the interests of 'the political caste' from those of the citizenry at large.[19] It would then be possible that members of constitutional assemblies enter into a coalition against their citizens. But if the citizens are the ultimate deciders on accepting the constitution, members of the constitutional assembly have more incentives to take the preferences of the citizens explicitly into account.[20]

Hypothesis #4: Inclusive participation in constitution-making enhances chances that the draft will be largely compatible with the ideal of the rule of law.
In short, we define the rule of law as that ideal in which the law is to be applied equally to all persons (*isonomia*), government leaders included. It is therefore also called government under the law. No power used by government is arbitrary, all power is limited. Drawing on Immanuel Kant (1797/1995), laws should fulfill the criteria of universalizability. Empirically, a 'perfect' or 'complete' rule of law has probably never been realized: men and women have been treated differently just as members of different races have been.

An (all) inclusive participation in constitutional deliberations is equivalent with a large heterogeneity of interests represented. If participants are to agree unanimously on a rule set, this will lead them to agree on process-oriented constitutional rules, which will tend to be universalizable. As long as not all relevant interests are

---

19 Frey and Kirchgässner (1993) report Swiss referendum results in which the population voted differently from what politicians had supposed.

20 Empirically, use of referenda to ratify entirely new constitutions or constitutional change seems to be most widespread in Africa (36 states have used referenda at least once for that purpose) and least used in Asia (only six such referenda have been reported).

represented at the convention, there is a greater danger that those present will agree on rules to the detriment of those not present.

Hypothesis #5: Inclusive participation in constitution-making will lead to high levels of power delegation.

Politicians who need to be reelected in order to stay in office are subject to various (time-)inconsistency-problems. In order to remain in office, they will use policies leading to (good) short-term results with, however, bad long-term consequences. Citizens have an interest in isolating their politicians from such situations. One possibility of securing that is to allocate competences to agencies that are not subject to the constraint of popular reelection, the most prominent one being an independent central bank.

It has been pointed out that there is a difference between rule-interests and act-interests (Vanberg and Buchanan, 1988): I might have an interest in a general rule against stealing. But if the general rule does not come with sufficiently severe sanctions against stealing, stealing might still promise utility gains. Taking up this distinction here, it might be argued that at the time of choosing constitutional rules, even politicians might be able to agree unanimously on delegating competences to bodies other than the legislature. This would mean, in other words, that with regard to the extent of delegation it does not necessarily make a difference whether participation is broad or not. But this counterargument is based on the premise that at the time of drafting the constitution, participants cannot with any certainty predict who will be the next government (because the party believing to be the next government would have less incentives to delegate competences). Alternatively, one would have to assume that the future is discounted with sufficiently small rates.

Hypothesis #6: 'Single issue participation' increases the chances that the constitution will be containing contradictory provisions.

An important function of constitutions is to allow all interested actors to form expectations concerning the processes of collective action in a given community that have a good chance of turning out to be correct. A crucial precondition for this to happen is the internal consistency of the document (Ordeshook, 1993 and 2002, emphasizes this point). Delegates to constitutional assemblies will have conflicting interests regarding the content of the constitution. General agreement will often only be attainable after package deals have been made. These do not, however, have to endanger the consistency of the entire document.

A different situation might prevail if the public at large is called upon to actively participate in the constitution-making process: if – for whatever reason – these proposals are reflected in the draft, the chances that it will be a coherent one will be lower than if the constitutional assembly is closed to active participation of the public.[21]

[21] Identifying inconsistencies in constitutions is tough work, yet it can be done. Ordeshook (1993) contains some examples from the 1993 Constitution of the Russian Federation.

Riker (1987) argues that more homogenous constitutional assemblies will prepare more coherent constitutional documents. Evaluated in terms of the criteria for successful constitutions, coherence improves chances that the constitution matters as well as that it lasts. Securing homogeneity of the assembly can thus increase chances that a coherent document will be produced. But if this is done by excluding relevant groups, this will supposedly be detrimental to the legitimacy of the constitution, which will be taken up as hypothesis #9.

4.2.2 Effects on the Success of the Constitution

Hypothesis #7: Inclusive participation in constitution-making will lead to less constitutional changes in subsequent periods.

Demands to renegotiate the contents of a constitution in later periods always arise if the bargaining power of at least one group has increased relative to that of others and this group now demands a larger share of the net surplus accruing from having a constitution. If broad public participation in the choice of constitutional rules is institutionalized, this secures that all the relevant interests will enter into the deliberation procedures, if not the constitutional document. This will reduce the probability that a society will be faced by renegotiation demands only a few periods after a new constitution has been passed.[22]

Hypothesis #8: Inclusive participation in constitution-making enhances the chances that the constitution will become effective in later periods.

If one reads the constitutions of the world, one can get the impression that the world is a democratic and just place. Unfortunately, the way many constitutions are enforced differs considerably from the text of the documents. It has been shown time and again that the contract theory of the constitution must remain unconvincing if it cannot show that the social contract called the constitution is a self-enforcing document (see Kirstein and Voigt, 2000 for an attempt to identify the possible scope of self-enforcing deals). The social contract notion as well as the critique thereof usually starts from the simple behavioral model of economics. But in the past couple of years, laboratory experiments have taught us that subjects in these experiments consistently deviate from the predictions based on the standard assumptions: PD-games are significantly more often solved cooperatively if the participants are allowed to communicate before playing the game. This holds true even if the participants are not capable of making binding commitments, i.e. even when their talk is only cheap. If participation is interpreted as a form of communication then this could also create additional constraints that make the relevant actors stick to the document later on.

---

22 For an empirical test of the hypothesis, one needs to control the differences in the possibilities to amend constitutions.

Hypothesis #9: Inclusive participation in constitution-making enhances the legitimacy of a constitution.

Economists have generally been reluctant to deal with issues of legitimacy. And if they have, they have dealt with it on a normative level such as normative constitutional economics. Models within positive constitutional economics that focus on the sustainability of a certain government or regime are usually not interested in issues of legitimacy. Hardin (1989) and Weingast (1995), for example, focus on the absence of opposition, the incapacity of actors opposing the current regime to coordinate their actions successfully in order to overthrow the current regime. Deliberation, consent, and participation are not part of those models. But the absence of organized opposition is obviously not sufficient to attribute high levels of legitimacy to a regime.

But one can turn this relationship on its head: a high degree of legitimacy will supposedly reduce the chances of opposition to materialize. If an individual attributes legitimacy to a regime that will not only influence her collective behavior (participate in opposition or not) but also her individual behavior, as an individual, she will be more likely to accept decisions by representatives of the state.[23] This will, in turn, lead to lower control, implementation and sanctioning costs of regimes attributed higher levels of legitimacy. In this sense, legitimacy can have important economic effects.

It is now hypothesized that the legitimacy of a regime is higher if its basic rules have been brought about with the possibility of large parts of the population participating. Even in small societies, meaningful direct participation in the deliberation processes will be difficult if not impossible. Legitimacy could then be generated if the mode according to which representatives to a constitutional assembly are elected is perceived as fair or bringing about an adequate representation of the various currents relevant in a society. Two empirical questions almost suggest themselves: (i) modes of participation can supposedly be ranked by some 'seriousness' criterion: being allowed to send a petition to an assembly is different from having a vote in the assembly. It would be interesting to know whether different degrees of legitimacy can be connected with different modes of participation. (ii) It would also be interesting to know whether different degrees of legitimacy can be caused by different modes of electing delegates to constitutional assemblies.

Up till now, we have assumed that legitimacy is a function of participation, i.e. can be explained by different arrangements securing (the possibility of) participation. Drawing on the distinction between constitutional and post-constitutional

---

23 For a more systematic treatment of legitimacy, it might be useful to distinguish between the legitimacy attributed to a regime (or the institutional arrangements on which it is based), on the one hand, and the legitimacy attributed to the concrete government that represents the regime at a given moment on the other. Additionally, the relationship between legitimacy and loyalty deserves attention: one could inquire whether regimes perceived to be legitimate would *c.p.* face a lower degree of exit in the sense of Hirschman (1970) due to higher degrees of loyalty that come along with legitimacy. Inquiring into the relationship between legitimacy and trust also promises to be of interest. All these issues seem closely connected to the rationality-assumption: how rational is it to attribute legitimacy to a regime or a government, how rational is it to be loyal or to trust somebody?

choice, one could inquire whether different levels of legitimacy have any effect on levels of using participation possibilities later on: a regime enjoying very low legitimacy levels might, e.g. be sanctioned by very low voter turnout. This leads directly to the next hypothesis.

Hypothesis #10: Inclusive participation in constitution-making induces high participation levels on the post-constitutional level.

We expect inclusive participation on the constitution-making level to have two effects, which could become relevant here: (i) inclusive participation will increase legitimacy, which would enhance the willingness to participate in day-to-day decision-making. This effect is, however, not in tune with economic theory which states that citizens would only participate if that activity were connected with an increase in their expected utility. It seems thus more plausible to assume the following: (ii) individual participation on the constitution-making level will lead to a high degree of formalized possibilities of participation. Whether they will indeed be used is an entirely different matter and hard to predict.

4.3 Endogenizing Participation

Until now, we have assumed possibilities to participate in the process of constitutional choice to be exogenously given. Factually, they are, of course, the consequence of some explicit collective choice on a pre-constitutional stage. In this section, we want to ask what factors influence this choice. Specifically, we are interested to learn (i) under what conditions constitutional assemblies with the only purpose of drafting a constitution will be created, and under what conditions a sitting parliament will simultaneously act as a constitutional assembly. (ii) Under what conditions the populace at large is called to participate in this process either by electing delegates to the assembly, by being encouraged to make proposals, or by being given a chance to participate in a referendum that is part of the ratification process.

The necessity of a new constitution regularly seems to arise after a war or a civil war but can also be the consequence of a revolution, or a coup that led to a new ruler etc. The recent constitutional transition processes in Central and Eastern Europe taught us that fundamental change can also be brought about by amending an existing constitution (the Hungarian way) or by an interim constitution that will only be replaced by a more fundamental new one after much of the uncertainty accompanying fundamental transitions has gone (the Polish way).[24]

---

[24] Note that the Polish approach is equivalent to a transparent veil. Although Rawls and Buchanan would opt for a thicker veil, less uncertainty concerning the strength of various actors – or groups of actors – can help to draft a constitution that takes their weight adequately into account which will make early renegotiation demands less likely. Salzberger and Voigt, 2002 contain an overview of the constitution-making procedures of eight countries of Central and Eastern Europe. Müller (1998) contains a more systematic precautionary argument against the consensus-enhancing function of a thick veil.

The above three arguments have been given in favor of having constitutional assemblies exclusively convened for that purpose. Despite these strong arguments, it has been noted that, historically, most constitutional conventions have been constituted from sitting parliaments.[25] This observation is not surprising. It is not that an all-purpose assembly might appear to save some time in such periods of radical changes (Mueller, 1996, ch. 21). It is, of course, the interests of the actors involved in collective decision-making which will make it very difficult to achieve this normative goal: no matter whether they represent an old or a new regime, they have their own conceptions of what the new constitution should look like. *Prima facie*, foreign powers who have just won a war might appear to have less direct interests in the concrete contents of constitutions. This would enhance the chances that they might convene or at least initiate the convention of a constitutional assembly. In Germany, U.S. interests acted as a constraint for the Germans involved in writing a proposal; in Japan, however, the constitution was written by a constitutional assembly convened by General McArthur (Inoue 1991). Thus, what needs to be explained are not all the cases in which a constitutional assembly was assembled out of parliament but those cases in which it was convened for the sole purpose of drafting the constitution.

Ackerman (1991), a legal scholar with affinity to Discourse Ethics has argued that there are 'constitutional moments' in which a group makes decisions not according to the standard self-interest rationale but according to special ones that are only valid in that very moment. 'Constitutional moments' would supposedly not only show while deliberating on the content of a new constitution but also prior to it, namely when somebody has to make a decision concerning a constitutional assembly. The low number of constitutional assemblies seems to imply that few people ever have constitutional moments.

Hypothesis #11: Demand for participation in constitutional choice is subject to a secular increase.

In '*Strukturwandel der Öffentlichkeit*' (1962/1990), Habermas describes how members of the *bourgeoisie* have changed the bases of power. Reading this study as a historic description, one could argue that the demand for more inclusive par-

---

25 But there have been constitutional assemblies in our sense. Even more, there have been constitutional assemblies that were convened subsequent to a referendum on their convocation: Venezuela's citizens were called to a referendum in order to vote on the composition of a constitutional assembly on April 25, 1999. In Ecuador, there was even a referendum that decided on the rule to be used to elect delegates to a constitutional assembly in 1997 (a majority voted in favor of having purely universal suffrage and against mixing it with giving organized groups the possibility to send delegates).

Regarding the extent of deliberation, the constitutions of Micronesia and the Northern Marianes are quite interesting: According to section XIV, Art. 2 of the Micronesian Constitution, a referendum on the convocation of a constitutional assembly needs to be held at least every ten years ('Shall there be a convention to revise or amend the Constitution?'). To make it convene, a simple majority of the votes expressed suffices. The Northern Marianes have a similar provision in their Constitution.

ticipation was the consequence of the development of a bourgeoisie. With hindsight, additional explanatory factors such as the example of other societies come to mind.

Hypothesis #12: Possibilities to participate are influenced by the values and norms prevalent in a given society.
Economists usually do not feel at ease with the concept of values, norms, and attitudes influencing individual behavior – and collective choice. Values have been defined as '... conceptions of the desirable, influencing selective behavior' (International Encyclopedia of the Social Sciences, entry values). Norms for conduct are sometimes differentiated from values: 'Values are not the same as norms for conduct. ... Values are standards of desirability that are more nearly independent of specific situations. The same value may be a point of reference for a great many specific norms; a particular norm may represent the simultaneous application of several separable values' (ibid.).

If relevant parts of the population are convinced that it is fate that is responsible for their lot, and not – at least to some degree – their individual actions, chances that considerable parts of society will ever demand the possibility to participate actively in constitution-making procedures appear to be slim. If there is no serious demand, possibilities to participate will supposedly not be supplied. Moreover, if decisive parts of the population adhere to organicist state conceptions that view the state as having a purpose that goes beyond the provision of public goods, demands to participate actively in constitutional deliberation seem to be misplaced. Similarly, the readiness to accept hierarchical structures is not equally distributed among societies. The more pronounced it is, the lower will be the possibilities to participate.

Values and norms are also one determinant of the degree of civil society in the sense of the number of voluntarily founded and horizontally structured associations. It follows that we hypothesize that the higher the degree of civil society, the higher the possibilities to participate in constitution-making.[26]

5 Towards Empirical Tests: Conclusion and Outlook

This is already a lengthy paper. Testing all the explicit – and implicit – hypotheses contained is a heroic task. Since we are no heroes, it will not be carried out here. But testing the hypotheses promises to be interesting.

In quantitative analyses, a lot of – potentially relevant – context is dropped by necessity. This is the standard reproach that representatives of less formally devel-

26 Relatedly, if the variance in the readiness to contribute voluntarily to the provision of public goods is based on differences in underlying values and norms and participation in constitutional choice has collective good elements, then actual participation will be influenced by the prevalent values and norms.

oped social sciences like to direct towards economists.[27] And in a certain sense, they are perfectly right: completely disregarding context often leads to predictions that are flatly wrong. Worse yet, it often leads to recommendations that make things worse: just think of the attempts to 'turn around' entire political and economic regimes in Central and Eastern Europe within a couple of hundred days. But parting from formal analysis entirely is like throwing the baby out with the bath water. In principle, context can be incorporated within formal models as part of the constraints that the actors are subject to. This is the main advantage that the New Institutional Economics – and Positive Constitutional Economics as a part thereof – has in comparison to more standard approaches.

Implicitly, we have assumed that contents and success of constitutions can be completely explained by drawing on a set of variables describing the procedures used to create a new constitution. Surely, there are other important determinants that will evade operationalization, just think of the role of political leadership (but see Riker, 1984 for the role of political entrepreneurship in constitution-making). At times, very practical reasons might dominate more theoretical considerations: the maximum number of delegates to a constitutional assembly might be determined by the size of the hall in which the convention is to be held (for a similar example, see Krastev and Peeva, 2002).

We started this paper with a quote from David Hume in which he says that the usual situations in which new constitutions are written are usually bad times for deliberation. Now, an entirely different process of constitution-making has been underway in Europe for more than four decades, namely the one that leads to a European Constitution. The marginal role of participation in that process must be very irritating to adherents of both Discourse Ethics and Normative Constitutional Economics. From the point of view of the economist, blaming politicians for creating very intransparent structures does not make sense. Rather, civil society does not seem to be strong enough to prevent technocratic constitution-making.

References

Aaken, A. van (2001) "Deliberative Institutionenökonomik oder: Argumentiert der homo oeconomicus?", in Panther, S., and W. Ötsch (eds.) *Ökonomie als Sozialwissenschaft*, Marburg (Metropolis).

Ackerman, B. (1991) *We the People, Vol.1: Foundations*, Cambridge, Ma. (Belknap).

Breton, A. and G. Gianluigi (1985) "Is Proportional Representation Always the Best Electoral Rule?", *Public Finance* 40 (1), 1-16.

Buchanan, J. (1954) "Social Choice, Democracy, and Free Markets", *Journal of Political Economy* 62, 334-43.

27 'Erkenntnis und Interesse' can be interpreted to be part of that critique.

Buchanan, J. (1959) "Positive Economics, Welfare Economics, and Political Economy", *Journal of Law and Economics* 2, 124-38.
Buchanan, J. (1975) *The Limits of Liberty – Between Anarchy and Leviathan*, Chicago (University of Chicago Press).
Buchanan, J. (1986) "Kommentar", in Koslowski, P. *Ethik des Kapitalismus*, Tübingen (Mohr), 81-92.
Buchanan, J. (1994) "Choosing What to Choose", *Journal of Institutional and Theoretical Economics* 150 (1), 123-135.
Buchanan, J. and G. Tullock (1962) *The Calculus of Consent*, Ann Arbor (University of Michigan Press).
Buchanan, J. and V. Vanberg (1989) "A Theory of Leadership and Deference in Constitutional Construction", *Public Choice* 61, 15-27.
Cross, J. (1965) "A Theory of the Bargaining Process", *American Economic Review* 55, 67-94.
Czeszjko-Sochacki, Z. and R. Machacek (1992) "Der Weg zu einer neuen polnischen Verfassung", *Europäische Grundrechte Zeitschrift* 19 (5-6), 93-98.
Elster, J. (1991) *Arguing and Bargaining in two Constituent Assemblies, The Storrs Lectures*, typescript.
Elster, J. (1993) "Constitution-Making in Eastern Europe: Rebuilding the Boat in the Open Sea", *Public Administration* 71 (1/2), 169-217.
Elster, J. (1994) "The Impact of Constitutions on Economic Performance", *paper presented to the Annual Bank Conference on Development Economics of the World Bank*, April 1994.
Elster, J. (1995) "Strategic Uses of Argument", in Arrow K., et al. (eds.) *Barriers to Negotiated Resolution of Conflicts*, New York (Norton), 237-57.
Elster, J. (1996) "The Role of Institutional Interest in East European Constitution-Making", *East European Constitutional Review* 5 (1), 63-5.
Elster, J. (1998) "Deliberation and Constitution Making", in Elster, J. (ed.) *Deliberative Democracy*, Cambridge (Cambridge University Press), 97-122.
Fink, E. and W. Riker (1989) "The Strategy of Ratification", in Grofman, B. and D. Wittman (eds.) *The Federalist Papers and the New Institutionalism*, New York (Agathon), 220-55.
Frey, B. (1979) "Economic Policy By Constitutional Contract", *Kyklos*, 32 (1/2), 307-19.
Frey, B. and G. Kirchgässner (1993) "Diskursethik, Politische Ökonomie und Volksabstimmungen", *Analyse & Kritik* 15, 129-149.
Frey, B. and A. Stutzer (2002) *Happiness and Economics – How the Economy and Institutions Affect Human Well-Being*, Princeton (PUP).
Habermas, J. (1962/1990) *Strukturwandel der Öffentlichkeit*, Frankfurt (Suhrkamp).
Habermas, J. (1968/1973) *Erkenntnis und Interesse*, Frankfurt (Suhrkamp).
Habermas, J. (1983) *Moralbewußtsein und kommunikatives Handeln*, Frankfurt (Suhrkamp).

Habermas, J. (1992) *Faktizität und Geltung – Beiträge zur Diskurstheorie des Rechts und des demokratischen Rechtsstaats*, Darmstadt (Wissenschaftliche Buchgesellschaft).

Hardin, R. (1989) "Why a Constitution?", in Grofman, B. and D. Wittman (eds.) *The Federalist Papers and the New Institutionalism*, New York (Agathon), 100-20.

Hirschman, A. (1970) *Exit, Voice and Loyalty – Responses to Decline in Firms, Organizations, and States*, Cambridge, MA (Harvard University Press).

Hume, D. (1777/1987) *Essays – Moral, Political, and Literary*, ed. and with a Foreword, Notes, and Glossary by Eugene F. Miller, Indianapolis (Liberty Classics).

Inoue, K. (1991) *MacArthur's Japanese Constitution – A Linguistic and Cultural Study of its Making*, Chicago (The University of Chicago Press).

Kant, Immanuel (1797/1995) *The Metaphysics of Morals* – Introduction, translation, and notes by Mary Gregor, Cambridge (Cambridge University Press).

Kirstein, R. and S. Voigt (2000) "The Violent and the Weak – When Dictators Care About Social Contracts", *Discussion paper 2000-2 Center for the Study of Law and Economics at Saar-University*, Saarbrücken.

Knack, St. and Ph. Keefer (1995) "Institutions and Economic Performance: Cross-Country Tests Using Alternative Institutional Measures", *Economics and Politics* 7(3), 207-27.

Krastev, I. and R. Peeva (2002) "Invisible Contexts, Invisible Constraints – The Limits of the Normative Explanation of Constitutional Change", in Voigt, S. and H.-J. Wagener (eds.) *Constitutions, Market and the Law*, Cheltenham et al. (Elgar).

Kreps, D. (1990) *A Course in Microeconomic Theory*, Princeton (Princeton University Press).

Kreps, D. (1998) "Bounded Rationality", in *The New Palgrave Dictionary of Economics and the Law, Vol. 1*, 30ff.

Macey, J. (1986) "Promoting Public-Regarding Legislation through Statutory Interpretation: an Interest-Group Model", *Columbia Law Review* 86, 223-68.

McCormick, R., and R. Tollison (1981) *Politicians, Legislation, and the Economy – An Inquiry into the Interest-Group Theory of Government*, Boston (Nijhoff).

Mueller, D. (1989) *Public Choice II*, Cambridge (Cambridge University Press).

Mueller, D. (1996) *Constitutional Democracy*, Oxford (Oxford University Press).

Müller, Chr. (1998) "The Veil of Uncertainty Unveiled", *Constitutional Political Economy* 9(1), 5-17.

Olson, M. (1965) *The Logic of Collective Action*, Cambridge, Mass (Harvard University Press).

Ordeshook, P. (1993) "Some Rules of Constitutional Design", in Frankel Paul, E., F. Miller and J. Paul (eds.) *Liberalism and the Economic Order*, Cambridge (Cambridge University Press), 198-232.

Ordeshook, P. (2002) "Are 'Western' Constitutions Relevant to Anything Other than the Countries they Serve?", in Voigt, S. and H.-J. Wagener (eds.) *Constitutions, Market and the Law*, Cheltenham et al. (Elgar).

Rawls, J. (1971) *A Theory of Justice*, Cambridge, Mass. (Harvard University Press).

Riker, W. (1984) "The Heresthetics of Constitution-Making: The Presidency in 1787, with Comments on Determinism and Rational Choice", *American Political Science Review* 78, 1-16.

Riker, W. (1987) "The Lessons of 1787", *Public Choice 1* 55, 5-34.

Salzberger, E. and S. Voigt (2002) "On the Delegation of Powers – with Special Emphasis on Central and Eastern Europe", in Voigt, S. and H.-J. Wagener (eds.) *Constitutions, Market and the Law*, Cheltenham et al. (Elgar).

Tschentscher, A. (2000) *Prozedurale Theorien der Gerechtigkeit: Rationales Entscheiden, Diskursethik und prozedurales Recht*. Baden-Baden (Nomos).

Vanberg, V. and J. Buchanan (1988) "Rational Choice and Moral Order", *Analyse & Kritik* 10, 138-160.

Vanberg, V. and J. Buchanan, (1989) "Interests and Theories in Constitutional Choice", *Journal of Theoretical Politics* 1(1), 49-63.

Vanberg, V. and J. Buchanan, (1991) "Constitutional Choice, Rational Ignorance and the Limits of Reason", *Jahrbuch für Neue Politische Ökonomie*, 10, 61-78.

Voigt, S. (1994) "Die kontraktorientierte Theorie der Verfassung – Anmerkungen zum Ansatz Buchanans", *Homo Oeconomicus*, XI (1994), 173-209.

Voigt, S. (1996) "Die konstitutionelle Ökonomik als Herausforderung für die Theorie der Wirtschaftspolitik – zugleich eine Skizze zur Weiterentwicklung einer ökonomischen Theorie der Verfassung", in Pies, I. and M. Leschke (eds.) *James Buchanans konstitutionelle Ökonomik*, Tübingen (J.C.B Mohr (Siebeck)), 157-83.

Voigt, S. (1997) "Positive Constitutional Economics – A Survey", *Public Choice* 90, 11-53.

Voigt, S. (1998) "Kants Gerechtigkeitskriterien, die Wirtschaftstheorie und die ökonomischen Transformationsprozesse in Mittel- und Osteuropa", in Dicke, K. and K.-M. Kodalle (eds.) *Republik und Weltbürgerrecht*, Weimar/Köln (Böhlau), 399-434.

Voigt, S. (1999) "Breaking with the Notion of Social Contract: Constitutions as Based on Spontaneously Arisen Institutions", *Constitutional Political Economy* 10 (3), 283-300.

Weber, M. (1922/1985) *Wirtschaft und Gesellschaft – Grundriß der verstehenden Soziologie*, fünfte, rev. Auflage, besorgt von Johannes Winckelmann, Tübingen

Weingast, B. (1995) "The Economic Role of Political Institutions: Market-Preserving Federalism and Economic Development", *Journal of Law, Economics & Organization* 11(1), 1-31.

Wicksell, K. (1896) *Finanztheoretische Untersuchungen*, Jena (Fischer).

---

* The author thanks the two discussants Michaela Haase and Horst Hegmann as well as the participants of the Conference, especially Anne van Aaken, Alois Stutzer, and Axel Tschentscher for stimulating discussion. The usual caveat applies.

Is There a Need for a Positive Constitutional Economics? Comment on Stefan Voigt

Michaela Haase

Voigt's paper is divided into two parts. In the first part, Voigt criticizes discourse ethics (DE) and constitutional economics (CE) for their disregard of (or at least their disinterest in) making their analyses suitable for empirical applications, and analyzes the reasons for this disregard. In the second part, Voigt concentrates on two aspects of popular participation in constitutional choice: first, on participation's effects on content, legitimacy, and success of a constitution; second, on the preconditions under which popular participation takes place. Not interested in the normative venture, as DE and CE 'are conventionally perceived' (p. 200), Voigt blends his 'conjecture that discourse matters for the choice and development of constitutional rules' (abstract) into testable hypotheses. These hypotheses are interesting, but many of them remain unrelated to the first, critical part of the paper. The paper also refers to the positive-normative distinction. While positive constitutional economics (PCE) has its origin in real deficiencies concerning empirical interpretations of concepts or in the lack of empirical applications of both discourse ethics and constitutional economics, this reference is unnecessary in order to handle the issues Voigt has presented.

Deficiencies of Constitutional Economics and Discourse Ethics

Voigt presents a couple of possible hypotheses and research questions related to the positive constitutional economics program. He claims that, in regard to content and success of a constitution, discourse matters, deliberation matters, and participation matters. Alas, those theories that have dealt intensely with these topics, namely, constitutional economics (CE) and discourse ethics (DE), include them only as '(implicit) hypotheses' (p. 200). Both approaches draw on procedures, but they 'have problems in transferring their procedural proposals into the real world' (p. 206). Both approaches draw on the notion of consent, whose meaning in real discourses is unclear. No wonder, then, that they have not been able to integrate participation into a systematic or convincing theoretical as well as empirical conceptualization. The scientist neglects either the analysis of procedures by referring to unanimity rules or veils of ignorance, or the analysis of non-idealized speech situations and communications in favor of ideal types of argumentation or discourse.

CE adheres to the unanimity rule but does not focus on procedures of participation, discourse or deliberation which may precede the state of unanimity. By contrast, 'agreement' is something that takes place within or at the end of a process. Voigt also reports that Buchanan has lost interest in the empirical interpretation of certain main CE concepts during the last decades. In contrast to advocates of constitutional economics, Habermas goes so far as to support an immunization strategy.

Habermas has not, in fact, encouraged empirical applications of the theory. However, the acceptance of an immunization strategy characterizes the intentions of a scientific community with the theory at its disposal rather than the empirical content of theory itself. The suitability of a theory for empirical applications can actually be investigated independently of a scientific community and its application intentions. Voigt has convincingly shown this by dissecting Elster's application of DE on the proceedings of two constitutional assemblies. Thus, the fact that a community proceeds with an immunization strategy does not imply the need for developing an alternative account.

Elster's Application of Discourse Ethics

Voigt examines the way in which Elster applies Habermas's notions to the analysis of two cases of constitutional choice. At first glance, Elster's results seem rather disappointing for several reasons. Notwithstanding his criticisms of Elster's analysis, Voigt extracts from it both a host of hypotheses and his own statement of the problem. For my argument, it does not matter whether Voigt's criticism of Elster's application attempt is justified or not. The main question is whether or not it is possible to work on the deficiencies and problems outlined by Voigt in order to make DE and CE suitable for empirical applications to a higher degree. As Voigt shows, Elster does not provide sufficient reasons in favor of, or against, his arguments. How can an approach that is still incomplete be completed by the provision of hypotheses? If we have, at least, no preliminary theoretical answers to the questions as given, for example, by Voigt on page 211, what, then, can we expect from answers that rest on empirical evidence? Voigt does not make explicit why we need a third approach beyond DE and CE, namely, *positive* constitutional economics, in order to deal with the theoretical and empirical shortcomings of the other two. Voigt's resuscitation of the positive-normative distinction is unnecessary because the epithet 'positive' does not provide an unequivocal characterization of any alternative theory.

Related to hypotheses # 2, # 7, and # 8 is Voigt's criticism that Elster disregards the importance of bargaining processes for constitutional choice as well as for its results. Voigt convincingly argues that bargaining is necessary to integrate the most powerful and influential actors prevailing in the discourse and deliberation processes, in order to bring about a self-enforcing constitution. It is possible to explicate the bargaining power of relevant interest groups in more detail by drawing on arguments grounded in social theory (Coleman, 1990). These arguments also find support among advocates of the new institutional economics (North, 1990) or the evolutionary economics strand (Langlois, 2001).

Behavioral Assumptions

Economic theories (of which constitutional economics is one part) refer mostly to behavioral assumptions that do not explicitly deal with the analysis of deliberation and communication. PCE also needs behavioral assumptions that are able to transmit the content of its hypotheses from the micro- to the macro-level of analysis. Voigt argues against DE's and CE's criticism of behavioral assumptions in economics. They reject the assumptions of utility maximization, of interpersonal utility comparisons, and of stable preferences as 'unrealistic'.

Voigt is right that economists use these assumptions out of methodological concern rather than in an attempt to provide realistic descriptions of reality. But this does not justify their use in every case, without pertinent regard for different ranges of intended applications of models, theories and their respective success. The same applies to the assumption of stable preferences which is, as Voigt puts it, 'not necessarily an impediment to a fruitful dialogue' (p. 203; italics omitted). Since in some cases of application the assumption may work with sufficient accuracy, whereas in others it may not, its use is not a question of principle, 'realism' or 'unrealism'; rather it is an empirical question. In some cases preferences may be stable, in others they are not. Additionally, preferences may be also specific to certain domains or even subdomains (Hahn, 1996).

If there is evidence that changes of preferences prevail, then a theory should be able to deal with them. As Ward commented 30 years ago, the importance of stable preferences is mainly due to the disappointing performance of economics in the area of consumer behavior: 'The present theory is far too weak to carry the additional burden of preference change. But this leaves ideology in the driver's seat, discouraging the search for a framework that could get at the issue ...' (Ward, 1972: 259, n. 6).

Voigt further argues with regard to stable preferences that discourse or communication helps actors in completing their information about known alternatives or in learning about the ex ante unknown consequences of alternative options. He points out that it does not make sense to interpret these two cases also as instances of unstable preferences; instead they are cases of incomplete information. Then, what does the assumption of stable preferences mean? It means that if people had complete information, or were in a state close to that, then there would exist no reason to correct a formerly undertaken decision.

There may exist situations which come close to this description. But how shall we deal with situations which are characterized by uncertainty, learning processes, and change? Independently of how it is labeled, the behavior of actors, then, may not result in stable patterns at the macro level. Today's rational-choice theory provides no satisfactory answer to this question. According to Voigt, we should focus on incomplete information and bounded rationality (p. 206). If, as he writes, the discourse notion is incompatible with complete information (perfect rationality), or if incomplete information is a necessary precondition for a useful dialogue (p. 204), then stable preferences prevail in idealized economic systems, but they need not matter very much for the analysis of non-idealized economic systems.

Idealization and De-Idealization

One often refers to the positive-normative distinction when actually the idealized-non-idealized distinction is at stake. 'Idealization' labels a procedure as well as its result, which allows the statement and analysis of 'real-world' problems in a counterfactual setting (Haase, 1995). However, 'idealized' is not synonymous with 'ideal'. That notwithstanding, the two terms are interrelated if the procedure of idealization is guided by reference to ideals. A theory that models idealized economic or political systems, situations, actors, or whatever is not necessarily normative. The same applies to a theory that is withheld from empirical applications, for whatever reason.

It is equally important to point out that the opposite of an idealized theory is not a 'realistic' one but, with reference to concrete assumptions, a de-idealized one. With regard to new institutional economics (NIE) or DE as examples, de-idealized theories result from the introduction of transaction costs or from the investigation in real speech situations, respectively. As Voigt has emphasized: In the social sciences it seems to be an impossible task to measure the deviation between idealized and non-idealized situations in terms of quantitative concepts. From this it does not follow, however, that the difference between idealized and non-idealized situations in the social sciences cannot be determined by the use of qualitative or comparative concepts.

The Positive-Normative Distinction

According to August Comte's declaration of the 'principles of positive philosophy', the term 'positive' means – among other things – that a theory is about reality and that it is committed to explanation and prediction but not to prescription. Both requirements could be met by idealized theories, too.

Albert (1965) argued that all theories are founded on value-laden decisions and that values themselves can be the topic of analysis. Hence, the 'normative' content can never be totally omitted. In spite of that, the problem of making value judgements for Albert is on a par with that of value-expressing statements. If we made use of an ostensibly 'positive' theory for matters of formation (Gestaltung) or for undertaking policy advice, then how would it differ from a 'normative' approach? The difference is simply reduced to the style of formulation, of not employing value-laden expressions in our sentences (Küttner, 1987). Exactly for this reason,

Voigt, following Elster, drops one 'value-laden' criterion of a successful constitution (p. 215). The flip-side of that coin is then putting the notions 'testable hypotheses' on a par with 'positive theory'. The answers to questions concerning the empirical content of a theory, as well as its empirical evidence, are complex. They cannot be reduced to the deduction or derivation of hypotheses and their empirical test.

The analysis of popular participation is not constrained to results of scientists' investigations, nor to their discourses over such. If scientific results need to be transferred into the heads and behavior of the members of larger communities, of committees, assemblies, etc., then we need to initiate or to support public discourse processes. Hence, CE needs to bring forth its own conditions of application. It needs to give rise to those procedures and processes that are the preconditions of a confirmation of his hypotheses (Gäfgen, 1979, p. 88). This is typical for the social sciences and should not trigger a resuscitation of the positive-normative distinction.

Outlook

After having moved out of philosophy, economics faces a lot of problems that it is unable to solve because they are now out of its range of objects. Take, for example, the question of social choice as mentioned by Coase in his paper on 'The Problem of Social Cost'. Because the development cannot be turned around, economics will remain a theoretical *and* empirical science. As a consequence, we have reason enough to examine theories from different disciplines, which could fill the gaps left by philosophical theories.

'Constitutional choice' designates a subclass of a larger class of institutional choices which is within the research interests of NIE. Voigt's view on CE as a part of NIE is therefore plausible. The NIE's research program regards mostly institutional choice as rational choice, too. According to Voigt, participation presupposes discussion which is a kind of communication. Generally speaking, communication is an important but nevertheless often disregarded concept in economics. As Suppes (1980, p. 177) has put it nicely: The Bayesian theory of rationality 'is meant to be a theory of rational action and not of rational talk'. Nevertheless, communication plays an important role in economic systems. Communication effects – to mention only a few examples – information distribution, learning processes, and the pay-offs related to games that are used to analyze collective action problems (Macy, 1997). As a matter of fact, the rise of prisoner-dilemma situations can be circumvented. We need to understand better how and why this happens. Norms are one possible explanation, but so are values, traditions, experiences, and, especially, the 'transaction history' of a community matters. As Denzau and North (1994) put it, it is necessary to take a closer look at concrete action situations, the belief systems and the learning processes of the actors. With regard to rational ignorance we will probably have not just one model that fits all cases of actual behavior.

Further, Voigt mentions Hayek's idea of the market process as a knowledge-distributing process. Following Voigt, discussion may create new ideas or hypotheses, that is, new or altered elements of the information set. Nonetheless, Voigt's view on information as a good is not compatible with Hayek's view on knowledge processes (Hayek, 1945). It is perhaps one step towards a solution of the problem of rational ignorance to treat information not as a good that is subject to cost-benefit calculations. With regard to constitutional choice, Hayek's idea can be converted into the question of how distributed knowledge might be integrated and focused on a specific topic, for example, on the discussion of a constitution. In answering this question we concentrate on *intended* results of deliberate action.

What does DE have to offer to an empirical approach? What possible role does DE play in the analysis of participation processes? Is there a difference between communication, discourse, and discussion? How important are uncertainty and incomplete information for constitutional discourses? What is the difference between constitutional discourses and those carried out within bargaining or managerial transactions? Perhaps DE could provide some useful insights for the formation of institutions at different levels and for different types of social systems, especially, for the analysis and formation of communication structures in transaction arrangements. Until now, however, the discourse concept has not been made empirically tractable in order to integrate it in hypotheses ready for empirical tests. What DE can contribute to economics is still open to discussion. I totally agree with Voigt that empirical studies matter; but, from my point of view, empirical work would be more promising if discourse and deliberation were integrated into the behavioral model, and if participation in constitutional choices were also subjected to dynamic analyses of the interrelations between choices and their respective outcomes. The analysis of constitutional procedures needs to rest on a broader, microanalytical base. However, Voigt's uncritical reference as to how economists would start, what they would attempt to do, and what they would prefer (pp. 211f.) could impede a fruitful dialogue with other disciplines.

References

Albert, H. (1965) "Wertfreiheit als methodisches Prinzip: Zur Frage der Notwendigkeit einer normativen Sozialwissenschaft", in Topitsch, E. (ed.) *Logik der Sozialwissenschaften*, Cologne and Berlin (Kiepenheuer & Witsch), 181-210.

Coleman, J. S. (1990) *Foundations of Social Theory*, Cambridge (Mass.) a. o. (The Belknap Press of Harvard University Press).

Denzau, A. and D. C. North (1994) "Shared Mental Models: Ideologies and Institutions", *Kyklos* 47, 3-31.

Gäfgen, G. (1979) "Zur Theorie kollektiver Entscheidungen in der Wirtschaft", in Pommerehne, W. W. and B. S. Frey (eds.) *Ökonomische Theorie der Politik*, Berlin a. o. (Springer), 83-129.

Haase, M. (1995) *Galileische Idealisierung – Ein pragmatisches Konzept*, Perspektiven der Analytischen Philosophie, vol. 4, Berlin et al. (Walter de Gruyter).

Hahn, F. (1996) "Some Economical Reflections on Ethics", in Farina, F., F. Hahn and S. Vannucci (eds.): *Ethics, Rationality, and Economic Behaviour*, Oxford (Clarendon Press), 13-21.

Hayek, F. A. v. (1945) "The Use of Knowledge in Society", *The American Economic Review*, XXXV (4), 519-530.

Küttner, M. (1987) "Deskriptive Modelle und Handlungsempfehlungen in der Betriebswirtschaftslehre", in Schmidt, R. H. and G. Schor (eds.) *Modelle in der Betriebswirtschaftslehre*, Wiesbaden (Gabler), 251-268.

Langlois, R. N. (2001) "Knowledge, Consumption, and Endogenous Growth", *Journal of Evolutionary Economics* 11, 77-93.

Macy, M. W. (1997) "Identity, Interest and Emergent Rationality", *Rationality and Society* 9 (4), 427-448.

North, D. C. (1990) *Institutions, Institutional Change, and Economic Performance*, Cambridge (Cambridge University Press).

Suppes, P. (1980) "Probabilistic Empiricism and Rationality", in Hilpinen, R. (ed.) *Rationality in Science*, Dordrecht a. o. (D. Reidel), 171-190.

Ward, B. (1972) *What's Wrong with Economics?* New York and London (Basis Books).

Constitutional Culture and Comparative Analysis: Comment on Stefan Voigt

Horst Hegmann†

Stefan Voigt's paper marks the starting point of a rather ambitious project. His aim is to assign the appropriate position to deliberation in Positive Constitutional Economics. After discussing the two strands of research he draws on, Normative Constitutional Economics as founded by Buchanan and Discourse Ethics as developed by Apel and Habermas, he then introduces deliberation into his own field of research in order to test empirical hypotheses on the causal relationship between popular participation in constitutional choice and the contents and success of the resulting constitution.

Leaving aside Voigt's discussion of Buchanan and Habermas, I will concentrate on this research project. Voigt starts with a critique of Jon Elster's more applied variant of Discourse Ethics. At first sight, it is surprising that in doing so he stresses Elster's distinction between deliberation, bargaining and the strategic use of argument, because he makes no further mention of them when outlining his own enterprise. This method of proceeding, however, becomes plausible when we remember that Positive Constitutional Economics is a branch of Public Choice Theory. Public Choice in turn is the application of conventional microeconomics to topics of non-market decision-making.

As Voigt rightly points out (pp. 204f.), deliberation makes sense only in a world in which not everything is known to everybody beforehand. Modern economic theory began with the assumption of perfect rationality, meaning that all relevant aspects of the situation are known to all participants. In a world in which everyone knows all other actors' preferences and the facts of their circumstances, it would not even be possible to engage in simple bargaining, let alone in genuine deliberation. Individuals would have no option but to react to the constraints they confront. They would take home their individual pay-offs with no more interaction than silent acts of exchange.

This ceases to apply when the actors do not know other people's preferences. If only the objective conditions are common knowledge, they may engage in bargaining, making offers and revealing thereby *peu à peu* their own preferences. Because these offers are the only indications of their preferences, individual pay-offs now not only depend on objective restrictions, but also on how cleverly each participant can bargain. If, in addition to the preferences of others, some aspects of the situation are also unknown, further need for interaction arises. However, all participants have as many common interests as conflicting ones. The bulk of the literature on New Institutional Economics deals with the design of institutions so that they create the right incentives under such circumstances. An obvious example here is the relationship between an employer and his agent. If the former cannot personally supervise the latter, they may both gain through the design of a contract motivating the agent to act in the interests of the employer. Without such a contract, the employer in turn may have no incentive to engage the agent in the first place. They both would lose by being unable to realise a Pareto-superior co-operation arrangement.

For a long time economists looked at constitutions along these lines. Politicians were depicted as agents of the people and constitutional choice was to deal with the design of an efficient constitutional contract. Appropriate rules were to provide the right incentives for the different branches of government. For citizens to agree on 'optimal' arrangements, however, it was assumed that everyone acts within the same informational frame. Because of asymmetrical information, each person may know different things, but the framework to organise their knowledge is the same everywhere. Only by dropping this optimistic assumption were economists able to reach an understanding of genuine deliberation. Only then could they start to perceive interaction not just as bargaining or a technical discussion but as a mutual assistance in the process of providing orientation in a widely unknown world.

From the viewpoint of a political actor this rather pessimistic view on available knowledge creates immense problems of trust. Under such circumstances, when somebody proposes a constitutional reform, his addressee lacks a measuring rod to check whether the change is an improvement or not. In response to this problem, different political cultures have emerged over time, systems of shared habits of thought and explicit rules providing guidelines for collective decision making in general and constitutional choice in particular. Seen from this viewpoint, a constitutional document makes sense only within the context of a political culture. It will not suffice merely to look at a constitutional document in order to understand how collective decision-making works in a specific society.

Voigt, of course, is quite aware of that fact. He does not ignore the intimate relationship between partly implicit habits of thought and explicit rules (see for example Voigt and Kiwit 1995), but his research project deliberately leaves such habits of thought out of the equation. Instead, he decontextualizes (Toulmin, 1990, pp. 21 and 45ff.) the written constitutional documents in order to isolate an independent variable (popular participation) and various dependent ones (concerning the contents and the success of a constitution). He thus replaces the organic traditions of preferences and cognitions embodied in a specific political culture with assumptions derived from a microeconomic model in order to derive hypotheses which he tests by looking at a great number of cases.

Now it becomes clear why Voigt can neglect the precise distinction between deliberation, bargaining and the strategic use of argument, so prominent in his critique of Elster's work. By contrast with Elster, Voigt is not really interested in proving the relative merits of deliberation compared with bargaining or the strategic use of argument. As long as he can show that deliberation may be more than just bargaining or a technical discussion on optimal institutional design, he is able to assume that human interaction can have an effect on the contents and success of a constitutional document beyond given preferences or restrictions.

Up to this point, Voigt's argumentation is quite straightforward. Starting from some rather pessimistic assumptions about individual stocks of knowledge, he constructs a microeconomic model of the situation, derives hypotheses from that model and attempts to test these hypotheses in a variety of cases. However, his last two hypotheses do not fit this schema. Hypothesis # 11 for example reads: 'Demand for participation in constitutional choice is subject to a secular increase' (p. 223). This hypothesis cannot be derived from Voigt's model. Of course, Popper taught us that it does not matter how we arrive at our hypotheses as long as we can falsify them, but Voigt's choice here looks decidedly arbitrary. He might just as well test the hypothesis of whether people in hot countries tend to have despotic governments. This was, after all, a serious assumption on the part of such eminent legal theorists as Jean Bodin and Charles-Louis de Montesquieu.

But hypothesis # 12 is still more problematic, it reads: 'Possibilities to participate are influenced by the values and norms prevalent in a given society' (p. 224). Again, this hypothesis cannot be derived from a microeconomic theory, moreover it contradicts the whole enterprise. Either Voigt decontextualizes constitutional texts in order to test hypothetical causal relationships for a range of different societies, or he analyses specific constitutions in their cultural contexts. He is inconsistent if he adds a hypothesis on political culture to a catalogue of hypotheses intended to test causal relationships leaving culture out of account.

Despite these criticisms, Voigt's whole enterprise is promising, provided he keeps its limits in mind. He himself mentions the sobering experiences with transition economics (p. 222). Here economists, some of them proponents of the New Institutional Economics in general and Public Choice in particular, believed for quite some time, that it would suffice to export a western legal framework to Russia and its former allies in order to start a new economic miracle. It was exactly the neglect of traditional habits of thought which frustrated the aspirations of this approach. In order to apply the results from quantitative, decontextualized research to specific cases, recontextualization is required. It depends on a society's political culture, whether a change in a given set of rules works as expected. The great political scientist of the 19th century, Alexis de Tocqueville, wrote in his 'De la démocratie en Amérique': 'Je suis convaincu que la situation (géographique; H.H.) la plus heureuse et les meilleurs lois ne peuvent maintenir une constitution en dépit des mœurs, tandis que celles-ci tirent encore parti des positions les plus défavorables et des plus mauvaises lois' (Tocqueville, 1986, p. 455). Decontextualizing economists alone are bound to fail, if they try to design better constitutions, they also need genuine deliberation with other holders of the knowledge dispersed throughout society.

References

Tocqueville, A. de (1986) *De la démocratie en Amérique*, Paris (Gallimard Folio).
Toulmin, S. (1990) *Cosmopolis: the Hidden Agenda of Modernity*, New York (The Free Press).
Voigt, S. and D. Kiwit (1995) "Überlegungen zum institutionellen Wandel unter Berücksichtigung des Verhältnisses interner und externer Institutionen", *Ordo* 46, 117-148.

Chapter 9

Bargaining over Beliefs*

Robert E. Goodin and Geoffrey Brennan

Abstract

Beliefs may lie in the background of bargaining, but they are not themselves the subject of bargaining, as it is ordinarily economically understood. Much of what goes on in actual social bargaining does, however, concern the negotiation and renegotiation of beliefs. Disputes over beliefs are sometimes resolved through persuasion, other times through negotiation. In the latter case, each still believes the truth of the proposition she was originally advocating; but all agree to treat certain propositions 'as if true', for the particular purposes at hand. That process of 'bargaining over beliefs' is a form of bargaining, on a par with any other, in ways that economists can and should take on board.

When sociologists, social anthropologists and philosophers of language talk of society as being a 'negotiated order', what they refer to is a system of shared beliefs and understandings. Comprehending the 'rationality' of social action is, for them, essentially a matter of elucidating the shared beliefs and understandings of the agents involved.[1]

When economists talk of a 'negotiated order' in society, what they envisage as being negotiated are not beliefs but rather distributions: paradigmatically of benefits and burdens, principally of a material sort. Beliefs of several sorts lie in the background of that sort of bargaining, to be sure.[2] But beliefs are not themselves the subject of bargaining, economically understood.

That constitutes a serious deficiency in economic understanding, though. Much of what goes on in actual social bargaining does indeed concern the negotiation

---

* With permission to reprint from *Ethics* 111, Jan 2001, 256-77 by The University of Chicago Press.

[1] This theme unites such otherwise diverse writers as Schutz, 1943; Berger and Luckmann, 1966; Wilson, 1970; Geertz, 1973; Taylor, 1985; Walzer, 1987; MacIntyre, 1988; and Searle, 1995.

[2] We have to believe that certain things will serve our desires (otherwise we would not want them); we have to believe we presently lack those things (otherwise we would not seek them); we have to believe that there are not enough of those things to go around (otherwise we would not compete for them); we have to believe that the distribution of those things is under the control of specific others (otherwise we would not try to strike a bargain with them).

and renegotiation of beliefs. That is what judges and juries are supposed to be arguing about, for example; that is what fact-finding commissions of inquiry are supposed to be arguing about; and that is at least part of what political parties are arguing about, in offering their rival election manifestos.

Such disputes over beliefs sometimes get resolved through persuasion. One side convinces the other of the truth of its beliefs, perhaps, or perhaps both come to see that the truth genuinely lies in some third proposition altogether (cf. Lehrer and Wagner, 1981). Other times, however, disputes over beliefs get 'resolved' through negotiation rather than persuasion. Each still believes the truth of the proposition she was originally advocating; but each sees the need to 'get on with it'; so all agree to treat certain propositions 'as if true', for the particular purposes at hand (cf. Lewis, 1979). The latter process is what we shall be calling 'bargaining over beliefs'. Our aim is to show that that is a form of bargaining, on a par with any other, in ways that economists can and should take on board.

In exploring that novel form of bargaining, our strategy is to proceed through the analysis of 'most different cases' cf. Mill (1843, bk 3, ch. 8). Ordinarily, many different forms of bargaining are intertwined, and the presence of the more familiar forms ('bargaining over distributions') blinds us to the presence of less familiar ones ('bargaining over beliefs'). To bracket out these confounding factors, we therefore focus on situations in which familiar forms of bargaining seem necessarily absent. We then show that even there bargaining, of a sort, might still occur. The sort of 'bargaining over beliefs' which stands out so clearly in relation to those aberrant situations, however, is not confined to them alone: having isolated the phenomenon in relation to extreme cases, we can perceive elements of it at work in more common sorts of social bargaining.

1 Bargaining: The Standard Story

Rational choice, economistically understood, is the joint product of belief and desire. Desires dictate the ends. Beliefs merely inform as to which means are best for serving them.

As with rational choice, so too with rational bargaining. Each agent is presumed to have a complete and consistent preference ranking over all the options which are potentially on the table; and that preference ordering is supposed to be unaffected by what is or is not on the table at any moment. Bargaining is supposedly a mere matter of each bargainer's deploying his skill and resources so as to induce the others to accept a joint solution which takes him as high up his preference ordering as possible.

Different mathematical models offer different 'solution concepts' defining which bargains ought rationally to be struck. But common across all those models is that central image of bargainers as coming to the table with independently given and settled preferences. Bargaining, as it is standardly conceived, is strictly over outcomes evaluated in terms of those settled preferences (cf. Luce and Raiffa, 1957, ch. 6; Young, 1975). Bargaining is not supposed to *change* people's preferences, desires – or beliefs, either. All that is taken as given, as exogenous to the bargaining process itself.[3]

2 Identical Interests, Different Perceptions: Bargaining over Beliefs

On the standard account, bargaining is driven purely by people's divergent goals. Bargaining comes about because people have opposing objectives. Those opposing objectives give rise to conflicts of interests (cf. Axelrod, 1970). To some greater or lesser extent, one person getting more of what he wants necessarily entails the others getting less of what they want. That, on the standard account, is the sort of situation that gives rise to bargaining problems.

Following the 'most different cases' strategy announced at the outset, we here focus on cases as unlike that as possible – cases where everyone has literally the same goals, where everyone ranks all the alternative possible outcomes in exactly the same way. In cases such as these, the most that they could possibly suffer would be a 'coordination problem' (cf. Schelling, 1960; Lewis, 1969). If everyone were literally agreed as to goals and indifferent to several equally good ways of attaining them, then the problem would simply be one of settling on one of those courses of action and communicating that choice clearly to everyone who has a part to play within that plan of action. The necessary information might not be easily conveyed; misunderstandings might arise; coordination and communication may be urgently required. But bargaining as such would have no role to play. Or so it is standardly said.

Even in that 'pure coordination game' scenario, however, we might still face an occasion for bargaining of a sort: 'bargaining over beliefs', as we shall call it. Consider the following variation on the basic 'coordination game' scenario – a scenario of 'identical interests, different perceptions'. Suppose that we face a coordination problem of the familiar sort. Everyone must go the same way, if any of us are to get anywhere at all. Everyone has the same goal: everyone wants to end up at exactly the same place. Everyone recognizes that it is a coordination problem: everyone appreciates that they must all proceed in the same direction if any of them are to get there. But imagine, now, that there is disagreement within the group as to which is the 'right' way to go to get there.

Imagine, for example, a convoy which for reasons of safety must travel together journeying across the Nullarbor desert of central Australia. Everyone in the party wants to reach Perth, but (these being the 1950s, before paved roads or reliable signposts) there is disagreement within the group as to which is the right path to take to get there. Or for another more real-world example, imagine members of the Federal Reserve arguing over the best way to control inflation without plunging the

[3] Formal models, of course, abstract from the messiness of the real world. There, hard bargaining is indeed interspersed with persuasive appeals; bargainers alternatively threaten and cajole; negotiators seek agreements that everyone can live with, rather than necessarily pressing their own bargaining advantage to the hilt (Midgaard, 1976; Raiffa, 1982). For present purposes, however, we will be sticking to those formalizations, to show ways in which those models can and should be amended and extended even in their own terms.

economy into a recession. Or for yet another example, imagine members of a firm's board of directors arguing over whether or not to buy out a rival firm.

Lest the model of 'identical interests, different perceptions' seem too contrived, note that that is precisely what underlies contemporary models of 'deliberative democracy'. According to the standard idealization, democratic deliberators are supposed to focus on what is in the common interest rather than what is in their particular personal or sectoral interests. Insofar as there is a single 'public' upon whose interests each deliberator is supposed to be focusing, the interests which each deliberator is supposed to be pursuing are identical to those interests which each other deliberator is supposed to be pursuing. Deliberation is necessary, in such circumstances, merely because each perceives the same public's interests differently. On those accounts, what deliberation is all about is resolving those differential perceptions of the public interest.[4]

In the ordinary course of events, we resolve factual disagreements by pooling our information or by conducting further experiments.[5] But where people have radically different prior beliefs, it ordinarily takes several rounds of Bayesian updating before those beliefs begin converging at all closely; and in practice we often have to take some joint action well before those processes have played themselves out. Similarly, incremental trial-and-error processes are often precluded, either by the pressures of time or by some other awkward feature of the situation (options are lumpy, or the response function is time-lagged, or whatever: Goodin, 1982, ch. 2). Let us call these cases of 'arrested convergence', and let us confine our attention to situations of that sort.

Finally, let us suppose that the people involved want a 'rationally-grounded decision'. Sometimes collective decisions represent just a pragmatic consensus, whereby everyone agrees on the same course of action, but each for his own very different reasons and with different ends in view (cf. MacCallum, 1966; Sunstein, 1995). Saying that people involved in a situation of 'identical interests, different perceptions' want a 'rationally-grounded decision' is to say that they want more than that sort of bare agreement as to what they should do. They want their collective action itself to be based on some collectively-agreed view as to why they are doing it, as to exactly how that action is supposed to work to produce the end in view.[6] They want this, in no small part, to ensure that any success they collectively enjoy will be sustainable, rather than the product of some unreproducible fluke.

---

[4] See, e.g.: Cohen, 1989; Dryzek, 1990, ch. 2; Benhabib, 1994; Bohman and Rehg, 1997. This model, like formal bargaining models in their very different ways, clearly represents an idealization abstracting from the real world. But even if legislators are actually pursuing personal or sectoral advantage, they feel none the less obliged to couch their appeals in terms of the public interest; and even if statutes really are just the senseless product of one log-roll after another, legislators feel none the less obliged to attach to them a 'preamble' which purports to offer a single, agreed rationale for their enactment.

[5] Modelled, variously, by Harsanyi, 1967-68; Aumann, 1976; Lehrer and Wagner, 1981; and Goldman, 1994.

[6] Note that the requirement of a 'rationally-grounded decision', as we here employ it, is a very weak constraint. All that it requires is this: for whatever course of action the group

Here of course we are focusing on cases of 'identical interests, different perceptions', so *ex hypothesi* everyone has the same ends in view and they differ only in their perceptions of how best to bring about those ends. Saying that the group wants a 'rationally-grounded' resolution of their quandary is, in those circumstances, therefore to say that they want a collective decision endorsing one or another of those differing perceptions as to how best to achieve those shared ends. The task of collective decision-making is to determine which it will be.

In the course of those deliberations, people with differing perceptions will naturally try to persuade one another of the greater accuracy of their own perspectives. But *ex hypothesi* they will have to act before they have been able to achieve full convergence of their perceptions. Wanting a 'rationally-grounded decision' in such circumstances forces them to opt for one of those sets of perceptions (and its concomitant action-plan and rationale), in preference to various other perceptions, action-plans and rationales that are still extant among some members of the group.

3 But is it Bargaining?

Spirited discussions inevitably ensue. Views diverge as to which way the group ought collectively to proceed, with some people championing one way and some another. Such discussions are naturally characterized by arguments and counter-arguments. All of that is broadly reminiscent of negotiation and bargaining behavior. But is it bargaining, strictly speaking?

There are two obvious (but opposing) respects in which such discussions might be thought to be radically unlike bargaining of the ordinary sort. Both are rooted in the observation that bargaining games are, paradigmatically, mixed-motive games. In any bargaining situation, there must be 'gains from trade': there must be motives for cooperation, as well as motives for competition. Absent either element – absent either elements of cooperation or elements of conflict – a situation could not involve bargaining, as it is ordinarily understood.

Objections to seeing cases of 'identical interests, different perceptions' as cases of bargaining might focus on the absence of one or the other of those essential elements of a mixed motive game. The first objection is that such situations of 'identical interests, different perceptions' do not contain enough conflict for them to qualify as a case of a mixed-motive or hence bargaining game. The second ob-

---

chooses, there must be some coherent story, based on the perceptions of some (perhaps just one) person, about how this course of action is supposed to lead to those results.

What the constraint is designed to rule out is the phenomenon of shifting coalitions leading to a series of partial decisions which, taken together, are simply incoherent. Thus, in the Nullarbor example, what we want to rule out is this. Suppose the track forks in three at three separate places. Jack thinks the convoy should go straight, then left, then right. Jill thinks it should go left, then straight, then right. James thinks it should go left at all forks. If they decided their route one step at a time, through majority voting, the convoy would go left, then left, then right. But *nobody* thinks that that is what they should do: that sequence of choices corresponds to no one's mental map of how to get out of the desert (Brennan, 1998).

jection is that there is not enough scope for cooperation. Both objections, we argue, are in error.

No Conflict of Interest?

In ordinary bargaining games, each player is trying to secure some narrow advantage for himself at the expense of someone else. Situations of 'identical interests, different perceptions' are 'most different' in that respect. There, what each person is trying to do is simply to promote interests which he shares with each and every other party to the discussions. In terms of the structure of the ultimate payoffs in view, the discussion must be classed as purely cooperative rather than competitive or even a mixed-motive one. And that being so, it seems not strictly speaking to be a situation that can give rise to 'bargaining' at all. Or so the first objection would go.

The lived experience of such situations is, of course, otherwise. Those discussions are, first and foremost, *arguments*. In them, each is trying to get his own way. In them, each is trying to prevail over others who are advocating a position opposed to one's own. True, what they are arguing about is what is best for all and each of us. But what we have in common (a shared concern for the interests of all and each) is eclipsed in our actual behavior by that about which we disagree (how best to promote that shared concern).

While there clearly is conflict, a persistent objector might reply, there is still no conflict of interest. No one stands to gain at anyone else's expense. (Indeed, ex hypothesi, in the situation in view, everyone will at the end of the day receive exactly the same identical payoff.) Game theorists take the 'division of spoils' to lie at the core of bargaining games; and for them, the very fact that everyone's fortunes rise or fall together means that this is not a game of dividing anything up, and hence not a bargaining game.

That objection seems to us to rest on a misunderstanding of what is going on even in the most standard of bargaining games, however. Consider this. Even when we pirates are bargaining over the division of spoils – gold for you, gems for me – what we are talking about is the extent to which each of us gets what he wants. What ultimate payoff each of us might get from getting what he wants is a separate issue, which is (rightly) left wholly to one side in any formal characterization of the bargaining game. Upon further inspection the gold may well turn out to be fool's gold and the gems to be cut glass, both worthless. As it eventually happens, then, we actually had no conflict of interest after all: there was nothing of any real value to any of us on the bargaining table, to start with. But we did not know that at the time we were carving up the booty. We each (however erroneously) valued everything that was on the table, and we each bargained hard with one another over the distribution of those (ultimately worthless) things.

The same is true in the case of 'identical interests, different perceptions'. We each *want* our group to adopt whatever course of action we perceive as being best for promoting our shared interests. And since we perceive things differently, we want the group to adopt different courses of action. Insofar as those are incompatible courses of action, my getting what I want precludes you from getting what you want. There is a 'conflict of wants'.

Furthermore, that 'conflict of wants' gives rise to a 'conflict of interests' that is perfectly genuine in the game-theoretic sense that is relevant in these circumstances. In situations of 'identical interests, different perceptions', different people perceive things differently. Because of our differing perceptions, each of us *expects* different outcomes from various courses of action. And our choice behavior must inevitably be governed by our *ex ante* expectations. Thus, even if ultimately we will all get the same payoff, *ex ante* I might expect that that payoff to each of us will be $2000 from our doing X and $1000 from our doing Y, and your expectations might be just the opposite.

At the end of the day, of course, each of us will actually receive exactly the same payoff, be it large or small. What we are haggling over, in bargaining based on our differential perceptions and different expected payoffs based on them, is simply which course of action is the right one for maximizing the payoff that will accrue identically to both of us. But that still leaves us plenty to argue over, at the time.

Looking at the payoffs from the perspective of some omniscient observer who knows how things will eventually turn out is to take the wrong perspective. Rather, we ought be looking at the situation from the point of view of the people who have to make the choice at the time. And in those terms, differing perceptions yield different expectations, which give rise in turn to differing 'expected utilities' and hence to a genuine 'conflict of interest' of the ordinary game-theoretic sort.

Whether that conflict is amenable to resolution by bargaining remains an open question. (We will be turning to that next.) The point, for the moment, is simply that the first objection is in error. Contrary to superficial appearances, a situation of 'identical interests, different perceptions' does indeed contain elements of conflict of the standard game-theoretic sort. It is not disqualified from being a mixed-motive (and hence bargaining) game on that score.

No Possibility of Compromise?

A case of 'identical interests, different perceptions' might seem not to involve 'bargaining', strictly speaking, for a second reason, opposite to the first. The first objection was that there was not enough conflict in the situation to ground a bargaining game. The second objection claims, conversely, that there is not enough scope for cooperation in them. Something in the nature of such situations, it may be objected, precludes compromise solutions of the sort which are essential in ordinary bargaining.

Of course, even in ordinary bargaining games each person is keen on getting his own way. But ordinary bargaining games are also characterized by a certain amount of 'give and take'. In the final analysis, each of us is prepared to settle for something less than he was initially seeking. That willingness to compromise is precisely what allows bargaining solutions to emerge.

Unless there is some scope, however limited, for each getting 'more or less' of what he wants, there would be no scope for bargaining among them. Suppose instead that the item at issue were utterly indivisible, and therefore has to be given entirely to one party or entirely to the other. Then they clearly have something to argue over, but they have nothing to *bargain* over – nothing to *divide* among themselves.[7]

Now, that may seem to be precisely the situation with respect to bargaining over beliefs as to 'what is best' in games of 'identical interests, different perceptions'. In the case of the travellers in the Nullarbor, the road to Perth is *either* the track going to the northwest or the one going to the southwest: it makes no sense to split the difference, going due west over the rocky plain where there is obviously no track at all. In the case of the quarrelling members of the Federal Reserve, one group has a model of the economy that recommends an increase of .5% in interest rates, while the other has a model which recommends an increase of 2%. But it makes no sense simply to split the difference, rising it 1.25%: there is simply no credible model of the economy presently on offer which can justify a move such as that. In the case of the quarrelling members of a firm's board of directors, one group has reasons for thinking it would maximize their profits to buy out their rivals while another group has reasons for thinking that that would do grievous damage to their own firm's bottom line. But it makes no sense simply to split the difference, buying a 25% stake in the other firm: neither group can think of any reason for thinking that that would maximize their own profits.[8]

In the fullness of time, more discussion or more experience might lead our perceptions to converge. But suppose circumstances require a decision before our perceptions have had a chance to converge. Then if we want a collective decision backed by a coherent collectively-endorsed rationale, we have no alternative but to opt for one or another of the contending perspectives on offer. In such a resolution, one side gets things all its own way – and other people's perspectives get ignored altogether. And all-or-nothing choices like that seem to leave us with no differences which can be split. In winner-take-all games, there seems to be no scope for compromise and hence nothing over which to bargain. That, anyway, is the essence of the second objection to viewing these sorts of situations as ones involving bargaining.

Once again, however, that seems to us to mischaracterize the situation. In the sort of scenario we have been sketching, it is certainly true that one of the contending sets of perceptions (and the concomitant action-plan and rationale underlying

[7] Supposing it is also temporally indivisible (so they cannot 'take turns' having it for fixed periods of time), that there is nothing else that these two people want from one another (so they cannot make sidepayments to one another in some other currency), and so on.

[8] Of course, splitting the difference in such ways might lead to moves which, fortuitously, prove to have been 'just right'. But if so, that would have been purely fortuitous. We have been given reasons for believing that each of the opposing recommendations might be the right thing to do, but we have been given no reasons for believing that splitting the difference between two incompatible models might yield the right results. Splitting the difference in such circumstances literally 'makes no sense'. There is no coherent model explaining why that might be the correct course for achieving our shared goals. And that course of action would therefore be rejected by a group which is seeking a 'reasoned decision', agreement not only on what they are going to do but also on why.

it) will have to be collectively endorsed, and all others set aside. In that sense, it may well be that one side will 'get things all its way', and other sides will get ignored altogether. But the point remains that the action being taken, while being based on one officially-endorsed perspective, might be to some greater or lesser extent 'in accord' with other perspectives which are being officially ignored. The practical upshot – the action-plan – may be more or less similar. Even the rationale that the favored perspective gives for those actions might itself be to some greater or lesser extent in accord with the rationales that would be given for similar actions by some of the other (disfavored) perspectives.

That is simply to say that the choice of perspectives upon which we will collectively act may not be an 'all or nothing' matter, after all. It is not necessarily a game which you either win completely or lose completely. Even once it has been decided that your own perspective will not be the one which is officially endorsed, you might nonetheless have preferences among the other perspectives, based on their affinities with your own. Insofar as you do, those 'preferences over perspectives not your own' create some middle ground of the sort required for a genuinely compromise, bargained solution.

The fact that people's perceptions have greater or lesser affinities with one another's creates the scope for people cooperatively coalescing behind some alternative or another. From the perspective of many of them, the alternative being pursued may be merely second- or third-best. But what even those people can agree on is that the alternative being pursued is much better than some of the other alternatives not being pursued. It is not at the top of their preference ranking, but it is not at the bottom either. It is, in short, a 'compromise' solution of just the sort which initially seemed unavailable in cases of 'bargaining over beliefs'.

4 The Nature of the 'Bargain'

The burden of our argument so far has been that situations of 'bargaining over beliefs' might contain both enough conflict and enough cooperation to qualify as 'mixed-motive games'. While bargaining games of any sort are a subspecies of mixed-motive games, however, not all mixed-motive games involve what we ordinarily think of as bargaining.

The sequence of moves and countermoves in an ordinary mixed-motive game just involves each player doing the best he can for himself, given what the other has done or is expected to do. Bargaining, in contrast, involves give-and-take aiming, ultimately, at an agreed joint action. Bargaining, when successful, ends in an agreement, whereas the most we get with ordinary mixed-motive games is an equilibrium.

To show that bargaining is indeed involved in cases of 'bargaining over beliefs', we therefore also need evidence that an agreement of some sort has been reached. This cannot be an agreement as to 'who is right', of course. *Ex hypothesi*, people cannot agree on that. Instead, the agreement is on 'what we will do' and 'why'.

The upshot of bargaining over beliefs is thus not any change in people's beliefs themselves. Assuming that belief is not something we can conjure up through an act of will (cf. Williams, 1973), we cannot bargain over what to will ourselves to believe, either. The upshot of bargaining over beliefs is not simply an 'agreement to disagree'.[9] The upshot of bargaining over beliefs is instead that bargainers settle on some course of action, and on some rationale as to how it is supposed to work to produce the desired results. In the course of so acting, we are treating certain beliefs 'as if they were true'. But we definitely do so in the subjunctive case – in the tentative and hypothetical way in which propositions being tested are treated in scientific experiments.

That is very different from the upshot of ordinary mixed-motive games, in which we do not form any views at all on what we collectively will do. Each merely has views as to what he will do, given what the others have done or are expected to do. Bargaining over beliefs, in contrast, leads us to treat certain beliefs as true, for purposes of our collective endeavours – which is to say, it results in a collective agreement as to what we will collectively do and why. The presence of such a collective agreement, rather than merely an equilibrium outcome, is what elevates the situation into that special class of mixed-motive games which we call 'bargaining games'.

There is nothing mysterious about this business of 'treating as if true, for the purposes at hand'. It is, on one famous account (Lewis, 1979), just what we do in ordinary conversations all the time. In trying to make sense of others' utterances, we apply a 'principle of charity'. We assume they are trying to talk sense; we assume that they are asserting propositions which they believe are true and relevant for the purposes at hand; and so on. As part of that process of trying to make sense of what others are saying, we implicitly agree to 'treat as true, for the purposes of the present conversation' that set of background conditions which would render most coherent the propositions which our interlocutors seem to be asserting. But of course what propositions we find ourselves provisionally 'treating as if true' in this way vary from conversation to conversation. In agreeing provisionally to treat them as if true in one context, we are not thereby committing ourselves to believing they are true, or even to acting as if we believe they are true in any other context.

5 Recasting Bargaining Models

How might we plausibly model differences in belief in the context of simple bargaining models? In this section, we attempt to address this question by appealing to an example. The example itself is simple, but can be easily built up to accommodate several dimensions of the idea of bargaining in belief-space.

---

[9] Literally, that makes no sense (Aumann, 1976). And simply agreeing to leave certain matters unresolved – which is what that phrase ordinarily actually involves (Sunstein, 1996) – is not what we actually do in the cases at hand.

A Simple Model

To begin, let us assume there are just two possible states of the world, A and B. For each state, there is an unique action that must be collectively undertaken which gives the highest available payoff if that state prevails. Denote these actions *a* for state A, and *b* for state B. The respective payoffs are O_A (if *a* is taken and A prevails) and O_B (if *b* is taken and B prevails). Otherwise, there is no payoff: the payoffs for actions-state of the world combinations (*a*, B) and (*b*, A) are both zero. In each case, the payoffs can be thought of as an identical sum that accrues to all members of the collectivity. We do not necessarily assume that the payoffs O_A and O_B are themselves equal. We do, however, assume that both O_A and O_B embody a (positive) sum for each player, which is equal across all individuals – and hence equally valued by all individuals. The collective decision to be taken is that of which action is to be pursued. Below, we shall specifically consider a number of alternative collective decision procedures; but we shall take it that, in the case where no action satisfies the decision procedure, no action is taken and the payoff is zero. Accordingly, there is an opportunity cost of failing to take an action (make a decision) – which is the payoff forgone in that period. The longer the time taken to reach a collective decision, the larger the number of periods in which the zero payoff accrues (cf. Rubinstein, 1982). Finally, all these matters are common knowledge (and subjects of total agreement). So far, there is complete commonality of interest and of belief.

To accommodate some divergence in belief, let it be the case that there is uncertainty about which state of the world applies; and that different individuals have different 'priors' about the likelihood of the two states applying. Suppose, for example, that agent 1 believes that A will prevail with probability p_{A1} and B with probability p_{B1} (where $p_{B1} = [1 - p_{A1}]$); while agent 2 believes that A will prevail with probability p_{A2} and B with probability p_{B2} (where $p_{B2} = [1 - p_{A2}]$). Suppose without loss of generality that $p_{A1} > p_{A2}$.

Suppose further that

$$p_{A1}\, O_A > (1 - p_{A1})\, O_B \tag{1}$$

and that

$$p_{A2}\, O_A < (1 - p_{A2})\, O_B \tag{2}$$

Accordingly, there is a corresponding divergence of belief over which action to pursue: A believes that *a* is best; B believes that *b* is best. How is this disagreement to be reconciled? Note that, by implication, reconciliation is desired by both parties. Since $(1 - p_{A2})$ and O_B are both positive, getting *b* is better for agent 1 than getting no agreement: the only difficulty is that the opportunity cost of choosing *b* as an action is a forgone, and agent 1 believes that *a* is better for everyone in expected terms.

Implicitly here, we are taking it that collective action requires the agreement of both agents 1 and 2: there is a decision rule of consensus. If this is so, we can plausibly take it that, in the absence of other factors,[10] whichever agent who sees himself (and, incidentally, sees all others as well) as losing most by giving in will be prepared to hold out the longest. We might ask, for example, in the spirit of Nash-Zeuthen models (cf. Harsanyi, 1965; 1966), what is the highest probability of non-decision ('conflict') each player is prepared to sustain in order to achieve his preferred collective action rather than the preferred action of the other player? Denote this probability q_i. Then,

$$q_1 = [p_{A1} O_A - (1 - p_{A1}) O_B)] / p_{A1} O_A \qquad (3)$$

and

$$q_2 = [(1 - p_{A2}) O_B - p_{A2} O_A] / (1 - p_{A2}) O_B \qquad (4)$$

The idea here is that it is not 'rational' (or, perhaps better, 'not reasonable') to expect another player to concede in circumstances where you would not concede yourself. If $q_1 > q_2$ then agent 1 would be prepared to accept continued non-decision in circumstances in which agent 2 would not. Accordingly, agent 2 will concede and action *a* will prevail. The two-person community acts *as if* agent 1's beliefs are correct.

Additional Players, Additional States of the World

Now we can augment the foregoing model in several dimensions. One relevant dimension is to add further players. Suppose, for example, we add agent 3, who is such that his beliefs over the likelihood of contingencies A and B are exactly the same as agent 2's. Note that adding a further such player has no influence on the outcome, *provided* that consensus remains the relevant test. Agent 1 will hold out when both 2 and 3 will concede: so agent 1's beliefs will still prevail as the decisive set.[11] Note equally, however, that this outcome would change if the consensus test were to be replaced by majority rule. Then, obviously, the 'weight of opinion' would favor action *b*, reflecting the fact that the beliefs of the majority support that action.

It is useful to augment the foregoing model by expanding the number of states of the world. Accordingly, consider the simplest model. The additional state is denoted C and calls for action *c* with corresponding payoff O_C. This payoff is a triplet $[O_C, O_C, O_C]$ to each of the (assumed three) players, designated 1, 2 and 3 as before. And payoffs under action/state combinations (*c*, A), (*c*, B), (*a*, C), (*b*, C) are all zero. The matrix of action/states is therefore as shown in Figure 1. Corresponding to Figure 1, there is a matrix of agents/beliefs – with the entries indicating the relevant agent's beliefs over the likelihood that the denominated state of the

[10] Specifically, in the absence of psychological considerations that induce some agents to place a higher premium on 'getting their way' than others, or that make some agents want the esteem of having been proven 'right' or some similar effects.

[11] This will remain true, however, many additional players with the same beliefs as 2 are added.

world will prevail. Since these three states are taken to be exhaustive of the possibilities, $p_{Ai} + p_{Bi} + p_{Ci} = 1$ for all *i*.

Figure 1

		state of the world		
		A	**B**	**C**
	a	O_A	zero	zero
action	***b***	zero	O_B	zero
	c	zero	zero	O_C

Let it be the case that:

$p_{A1}\, O_A > p_{C1}\, O_C > p_{B1}\, O_B$

and

$p_{B2}\, O_B > p_{C2}\, O_C > p_{A2}\, O_A$

and

$p_{B3}\, O_B > p_{C3}\, O_C > p_{A3}\, O_A$.

Further, let it be the case that:

$$\Sigma_i\, p_{Ci}\, O_C > \Sigma\, p_{Ai}\, O_A > \Sigma\, p_{Bi}\, O_B$$

In this sense, one could say that there is maximal epistemic warrant for choosing action *c*. Each knows that all agents cannot be *right*. But if procedures are such as to treat the beliefs of all agents equally and on a par, belief by some agent becomes a reason for action according to that belief. Treating agents with equal respect entails – in the absence of any further considerations – a collective decision procedure that weights each set of beliefs equally. On this basis, the ideal procedure will generate a collective decision according to the sum (or equivalently, average) of the columns in the matrix in Figure 2. And on that basis, *c* emerges as the 'best' choice – the one best supported by the 'beliefs of the community'.

Figure 2

		beliefs as to likelihood		
		A	**B**	**C**
	1	p_{A1}	p_{B1}	p_{C1}
agent	**2**	p_{A2}	p_{B2}	p_{C2}
	3	p_{A3}	p_{B3}	p_{C3}

Now, were *c* to emerge as the collectively chosen action, it seems reasonable to say that the process that generated *c* involves bargaining over beliefs. After all, no agent actually believes that *c* is the best choice: agent 1 thinks *a* is best, and 2 and 3 think that *b* is best. Action *c* presents itself as an optimal compromise only because all agents prefer to secure consensus on something rather than not to act at all; and *c* is the action that, given the pattern of beliefs, is believed in aggregate to have the highest expected payoff. In the special case where $O_A = O_B = O_C$, the *only* consideration is beliefs about the likelihood of different states of the world (which in turn drive preferences over collective actions. In this case, C is the state of the world that is believed to be the most likely to prevail, in aggregate. And where collective decision arrangements are such that the decision-making agents must not only decide on an action but also provide a coherent *rationale* for that action (for example, in the case of a bench of judges, or a political party arguing for a policy), then the belief on the basis of which action *c* is best is entailed in the compromise choice of action *c*.

There remains a question, of course, as to whether *c* is 'institutionally accessible'. As before, majority rule will deliver *b* (since agents 2 and 3 can outvote 1). And a direct run-off between perceived 'best' options – *a* and *b* – will generate *a*, because (continuing the previous assumption) agent 1 is prepared to hold out longer (or equivalently endure a higher probability of inaction) than are agents 2 and agent 3. Nor, it seems, does a bargaining process necessarily guarantee *c*, because it is perfectly possible that, say,

$$(p_{A1}O_A)(p_{A2}O_A) > (p_{C1}O_C)(p_{C2}O_C)$$

and equivalently

$$(p_{A1}O_A)(p_{A3}O_A) > (p_{C1}O_C)(p_{C3}O_C)$$

even though

$$\Sigma\, p_{Ai}O_A < \Sigma\, p_{Ci}O_C.$$

As we earlier noted, if agents 2 and 3 have identical beliefs they will have identical threshold probabilities of conflict and will *both* equally defer to 1's intransigence.

In cases of bargaining over beliefs, then, no less than in cases where negotiation arises out of conflicts of interest with common beliefs, the institutional arrangements for achieving collective decisions matter. And indeed, there may exist no collective decision procedure which will robustly deliver what, on independent grounds, appears to be the best course of action, given the prevailing beliefs of community members.

Additional Actions

It would, finally, be possible to augment the basic bargaining over beliefs model by adding to the set of actions, qua actions. Return to the case where there are two mutually-exclusive states of the world, A and B. Suppose there is a continuum of actions, all of which involve some positive payoff in states A and B: *a* is best if A prevails, and *b* is best if B prevails, as before. But now, agent 1's most preferred action will be *d*, where $p_{A1}O_D{}^A + (1 - p_{A1})O_D{}^B$ is maximized; and agent 2's (and 3's) most preferred action will be *f*, where $p_{A2}O_F{}^A + (1 - p_{A2})O_F{}^B$ is maximized. Somewhere 'between' *d* and *f* (in the sense that the payoff under A is lower and under B higher than at *d*, and the payoff under A is higher and under B lower than at *f*) there will be an action *e*, such that:

$$[p_{A1}O_E{}^A + (1 - p_{A1})O_E{}^B]\,[p_{A2}O_E{}^A + (1 - p_{A2})O_E{}^B]$$

is maximized. This action *e* will represent a bargaining equilibrium for agents 1 and 2 – and hence, by argument analogous to the foregoing, for 1, 2 and 3 as well. At this point, the threshold probability of continued conflict, q, will be the same for both 1 and 2. And hence for 1, 2 and 3.

Needless to say, the action outcome *e* corresponds to a set of beliefs held by no one at all. Bargaining settles on a compromise action, and since the only source of possible gains from perceived compromise lies in the fact of differing beliefs, we might plausibly describe this as a case of bargaining over beliefs as well. This description is particularly apt when arrangements are such that some coherent rationale for action must be found, and articulated publicly.

This last case, because it involves continuity within the choice set, most clearly resembles the case of interest-based/preference-based exchange. The equilibrium analysis in this case is the same, whatever the source of conflict. But since, in the belief case, interests as such are identical, *belief* is the only instrument of bargaining available for the purposes of the exercise: even here, we have a kind of 'bargaining in belief'.

A Caveat

Although the focus of our discussion so far has been directed at pointing out the similarities between bargaining over beliefs and bargaining over interests, there is one aspect in which the two kinds of bargaining differ. In the normal (interest-based) case, options that are 'close' to one another in description are taken to be close to one another in value. So, for example, if the collective decision is taken to be the level of provision of some desired 'public good' (education, say), then levels of education provision that are very close are standardly taken to give rise to agent valuations that are correspondingly close.

No such presumption holds in the case of beliefs. The probability that proposition V is true may be held by agent 1 to be quite high, but there is no presumption that proposition V^1 ('close' in some sense to V) will be assigned a similar probability of being true. There is, in this sense, no analogue in 'belief space' to the continuity property of utility functions. This fact may complicate bargaining over beliefs: but it does not render the notion of bargaining over beliefs incoherent.

6 Different Currencies

To this point, our models have all been assuming that people's payoffs are purely a function of outcomes, and agency is irrelevant. That is to say, those models have been assuming that if action *a* is performed and state of the world A eventuates, then everyone involved receives the identical payoff of O_A, whether they had been the ones arguing for action *a* or not.

In the real world, of course, that is not true. People often take personal satisfaction in 'getting it right' and shame in 'getting it wrong'. These involve private payoffs accruing to the individuals concerned, over and above the O_A payoff which accrues to everyone who is a member of the group. Furthermore, social institutions of credit and blame are standardly imposed to encourage people trying to influence the group's actions to get it right and discourage them from getting it wrong. Those incentive side-payments, too, accrue as private payoffs to those responsible for taking the lead in guiding the group down one path rather than another.[12]

On the face of it, all those sorts of private 'responsibility' or 'agency-based' payoffs might seem to be all-or-nothing affairs. The 'bounty' paid, as a private agency-based side-payment, might be a function of the value of the public payoff that their wisdom and steadfastness turned out to achieve for the group as a whole; and if it is, then different people might anticipate themselves getting different sized private agency-based payoffs, simply because they anticipate leading the group to more or less rewarding shared payoffs (O_A etc.). But at the end of the day, the group has to perform one action rather than another, and any given agent is either responsible (in the sense of having advocated that course of action) or not. And with an all-or-nothing payoff structure of that sort, it would seem that there is minimal scope for compromises, tradeoffs or hence bargaining among the various players.

[12] Insofar as people cannot change their beliefs through any act of will, it would be odd to hold people responsible for what beliefs they have (cf. Stocker, 1982). Notice, however, that what we are holding people responsible for is not what beliefs they hold but, rather, for encouraging others of us who do not share those beliefs to permit them undertake actions on our collective behalf which are predicated on the assumption that their beliefs are correct.

Even with payoffs calibrated in terms of these different agency-based currencies, however, there may be scope for compromise and hence bargaining. All we need do here is to suppose – perfectly plausibly – that there are generally at least two levels of agency-based private payoffs involved in such situations. Those who 'take the lead' in advocating a particular course of action get a relatively larger share of the credit or blame, satisfaction or shame, for what happens as a result of the group's following their lead. But while the lion's share of credit or blame goes to the leaders, a certain measure of credit or blame goes to their 'junior partners' in the coalition advocating that course of action. Or, where the group decides what to do by looking at which choice of action has the highest 'epistemic warrant' by pooling everyone's expected utilities, each player would receive a share of credit or blame for the ultimate outcome in proportion to the extent to which her expected utility estimates contributed to that epistemic warrant.

And even without compromise in this 'agency' dimension, there may still be bargaining of a sort involved. If agent 1 derives a private payoff from 'having his way' and cares nothing for the shame of being proven wrong, whereas agent 2 would be mortified if he were responsible for what turned out to be the 'wrong' choice and derives little personal satisfaction from 'winning the argument', these factors will shift any bargaining solution towards *a* (in those cases where multiple states of the world or multiple actions are on offer). But in general agent 1 will get things only 'rather more' his own way; and even if agent 1 is utterly decisive and *a* is chosen, this outcome too would simply reflect the relative positions of the two 'bargainers'.

7 Extending the Model

To isolate 'bargaining over beliefs' as a distinct category of bargaining behaviour, we have here been deliberately focusing on cases 'most different' from the cases of conflicts of interest which give rise to most ordinary bargaining. But as we said at the outset, most real-world bargaining games involved elements of both 'partially conflicting interests' and 'differing perceptions'. People are bargaining, at one and the same time, both over distributions and over beliefs.

In a literally zero-sum game, any error that your opponent makes in pursuing his interests inevitably rebounds to your own advantage: there is no advantage to you, there, in helping correct any false beliefs that others might be harbouring. But most games in the real world are no more pure-conflict games of that sort than they are purely-cooperative ones of the sort we have here been discussing.

Many real-world bargaining games can be aptly characterized as 'unequal coordination games', the classical instance of which is the Battle of the Sexes. This is a coordination game, in the sense that each of us prefers that we do something together rather than go our separate ways. But it is an unequal coordination game, in the sense that each of us has our own preferences as to what that should be. You want to go to the wrestling, I to the opera; but you would prefer to go to the opera with me than to the wrestling by yourself, and I would prefer to go to the wrestling with you than to the opera by myself.[13]

In situations like that, we do not have literally 'identical interests' any more. But diverge though our interests may at the margin, everyone's overriding interest in such situations coincides. Attracted though each of us may be by our own preferred activities, most of all each of us wants to do something together. There is in such situations a dominant interest in cooperation which overrides any subordinate interests we have which conflict.

Now, suppose in such situations we have 'different perceptions' as well. Suppose I think that this opera is one you would really enjoy, and that that wrestling match is one I would find particularly silly; and you have just the opposite perceptions. Given our shared interests in doing something or other together, each of us has a reason to try persuading the other of the accuracy of our own perceptions in that regard. But given those shared interests in doing something or other together, each has a reason to yield – acting on the other's perceptions as well as on the other's preferences – if that is the only way for us to do what we both want to do, which is to go somewhere together.

That looks very much like a case of 'bargaining over beliefs', as discussed above. We jointly agree to 'treat as true' the perceptions of one or the other of the parties. The party who won is held responsible for being right, and if things turn out otherwise that party is the one to blame; and someone else's perceptions will be the ones we act upon in future.

Because it is not a purely cooperative game, that is not quite all there is to the story. In 'unequal coordination games', just as in zero-sum games, there are conflicting interests which might tempt us to mislead one another, professing beliefs we do not in fact hold about how attractive the other would actually find our preferred activity. But in repeated games of unequal coordination, such temptations are minimized by the realization that those whose perceptions are acted upon will be held responsible for the accuracy of those perceptions. If we have been intentionally misleading (or even just simply mistaken), we are likely to pay the price in future rounds of the game by having our perceptions not be the ones upon which collective action is based.

References

Aumann, R. J. (1976) "Agreeing to Disagree", *Annals of Statistics* 4, 1236-9.

Axelrod, R. (1970) *Conflict of Interests: A Theory of Divergent Goals with Applications to Politics*, Chicago (Markham).

Benhabib, S. (1994) "Deliberative Rationality and Models of Democratic Legitimacy", *Constellations* 1 (#1: April), 26-52.

Berger, P. L. and T. Luckmann (1966) *The Social Construction of Reality*, Garden City, N. Y. (Doubleday).

[13] Luce and Raiffa, 1957, p. 90. For a more politicized application, see Hardin's (1983) discussion of Pax Romana solutions to deterrence games.

Bohman, J. and W. Rehg, (eds.) (1997) *Deliberative Democracy: Essays on Reason and Politics*, Cambridge, Mass. (MIT Press).
Brennan, G. (1998) *Collective Irrationality and Belief*, Mimeo, Research School of Social Sciences, Australian National University.
Cohen, J. (1989) "Deliberation and Democratic Legitimacy", in Hamlin, A. and P. Pettit (eds.) *The Good Polity*, Oxford (Blackwell), 17-34.
Dryzek, J. S. (1990) *Discursive Democracy*, Cambridge (Cambridge University Press).
Geertz, C. (1973) *The Interpretation of Cultures*, New York (Basic).
Goldman, A. I. (1994) "Argumentation and Social Epistemology", *Journal of Philosophy* 91 (Jan), 27-49.
Goodin, R. E. (1982) *Political Theory and Public Policy*, Chicago (University of Chicago Press).
Hardin, R. (1983) "Unilateral versus Mutual Disarmament", *Philosophy & Public Affairs* 12, 236-54.
Harsanyi, J. C. (1965) "Bargaining and Conflict Situations in the Light of a New Approach to Game Theory", *American Economic Review* (Papers & Proceedings) 55, 447-57.
Harsanyi, J. C. (1966) "A General Theory of Rational Behavior in Game Situations", *Econometrica* 34, 613-34.
Harsanyi, J. C. (1967-68) "Games of Incomplete Information Played by Bayesian Players", *Management Science* 14, 159-82, 320-34, 486-502.
Lehrer, K. and C. Wagner (1981) *Rational Consensus in Science and Society: A Philosophical and Mathematical Study*, Dordrecht (D. Reidel).
Lewis, D. (1969) *Convention*, Oxford (Blackwell).
Lewis, D. (1979) "Scorekeeping in a Language Game", *Journal of Philosophical Logic* 8, 339-59.
Luce, R. D. and H. Raiffa (1957) *Games and Decisions*, New York (Wiley).
MacCallum, G. C. Jr. (1966) "Legislative Intent", *Yale Law Journal* 75, 754-87.
MacIntyre, A. C. (1988) *Whose Justice? Which Rationality?* Notre Dame, Ind. (University of Notre Dame Press).
Midgaard, K. (1976) "Co-operative Negotiations and Bargaining: some Notes on Power and Powerlessness", in Barry, B. (ed.) *Power & Political Theory*, London (Wiley), 116-37.
Mill, J. St. (1843) "A System of Logic", in Nagel, E. (ed.) (1950), *John Stuart Mill's Philosophy of Scientific Methods*, New York (Hafner), 3-358.
Raiffa, H. (1982) *The Art and Science of Negotiation*, Cambridge, Mass. (Harvard University Press).
Rubinstein, A. (1982) "Perfect Equilibria in a Bargaining Model", *Econometrica* 50, 97-109.
Schelling, Th. C. (1960) *The Strategy of Conflict*, Cambridge, Mass. (Harvard University Press).
Schutz, A. (1943) "The Problem of Rationality in the Social World", *Economica* 10, 130-49.
Searle, J. R. (1995) *The Construction of Social Reality*, New York (Free Press).
Stocker, M. (1982) "Responsibility Especially for Beliefs", *Mind* 91, 398-417.

Sunstein, C. R. (1995) "Incompletely Theorized Agreements", *Harvard Law Review* 108, 1733-72.
Sunstein, C. R. (1996) "Leaving Things Undecided", *Harvard Law Review* 110, 4-101.
Taylor, Ch. (1985) *Philosophical Papers*, Cambridge (Cambridge University Press).
Walzer, M. (1987) *Interpretation and Social Criticism*, Cambridge, Mass. (Harvard University Press).
Williams, B. (1973) "Deciding to Believe", in *Problems of the Self*, Cambridge (Cambridge University Press), 136-51.
Wilson, B. (ed.) (1970) *Rationality*, Oxford (Blackwell).
Young, O. R. (ed.) (1975) *Bargaining: Formal Theories of Negotiation*, Urbana (University of Illinois Press).

Final Remarks: Deliberation and Decision – Perspectives and Limitations

Christian Kirchner

1 Introductory Remarks

A summary which discusses perspectives and limitations of a dialogue between constitutional economics and discourse theory has to compare the original goal of the conference with the outcomes. Has it been a *dialogue* between these two social science approaches? Was it a dialogue between constitutional economics and discourse theory or rather deliberative theory? Did the conference lead to an approximation of the two approaches?

It has become clear from the very beginning of the discussion that all participants – and the relevant papers – were interested in constitutional economics and deliberative democracy/deliberative theory. And it was evident that the approach of the conference should be a more modest one: to identify intersections between both approaches, to propose translations and to discuss potential modifications of one approach in the light of given or assumed comparable advantages of the other.

2 Clarifications of Positions

2.1 Constitutional Economics

'Constitutional economics' stands for an economic approach which looks into the working of institutions, more precisely a subset of institutions: constitutions and constitutional rules, rules which are essential for the organisation of society.

For research purposes it makes sense to distinguish between a positive and a normative theory of constitutional economics (see Stefan Voigt's paper). Even if one limits the research agenda to the study of the legitimacy of constitutions, the decision on which concept of legitimacy is preferable is a normative issue. This can only be discussed in the light of testing various concepts of legitimacy in the real world.

The *positive analysis* has to answer the question of how alternative institutional/constitutional designs are working not only under real-world constraints, but under given preferences of individual actors and under certain assumptions on how these individual actors respond to alternative institutional/constitutional designs.

The *normative analysis* – which according to the understanding of some representatives of constitutional economics is the core of the approach – discusses suitable institutional/constitutional designs as a result of a cooperative venture for mutual gains. But this normative analysis can only work within a framework of positive constitutional analysis, because the suitability of an institutional/constitutional design can only be judged on the merits of its expected outcomes.

2.2 Deliberative Theory

In deliberative theory *deliberation* is the essence of democracy. The approach is interested in the legitimacy of decisions; in the discussion Philip Pettit has introduced the term *discursive legitimacy* (and *discourse compatibility*). The deliberative model is a dynamic rather than a static one. Preferences are shaped and developed within the deliberative process; their definition is broad and contains as well the element of 'interest' as that of 'theory'. Deliberation is supposed to be a social process in which the participants are searching for the common interest, i.e. the common interest of a given society. The approach contains various prerequisites (rather than 'constraints', which could be a misleading term in a dialogue with constitutional economics). Among these prerequisites are reciprocity, publicity and accountability/contestability.

3 Incommensurabality

Constitutional economics is searching for procedural rules and is interested not so much in direct justifications of outcomes but in indirect justification (proceduralism) aimed at specifying proposals of institutional reforms and testing them in a positive analysis (see Andreas Suchanek's paper) in order to find out whether or not a mutual advantage can be attained. Deliberative theory, by contrast, is interested in defining the agenda for decision making in the public sphere.

Both approaches question which variables are changing. But whereas constitutional economics looks into the variables institutions, constraints, information of individual actors, deliberative theory looks into the variables preferences (from individual goals to common interest), decision making rules and general conditions such as publicity, accountability/contestability.

4 Meeting Points

There are options of approximation between both approaches to be found in some papers.

The *van Aaken paper* asks how to improve the rationality assumption. She is not just interested in substituting full rationality by bounded rationality, but looks for solutions of anomalies. She is very close to constitutional economics and deliberative theory, as she aims at forming institutions so that a learning process (in the sense of deliberative theory) may take place. Her question is: 'Are institutions "discourse compatible"?'. The issues raised in her paper may be a bridge between constitutional economics and deliberative theory. The institutionalist concept of proceduralism may be a tool to create a framework in which the individual actors can not only form superior constitutional rules but also create a discourse which improves the probability of finding such superior institutional devices.

The *Dryzek paper* responds to the often held view that, among different sources of social order, constitutions are the only ones which can be systematically influenced. The paper identifies some alternative sources of social order, arguing that some of these can also be the target of informed and systematic reconstruction in the interest of better social outcomes. Amongst these alternatives, the paper focuses on the role of discourses and deliberation.

The *Pettit paper* first sketches some of the ideals of deliberative democracy, including non-domination, publicity and accountability/contestability. Then the paper introduces a 'discursive dilemma', which highlights a problem of aggregating individual judgments into collective ones. Pettit points out that it is not at first sight clear how the dilemma can be resolved in a deliberative democracy, but argues that the republican approach provides a compelling argument for resolving the dilemma in one particular way: a deliberatively democratic group should adopt a method to ensure that collectively endorsed judgments are consistent and rational.

The *List paper* also addresses the problem of aggregating divergent individual inputs into collective decisions, focusing on both classical preference aggregation problems and judgment aggregation problems similar to the ones discussed by Pettit and Bovens and Rabinowicz. The paper develops a taxonomy of two concepts of agreement, agreement at a substantive level and agreement at a meta-level, and argues that the second concept points towards a possible deliberative-democratic response to the impossibility problems of social choice. The key hypothesis is that deliberation may generate agreement at a meta-level, which in turn facilitates consistent aggregation.

The *Bovens and Rabinowicz paper* first introduces a complex social decision problem similar to one leading to the 'discursive dilemma' discussed by Philip Pettit. While the Pettit paper is mainly concerned with the procedural merits of different proposed solutions to that decision problem, the Bovens and Rabinowicz paper focuses on their epistemic merits, i.e. on their performance at 'tracking the truth'. Starting from the Condorcet jury theorem, the paper identifies conditions under which the so-called premise-based procedure is the better truth-tracker and conditions under which the conclusion-based procedure is the better truth-tracker.

The *Suchanek paper* argues that the concept of consent should be self-enforcing, and discusses two different approaches of achieving self-enforcement. The first approach is broadly normative, while the second is based on economics. The paper argues that the first approach is inferior to the second one in that it leads to 'normativistic fallacies', whereas the second approach may serve as a useful heuristic for improving the preconditions of social cooperation.

The *Voigt paper* attempts to reformulate certain aspects of deliberative theory in order to test them in a positive analysis (positive deliberative theory). Then constitutional economics and deliberative theory are on the same level and can be better compared. But such a positive analysis falls short of being able to formulate normative postulates, which is the heart of constitutional economics. But on the other hand any valid normative social theory should be based on a solid foundation of positive analysis.

The *Goodin and Brennan* paper contrasts the way in which anthropologists and philosophers interpret the notion of 'society as a negotiated order' with the way in which economists interpret that notion. The former refers to a negotiated system of shared beliefs and understandings, while the latter refers to a negotiated system of benefits and burdens. Bargaining theory, as developed in economics, concerns mostly material benefits and burdens, and not so much beliefs. The paper argues that that constitutes a deficiency in economic understanding, and proposes that bargaining theory should be extended so as to address not only disputes over resources but also disputes over beliefs.

5 Conclusion

A reciprocal learning process between constitutional economics and deliberative theory has been initiated. The conference has led to a clarification of differences in questions and methodological concepts. Proposals have been discussed of how to extend the research agendas of both approaches. A potentially fruitful dialogue between two approaches has been started, which should not blur the continuing differences but which may enlighten the process of methodological reflection on both sides. This conference has only been the first attempt, which may be viewed as an invitation to proceed on this path.

For Product Safety Concerns and Information please contact our EU representative GPSR@taylorandfrancis.com Taylor & Francis Verlag GmbH, Kaufingerstraße 24, 80331 München, Germany

Batch number: 10726007

Printed by Printforce, the Netherlands